S0-BNF-535

A REBIRTH OF
IMAGES

A REBIRTH OF IMAGES

The Making of St John's Apocalypse

BY

AUSTIN FARRER

State University of New York Press

First Published in 1949
Printed in Great Britain by Robert MacLehose and Co. Ltd.
University Press, Glasgow

Published by
State University of New York Press, Albany

© *1986 Trustees of Mrs. K.D. Farrer*

For information, address State University of New York
Press, State University Plaza, Albany, N.Y., 12246

Library of Congress Cataloging in Publication Data

Farrer, Austin Marsden
  A rebirth of images.

  Originally published: Great Britain: University
Press, Glasgow, 1949.
  Includes index.
  1. Bible, N.T. Revelation—Criticism, interpretation,
etc. I. Title.
BS2825.F36   1986   228'.06   85-26219
ISBN 0-88706-271-7
ISBN 0-88706-272-5 (pbk.)

10   9   8   7   6   5   4   3   2   1

CONTENTS

PREFACE

Nothing justifies the writing of prefaces, except that they are in fact epilogues: one puts them at the beginning, as a concession to the common vice of reading books backwards. The preface is written last, and so it may serve as a vehicle for those general observations one feels moved to make on the scope and nature of the work as a whole, after it is finished and done with. Now that I have detached my mind to some extent from my task, I may be able to say a few things which will prevent the reader from being misled or imposed upon.

When I look back on the course of my study, I see how many different positions I have confidently adopted and passionately maintained in the course of the seven or so years during which it has engrossed me. There is nothing in this to be distressed about: the only way to arrive at a right construction is to try every hypothesis in turn, to do one's very best for it, and to break it against the facts. And it is some comfort against scepticism to see that what appeared most convincing in the earlier hypotheses has a way of nestling into the frame which the later hypotheses provide; so that it has not been simply a matter of abandoning position after position in face of inexorable evidence and fighting a continual rearguard action against the encroachment of intractable fact. At the same time it is impossible, in view of such a history of instability, to claim finality for the present stage of interpretation. Although I can see no further than I have got, I must realize that anything I can publish is no more than an interim report.

If so, why publish now? Because one tires of pursuing novel and exciting investigations by oneself in a corner, or talking about them with people who are not in a position to be as severe as they ought, not having the whole matter in black and white before them. There is no way of bringing other minds to bear, except by publishing in full. Even the first stage of publication brought my typescript into the hands of an acute and painstaking critic, whose

5

reactions gave me so much to think about, that I almost rewrote the book. So what may I not expect from actual publication? The book will be thoroughly pulled to pieces, which will be all to the advantage of the truth.

It will be to the advantage of the truth, on one supposition—that the task which I have taken in hand is a genuine and important task, a task which has got to be finished, however imperfectly I have begun it. This is the last stronghold of vanity, to believe that one has at least got hold of an important issue. If it is vanity—for one cannot pretend to doubt the seriousness of a study to which one has given so much time and attention.

Whatever success I may have had with the interpretation, my wrestling with the Apocalypse has convinced me of this: it is the one great poem which the first Christian age produced, it is a single and living unity from end to end, and it contains a whole world of spiritual imagery to be entered into and possessed. It may well be that what I have just said about St John's vision may not seem to some readers any very solid support for its position in the New Testament. No one, after all, has proposed to include Dante's *Commedia* in the body of inspired scripture. I do not propose to discuss here the right of the Apocalypse to its place in the Canon. I shall merely observe that those who wish to understand the mind of the later New Testament age must embrace the study of a great and vividly imagined poem, in which the whole world of that age's faith is bodied forth.

I began my work on the Apocalypse in reaction against the attitude of the commentators I read. It appeared to be too easily assumed that the several paragraphs of the book could be interpreted piecemeal, and by reference to what lay outside St John's own work. Here he was accused of rehandling a pagan myth, there of imperfectly adapting a scrap of 'apocalyptic tradition', postulated *ad hoc* by the commentator. I began with the resolution to find out if I could what St John was doing, thinking, imagining in his own mind, and, if I could, to see each vision as the appropriate expression of his mental act. St John's mind, I thought, was not a sort of rag-bag which had got stuffed with all sorts of contents from various sources, it was a living act. When one could see what St John was doing, one might hope to see that he did it

6

well, and that his 'borrowings' no more disfigured his work than Virgil's or Milton's disfigure theirs.

But what was St John doing? I observed two facts. There appeared to be in several parts of his book a more continuous, hard-headed and systematic working-out of Old Testament themes than had been recognized; and St John's finished work exhibited an extremely elaborate and varied cyclic pattern, both in the regular recurrence of themes, and in the form of their visionary presentation. These two facts provided my original hypothesis. I would suppose that St John believed Ezekiel, Zechariah and Daniel to express the form of things to come, that he laid the three prophecies side by side and went straight through, meditating the triple strand of visions into unity at each point of his progress, in the light of the Christian revelation. And I would further suppose that he wove the resultant new vision into a cyclic rhythm of his own, a sort of mental music. These two suppositions, I hoped, might account for the facts.

They did not. But the attempt to work them out led to a great deal of wholesome exercise in the appreciation of the structure of the cyclic rhythm, and in the recovery of St John's way of working with the Old Testament. My attempt to force the hypothesis of a continuous use of the principal ancient prophecies led to a lot of impossibly artificial interpretation. But at the same time as I was forcing upon St John my continuous exegesis of Ezekiel and the other prophets, I was recognizing how much else from the Old Testament St John used; while I tried to make out that his starting-point was always in the texts I had chosen for him, I had to admit that he called in a great deal besides by way of parallel, even from the 'wrong' parts of Ezekiel, Daniel or Zechariah. Gradually my 'text' of continuous exposition grew thinner and my 'foot-notes' of parallel matter more hopelessly disproportionate, and the hypothesis capsized. The continuous exposition vanished, and I was left with the footnotes, which I had anyhow arrived at by accident and honestly, without any axe to grind. So I had to find a new soul of continuity to animate and knit together these *disjecta membra*.

The principle of intelligible continuity has (to cut a long story short) turned out to be absolutely one with the musical formality

7

of the design. St John was not imposing rhythmic form on some intelligible matter alien to it; the rhythmic form simply expresses the intelligible progress of the sense. And this form, both rhythmical and intelligible, turns out to be—it was the last thing I wanted or expected to find—thoroughly Rabbinic, and not a little Gnostical. St John does not see the scriptures in what seems to us to be their 'own' pattern, he sees them artificially arranged in the Jewish sacred calendar, with its feasts and its lessons: and he imposes further elaborations of pattern upon the calendar itself, quite alien from the spirit of the Old Testament, and still more alien from the common sense of the modern world.

It is the ever clearer emergence of the Rabbinic factor in the pattern of the book which has, more than anything else, made it clear to me that I must publish what I have got and hand the investigation over. I am not, and shall not probably become, a competent Rabbinic scholar, and the questions involved are of the most intricate kind. So what I have written is no doubt most unscholarly. Let me mention a single point by way of illustration. The Jewish synagogue of the First Century A.D. read the scriptures according to a lectionary which has since gone out of use, and has to be conjecturally reconstructed. The late Dr Büchler, a learned Jew, made what appeared to be a very workmanlike reconstruction,[1] but it is in fact challenged by others. St John sees the scriptures through the pattern of the feasts and their lessons. Some of the most important festal lessons are, fortunately, beyond dispute, but there is much uncertainty about others, especially about the readings from the prophets. Now I am not competent to touch these most intricate questions. The best I can do is to build upon the agreed points, and for the rest to show what texts St John in fact used in several parts of his book. Others will, I hope, be able to weave many of these texts into the lectionary pattern. But I realise that, in doing so, they may see themselves constrained to pull parts of my pattern to pieces. I can only hope that the principal pegs of my structure are firmly and truly driven.

The cruciality of some of these Rabbinic points has (to make a clean breast of it) come home to me since I became committed to the publication of this book. I cannot make myself competent to

_____
[1] *Jewish Quarterly Review*, Old Series, v, 420 and vi, 1.

settle them for myself before I let it go into the press, and so I let it go as it is. For I feel a reasonable confidence that I have been able to see from within St John's work what St John is doing in the main, and the whole thing is not going to be overthrown by more exact Talmudic learning. The Talmudists may call me, with justification, several hard names, of which 'unscholarly' should be the first: but I hope they may find something here that they can use.

I trust that nothing I have written may appear to show lack of appreciation for the work of previous commentators. Nearly all the facts one requires have, in truth, been collected and piled conveniently to one's hand by the admirable and massive learning of men like Dr R. H. Charles, a learning which I have no pretentions to emulate. The next stage belongs to our generation; it is for us to reap the harvest of their labours by working the puzzle for which they have provided the pieces. If we could hope to discharge the task that falls to us as well as they discharged theirs, we should be well content. We have not got to go down the mine and dig out the metal: one thinks of Charles and his collaborators at work on hitherto untranslated and unpublished Jewish apocalyptic writings, recovered out of all sorts of corruption and disfigurement, and from under the disguise of Ethiopic or Old Slavonic versions.

From contemporaries I have received all sorts of encouragement and kindness, and not least from Fr Richard Kehoe, O.P., who looks into the spirit of scripture with marvellous discernment. But there is, I think, only one person whom I have plagiarized wholesale, my former pupil, Miss Aileen Guilding, whose suggestions I should now find it difficult to discriminate from the rest of my work. She is now studying St John's relation to the ancient Jewish lectionary under Dr Herbert Danby's direction, and whatever I have got right in the matter of the lectionary I probably owe to her directly; how much to Dr Danby indirectly I cannot say. He has been very kind in answering particular questions which I put to him. Miss Guilding has not only steered me in the matter of the lectionary; she has made several acute observations about St John's use of particular texts from the Old Testament, which she appears to know backwards and inside out. She is not to be held responsible for my errors.

9

My sister has typed and typed again the several rewritings of this book with unfailing patience and care. My father has made me an index. Miss Adams, of the University Observatory, has explained to me such points of astronomy as I have supposed to be involved in St John's symbolism.

I wish that my book did more credit to so much kind assistance, as well in form as in substance. As to the form, I have several times tried to write the thing out pleasantly and consistently, but it would keep demanding to be patched and rewritten piecemeal, and the result may not be very smooth. Perhaps it will be remembered that my task has been considered for the last seventeen centuries to be one of peculiar intricacy. There are, I hope, no material inconsistencies. There are apparent inconsistencies: different reasons are given in different places for St John's having written this or that sentence in the way he did. But the reader will no doubt realize that there is no such thing as *the* reason for the occurrence of any line in a poem. Why does Shakespeare make Hamlet say such-and-such a thing? Because it belongs to Hamlet's character; because the circumstances demand it of him; because it expresses the quality of human destiny; because it fulfils the design of the plot; because it falls in with the traditional fable. One may give the answer appropriate to one's point of view at the moment. My various answers do nothing but relate St John's words to different aspects of his symbolism and different parts of his context. At least, I hope so. If I have contradicted myself, I have contradicted myself.

Enough of apologies and excuses. I hope I have been able to express what has excited me so much, and that a great deal of it is true.

Oxford
January 1948

CHAPTER I

(1)

The human imagination has always been controlled by certain basic images, in which man's own nature, his relation to his fellows, and his dependence upon the divine power find expression. The individual did not make them for himself. He absorbs them from the society in which he is born, partly through the suggestion of outward acts and the significance of words, partly, it would seem, by some more hidden means of appropriation. The contents of other people's minds flow into ours at a subconscious level, even across gaps in time and space, a fact constantly evidenced, and as constantly disbelieved. The ancestral images of which we speak may, it would seem, be carried and communicated to the next generation by those who are unaware of their existence at the conscious level. Our ignorance of what we are does not make us cease to be, and our unawareness of the profound levels of our imagination neither abolishes them nor prevents them from acting upon our wills, nor, even, on the wills and minds of others.

Who first saw life as a springing fountain, or guilt as dirt needing to be purged away? When did favourable deity begin to be an irradiating light, or divine sanctity a jewel wrapped by a veil within a veil, and guarded by jealous hands from the profane? When did the sky first marry the earth, to generate her fruits? Which was the clan or family first seen to be a sacred body with a common blood, the ties of kindred being its arteries: so that if any of the blood was spilt, sacrilege was done to the communal person, only to be expiated with the blood of the bloodshedder? Where did the traditions of the elders or the justice of a king first seem to be the act of an authority controlling the stars?

In ages for which religion and poetry were a common possession, the basic images lived in the conscious mind; men saw their

13

place and destiny, their worth and guilt, and the process of their existence, in terms of them. Being externalized, the images taken for the reality of the divine became idolatry, and taken for the reality of nature became a false science. The rejection of idolatry meant not the destruction but the liberation of the images. Nowhere are the images in more vigour than in the Old Testament, where they speak of God, but are not he.

The images are not through all ages absolutely invariable, and there is no historical study more significant than the study of their transformations. Such a transformation finds expression in the birth of Christianity; it is a visible rebirth of images. This should be common ground to believers and unbelievers. Some may regret the nature of the transformation which then took place, if regret has any meaning in such a case; but no one can regard it as trivial. The historian will see the transformation as gradual, prepared for within Judaism and outside it: but it precipitated itself in the thought and action of Jesus Christ. It is strange that his part in the process should be doubted by historians; from a purely secular point of view, there is no superiority in the common hypothesis that the transformation took place first in the minds of the disciples and was projected back upon him.

This elaborate and uneconomical supposition was the product of a prejudice which ought to be outworn now. It was supposed that the Christian Faith could be divided into two parts, a vital content of ethical spirituality, and a mythological or theological frame constructed to set it off and give it emphasis. The spirituality, as being the primary fact and real motive cause, was then assigned to Christ; the theology could naturally be left to accumulate round it in the course of the Church's life. We shall not now accept such a distinction as corresponding with historical realities. It is, no doubt, always the pressing concern of religion to seek after and seize its own vital essence and spiritual centre, but that is a poor reason for supposing that spirituality came naked into the world, or could exist without the images which condition it. Given a system of religion, we may distil spirituality from it, but this distilling will not effect a transformation of religion. Religion is transformed when the images are transformed, and their transformation will determine the character of spirituality. Christ did

14

not distil the essence of Judaism; still less of religion-in-general, for there is no such thing.

Since, then, we must regard the Christian revolution as essentially a transformation of images, it is not reasonable to leave Christ himself out of the transforming work. There had arisen in Judaism the image of heroic and unmerited suffering for God's glory and the good of the brethren, especially in the figure of Joseph: and this image was tending to fuse with that of the blood-offering in atonement of sin. There was also the image of the Messiah, in whose enthronement the Kingdom of God would be manifested on earth. There were also images of the divine power and presence—God is in heaven, but his 'Name' is in the temple, his Wisdom or Word or Spirit is in the mind of the prophet, or, in some degree, wherever there is a mind alive with the divine law. There was an image of divine sonship, belonging primarily to the chosen people. In Christ's very existence all these images fused. Joseph the saint of sacrificial loving kindness, the ritual Lamb of the atonement, David the viceroy of God, the word of God's presence and power, Israel the Son of God, Adam the new-created Image of God: all these were reborn in one divine Saviour out of the sepulchre of Christ. All this he was by right and in fulness, all this the Christians were to be by grace and by participation.

If it is unreasonable to deny that the primary rebirth of images took place in the thought and action of Christ, it is equally unreasonable to suppose that it was so simply accomplished in him once and for all, as to require nothing but tranquil appropriation on the part of his disciples. The decisive act of transformation had taken place in him, but the whole furniture of images had to be touched and leavened by it, all had to be reborn with Christ. This process was one of great ferment and profound disturbance, and has much to do with the phenomena in which the primitive Church recognized the presence of the Holy Ghost.

The presence of the Spirit is recorded to have been first recognized in the outbreak of compulsive and ecstatic utterance. This phenomenon later became somewhat of an embarrassment, when the knowledge that it could occur led to its inducement by auto-suggestion: but its sheer and unforeseen outbreak on the day of

Pentecost remains none the less impressive. We may compare the phenomenon of the *stigmata*. It is uninteresting that mystics nowadays produce by meditation the appearance of the wounds of Christ on their own bodies, because they know it may happen. The appearance of them for the first time in the body of St Francis remains an impressive evidence of the whole-heartedness of his meditation on the passion of Christ.

Of what was the compulsive Pentecostal utterance the symptom? It might, no doubt, be the symptom of several things, but it could not be the symptom of anything whatsoever; hardly, for example, as some would wish to suppose, of a sudden and lively disposition towards civic and domestic virtue. The Christians themselves connected it with a parallel phenomenon, prophecy, in which inspired utterance took on intelligible form and was the clear expression of compulsive thinking. Prophecy, no doubt, often had a particular and quite practical address, but it was distinguished from mere exhortation by ultimate dependence on the pressure of supernatural mysteries within the mind, and the sense that these mysteries were revealing themselves for the first time. This was the work of the Spirit. Christ in his earthly life had made the decisive transformation of the images, and he had given his Spirit to continue the work in the minds of the disciples, to lead them into the knowledge of all the truth.

The vigour of this process in the first Christian generations could scarcely be exaggerated. We experience it in the pages of the New Testament. The results are, for the modern historical scholar, extremely disconcerting. The most primitive of the Evangelists cannot narrate the story of Christ without coming under the constraint of the Spirit, obliging him to set forth the image of Christ as what the Spirit now shows it essentially to have been, rather than as what it could have been seen at the time to be. A second evangelist takes up the story of the first, and refashions it under the compulsive breath of his own inspiration. Yet all this is the effect not of the lack of traditions about Christ, but of their uncontrollable creative force. The breath of the Spirit is equally evident in the Epistles. St Paul is writing on some purely practical matter, but presently it touches the living image somewhere, and a marvellous fusion and rebirth of scriptural figures fills his page

16

before he can return in the authority of his vision to give his ruling on the business in hand.

Since the process is of the rebirth of images, it is to the matrix of images, the Old Testament, that the Spirit continually leads: for here are the images awaiting rebirth; all this is Christ, could we but see how and why; the Spirit will teach us. The work of reinterpretation may include much hard and close intellectual effort, there is nothing dreamy or sentimental about it; but it is obvious that the calculative reason alone can do nothing here. The images must live again in the mind, with the life of the image of Christ: that is inspiration.

The rebirth of images can be studied everywhere in the New Testament, but nowhere can we get so deep into the heart of the process as we can in St John's Apocalypse. For nowhere else have we a writing which is so simply devoted to the liberation of the images as this is. The Evangelists clothe their history with the images, but they are restricted by the historical actuality upon which they fit them. The Epistles find their inspiration in the images, but they express them only in so far as serves the purpose of instruction or exhortation. But the Apocalypse writes of heaven and things to come, that is, of a realm which has no shape at all but that which the images give it. In this room the image may grow to the fulness of its inborn nature, like a tree in a wide meadow.

The teaching of Christ contained both the unfettered images of apocalypse and the applied images of history and doctrine. In the thirteenth chapter of St Mark, and in the words of Christ to the High Priest in the fourteenth, the tremendous figure of the Son of Man expands to fill the skies of future Advent. Elsewhere in the Gospel we have the figure confined by particular circumstance, for instance, the narrow walls of a sepulchre—the Son of Man must suffer; or made an example of moral instruction—the Son of Man came to minister. We read the Gospel as one, and the applied image colours the free image also. St John sets free the images again, but now they are through and through transformed by what happened after Christ-in-the-flesh had ceased to prophesy, and begun to suffer. When St John's spirit flies up through the door of heaven, he sees a Lamb, standing as slaughtered: a symbol

17

as pregnant for the new faith as that which Moses saw in the old, the flame of a bush, burning unconsumed.

St John simply yields himself to the images, that is to say, to the Holy Ghost. Nowhere in the New Testament is an author's consciousness of writing under spiritual constraint more evident, or more effectually communicated to his reader. His book is 'a prophecy'; blessed is he who reads it, and those who hear. Christ manifest in presence commands him to write to the Churches. Let him that hath an ear hear what the Spirit says. St John is directed by the heavenly voice as to what he shall write and what withhold, and assured that the words are true and faithful words of God. Woe betide the man who changes a syllable of the writing: he has committed sacrilege against the divine word. For he that testifies to the things written is Jesus, the Root and Child of David, the bright and morning star.

We can study in this book not only the images, but the process of inspiration by which they are born in the mind. Indeed the two studies are one. An image thrown in isolation on the screen means nothing, because it may mean anything: and everyone who has touched the interpretation of images has experienced this bewilderment. In a long concatenation of images, each fixes the sense of the others, and is itself determined by them. If we appreciate the connexion rightly, we feel the new image emerging out of the hidden mind under the evocation of the images already in place, as St John saw the figure of the Beast come up out of the deep when the Dragon's feet touched the sand of the sea.

At a first reading the complexity of images in the Apocalypse may baffle and confuse us, but if we persevere we shall become thankful for it. It means that no image stands alone, but has its place and sense determined by a whole surrounding world of images. In the Apocalypse every image is bound to all the others by a delicate web of interrelated significance, almost as every point in physical nature is bound to the rest by lines of causal force. It is an intricately planned paradise, which we can make the home of our thoughts for a while, and explore from end to end; every detail will bear examination, down to the wings of the butterflies and the blades of the grass.

The study can be exact, it can escape from the suspicion of phantasy, for two reasons; first, because of the breadth and complexity of St John's edifice, and second, because the material from which it is built lies open to us. It is all in the Old Testament. St John used other writings and oral formulae, but always as a rule for the interpretation of Scripture, never as a substitute for it. We have several writings that he used, for instance I Enoch, the Twelve Testaments, the Gospels of St Mark and St Matthew, certain Epistles of St Paul: we know something of oral teaching by which he was guided, from rabbinic sources later written down. All this may be of service, but we do not have to wait for an exhaustive knowledge of his bibliography before we can proceed to assured results. For he is always doing something with the Old Testament, and we can see what he does, so long as we have a sufficient guide from his contemporary world and literary background to set us on the right paths. He makes considerable use, for example, of I Enoch. And yet, if that work were lost to us, we could still see without it what St John is doing: and if an apocalyptic writing, previously unknown, were to be discovered tomorrow, and prove to have been largely followed by St John as a canon of interpretation, we should be interested to observe the fact, but we should very likely add nothing material to our knowledge of what St John did and meant. For, whether he interpreted by a guide or without, he interpreted: he never copied out 'sources' or used undigested matter or stopped short of the grasp of the ancient scripture which was to be reborn through his inspiration.

For the reasons we have given, St John's images do not mean anything you like; their sense can be determined. But they still have an astonishing multiplicity of reference. Otherwise, why write in images rather than in cold factual prose? It has been said that the purpose of scientific statement is the elimination of ambiguity, and the purpose of symbol the inclusion of it. We write in symbol when we wish our words to present, rather than analyse or prove, their subject-matter. (Not every subject-matter; some can be more directly presented without symbol.) Symbol endeavours, as it were, to *be* that of which it speaks, and imitates reality by the multiplicity of its significance. Exact statement isolates a single aspect of fact: a theologian, for example, endeavours to isolate the relation in which the atoning death of Christ

19

stands to the idea of forensic justice. But we who believe that the atoning death took place, must see in it a fact related to everything human or divine, with as many significances as there are things to which it can be variously related. The mere physical appearance of that death, to one who stood by then, would by no means express what the Christian thinks it, in itself, to be; it took many years for the Cross to gather round itself the force of a symbol in its own right. St John writes 'a Lamb standing as slaughtered' and significances of indefinite scope and variety awake in the scripture-reading mind. There is a current and exceedingly stupid doctrine that symbol evokes emotion, and exact prose states reality. Nothing could be further from the truth: exact prose abstracts from reality, symbol presents it. And for that very reason, symbols have some of the many-sidedness of wild nature.

The purpose of symbols is that they should be immediately understood, the purpose of expounding them is to restore and build up such an understanding. This is a task of some delicacy. The author had not with his conscious mind thought out every sense, every interconnexion of his imagery. They had worked in his thinking, they had not themselves been thought. If we endeavour to expose them, we shall appear to over-intellectualize the process of his mind, to represent an imaginative birth as a speculative construction. Such a representation not merely misrepresents, it also destroys belief, for no one can believe in the process when it is thus represented. No mind, we realize, could *think* with such complexity, without destroying the life of the product of thought. Yet, if we do not thus intellectualize, we cannot expound at all; it is a necessary distortion of method, and must be patiently endured by the reader. Let it be said once for all that the convention of intellectualization is not to be taken literally. We make no pretence of distinguishing between what was discursively thought and what intuitively conceived in a mind which penetrated its images with intelligence and rooted its intellective acts in imagination.

What we are proposing to do is to introduce into the field of scriptural divinity a known method of poetical analysis. It will not be reasonable if the admitted and inevitable complexity of the method is made the especial crime of our essay in it. Not only in

20

St John's writings, but wherever we go behind the finished surface of poetical creation we reach an astonishingly manifold web of imaginative association. As the animal body appears intelligible and satisfyingly unified to our eyes, and yet has built itself up out of an unimaginable chaos of ingredients by the silent magic of its nutritive life, so it is with the product of poetic imagination. It gathers and unites its materials with a subtlety which no conscious contrivance could aspire to. If we try to trace it back to its sources, we may spend years in putting asunder what an intuitive instant sufficed to join. An instructive and well-known example is J. L. Lowes's examination of the imaginative process which lies behind a few of Coleridge's poems. He had access through Coleridge's notebooks to the things Coleridge read: and we have access to St John's library, that is to say, the Old Testament and a few other writings.

In view of what has been just said we may deal with an apparently formidable objection. The reader who perseveres through the analyses which follow may naturally ask, 'How much of all this did the congregations of the Seven Churches comprehend, when the apocalyptic pastoral of their archbishop was read out to them?' The answer is, no doubt, that of the schematic analysis to which we resort they understood nothing, because they were listening to the Apocalypse of St John, and not to the lucubrations of the present writer. They were men of his own generation, they constantly heard the Old Testament in their assemblies, and were trained by the preacher (who might be St John himself) to interpret it by certain conventions. And so, without intellectual analysis, they would receive the symbols simply for what they were. They would understand what they would understand, and that would be as much as they had time to digest.

They would not, of course, understand all. St John was writing by simple inspiration, he was not studying his audience. The words he hears are holy and divine, and he has been commanded to address them to the Seven Churches: what their value for instruction or exhortation may be is no responsibility of his. We could not make a comparison more misleading than that with a modern bishop sitting down to compose something edifying for the lay people to read during Lent. St John even studies to inlay the

21

plainer outline of his vision with riddles and mysteries, so that his book may be an inexhaustible mine of truth to those who ponder it. He certainly did not think it was going to be read once to the congregations and then used to wrap up fish, like a pastoral letter.

(2)

If the study of the Apocalypse is of inestimable value for the understanding of the New Testament as a whole, it is especially so for the appreciation of the other Johannine writings. It is a subject for sorrow that a critical dogma of plural authorship should have taken such hold as to bar the way to a fruitful and natural comprehension of the unity and development of St John's work. Such an opinion, when it has remained unchallenged by serious argument for forty years, becomes as deeply rooted as the articles of the creed; it comes to rest upon something more powerful than reason, mental habit; but it rests on reason too, being rationally deduced from existing assumptions. It is folly to suppose that we shall quickly eradicate it.

The evidence for the unity of the Johannine writings cannot even be supplied here: it must await a full study of the Gospel. For it essentially lies in the identity of image-pattern in the Gospel and the Apocalypse, and this can only be exhibited by making an analysis of the Gospel like the analysis we have endeavoured to give of the Apocalypse here. The identity is so subtle and at so profound a level, the pattern is so naturally adapted and developed in the Gospel, as to make the hypothesis of imitation by another hand fantastic. Why, then, is the dogma of separate authorship so prevalent? Not, of course, through the inability of intelligent men to give the correct answers to their own questions, but by the right questions not being asked. If, for example, we ask: 'Is the style of the Apocalypse that of the Gospel?' the answer is, plainly, 'No.' If we ask, 'Is the attitude to the Advent Hope the same in the two works?' the answer is, again, 'No.' But since the style of the Apocalypse is completely artificial and antiquarian, to refuse to allow St John ever to write in more ordinary speech is like refusing to recognize the authenticity of my everyday writings, because I once composed a collect in what I supposed to be the style of

22

Archbishop Cranmer. And as for the attitude to the Advent Hope in Apocalypse and Gospel, let us get on to the time-machine, fly back to Patmos, and put our question to St John himself, at work on his Revelation:

'Are you not developing a somewhat one-sided eschatological emphasis?' 'Let me be,' the Saint replies. 'I am making my meditation on the Last Things. I shall meditate on the Incarnation tomorrow.'

It seems best to state first in a few words what the relation between the several Johannine writings appears to have been, and then to give a sketch of the really quite simple history of what happened to the tradition about them.

St John of Ephesus flourished (in authorship) at the very end of the First Century. He writes as one who had spent many reflective years in the synagogue before his conversion, and since his conversion he has attained to a position of leadership in the Asian Churches, unlikely to have been reached in a day. So, if we put together his Jewish and his Christian periods, we may be wise to suppose that he is over fifty years old when we first hear of him. On the other hand it would be surprising if what happened in the mind of St John as he wrote the Apocalypse (or the Gospel, for the matter of that) happened to a man of really advanced age. His position of authority probably means that he was formerly companion and coadjutor to one or more of the heirs of the apostolic mission, let us say St Timothy, while St Timothy lived.

By the time that St Ignatius of Antioch made his triumphal progress through the cities of Asia on his way to martyrdom at Rome, it seems clear that St John had disappeared, or St Ignatius could hardly have failed to address him or speak of him in his letters to the Churches. St John had been a 'great light', doubtless, but he had now 'fallen asleep'; he had been an apostolical man, but not an Apostle, and there is no reason why St Ignatius should mention him beside SS Peter and Paul. He mentions both, especially St Paul, of whom he speaks as founder of the Asian Church; but never St John. Ignatius's journey is commonly dated about A.D. 115. If St John had just died at the time, perhaps St Ignatius would have been likely to mention it. Let us say, for the sake of saying something, that he was gone by 110. St Irenaeus says that

23

he saw the Apocalypse under Domitian: we shall naturally suppose in the later and gloomier years of that monarch, say in 95. There is plenty of room between the two dates to accommodate the Gospel and the Epistles. As likely as not, they were all written by 100.

St John's activity as a Christian writer began, so far as we know, with the Apocalypse. Initiated by this inspired labour, he proceeded to the tranquil composition of the Gospel. The Apocalypse explains to us how its author took to the literary medium. He was the prophetical leader of the Seven Churches, but, for the while, he was in the concentration-camp at Patmos. Quite apart from his own will, he was compelled by spiritual rapture to address with the pen those he could not reach with the living voice. And so he wrote the Vision of the Second Advent. It was only natural that he should presently balance it by writing the Vision of the First, his 'Spiritual Gospel'. In the Revelation the Old Testament material is still rough from the quarry, in the very form and phrase of its originals, so much so that St John adopts an artificial language, Septuagintic Greek, in which to handle it. Dr Charles has said what is necessary about this extraordinary style in his Commentary. It is certainly not the dialect of the Asian Ghetto, but an elaborate archaism. The suggestion that St John wrote like this because he knew no better may be dismissed out of hand. He was writing a Christian Ezekiel or Zechariah in the phrase of the old. There is a great deal of such writing in the New Testament, for example, in parts of St Luke; but nowhere else is it done with the thoroughness and consistency of St John. If a simple-hearted Bible-reading sect of the present day were to produce a prophet who wrote in a state of rapture, how surprised would you be to find that his book was, as near as he could make it, in the language of the Authorised Version?

The rapture through which St John wrote the Apocalypse was not an inspired lesson in propaganda but a personal revelation: he was not the same man after it as he had been before. It makes more difference to a poet, as poet, to compose a great poem in six weeks, than to look at sunsets and mountains for six years without composing. By the time that St John had seen the Vision of the Bride, and bowed before the Throne of God and of the Lamb

24

planted in the heart of the redeemed creature, he was ready to begin writing the Gospel, whether weeks, months or years in fact elapsed between the compositions of the two works. We have probably been wont to ask ourselves, 'Could the man who wrote the Gospel *go and write* the Apocalypse?', and to answer, very properly, 'No.' But if we ask, 'Could the man who saw the Apocalypse go and write the Gospel?', the answer is that that is the very thing that he would be most likely to do. It has often been very sensibly observed that the First Epistle of St John goes on from the heights reached in the Gospel, especially from the Supper-Discourses. The relation of the Gospel to the Apocalypse is much the same.

When St John comes to write the Gospel, he is writing not a new Ezekiel, but a new Mark, and with the model the style changes. When he comes to the Epistles, he is free from models, and, as Dr Dodd has acutely observed (in the interests, indeed, of a contrary argument)[1] the style changes once more; it is more modern, it throws off the last fetters of scriptural form, and uses certain devices of secular rhetoric. The differences of style are differences of *genre*: in the Apocalypse it is proper to write, 'Thus saith the Amen,' and in the Gospel, 'I am the Truth.' But under all such differences something remains constant. The hand-writing experts are able to distinguish between the forms and flourishes which a forger may vary at will, and a basic quality of line and curve which he can hardly modify. The same distinction may be observed in differences of style. At bottom, language is the instrument of thought, and a man cannot vary the fundamental shape of his thinking, for that would involve the power not merely to act someone else but to become another man. I may indeed by sympathy fall into the rhythm of another mind in order to think his thoughts after him, but when I think creatively for myself I shall think in my own rhythm. Both Apocalypse and Gospel are inspired writings; by a divinatory process the author shapes new images out of old words. He thinks with his pen, he

---

[1] Dr Dodd argues that there are different doctrines and opinions in the Epistle. We do not dream of contesting his judgement; but we see the constant factor of St John's mind elsewhere: not in doctrinal formulations, but in a stock of living images which are continually fertile in fresh applications.

does not expound ideas long ago formed. In both books the rhythm of his thought is plainly visible, and that rhythm is the same, and it is unlike that of any other New Testament author. Everyone has felt the common personal quality of the Johannine books, but everyone allows himself to be argued out of his perception by exact demonstrations of stylistic and ideological differences, correct in their form, but irrelevant in their conclusions.

The characteristic rhythm of St John's thinking is the direct expression of his divinatory brooding. He takes up a phrase or a word, plays with it, repeats it, turns it inside out, then drops it and revolves in a similar way round another, very often one that has been thrown up in the process of handling the first. We have to come to terms with this and accept it, otherwise we are simply baffled and irritated by his refusal to make his points and advance in an orderly manner. He uses the method we have described both when he is developing ideas, as in the Epistle, the Gospel-discourses, and the Voices of the Apocalypse, and also when he is elaborating quasi-visual imagery, as in many apocalyptic passages. The analysis of his text reveals a chain of stanzas, each centred round a word or phrase. Here are some examples:

'Behold the *tabernacle* of *God* is *with men*
And he will *tabernacle with them*
And they shall be his people
And *GOD-WITH-THEM* himself shall be their *God.*'

(Apoc. XXI, 3).

'And *temple* saw I none therein
For the Lord God Almighty is the *temple thereof, and the Lamb,*
And the city hath no need of the sun or of the moon to shine on her
For the *glory* of God hath *lightened* her and the *lamp thereof is the Lamb*
And the nations shall walk in the *light* of her
And the kings of the earth bring their *glory* into her.'

(Apoc. XXI, 22–24).

In the beginning was the *Word*
And *the Word* was with *God*
And *God the Word* was.

26

He was *in the beginning* with *God*
All things through him *were made*
And without him *was made nothing.*

What was made in him was *life*
And the *life* was *the light* of men
The light shineth in the *darkness*
And the *darkness* overtook it not.

(John I, 1–5).

Amen, amen I say to thee
That what we know we speak
And what we have seen we witness
And our witness ye receive not.

If I have told you the earthly and ye do not believe
How if I tell you the heavenly shall ye believe?
And none hath ascended into heaven
Save he that from heaven descended
The Son of Man that is in heaven.

And as Moses uplifted the serpent in the wilderness
So uplifted must be the Son of Man
That every believer on him may have life everlasting.
For so God loved the world
That his only begotten Son he gave
That every believer in him might not perish
But have life everlasting.

(John III, 11–16).

I know thy works and thy *weariness* and thy *endurance*
And that thou canst *not bear* the wicked
And hast tried these that call themselves apostles and are not
And hast found them false
And holdest *endurance* and hast *borne* for my name's sake
And hast not *wearied.*
But *I hold* against thee that thou hast *let go* thy *first love*
Remember then whence thou art fallen and *repent*
And do the *first* works
Else I come to thee and will move thy candlestick out of its place
Except thou *repent.*

27

But this thou *holdest* that thou *hatest* the works of the
   Nicolaitans
Which I also *hate*.
                                        (Apoc. II, 2–6).

Beloved, no new commandment write I unto you
But an old commandment which ye had from the beginning
The old commandment is the word ye heard.
Again a new commandment write I unto you
Which is true in him and in you
For the darkness passes and the true light already shines.
He that saith he is in the light and hates his brother
Is in the darkness to this day.
He that loveth his brother abideth in the light
And with him is no stone of stumbling
But he that hateth his brother is in the darkness
And in the darkness he walks and knows not whither he goes
Because the darkness hath blinded his eyes.
                                        (I John II, 7–11).

This is he that came by water and by blood, Jesus Christ
Not by the water only but by the water and the blood
And the Spirit is the testifier because the Spirit is the truth.
For three there are that testify, the spirit the water and the
   blood
And the three agree in one.
If the testimony of men we receive
The testimony of God is greater
For this is the testimony of God that he has testified of his Son.
                                        (I John v, 6–9).

And I saw a star from heaven fallen to earth
And there was given him the key of the pit of the abyss
And he opened the pit of the abyss
And there went up smoke from the pit as smoke from a great
   furnace
And the sun and air were darkened from the smoke of the pit.
And from the smoke there issued locusts upon earth
And there was given to them power
As have power the scorpions of earth

And it was told them not to hurt the grass of earth
Nor any green nor any tree
But only the men that have not the seal of God in their fore-
heads.

(Apoc. IX, 1–4).

There is of course a perceptible difference in the form of this repetitive rhythm in the three works. In the Apocalypse the pattern is more varied and intricate, but then the Apocalypse is far more consciously poetical. The antitheses and inversions go hand in hand with the archaic diction. The Epistle is at the other extreme—the use of the repetitive rhythm is almost monotonous, and less effort is made to vary it. This may represent the exhaustion of age, or it may be simply part of the more pedestrian character of the Epistle.

The simile of the handwriting expert with which we began this stylistic argument must not be pressed to the point of absurdity. It is healthy for would-be forgers to believe that the handwriting expert will be able to see through all their disguises. But it would be vain for us to pretend that we can so penetrate the screen of archaism as certainly to detect the writer of the Fourth Gospel in the author of the Apocalypse. The sort of examination of which we have given a few specimens just now can at the best shift the burden of proof. It may shew that the Fourth Evangelist is a perfectly credible author for the Apocalypse, more credible, let us say, than any other primitive Christian writer known to us. But that is the most it can do. We shall not pretend to say of the Apocalypse on stylistic grounds alone, 'No one but the Fourth Evangelist could have written that.' Happily we are not limited to stylistic arguments.

St John's style, we have said, varies with the *genre* of his writing, but there is an underlying identity of rhythm. So it is with the working of his images. The same images are there, making the same kinds of pattern, drawing by preference on all the same Old Testament sources: but in the Apocalypse they are rough, new-minted, visibly presenting the type from which they are taken along with the antitype to which they are referred. In the Gospel they have shed the inessential and have simply become the figures

29

of Christ and the Church. In the Epistle they are hardly themselves the objects presented: it is the spiritual precepts and general truths flowing from them that St John sends to his disciples.

We must not suppose that because there is a progress perceptible through the Johannine writings we can therefore afford to neglect the first stage, the Apocalypse. The progress of St John is that of the mystic, from the multitude of vigorously conceived images towards the point of ultimate simplicity, the being in God through Christ. But the significance of the simplicity cannot be divorced from the variety out of which it was concentrated. It is the centre of the circle of meanings, because the circle is there of which it is the centre; otherwise it would be the centre of nothing. If we wish to understand St John, we cannot start with the central simplicity, we must work to it from the circumference of images, and we must repeat this inward movement again and again. It is by meditating the sharp diverse images of the Apocalypse that we shall appreciate the fused images of the Gospel, and the mystical perceptions beyond all images.

Let us turn now to the history of the tradition. St Irenaeus, an Asian Christian, is the true heir of the Johannine theology, but he is no Jew, and does not understand all St John's thought-processes in detail. He writes after he has migrated from Asia to Gaul. He attributes both Apocalypse and Gospel to John. He cites Polycarp, the long-lived bishop of Smyrna, for personal memories of John in Asia. St Irenaeus is emphatic that he cannot be mistaken: he listened to Polycarp when he was a youth, and remembers exactly what he said. It is absurd to dispute such testimony: no doubt Polycarp had been in Asia with John, the great John, the only John of apostolic stature who had ever been there, the writer of the books. He was simply 'John' to Polycarp: there was no need to particularize.

When, however, St Irenaeus proceeds to identify this John with the Son of Zebedee, we may legitimately wonder whether we are listening to the voice of Polycarp or merely of St Irenaeus himself, especially as he couples Polycarp's testimony with that of Papias, which he has apparently misinterpreted on this very point. Papias, a younger contemporary of Polycarp, is cited not for what he said but for what he wrote in a book which the historian Eusebius

30

still possessed, and Eusebius confuted St Irenaeus from Papias's text. Papias had distinguished the Son of Zebedee, about whom he claimed to know no more than about other apostles, from an Elder John whose words he claimed to retail, though at second hand. The conclusion Eusebius ought to have drawn is plain: Polycarp and Papias were referring to the same John, the Elder; that is to say, the man who had signed himself 'John' in the Apocalypse and 'Elder' in the Second and Third Epistles.

Eusebius did not draw this conclusion. We must turn to consider why. There was not (let us get this clear above all) any good early tradition of an author for the Apocalypse other than the author of the Gospel. St Irenaeus assigned both to the great John who had taught in Asia, believing this John to be the Apostle; and if Papias had divided the authorship of the two books, there is no fact that Eusebius would have been more delighted to retail. Some Churches rejected the Apocalypse from their Canon, as being difficult, unprofitable, or dangerous to read out whole to the congregation, a view which appears to be shared by the makers of modern lectionaries. Rejection from the Canon automatically carried with it a denial of 'apostolic' authorship: but there was no alternative tradition of origin. One simply said, 'Whereas others read an apocalypse reputed to be St John's, we account it spurious.' The Third Epistle was rejected by others, for the obvious cause that it appeared to be trivial and to add nothing to the Johannine canon. That it is in the same style and form as the Second Epistle, and that no one would have bothered to forge such a scrap of writing, is evident; yet if a Church did not use it, she was held to deny its authenticity.

Scholarly argument for dual authorship was first produced by the disciples of Origen. They were scholarly, but, like some other scholars we have read, they were not disinterested. The spiritualising theology of Origen found its supreme authentication in the Gospel of St John, read through Alexandrian eyes, and in separation from the Apocalypse. The Origenists were confronted by some very stubborn and literal-minded Second Adventists dubbed 'Millennarians', who attempted to tip the balance their own way by appealing to the work in which St John had emphasized a complementary aspect of the truth. So the Origenists began to make a

31

case against the Apocalypse. Not that they admitted that the Millennarians were interpreting the Apocalypse correctly: the Apocalypse was a holy, if somewhat bizarre and (if one dared to say what one thought) indiscreet book: but if it was interpreted by the standard of the Gospel, it was profitable, indeed, highly edifying. One could establish the Gospel as the norm for the interpretation of the Apocalypse if one could show that the Apocalypse was not fully apostolic, whereas the Gospel was. That the Gospel was apostolic, needed by this time no demonstration. Everyone accepted Irenaeus's testimony about that, and indeed Irenaeus's confusion of Evangelist and Apostle was very natural, in view of the extreme subtlety of St John's hidden signature to the Gospel, in which he identifies himself with the name and spirit of the Son of Zebedee. So much for the apostolicity of the Gospel. The non-apostolicity of the Apocalypse could be shown simply by demonstrating the difference of style, which is not at all difficult to do. Who then was the author? Since the Gospel goes to the Son of Zebedee, why not give the Apocalypse to Papias's other John, the Elder, so that he may not have a completely dumb part in the play? Eusebius added a really brilliant confirmation. There were two vergers in Ephesus each of whom claimed to exhibit the tomb of St John. Each, indeed, thought it was the one and only John that he had: it was very stupid of them, for how could it be? Not all the skulls reputed to be Oliver Cromwell's can be his: evidently there must have been several distinguished generals of the same name about the same time.

There, really, the matter rests. The moderns have many of them realized the improbability of the Fourth Gospel's being the work of the Son of Zebedee, and have seen that it must be assigned to the extreme end of the First Century. Has this led them to draw the inevitable inference, and to assign it to the only John of Asia, the prophet of the Apocalypse? It has not. They have not shrunk from the hypothesis of two archiepiscopal Johns, operating in the same region and in the same decade, the Elder who writes the Gospel and the Epistles, the prophet who sees the Apocalypse. The ground for so perverse a judgement is still fundamentally what it was with the Origenists; the Apocalypse is barely tolerated, because of its (apparently) crude Adventism, and the Gospel is loved, because of its (apparently) philosophic spirituality. The moderns are convinced that the 'spirit' of the two books is completely different; they could not come from the same hand.

It is a little difficult to see what this argument, if it is pressed, really amounts to. No one of even moderate learning can really suppose that the Author of the Fourth Gospel was a philosophic humanitarian who disbelieved the Second Advent with its traditional mysteries, or disbelieved the everlasting punishment of the damned. Presumably it is thought that, if these things were put to him, he would have replied like the old-fashioned mamma to the young girl, 'Why yes, my dear, but there is no need for us to dwell upon these matters.' Is such prudery really conceivable? What possible motive was there for it? If St John believed in these things, he must have thought them very important and solemn facts, to be deeply weighed and to be meditated upon occasion. Presumably the Patmian exile was the occasion. If we say, 'But in the Gospel he contents himself with allusions to them,' we are, of course, begging the question, because the retort is easy: 'He contents himself with allusions in the Gospel because he is writing it as a companion-piece to the Apocalypse.'

The root of the trouble is the doctrine of punishment: this is the nettle that needs to be grasped. Perhaps a remark or two about the primitive attitude to this will do more than direct argument to remove prejudice against the authenticity of the Apocalypse.

The prejudice arises from the usual cause: we are misinterpreting the apostolic age in accordance with our own views. We see the human conscience as something completely separate from the divine judgement, and the divine judgement as, again, separate from the penalty, if any, which sanctions it. They made neither of these separations. The conscience is, to them, a mirror in which we see, though darkly, the judgement of God,[1] and the judgement of God is not an ineffectual registering of disapproval but is the act of punishment, for all God's words are of themselves efficacious.

[1] The righteous gentiles 'show the work of the law written in their hearts, their conscience giving attestation to it, and their thoughts doing battle with one another as prosecution and defence, in the session at which God judges the secrets of men, according to my preaching, through Jesus Christ.' (Romans II, 15–16).

Thus, what our consciences feel when they feel guilt is the coals of fire piling up over our heads: it is the special act of divine mercy to withhold them while we repent. If the man who is wronged returns good for evil, he is 'leaving the vengeance to God', he is 'piling coals of fire over the head' of his enemy. That, you may say, is not a very amiable thing to do. No, not if the piling up of the coals is invisible to the offender: but it is not. He has a conscience, which is gradually overwhelmed (let us hope) by the evident adverse score you are piling against him by your charitable forbearance (Rom. XII, 19–21).

There is, therefore, nothing amiable about refusing to awaken the consciences of your impenitent neighbours to the impending coals of fire and nothing virtuous about refusing to observe the coals piling against yourself. In particular, when nature breaks forth in singular disasters or when the madness of man is permitted to break loose in war and its attendant horrors, we ought to see that the angels who are the motive-forces of nature and the controllers of history are warning us of what the arm of the Almighty cannot for ever withhold. If St John were to return to us now, he might say: 'I warned you that the day would come when for the folly and sin of men fire would fall upon them from the sky. Well, it has fallen. You complain that it was vindictive of me to give you the warning. If you had repented in time, you would have had cause to be grateful. And if you still think that God will build into the stainless city any that loves or works a lie, rather than cast him on to the everlasting fires without the gate, I advise you to look into your consciences.' Such was the mind of the whole apostolic Church. But we evade the evidence where we can, and hate the book in which the evidence cannot be evaded.

How are we to proceed? We have not given a demonstration of the unity of the Johannine writings, but at the most a sketch for the demonstration. There is no sufficient reason why the reader should believe us, but we are sure in our own minds, and wish to be free to illustrate the Apocalypse from the Gospel on the assumption of common authorship. Perhaps the reader would like, at this stage, to compromise with us. The Apocalypse and Gospel are both, let us say, Ephesian books, the Gospel being written after the Apocalypse by one who knew it well and lived in the same

34

thought-world, so that such images and ideas as seem to be taken up in the second work from the first have as likely as not been taken from it in fact.

The reader of the chapters which follow perhaps knows the Apocalypse and the substance of the Old Testament by heart. If he does not trust his memory, he would be well advised to have a complete Bible at his elbow, the Revised Version by preference. The references given are all to the chapters and verses of the English Bible. In quoting the Old Testament, I have sometimes made omissions, and sometimes substituted a translation of the Septuagint Greek version, which, for the most part, St John was following. Wherever my wording differs materially from the Revised Version, it represents the Septuagint. The reader who wishes to check it can go to the Septuagint Greek. Quotations from the New Testament are often freshly translated from the original, not to quarrel with the standard version of the text in question, but to emphasize an appropriate aspect of the sense of the Greek. The last part of this book is a text of the Apocalypse, but it will be very awkward to use for reference, being in the same volume as the exposition, and noting neither chapters nor verses. The purpose of it is to enable the reader who has mastered the exposition to read the Apocalypse with the maximum of pleasure. It is the Authorised Version with all serious errors removed, and divided in accordance with the proper pattern of the book. Behind it is a diagram, which can be pulled out and used as a constant guide through VIII; and also a pull-out analysis of the Apocalypse, which will save the reader from ever getting lost in St John's text.

CHAPTER II

The Apocalypse has a great deal of framework; no one can miss that. It bears the promise of formal consistency, of a continuous grand architecture spanning the whole book, into which all the visionary detail is to be fitted. Yet, as we advance, it does not appear to us that the promise is fulfilled. The lines of the schematic architecture elude us, and the work seems in danger of disintegrating into a mere pile of visions and oracles. Then architectural elements reappear, yet not in such order as plainly to make up the unity of a single edifice. We are left unable to reconcile ourselves either to the hypothesis of formal order or to the hypothesis of its absence. Must we conclude that St John attempted form and broke down in the execution of it? Or must we accept the supposition of a demon-editor who has broken up St John's noble building by his senseless omissions, rearrangements and additions?

Before we capitulate to either of these desperate conclusions let us make one more attempt to construe the formal pattern as it stands. Perhaps a little more flexibility of approach, a little more attention to St John's parallelisms of phrase may yet succeed. Evidently his architecture was not fully successful, in a literary sense, or it would not have proved so baffling to his readers from the second century onwards. He was, perhaps, over-subtle; yet that does not mean that the recovery of his form, if indeed we can recover it, will be unrewarding. There is no absurdity in entertaining hope of the attempt, for we are now possessed of methods and materials for the reconstruction of the Jewish-Christian mind in the first century which the Christian exegete has lacked ever since the second.

In I–XI there is a firmly built structure: it is at XII that we lose our way. It seems best, then, to analyse the structure so far as we can already see it, in the hope that a better acquaintance with it here may help us to trace it where we cannot see it yet.

The pattern in I–XI is based on three series of sevens: seven messages, seven unsealings, seven trumpet-blasts. But the form of the seven-term cycle does not simply repeat itself; it becomes elaborated and modified with each repetition, as we shall proceed to show.

The first seven (I–III) is straightforward enough. The seven things are introduced all together in the opening vision. The Son of Man stands among seven candlesticks, which are the seven churches. He holds in his hand seven stars, which are their guardian angels; and to these angels the seven messages are one by one addressed. The serial idea is contained in the very notion of the seven luminaries, for in the universally known Chaldaean system, seven luminaries give their names to the series of seven days, the week:[1] and St John has just told us that his vision falls on the first of the week, the Lord's Day. So the seven messages spell out that favourite apocalyptic period, the symbolical week. The detail of the messages is not, however, prescribed by the special characters of the seven week-days, except for the last, where the sabbath-note is unmistakably heard. Here Christ, significantly named the Amen, the fulfilment and end, stands at the door and knocks, that he may enter and sup with the true believer in a holy sabbath feast.

The introduction to the second seven (IV–VIII, 6) places it carefully in line with the beginning of the first. Again the trumpet-like voice and the spiritual rapture introduce a theophany. In the former vision the Son of Man stood on earth as the apostle of the Ancient of Days, whose features therefore he wore. In the latter, the enthroned Glory himself is seated in heaven, and the Son of Man appears accessory to his throne, a Lamb endued with his Spirit. There is evident climax here—from the Messiah we proceed to the Glory, from earth we rise to heaven. Again the seven things appear together—the seven seals of the book, and the seven Spirits whereby they are opened. Again the serial treatment of the seven follows—the seven seals are broken one by one, to the accompaniment of visions. And again the seventh is sabbatical in

---

[1] The sun to Sunday, moon to Monday, and so on with the remaining five planets, or planetary gods. We have the names teutonised, except for Saturday, which is Latin = dies Saturni. The seven stars have another sense besides; see p. 225 below.

37

character, introducing a heavenly silence, a sabbath-pause (VIII, 1).

So far the pattern is the same: but when we look at the structure of the six week-day visions (VI–VII) we find much elaboration which had no counterpart in the messages to the Churches. The first four are marked off from the rest and grouped together, by the following features. (a) In addition to the rubric common to the whole series, 'I saw when the Lamb opened the first seal,' or 'the second', or whatever the number may be, they have the additional rubric, 'I heard the first, second, etc. beast say: Come,' a cry to be understood in the sense of the Church's prayer for Advent, 'Maranatha,' 'Come, Lord Jesus' (cf. XXII, 20). (b) This rubric is in each case followed by the appearance of a horse of distinct colour bearing a rider; the further descriptions of the several horsemen are written in careful stylistic parallel to one another. (c) The four visions have their own joint conclusion, when the powers of all four horsemen are epitomised in the fourth: 'and there was given unto them (i.e. to the fourth rider and his companion) authority over the fourth part of the earth, to kill with the sword, the famine and the death, and by the wild beasts of the earth.'

The fifth vision lacks the peculiar features of the first four, and is about twice as long. The Maranatha-prayers of the four cherubim are here paralleled and expanded in the more potent prayers of the martyr-souls run down in blood beneath the altar of their sacrifice, and crying, 'How long?' Their prayer is not, like that of each cherub, immediately followed by a partial vengeance: it receives the assurance of complete vindication soon to follow.

The sixth vision is a pair to the fifth in length, and carries out its idea, for the signs of the Last Day are now manifested to appal the kings and the mighty men of earth. 'The great day of wrath is come: and who is able to stand?' This verse, being the last of the vision, brings us to the most surprising feature of the whole series of unsealings. The sixth unsealing is not directly followed by the seventh, but by a pair of intrusive visions which are not numbered (VII, 1–8, VII, 9–17). We might well begin to think that the series of unsealings is finished and that we are passing into another series altogether, except that we know that the seventh unsealing must yet be fulfilled.

The two intrusive visions do to some extent run on from the

38

sixth unsealing. 'And I saw when the Lamb opened the sixth seal, there was a great earthquake . . . and the stars of the heaven fell to earth as a fig-tree casteth her unripe figs when she is shaken of a great wind.' So the sixth unsealing begins: and the first intrusive vision thus : 'After this I saw four angels standing at the four corners of the earth holding back the four winds of the earth, that no wind should blow on the earth, or the sea, or any tree: and I saw another angel ascend from the sunrising with the seal of the living God.' So the winds of destruction released by the sixth *unsealing* are after all restrained a while for a contrary operation, a *sealing*, to take place. The imposition of the divine seal protects the righteous against the plagues which the breaking of the (seventh) divine seal will let loose upon the wicked. We are given the number of the sealed, and so proceed to the second intrusive vision, there to catch a glimpse of the saints' final bliss, in which their sealing is to have its full effect. The opening phrase is placed in line with that of the sealing vision: 'And after this (vision) I saw four angels . . .'—'And after these (visions) I saw, and lo, a great multitude. . . .'

We have called the vision of the great multitude a glimpse of final bliss. In being this it cannot help being an anticipated conclusion to the whole apocalypse. This fact may afford us a clue to the significance of the two intrusive visions. St John leaves them unnumbered, but the reader is broken in to enumeration by this time, and counts them for himself: they may not be *the* seventh and eighth, but they are *a* seventh and an eighth. Now the Christian, unlike the Jew, sees the climax of the week in the Sunday, not the Sabbath, in the eighth day which is a new first, and not in the seventh. This has already been exemplified in I–V. It is on a first Sunday that the Son of Man appears to St John. The appearance articulates itself into a whole 'week' of messages, formally concluding in the seventh. What follows upon it as an eighth is a new Sunday and a new theophany (IV–V); and this in its turn articulates itself into a 'week', the series of seven unsealings (VI ff.). In the sixth unsealing we reach a climax of action, with the cosmic earthquake. The first intrusive vision follows it up with a sabbatical pause; the work of judgement rests while the saints are sealed. The second intrusive vision adds a spectacle of heavenly glory and

39

final redemption, closely echoing the triumphs and blisses of the Sunday-vision in IV–V, and itself to be understood, surely, as a Sunday-vision.

What St John has done, then, is to permit the week of judgements, which sprang from the breaking of the seals, to run on through a sabbath into a Sunday of final consummation. So he lets us see what the movement of the week is striving after, what its form really signifies. Yet it is not for *this* week to fulfil the movement so perfectly, or reach so absolute a consummation. The two visions after the sixth are therefore left unnumbered, and when the seventh seal is formally broken they are forced back into the position of a cancelled conclusion, and allowed to stand as a mere interlude, an anticipation of the supreme end. Meanwhile the numbered seventh vision introduces a more modest sabbath—the half-hour's silence of incense-offering—and a more modest Sunday—the trumpet-blowing (VIII, 1–6).

We have now to examine the structure of the third seven (VIII, 7–XI, 19). An innovation here, to begin with, is the dropping of the introductory theophany. This is plainly necessary, for the second theophany has already touched the height of theophanic climax. We can proceed from Messiah on earth to the enthroned Glory in heaven, but there is nowhere further to go, no theophany could be an advance on this, unless it should be that of the Last Day; and we have just been made to understand that the Last Day is not yet. Since mounting climax must nevertheless maintain the tension of the Apocalypse until the final consummation relaxes it in everlasting peace, St John finds another stair by which to climb. The theophany of the enthroned Glory took effect in the opening of the book: and this was a process of seven stages, the breaking of the seven seals. Now if one is breaking seven seals to open a scroll, nothing has really been effected until the seventh is broken: for then the scroll is open, and until then it is not. Thus the visions which accompany the six unsealings are by their very position preparatory in character; it is the seventh seal which unseals apocalypse, and the fresh seven in which it proliferates are the proper content of revelation. Now the day arrives, now the seven-fold trump of the archangels is blown.

Just as the simple Maranatha-cries of the four cherubs prepared

40

us for the more expansive treatment of petition in the martyrs' cry from beneath the altar, so the trumpet-like voices which introduce the two theophanies of I and IV prepare us for the vision of the seven trumpet-angels which takes the place of theophany in VIII, 2-6. As the winds were checked until the saints were sealed, so the trumpeters stand by while the prayers of the saints, carried from the altar of slaughter where we heard them at the fifth unsealing, are offered in angelic incense at the golden altar of perfume within the shrine. When the saints' prayers have been thus presented, and cast back in coals of fire on the heads of their persecutors, then the first of the seven trumpet-blasts shatters the quiet of celestial liturgy, and brings down hail and flame upon the wicked earth.

The seven trumpets are presented all together in VIII, 1-6, and then drawn out serially, like the messages and seals: and the last of the serial seven has that sabbatical character which the pattern hitherto has led us to expect. The seventh trumpet is greeted with shouts of heavenly worship, and there follows a heavenly liturgy —the opening of the temple to reveal the ark (XI, 15-19).

All sabbaths, as we know, represent the seventh day of creation-week, when after his six days' work God entered into eternal rest: and it is a simple development of this idea to consider our six working days as representing his six creative labours. In the trumpet-series St John makes this development. The series expresses divine judgements, not divine creations: but he can still draw six judgements into correspondence with six creative works by representing the creatures made in the genesis as used one by one in the judgement to plague the wicked. The works of the six days are these:

1. Elemental light.
2. Firmament.
3. Land, sea and waters, vegetation.
4. Luminaries.
5. Sea beasts.
6. Land beasts.

The first two present difficulties.[1] How can light itself, the light

---

[1] There is a more interesting reason for the omission of the first two days' work which will appear presently (p.61).

41

before the sun, which expresses the eternal Word, be made the substance of a plague? And how can the firmament, the very floor of heaven? St John profits by the manifold character of the third day's work, and by dividing it can still obtain a list of six, though he lets go the first two works on the Genesis list. Here is St John's:

1. Land, vegetation.
2. Sea.
3. Waters.
4. Luminaries.
5. Beasts from the abyss (of sea).[1]
6. Beasts from the land.

The first four, being inanimate, are simply smitten, the land with hail and lightning, the sea and waters with corruption, the luminaries with darkness. The last two play a more active part: demonic monsters swarm first from the abyss, then from the confines of the earth, to vex and slay the enemies of God.

We see, then, that the idea of the week, which had its germ in the two previous series, has its expansion in the series of the trumpets. Two further features of the series of unsealings find their counterpart in the trumpets: the division into a group of four and a group of three; and the intrusive visions between the sixth and the seventh. As to the division of the seven into a four and a three, we have already seen the first four trumpet-plagues grouped together by subject-matter, as simple smitings of four world-elements. They match one another in treatment, and also in brevity. The remaining three are separated from them not only by greater length and expansiveness of style, but also by the insertion of a separate heading: 'I saw and heard an eagle (vulture) flying in mid-heaven,[2] saying with a great voice: Woe, woe, woe to

---

[1] The sea and the infernal abyss are one in Old Testament imagery, and they are equivalents, for St John. xi introduces 'the beast from the abyss' to be understood, presumably, from Daniel vii which says 'sea'. In xiii he appears as a beast rising from the sea; in xvii he comes up out of the abyss. In xxi we learn of new heaven and earth, but no more sea; neither sea nor abyss has any part in the world to come.

[2] The vulture flying in mid-heaven is a proper introduction to a plague by the creatures of the fifth day: for on the fifth day God made not only the monsters of the sea, but also the 'fowl to fly above the earth on the face of the breadth of heaven'.

42

the dwellers upon earth, for the remaining trumpet-blasts of the three angels still to sound' (VIII, 13). This heading is picked up in a heading to the sixth trumpet, 'The first woe is past; behold there come yet two woes hereafter' (IX, 12) and in a similar heading to the seventh: 'The second woe is past: behold the third woe cometh quickly' (XI, 14). And when the third woe comes in Satan's descent to earth, there is a heavenly voice: 'Woe to the earth and to the sea,' closely followed by a vision of Satan's pursuit after the Mother of Messiah, to whom are given 'the two wings of the great eagle, that she may fly into the wilderness' (XII, 12–14). The eagle's voice proclaimed threefold woe to the inhabitants of earth, the eagle's wings prevent the third woe from being misdirected upon an inhabitant of heaven: only the wicked are destroyed by the Satanic invasion.

Now as to the intrusive visions after the sixth trumpet-vision. The sixth trumpet-angel looses 'the four angels bound at the great river Euphrates, prepared for the hour and day and month and year, to slay the third part of mankind', which they proceed to do with the aid of their two myriad myriads of land-demons. The theme of the hour, day, month and year is carried on into the intrusive visions. We have been shown the predestined moment of a third-part judgement; which may well have set us wondering about the moment of the last and total judgement. The next vision brings us the answer: 'Another strong angel descending from heaven arrayed in a cloud and the rainbow over his head, his face as the sun and his feet as pillars of fire' (X, 1) for no other purpose than to swear the oath 'that there shall be delay no more, but in the days of the seventh angel when he shall sound, the secret of God is accomplished'. He carries in his hand a scroll, in which we presume that his essential message is expressed more in detail: there we should find written the history of 'the days of the seventh angel', the series of events leading to the accomplishment of the secret of God, in other words, the substance of the rest of the Apocalypse. St John, like Ezekiel, is told to eat and digest the scroll of revelation.

At the same time he is given a reed (XI, 1). 'Reed' when placed in parallel with 'scroll' obviously means 'pen'; compare the phrase in St John's third epistle, 'Many things . . . I am unwilling to write to thee with ink and reed, but hope shortly to see thee.' 'Take the

43

scroll and scan' was too straightforward for Ezekiel; 'Take the reed and write' is too straightforward for St John. 'Take the scroll and eat' says Ezekiel, and St John after him: 'Take the reed and measure the Temple of God,' says St John, for the reed, *calamus*, is also a measuring-rod. The digesting of the scroll is a metaphorical reading, the measuring of the temple will be a metaphorical writing. St John the inspired prophet by his written prophecy is to effect what the 'measuring' describes: those who heed the word of God become the living sanctuary of God, but those who find their condemnation in the word are left outside the sacred enclosure, to be profaned by invasive heathendom. An oracle which St John hears proceeds to treat of those within, letting go those without. The candles of the sanctuary, it says, are the Lord's two witnesses, prophetic figures like St John himself. His potent reed, 'a reed like a staff,' becomes in their hands the rod of Moses, to 'smite the land with every plague'. They do the works of Moses and Elias[1]; the oracle goes on to tell of their martyrdom and assumption into heaven.

The history of the two witnesses is, indeed, a summary of the reign and fall of Antichrist, of the persecution and final redemption of the saints. These things will be more fully set out in the remaining visions of the Apocalypse. What we have in XI is a foreshortened and premature conclusion, cancelled, and yet permitted to stand by way of interlude; a close parallel, in fact, to the 'intrusive eighth vision' in the series of seals. The sixth trumpet-vision reached a climax of action in the slaughter of a third part of men. Then come the unnumbered visions—first a pause from action, devoted to the 'eating of the scroll', i.e. scriptural meditation: next, in the vision or oracle of the Reed, an action extending through the reign of Antichrist to the brink of Advent. Lastly, the premature conclusion of the trumpet-series offered by x and XI, 1–13 is firmly cancelled when the authentic seventh trumpet sounds (XI, 15).

The very meaning of such a cancellation is, that the week in question (in VI–VIII that of the seals, in VIII–XI that of the trumpets) is not the final week; it aspires, but is not permitted, to be this. So when the seventh trumpet and its sabbath have past, we must expect to find another week stretching out before us towards the ultimate goal. We turn therefore to the sequel (XII, 1 ff.) in the

[1] See below, p. 132.

44

hope of finding a new sevenfold series, bearing some of the marks which the previous sevens have taught us to recognize.

With this clue in our hands we step forward into unmapped country; for with the seventh trumpet the explicit counting of sets of seven breaks off. St John has warned us that it will be so in x. When the Angel of the Oath exerts his lion-like voice, the Seven Thunders speak. With our experience of the seven seals and the seven trumpets, we naturally expect a thunder-apocalypse to follow, seven visions each initiated by a word of thunder. Were not the breakings of the first four seals each accompanied by the cries of a cherub, with a voice like thunder? But St John is told to 'seal' the thunder voices and not write them: there is to be no more delay, no more sevenfold sets of portents are to unroll before the great event begins. In the days of the seventh trumpet-angel when he shall sound, the secret purpose of God is fulfilled. It is this fulfilment, divested of the form of *numbered* series, that we have now to examine. It will be a seven, but not a numbered seven.

Let us pause and consider our situation. Our first inclination may be to complain that St John, after providing us with a clear plan in the three sevens of I–XI, has suddenly let us down. But a little reflection may suggest that he has not really treated us so unkindly. I–XI are roughly the first half of the work, and they consist of the three roughly equal sections which we have analysed, I–III, IV–VII, VIII–XI, 14, the core of each section being a counted seven. In the second half of the book (XI, 15–XXII), and roughly in the middle of it, there occurs a counted seven, the vials (XVI), which, with its exordium and closely attached appendix, occupies roughly a third part of it (XV–XVIII). Thus, all we have to do is to mark off the four counted sevens with their attached material, and the whole book is divided into six equal parts, the four sevens and the two blanks, thus:

> Seven Messages, I–III. (125 lines in my Greek Bible.)
> Seven Seals, IV–VII. (133 lines.)
> Seven Trumpets, VIII–XI, 14. (122 lines.)
> ... XI, 15–XIV. (144 lines.)
> Seven Vials, XV–XVIII. (159 lines.)
> ... XIX–XXII. (148 lines.)

45

St John has not, surely, put too severe a strain on our ingenuity by leaving us to realize for ourselves that the two blanks are sections comparable with the others, and that his whole work falls into six divisions.

It is with the former of the two blanks that we have to do at present. What guidance have we for mapping out its interior structure? We have just above obtained some directions, from what precedes the blank. We have seen that the sense of the 'cancelled conclusion' to the trumpets requires that another seven should directly follow the seventh blast, though it be an uncounted seven. We may derive a similar indication from the other end of the gap. The seven vials are introduced by a sabbath-vision (xv) which is written in the closest possible parallel to the two sabbaths which follow the seventh seal and the seventh trumpet respectively. The conclusion is obvious: xv is the sabbath-vision to the visions in the blank (xi, 15–xiv); in it a sevenfold series ends, just as a sevenfold series (the vials) opens out of it.

But before we proceed to analyse the series in the blank, let us exhibit the parallel between the three sabbath-visions, viii, 1–6, xi, 15–19, and xv, 1–xvi, 1. In the last of these, as in the first, the seven angels of the seven coming plagues (the trumpets, the vials) are first introduced, and then left to stand by while a liturgy is performed. When it is finished, the trumpet-angels prepare themselves to blow, and the vial-angels are commanded to pour. In viii the liturgy is an incense-offering, in xv it is levitical psalmody followed by the opening of the temple and the entry of the Glory-Cloud. The two ceremonies could not, you might say, be more different, and yet they are firmly tied together by the highly significant common use of Ezekiel x. The incense-offering of viii becomes a scattering of fiery coals over the doomed city of earth by the angelic minister, as we read in Ezekiel. The liturgy of xv is even closer to Ezekiel—it is an entry of the temple by God's Glory, at which a cherub puts liquid fire (the vials of wrath) into angelic hands, to be outpoured upon the world. Now as to the parallel between xv and xi, 15 ff.: xi, 15 ff. is a two-part liturgy, the shouting of heavenly worshippers followed by an opening of the temple of God in heaven, to reveal the Ark of his covenant.

The liturgy in xv is equally of two parts, the song of heavenly worshippers, followed by the opening of the 'temple of the tabernacle of the testimony' in heaven, to admit the Glory.

Let it be accepted that the parallel between the three sabbaths needs no more argument. xv, being so careful a match to the two previous sabbath-scenes, is itself the sabbath of the series in the blank: what we have to do is to identify the previous six visions to which it acts as seventh. But what are we to look for? Just six visions, or, as in the seals and trumpets, six visions followed by a set of 'intrusive visions'? Surely there can be no question of 'intrusive visions' here, for the very possibility of intrusive visions depends on the explicit counting of the rest of the series. It is because they are by contrast uncounted that we know them to be intrusive: it is because after them we return to the counting that we know the intrusion to be over. In the section we are examining there are no counted visions, and therefore no intrusion. We have to look for six visions, and no more. And, if we feel inclined to say that the feature of the intrusion, carefully built up and elaborated in vii and x–xi, cannot be allowed to die, a glance at the vials (xvi) may suffice to set us right. Here is a counted series, but the seventh directly follows the sixth. The intrusion-feature has died by this time anyhow. What more likely than that it died in the previous series (xi, 15–xiv), where the absence of counting was of itself enough to kill it?

In dividing the six visions of xii–xiv let us allow ourselves to be guided by the most objective and mechanical of tests. If St John does not mark the introduction of a fresh vision by the numbering of its angel or seal, how does he mark it? By the use of the rubric 'And I saw', for which 'And there was seen' (xii, 1) may be accepted as an equivalent. If we use this simple test, we get the following result:

(i) And a great sign was seen in heaven, a woman . . . and there was seen another sign in heaven, and behold, a dragon . . . (xii, 1–3).

(ii) And I saw a beast coming up out of the sea (xiii, 1).

(iii) And I saw another beast coming up out of the earth (xiii, 11).

(iv) And I saw, and behold, the Lamb standing upon Mount Zion (XIV, 1).

(v) And I saw another angel flying in mid-heaven (XIV, 6).

(vi) And I saw, and behold a white cloud, and on the cloud sitting as a Son of Man (XIV, 14).

(vii) And I saw another sign in heaven great and marvellous, seven angels having seven plagues (XV, 1).

The only informality here is the repetition of the rubric in XII, 3, so that the first vision is made double: it is the vision of the woman, and the vision of the dragon. But it would surely be absurd to cut off the first two verses of XII and call them a separate vision, the vision of the woman: the fortunes of the woman and the dragon are intimately linked throughout the long chapter: it is a single two-headed vision. It is not the only such in St John's book: cf. XXI, 1-2, where we read: 'And I saw a new heaven and a new earth: for the first heaven and the first earth are passed away, and the sea is no more. And the holy city, new Jerusalem, saw I descending out of heaven from God....'

The conclusion derived from the examination of beginnings is confirmed by an examination of endings, for these link into a system of refrains.

(i) And the dragon waxed wroth with the woman; and he went away to make war with the rest of her seed, which keep the commandments of God, and hold the testimony of Jesus; and he stood on the sand of the sea (XII, 17).

(ii) If any man hath an ear, let him hear. If any is for captivity, into captivity he goeth, if any to be killed with the sword, with the sword must he be killed. Here is the patience and faith of the saints (XIII, 9-10).

(iii) Here is wisdom: he that hath understanding, let him count the number of the Beast: for it is number of man. And his number is six hundred and sixty-six (XIII, 18).

(iv) These are they which were not defiled with women, for they are virgins; these are they which follow the Lamb whithersoever he goeth; these were purchased from among men, first fruits

48

to God and the Lamb, and in their mouth was found no lie: they are unblemished (XIV, 4-5).

(v) Here is the patience of the saints, that keep the commandments of God and the faith of Jesus. And I heard a voice from heaven, saying, Write, Blessed are the dead that die in the Lord, and that presently. Yea, saith the Spirit, let them rest from their labours, for their works accompany them (XIV, 12-13).

(vi) And the winepress was trodden without the city, and there came out blood from the winepress even to the bridles of the horses, to the distance of furlongs a thousand and six hundred (XIV, 20).

We observe the theme of the sufferings and merits of the saints (i, ii, iv and v) and the two mysterious figures with sixes in them, which express the apostasy of the wicked and their punishment respectively (iii and vi). The dramatic 'Here is' formula appears in (ii), (iii) and (v).

So much for the beginnings and endings. Let us turn to the substance of the six visions. What we have is this:

> The Woman and the Dragon
> The Beast
> The Second Beast; a false Lamb
> The True Lamb and his followers
> Three flying angels with proclamations
> The Son of Man on clouds, and three angelic harvesters.

The first four form a group, being held together by the theme of Beast-Figures. The first is the vision of (the Woman and) the Dragon, the second is of the Beast, the third of the False Lamb, the fourth of the True. To appreciate the closeness of this sequence one must recall that 'dragon' is the LXX version of 'Leviathan' and 'beast' ($\theta\eta\rho\iota\upsilon$) of 'Behemoth': or rather, 'Behemoth' is translated by the completely non-Greek 'plural of majesty' $\theta\eta\rho\iota\alpha$, 'beasts.' So 'Leviathan and Behemoth' will be 'the Dragon and the Beasts'—the two Beasts, says St John. The opposite of the Beast ($\theta\eta\rho\iota\upsilon$) is the Lamb ($\check{\alpha}\rho\nu\iota\upsilon$), whose appearance therefore brings the procession of animal-figures to a close. The real theme is as continuous as the apparent form—the four visions are concerned with the persecuting tyranny of the instruments of Satan,

49

and the sacrificial loyalty of Christ and the Saints. The last vision of the four both belongs to its predecessors, and is their antithesis; it begins the movement in which divine power reacts against bestial usurpation.

The presence of the Lamb on Mount Zion is to be understood spiritually. It does not represent the Millennium: Zion is that spiritual 'place', neither Jerusalem nor Gerizim, where God through Christ is worshipped in spirit and in truth. The vision does not show the replacing of the throne of the Beast by the visible throne of Christ; it simply reveals the spiritual kingdom of Christ on earth which the Beast's tyranny is powerless to touch, and to which it is destined to succumb. There stand Christ and the saints, signed with the Holy Name, in defiance of the kingdom of the Beast's worshippers, who bear his blasphemous mark. If the primitive Christian wished to image Christ in the act of supplanting the Beast's usurpation, there was only one figure under which he could see him—not the figure of the Lamb, but the figure of the Son of Man on clouds: for this was the figure which Daniel had seen supplanting the Beast from the Sea, in the great vision of his seventh chapter, a vision which evidently supplies the most part of the material to Apocalypse XIII. And so the four beast-visions (XII–XIV, 5) are followed by a pair of visions (XIV, 6 ff.) which culminate in the figure of the Son of Man on clouds, with his attendant reapers and vintagers. That is the sixth vision: the fifth is supplied by forerunners of the Rider on the cloud, angels with warning cries, flying in mid-heaven.

When we were examining the six trumpets, we found there the series of God's creation-works, earth, sea, rivers, luminaries, living things of sky and water, living things of dry land. In the Beast-Visions (as we will now begin to call the whole series in XII–XIV) the theme of the six works reappears, though the first four are taken in reverse order. Why in the world St John should make the reversal, is a question we will reserve for the present: let us rather attend to the facts. The first vision, that of the woman and dragon, is firmly placed among the heavenly luminaries. The woman is a great sign in the sky, clothed with the sun, standing on the moon, and crowned with twelve stars. The dragon is also a celestial sign, and his tail sweeps up a third of the stars and casts them to the earth. When he is himself cast by Michael out of heaven, he must be thought to fall like a star: 'How art thou fallen from heaven, O Lucifer, son of the morning!'

Expelled from the region of the *stars,* he does not abandon his attempts at playing omnipotence: he tries to overcome the woman by shooting after her a *river of water.* Here too he is foiled: the earth swallows the river. His next attempt at mischief is to evoke the Beast out of the *sea,* and this is followed up by the emergence of the False Lamb from the *land.* The futility of his efforts is shown by the True Lamb and his followers, standing on Mount Zion.

So much for the four elements of the world, taken as they are in the reverse of their true order. The first of the flying angels, who initiates the fifth vision, epitomizes the four, calling on men to worship the God who really wields the world, 'the maker of heaven, earth, sea, and the fountains of water.' But this flying angel, while he epitomizes the four previous works, is himself the representation of the fifth work. On the fifth day God made not only living things of the water, but also birds to fly over the breadth of the firmament: and for that reason the plague of the fifth trumpet was introduced by 'an eagle flying in mid-heaven'. The phrase is echoed in the description of our angel, 'flying in mid-heaven', $\dot{\epsilon}\nu\ \mu\epsilon\sigma o\upsilon\rho\dot{\eta}\mu\alpha\tau\iota$. The eagle cried triple *woe* to the inhabitants of earth from the plagues of the three trumpet-angels yet to sound. Our angel is himself one of three, and proclaims everlasting *gospel* to the dwellers upon earth. That he is the conscious antitype of the flying eagle is evident. He flies like a bird, a form of motion not attributed to an angel anywhere else in the Apocalypse, nor are any other angels even said to be winged, except of course the cherubim of Apocalypse IV.

We might conclude, then, that the angel of this fifth vision is represented birdwise in allusion to the creation of birds on the fifth day of Genesis; but there is more to it than that. For it was a subject of speculation with the Jews, on which day of creation the angels were made, since scripture says nothing of the matter. There were allowed to be two 'probable answers': either they were made with the firmament of heaven, for it is their country, or else they were made with the birds, for they are included in the

51

description 'winged fowl'. So angels, in so far as birdlike, are actually to be taken as creatures of the fifth day.[1]

From the fifth day we pass to the sixth, from (fishes and) birds to (beasts and) the son of man. As St John's fifth vision takes the second work of its day, so does his sixth. And both consider the work they take in its highest excellence: not any birds, but angels; not any man, but the New Adam, Jesus the Son of Man.

The visionary series of Apocalypse XII–XIV is of peculiar interest, because here St John places the famous symbol of the Son of Man back in that same Genesis-context from which the writer of Daniel had first drawn it; and it is of the highest importance for the understanding of the doctrine of Christ, that we should know his followers to have been still in possession of the clue to the Son of Man riddle, its relation to Genesis 1. Daniel VII is, of course, a spiritual exposition of Genesis 1, 20–28. The seer sees himself in, as it were, the fifth 'day' of the world's history, the day of the monsters which 'come up out of the great sea', always, to the Semitic mind, the symbols of chaotic and godless violence. But he knows that their time is appointed, and the day will come when the Ancient of Days will establish the everlasting dominion of the Son of Man 'over the fishes of the sea and the birds of the heaven and all cattle, over all the earth and all that crawl the earth' (Gen. 1, 28). Of this dominion there can be no end, for the Son of Man is the last work of God. He is not spawned either out of the sea or out of the land, but is especially the creature of heavenly God, made in his image and likeness: so whereas the beasts come up out of the sea, the Son of Man comes with the clouds of heaven. Daniel applies his parable to the history of mankind. There is the age in which the image of Leviathan reigns; the age is coming when the image of Adam will reign, and Adam is the image of God. The image of Adam, for the mere Jew, is to become incarnate in a regenerate Israel, of which Messiah is the representative head. For the Christian, Christ is primarily the image of Adam, and Christians derivatively his members. Allowing for this difference, there is no reason to think that the special title 'Son of Man' ever meant anything else from the time of Daniel to the time of St John, than what it means to both of them.

[1] See Moore, *Judaism*, I, 381.

52

A fact which must immediately strike us about the visions in Apocalypse XII–XIV is the new distribution of emphasis. Both the seals and the trumpets run into a climax: their first four visions are preparatory, the weight is in the fifth and sixth. But in the beast-visions the weight is in the first four. The tyranny of the beasts is expansively treated, the triumph of the Son of Man is barely sketched. This curious fact needs to be brought into relation with another, which we have discussed already—the absence from XII–XIV of any 'intrusive visions'. The function of the intrusions after the sixth seal and the sixth trumpet was to carry an 'anticipated conclusion', a foreshadowing of how the whole apocalypse will end; with the result that the series of six seals or six trumpets *plus* the intrusive visions belonging to each could be read each as a complete apocalypse, though with a somewhat shadowy conclusion. Now the same thing can be said of the beast-visions: they provide a complete apocalypse, extending from the Incarnation (Birth of the Man Child) to the Second Advent (Son of Man on Clouds). But the conclusion is a mere shadow, a mere anticipation. The centre of XII–XIV is the Tyranny of Antichrist. The proper place of the Advent is in XIX. There are, as we said, no 'intrusive visions' in XII–XIV, but there is an 'anticipated conclusion' never the less.

We have now crossed the unmapped territory of XII–XIV. With the vials there begins once more a country of fields, lanes and hedgerows. The vials are most carefully modelled on the trumpets. The parallel begins, as we saw, in the sabbaths out of which the two weeks open (VIII, 1–5, XV). It is continued in the detail of the sevenfold series. The four first vials, like the four first trumpets, smite the four elements of the world, and in the same order: earth, sea, waters, luminaries. The fifths also match, though not so simply. The fifth trumpet released the smoke of the pit, whereby the sun and the air were darkened. If this had been the substance of the fifth trumpet-plague, it would have merely duplicated the fourth, in which all the heavenly lights were already darkened by a third part. But in fact the darkening of the air in the fifth trumpet is a mere prelude to a plague of locust-demons. In the fifth vial, no such development takes place: the darkening of the Beast's kingdom is the substance of the plague. To avoid any mere

53

duplication of a precedent darkening of luminaries in the fourth vial, St John completely alters the character of the fourth vision. The sun, touched by the angel's fiery libation, is not darkened, but quickened to an intolerable heat.

In the sixth vision trumpets and vials closely correspond: armies from behind Euphrates are let loose for a predestined day of battle. ('The hour and day and month and year to slay the third of mankind'—'The battle of the great day of God Almighty: behold, I come as a thief'). In the trumpets the soldiers are demons, in the vials they are men.

So much for the six vials. There are, as we have said, no 'intrusive visions' after the sixth. We proceed straight to the seventh, which none the less reflects the character of the seventh trumpet-vision. The seventh trumpet-vision was 'great voices in heaven', declaring that the kingdom had come; and an opening of the temple, to the accompaniment of lightnings, voices, thunders, earthquakes, and great hail. At the seventh vial, a great voice comes out of the temple, saying, 'It is done,' to the accompaniment of lightnings, voices, thunders, earthquakes, and great hail. At the seventh trumpet the accompanying portents are a simple list, but at the seventh vial the two last items are expanded: the earthquake shakes down the cities of earth, cleaving Jerusalem and overthrowing Babylon; the hail falls in stones of a talent's weight, provoking blasphemy from unrepentant man.

This ingenious variation on the theme of the earlier vision is both characteristic of St John, and appropriate to its place. The seventh trumpet is widely separated from the first six, and does not really continue the sequence of judgements: it is rather the liturgy out of which the next sevenfold series opens: it is purely sabbatical in character. It is otherwise with the seventh vial. It is an immediate part of a continuous series, just as the seventh message is, and should conform to its series. And it is widely separated from the next sevenfold action by an interlude: it is not a sabbath-liturgy out of which a new week opens. St John does justice to such sabbatical character as it has by making the great voice 'It is done' the substance of the vision: but he conforms it to the series of active judgements of which it is the conclusion by developing its accompanying portents of earthquake and

54

hail[1] into plagues on their own account. The trumpet plagues, being six, covered four elements of the world and two creations of living things. The vial-plagues are seven, and so the seventh vial requires a seventh sphere of action in which to take effect. It falls on none of the regions of whose creation Genesis makes specific mention, but on the air. On which day was the air created? Let us leave the question to the Rabbis who discuss the occasion of the making of angels.

With the seventh vial the system of numbered visions finally ends, and we step off the map for good. But we have little excuse for getting lost; an interpreter-angel steps forward to be our guide. He is explicitly said to be one of the seven vial-angels, and his business is to shew us in greater detail a mystery all too briefly touched in the seventh vial, the overthrow of Babylon. We may safely, therefore, consider him and the vision he has to shew as an explanatory appendix to the vials: the appendix could scarcely be more emphatically attached than it is. So much for the beginning of it: but where does it end? The interpreter-angel promises a vision of 'the judgement' (i.e. punishment) 'of the great harlot enthroned upon many waters'. But the vision, as it opens, hardly does justice to the description. It is not a shewing of the harlot's punishment, but of her queenly enthronement. True, the *comment* is added that such an enthronement will prove her certain ruin at last. But this comment, even among the comments offered, is not specially prominent: it cannot justify the description of Apocalypse XVII as 'a shewing of the punishment of the great harlot'. The discrepancy between title and contents is no mere clumsiness, however; it is simply another of St John's devices for sustaining climax and preserving continuity. The theme of the harlot's punishment overflows the *Angelus Interpres* vision. Very well, then let supplementary visions do justice to it. Let another angel descend from heaven with the proclamation of Babylon's doom, let voices from the sky exult over the smoke of her burning, let

---

[1] The hail has room made for it by the rehandling of the previous plagues. In the trumpets, the first plague smites earth with hail and fire. In the first vial, a plague of boils is substituted, arising out of the infection of the dust of the earth. So the hail is left for the seventh vial, and the fire for the fourth (the sun scorches, instead of being darkened, as we have seen above).

the sinking of a millstone confirm her everlasting annihilation, let the dividing clouds reveal a heavenly host triumphant in the victory of God (Apoc. XVIII–XIX, 10).

The appendix to the vials trails out to a great length, but then the vial-series itself is very brief, and so the whole vial-section, series *plus* appendix, is still not disproportionate to the other five sections out of which the Apocalypse is made up. We need be in no doubt where it ends. XIX, 1–10 builds up into a great scene of heavenly sabbath, an unmistakable companion-piece to the scenes out of which the seals, trumpets, beast-visions and vials each take their spring. And the new series which rises from it is nothing but the Advent itself. When the first seal was broken, and the first cherub cried 'Come', there appeared *a* rider on a white horse. It was not he for whom the cherub prayed, and the saints still cried, 'How long, O Lord?' But here at length is *the* Rider on the White Horse. He initiates the sevenfold series of the last things: there is nothing left for which the saints should pray.

We have now to attempt the formal analysis of this sevenfold series. Let us follow the same procedure as we did with the previous unnumbered series in XII–XIV. First we fix its limits: then we divide it up by the mechanical method of counting 'And I saw's. As to fixing the limits, we already have the beginning, the white-horsed rider of XIX, 11. No less evident is the end, for everyone knows that the Apocalypse concludes with a Jerusalem-appendix set in careful balance against the Babylon-appendix to the vials. The comparison is enforced by the introductory phrases of the two appendices. 'And there came one of the seven angels that had the seven bowls, and spake with me, saying: Hither, and I will shew thee the judgement of the great harlot that sitteth upon many waters. . . . And he carried me away by the spirit into a wilderness' (XVII, 1–3). 'And there came one of the angels that had the seven bowls . . . and spake with me, saying: Hither, and I will shew thee the Bride, the Lamb's Wife. And he carried me away by the Spirit to a mountain' (XXI, 9–10). The relation of the two appendices to the previous texts on which they severally hang is the same. The 'judgement of the great harlot' sets forth in detail that fall of Babylon of which there was briefest mention in the last preceding vision (XVI, 19), and the vision of the Bride sets forth at

56

length the establishment of Jerusalem, barely stated in the vision directly preceding (XXI, 2).

We have our end, then (XXI, 8) and we have our beginning (XIX, 11). It remains to count the series. Since XXI, 9 ff. is not a sabbath, but an appendix, we ought to suppose that the Last Things, like the Vials, are a complete seven, comprising their own sabbath. Without more ado, let us count the 'I saw's.

(i) And I saw the heaven opened, and behold a white horse (XIX, 11).

(ii) And I saw an angel standing in the sun (XIX, 17).

(iii) And I saw the Beast and the kings of the earth (XIX, 19).

(iv) And I saw an angel descending from heaven (XX, 1).

(v) And I saw thrones, and they sat on them (XX, 4).

(vi) And I saw a great white throne, and him that sat upon it (XX, 11).

(vii) And I saw a new heaven and a new earth . . . and the holy city saw I, New Jerusalem (XXI, 1, 2).

Nothing could be more formally beautiful than this series. There are four visions of the great battle, then two of the kingdom, the many millenial thrones and the one great throne of judgement. Then there is a seventh vision of the final sabbath, in which God will abide with men in a renovated world. The four visions of the battle are perfectly arranged. First there is a vision of the heavenly host, followed by a vision of the angel summoning the kites. Then there is a vision of the earthly host, followed by a vision of the angel haling off the defeated Dragon to his prison. As in the trumpets, beast-visions and vials, these four first visions set forth four elements of the world: here they are taken in vertical order, to express the invasion from above. The firmament opens to let forth the heavenly warriors, on their downward path is an angel standing in the sun to summon the birds who fly below. On earth stand the Beast and his allies: the abyss beneath is opened for Satan, and sealed over his head.

A second battle, the destruction of Gog, is not allowed to appear as a vision on its own account, but is compressed into a narrative appendix to the vision of millennial thrones. In that position, never the less, it makes a certain balance between the visions of the

57

battle (I–IV) and the visions of the kingdom (V–VI). The judgements meted out after the battle become parallel to the judgements meted out after the defeat of Gog, at the Great Assize. In each of the preceding 'weeks' there has been a climax of judgement in the sixth vision. Here in the sixth sixth is the climax of climax, the Last Judgement itself. And so the sabbath which succeeds, and the appendix which, as an eighth, completes the whole, have no longer anything anticipatory about them. This is fulfilment: the throne of God and of the Lamb is set in the heart of the city, and the river of the Holy Ghost pours from beneath their feet to water it with eternal life. The saints look up, and their faces reflect the radiance of the Face of God.

This chapter has contained no more than a provisional sketch of the scheme to which St John writes. Even as such it is unsatisfactory, full of makeshift explanations and loose ends. The loose ends shall be tied in, and the makeshifts replaced by more solid building, in the chapters that follow.

CHAPTER III

(1)

The Apocalypse consists, we have said, of six sevens, the messages, unsealings, trumpets, beast-visions and last things. Why does St John repeat the same form just so many times? The number interior to each series we have seen to be significant; perhaps the number of series is significant too. The number interior to each series is a six of work-days *plus* a sabbath. Perhaps the number of series has the same meaning—perhaps it is a sixfold work, which, culminating in the sixth vision of the sixth series, gives place at the seventh vision to the everlasting sabbath of God.

Hitherto we have confined our attention to the numbers interior to each series. In three of them, in the trumpets, beasts, and vials, we found the rhythm of the creation-works: the six first visions were analogous to the six works of Genesis, the seventh to God's sabbath. Now the easiest verification of the hypothesis that the six series are themselves a working-week of God's judgement would be the demonstration that the six series illustrate the themes of the six creation-days one by one. Supposing that it turns out not to be so, it may still be that St. John is using the pattern of a working 'week' of weeks, but we shall have to test for it in some other way. Supposing on the other hand that it does turn out to be so, the hypothesis will be sufficiently established.

It does appear to be so. The scheme of the six works is manifest in the introductions or beginnings of the several weeks. The first work of Genesis is the creation of that elemental light which, according to St Paul and to St John in his Gospel, expresses the generation of Christ himself. The first week of the Apocalypse is introduced by the vision of the sevenfold candlestick. Zechariah (IV) saw the candlestick of the Lord alight in Israel, with Zerubbabel the prince and Jesus the priest standing on either hand, to supply from their anointing the oil of its light. This vision is the proper expression of the theology of the old covenant: it under-

59

goes radical alteration in the new. Jesus is both prince and priest, and what is more, he is primarily and archetypically Israel. He therefore stands in the midst, and the seven candles of the worshipping Church are planted on the ground about him, to shine with derivative light.[1] He, the fount of light, has a countenance shining as the sun, and holds in his hand as stars the angelic rulers of the seven candles. The seven messages are addressed to them, in judgement on their management of the lamps under their care. The whole vision is concerned with light: it tells how Christ, the elemental light of the first day, 'the Beginning of the Creation of God,' has replaced the sevenfold candlestick of the old covenant with himself and with those who derive from him. It is certainly a vision of the first day, the Lord's Day, says St John, the day of resurrection: but also Sunday, for Christ's countenance is shining as the sun shines in his strength.

The work of the second day is the firmament, of which Genesis says that it was made to divide the upper from the nether waters: it was conceived as the floor or curtain between the heavenly and the earthly. St John's second week begins with the passage of this barrier: the seer ascends through a door in the heavenly vault to penetrate above the veil and see the glory of God. Among the wonders represented there he finds the great 'sea' (i.e. laver) of glass which holds the upper waters. The drama which follows of the unsealing of the sealed book is a duplication of the penetration of the hidden and heavenly things: whether we pierce the curtain or have the scroll unrolled for us, it is all one. The two images flow together in the sixth unsealing: when the Lamb opened the last seal but one on the seven-sealed scroll, there was a great earthquake, and the sky departed as a rolled-up scroll, leaving the kings and the mighty under the immediate threat of naked heaven. The unrolling of the book is equivalent to the rolling up of the sky: both are revelation.

The third week (the trumpets) has no introduction at all

[1] There is a slightly different midrash on the same text in Apocalypse XI. Christ the 'Lord of the whole earth' is still the central light: but the priestly and royal supporters on either hand are the derivative royalty and priesthood of the apostolic Church: they are not only 'anointed stocks' but also (derivative) candlesticks.

60

sharply distinct from the sabbath of the previous week, out of which it almost immediately unfolds. It consists itself of judgements by means of the successive creation-works but, as we saw when we were analysing the series, it starts from the works not of the first day, but of the third. The number three is prominent throughout the whole seven: always a *third* is smitten by divine judgement. This contrasts with the *fourth* smitten by the four horsemen. The 'four' is there the number of destructive agents employed: but the only 'three' to which the constantly repeated 'third' of the trumpets can correspond is the ordinal number of the whole trumpet series. Again, the eagle's cry attaches peculiar terrors to the last three trumpets when they shall sound. Elsewhere the last three of the sevens are grouped together, but here alone St John emphatically proclaims that it is so.[1]

This third week presents us with a new problem, because it is preceded by a pair of 'intrusive visions' (VII) in the previous week. The intrusion seems to be of a preparatory and forward-looking character. We must ask, therefore, whether or not the creation-work proper to the third day already appears in it. Clearly it does. The 'intrusion' begins with the withholding of the winds from blowing on land, sea or any tree: land, sea, and vegetables are the works of the third day: land, herbs and trees are smitten by the first trumpet, and sea by the second.

The fourth week is that of the beast-visions. Here Leviathan, the false God, pretends to exercise divine power over the four parts of nature: first he is running riot among the heavenly luminaries, then he tries to make a river of water the instrument of his vengeance. After that the sea yields him an accomplice, then the land another. It is noticeable that the order of works in the trumpets, which is also the order of Genesis, has been exactly reversed: the luminaries are placed first. But the luminaries are the work of the fourth day. The series starts in the luminaries with all

[1] Other numbers in the series are readily explicable. The demons of the *fifth* trumpet-plague were to range for *five* months: *four* angels lead the two myriad myriads of demons in the sixth, because these are the slayers against whom above all the faithful were sealed while the *four* winds of destruction were restrained. (In the Ezekiel archetype, it is against slaying angels that the saints are marked on the forehead.)

61

the emphasis one could desire: a great sign in the sky, a woman clothed with the sun and the moon beneath her feet and over her head a crown of twelve stars.

Once more, the preceding 'intrusion' (x–xi, 13) of which the forward-looking character is so marked, anticipates the special creation-work of the day that follows it: the Angel of the Oath anticipates the astral description of the travailing woman: 'a strong angel descending from the sky, clothed with cloud and the rainbow over his head, and his face as the sun'. Genesis says that the luminaries were created 'for signs and seasons and days and years', and the message of the sun-angel is in accord with this. He comes to declare that the blowing of the seventh trumpet will mark a period of great significance in the fulfilment of the secret purpose of God.

The 'intrusive visions' in the seals and trumpets appear to act as preludes to the series which follow. If the following series is, as we are suggesting, to be reckoned as a 'day', then the preceding intrusive visions should perhaps be considered as the eve to that day. The Jews reckoned their days from evening to morning, and the account of creation-week in Genesis I conforms to this style, 'And there was evening and morning a first, second, etc., day.' And so St John counts his day from evening to morning when he begins the theme of land, sea and trees in the extra seal-visions, and continues it in the trumpet-visions, or when he begins the theme of luminaries in the extra trumpet-visions, and continues it in the beast-visions.

But if so, what is to happen about the 'days' which are preceded by no extra, or intrusive, visions? For intrusive visions are confined to the seals and trumpets. Are there to be no other eves? That would be surprising. Genesis reckons the days in two parts, evening and morning. Where there are 'intrusive visions' these become the 'evening' of their series, because in fact they make up in bulk roughly the second half of it: the numbered seal-visions (vi) are balanced by the unnumbered (vii), and it is the same in the trumpets, viii–ix being balanced by x–xi, 13. Where there are no intrusive visions, the whole section in which the seven occurs is never the less divided. The first section contains the candlestick-vision *plus* the messages, the second the vision of heaven *plus* the seals. The beast-visions we saw to have a division between the first four and the anticipatory fifth and sixth: the vial-section consists of the vials themselves *plus* a long appendix, and the last things similarly have their appendix.

The correct account would seem to be this. St John, obliged to start with day 1, and not halfway through day 0, treats the theophany (I) as the evening, and the messages (II–III) as the morning. He continues this form in the second day, the theophany (IV-V) being again the evening, and the unsealings (VI) the morning. But from this point onwards he varies his style: the next evening is not supplied by a third theophany, but by a new feature, the intrusive visions: and the fact that the evening is the evening of its own day as well as the eve of the day following finds expression in the stretching of the seal-series to cover the intrusive visions—for the seventh seal is withheld until after them. This form is repeated for the next day. But now the reader is used to the idea of an eve included within the preceding day, and in the beast-visions St John leaves us to see for ourselves that the second part of the straight series is the evening of its own day, and therefore the eve of the next. In the vial-section we have an appendix, which is doubtless an evening besides, and if an evening to its own day, then presumably an eve to the day following.

The eve to the vials, then, should begin at the second half of the beast-visions, that is to say, with the angel flying in mid-heaven (XIV, 6). We had occasion above to point out that the bird-like angel is the creature of the fifth day: and the vials are the fifth series. So much for the eve: but what of the morning? The creatures of the fifth day are the natives of the water, as well as the flying fowl. We have had the flying fowl in the eve: we may expect the morning to show us the living things from the water. 'Life from the water' is a great Johannine theme, as readers of the Gospel know; nor does the Apocalypse neglect it. 'The Lamb shall guide them unto fountains of waters of life' (VII, 17). 'I will give him that is athirst to drink of the fountain of the water of life freely' (XXI, 6). 'A river of water of life . . . proceeding out of the throne' (XXII, 1). 'He that will, let him take the water of life freely' (XXII, 17). In the Gospel the water both quenches spiritual thirst, and regenerates in the baptismal font. The Apocalyptic citations

63

which we have just given are all concerned with the water which quenches thirst: in the introduction to the vials we find the regenerating font, and this is proper to the symbol of the fifth creation-work. God commanded the water to bring forth living things: now he commands the font to bring forth men alive with the life of the world to come. Because of this analogy, the symbol of fish for baptised Christians was current in the primitive church; and Christ himself, as the prototype of Baptism, was specially designated by it.[1]

The vision of the vials begins with a vision of the font or laver of the heavenly temple, the 'sea' of glass; and over it, perhaps as risen from it, are the saints, equipped as levitical harpers. It was in the 'sea' of Solomon's temple that the priestly personnel performed their ritual ablutions. These heavenly musicians are to be understood as newly purified. They are martyrs, and the baptism they have undergone has been a baptism of fire: the fontal 'sea' is filled with a fiery mixture. In the sequel we see a fiery baptism poured by angel-hands upon the heads of their persecutors; but they do not repent.

In the pouring of the six vials there are two climaxes, the third and the sixth, and both are concerned with waters. The plagues on earth and sea are brief, and pass without comment; in the sea every living soul died, for the water was corrupted to blood. The third plague is equally brief in itself: it simply extends the same ghastly change to the rivers and fountains, but now a dialogue of angelic voices adds a comment. The angel of the waters justifies God for giving them blood to drink who had shed the blood of saints and prophets, and the voice of the slaughter-altar says Amen. Now they drink the river of death, they shall presently swell it: in the anticipatory vision of the eve to the vials we have already seen a premonitory shadow of a ghastly vintage, which will run blood to the height of the horses' bridles, and to a distance of two hundred miles.

The fourth and fifth vials pass as undistinguished as the first and second, but when the sixth brings us to the waters of Euphrates there is a fresh climax. Frogs, the living children of water, are spawned from the mouths of the Dragon and his two associates:

[1] The name $IX\Theta YC$ for Christ was also a play on letters, but it would not have been made unless the result had appeared to mean something.

64

they are evil spirits which go forth to summon the Armageddon muster, especially from behind the Great River.

We see, then, that the vials are full of the images of life from the water and death from the water. The theme continues in the introduction of the appendix-vision. One of the angels of the bowls shows Babylon as a harlot sitting on many waters, with a cup in her hand from which her lovers drink damnation: she is drunk herself with the blood of the saints. Her annihilation is sealed at last by the fall of a millstone into the sea.

Let us turn now to the work of the sixth day, the creation of the beasts of the earth, but more particularly of Adam. The things said about Adam in Genesis I are that he is directly created (not evoked from water or land), he is made in the image of God, he is made king over all the works of God's hands, and he is given a consort (male and female created he them). The Christ of the sixth morning (XIX, 11 ff.) appears from heaven, wearing the Name and nature of God. He appears as the Bridegroom of the Bride, and as the King of kings. The themes of the kingdom and the Bride continue in the sequel, and receive their full expression in the final vision, where the Throne of God and of the Lamb is planted in the heart of a city which is no other than the Bride.

The figure of Eve has appeared already, but as the mother of the seed who rises to bruise the serpent's head, as the bearer of the messianic Son, not as the bride of the messianic Adam (XII, 1). The figure of Eve the bride belongs to the sixth part of the Apocalypse. It is, however, anticipated, as is very proper, in the preceding eve (XVII–XVIII). Before we hear of the true Bride, we are shown the false, Babylon, the Beast's whore. The Beast's multiform figure is at the same time expounded to us as a confederacy of kings, destined to fall, because they must meet the Lord of Lords and King of kings—the very title borne by the warrior Bridegroom when he at length appears (XVII, 14; XIX, 16). The overthrow of the great whore makes room for the marriage-supper of the Lamb (XIX, 2, 7).

From our investigations, then, it results that the Apocalypse consists of six evenings and mornings, *plus* a final sabbath-eve (XXI, ff.). Not only are the creation-works regularly disposed through their proper days, but this disposition of them explains in addition certain irregularities in the creation-work rhythms interior to the separate series. We can now see why the series of the third day begins with earth, sea and waters instead of light, heaven and earth, and we can see why in the fourth day the order of the first four is reversed: luminaries, waters, sea, earth, instead of earth, sea, waters, luminaries.

However distant we may be from Jewish ways of thought, we are presumably able to appreciate the naturalness to a Jewish mind of conceiving the work of judgement which accomplishes the world as a week of divine labours. In six days God made this world, in six he is to fulfil it: and that will bring in the World to Come, the sabbath in which not only God himself, but also the saints will rest, as the Author to the Hebrews teaches: 'They shall enter into his rest.' Jewish Rabbis contemporary with St John applied the scheme of the week to the whole process of history. In a little week God had created the world, in a great week his sustaining providence guides it from its beginning to its destined end: the days of this great week are each, perhaps, a thousand years, as it is written, 'A thousand years in thy sight are as yesterday' (Psalm XC, cited in 2 Peter III, 8).

The speculation about the Millennium appears to have been integral to this scheme of history. If the days of Messiah were, as one school taught, to be a thousand years, it was because the days of Messiah are the last 'day' of history itself. St John accepts the belief in the Millennium, and with it, we must suppose, the scheme of a six-thousand-year world-history. According to the vision of Daniel the fifth day of history, the day of the monsters from the sea, is the age of persecution extending from Nebuchadnezzar onwards; the sixth day, the day of the Son of Man, is the age of the kingdom of the saints. St John, as we have seen in our examination of Apocalypse XII–XIV, understood perfectly the relation of Daniel's vision to Genesis I. We must suppose, then, that for him the Millennial Reign is the sixth age of history. There is no doubt whatever that he applies Daniel's vision to his Millennium. Daniel tells us that the enthronization of the Son of Man means that 'judgement is given to the saints of the Most High': and thus St John's millennial vision begins: 'I saw thrones, and they sat on them to whom judgement was given.'

66

St John, we must suppose, accepts a history of six thousand ages, the Millennium being the sixth:[1] and he places the Millennium in the sixth of his apocalyptic 'days'. And yet it is plain enough that the six great 'days' which compose his book do not represent the six ages of world history. On the contrary: the first five 'days' must all of them fall within the latter part of the fifth historical age, for they deal with that 'little while' which (for the primitive Christian imagination) was to elapse between the First Advent and the Second. It was 'in the end of the ages' that Christ had been first manifested: and though some theologians contemporary with us have made this mean something highly mysterious, the primitive Christians meant by it exactly what it appeared to say. For St John, to make the matter precise, Christ had come towards the end of the fifth age: the sixth would be the Millennium, initiated by the Second Advent, and terminated by the Last Judgement.

It follows from this that St John's six 'days' are grossly disproportionate to one another. It is rash to affirm anything of the exact length of perspective which St John allowed himself when he looked into the future, but there can be no doubt that he *writes* as though the interval between the two Advents were less than a hundred years. Within this period all the first five 'days' of his Apocalypse must be found: the sixth is a thousand years. A striking disproportion, yet nothing compared with the disproportion of the sixth to what follows it; for what are a thousand years to the days of eternity?

St John's six days begin with the Resurrection, with the Easter-Christ, 'the Living God who died, and is alive unto ages unending.' He stands among the Churches, their light, their master and their judge. And the six days end with the Advent, the Rider on the White Horse, the victor of the great battle. On these two days, the first and the sixth, Sunday and Friday, we have Christophanies. The figure of Christ is of course very frequent throughout the Apocalypse, but elsewhere he appears as a simple emblem,

---

[1] According to ordinary Jewish opinion, the Millennium would be the seventh, and this can be squared with Daniel; for since the *creation* of Adam is the last work of the sixth day, the *reign* of Adam may well fill the seventh. St John's scheme is presumably just Christian: for the Church, Friday and Sunday, not Saturday, are the days of the Son of Man.

67

a Lamb standing as slaughtered, a Harvester seated on a cloud. Only in the Son of Man among the Candlesticks and the Rider on the White Horse does St John give full rein to the ardour of his devotion, and lavish upon Christ the attributes of salvation and of majesty. For Sunday and Friday are the days of Christ. On Friday he won the victory of the cross over all 'principalities and powers', demons and men: and on Friday he returns to conquer in the visible sphere, as he already has in the invisible. On Sunday he rose, and on Sunday St John, in the spirit, beholds the Resurrection and the Life.

The Christ of Sunday and of Friday is the beginning and the end of the work of God, the A and the Ω, and St John sees this to be prefigured in the story of Genesis. For the noblest of the works were the first and the last, and each of them most evidently the type of Christ. The first work was the light which first conquered chaos and darkness, not the light which, as sun, moon, and stars, became part of the world, but an elemental light more ancient than heaven or earth, the true spiritual 'candle of the Lord'. And the last work was Adam, made in God's own image and likeness. How evident it is, then, that Sunday and Friday belong to Christ. St John's Gospel has no other doctrine: it begins with the Word which said, 'Let there be Light,' which Word is God the Son, and the light is his incarnation. And it leads us on to a great Friday when Christ conquered death as a new Adam, hailed by Pilate with the words 'Behold the Man' and 'Behold your King'. From a garden he went to his Passion, and in a garden St Magdalen saw him after it, as it had been a gardener, such as unfallen Adam was.

The moment of judgement in the Passion was the sixth hour of the sixth day, when the Jews looked into the face of their Creator and said, 'We have no king but Caesar,' and condemning him to be crucified, were themselves condemned. And the moment of judgement in the Advent is the sixth vision of the sixth day, when before the face of Enthroned Glory earth and heaven fly, but not the souls of men: they must stay and behold. After the judgement in the Passion Jesus brought all things to fulfilment on the cross, and saying 'I thirst' and 'It is finished', he died, and poured blood and water from his smitten side. No sooner is the judgement past in the Apocalypse than we hear the voice of him who makes new

68

the heaven and earth, and thus he speaks. 'These words are faithful and true; and they are done. I am the A and Ω, the beginning and the end. I will give to him that is athirst of the fountain of the water of life freely.' He continues: 'He that overcometh shall inherit these things: and I will be his God, and he shall be my Son.' We remember how, at the Cross, that disciple who, in the language of the Apocalypse, 'overcame,' that is, was steadfast in the day of persecution when Peter denied and fled—that solitary victor, hearing the words, 'Son, behold thy Mother,' was made the adoptive brother of the Son of God, of him who was able for himself to say, 'Be of good cheer: I have overcome the world.'

This is not the place to elaborate the parallel between Apocalypse and Gospel. It will be more relevant to observe that the voice, 'It is finished' or 'The words of God are done,' is proper to the sixth day, according to the scheme of Genesis. For on that day 'God saw all that he had made, and behold, it was very good. And there was evening and there was morning a sixth day. And the heaven and the earth were finished, and all the host of them'. When God says, 'They are done,' in the last vision of the sixth apocalyptic day, the heaven and the earth, and all their host, have just been new-created.

The Christians honour Sunday and Friday, but not most naturally in that order. It is the Sunday which follows the Friday, the Resurrection which follows the Passion, the eighth, not the first of Holy Week that they revere. In a Christian work we should expect to find the week in the form of an octave.

But how is St John to reconcile this Christian octave with the Jewish scheme of the week, which appears to end with such finality in the sabbath-rest of God? Jewish theology itself contains the suggestion he requires. God entered into rest on the seventh day of the genesis, yet this was a rest only in respect of the work of primary creation. He who slumbers not nor sleeps is active in sustaining, guiding and redeeming his creatures.

This piece of theology is directly invoked by the Christ of the Fourth Gospel, when he is accused of healing on sabbath. 'My Father worketh hitherto,' he says, 'and I work.' Sabbath is for men, in commemoration of the divine rest after the labour of Creation. But it does not bind the Creator. Though he has rested

69

for ever from the primary creative work, he works continually in the sustenance and restoration of his creatures, whether men work or rest, wake or sleep. And the Son's acts of healing are part of the Father's continual work in the history of men.

The eternal rest of the seventh creation-day is the womb out of which issues the work of history. But if history itself is to be conceived as making up a week, and so as attaining its own sabbath, may not we think of this sabbath in the same way? Is not God's sabbatical rest from the work of history the womb out of which a greater work comes? God rests, perhaps, from the guidance of his first creation, but this rest is itself the changeless act of uttering a new creation, and filling it perpetually with himself. God is not inactive through the eternity of the World to Come.

The Sabbaths of God are just as much the eternal repose out of which his action breaks, as they are the eternal repose into which his action resolves. There is for him no mere repetition of weeks with similar form and content, each renewing and continuing the labours of the last. For each process of divine act is complete, and shapes its own week. When the next is born, it is a new level of act, and constitutes as it were a new dimension of time, springing direct out of God's eternity, rather than out of any series of successive events. The Sabbaths of the Apocalypse conform to this system of thought. We never find one week running on into the next at the same level, as our human weeks do. Sometimes eternity is unveiled between one week and the next, as happens between the messages and the seals, and again after the vials. Sometimes the Sabbath of the previous week itself becomes a vision of heaven, out of which the new action of the succeeding week springs, and this is what we find at the seventh trumpet and the seventh beast-vision. In such cases as these, St John treats the Sabbath as belonging quite as much to the process to which it gives birth, as to the process which it terminates.

Sunday is the day of Resurrection. The 'week' with which the Apocalypse deals extends from the Resurrection of Christ to the General Resurrection, when death has been destroyed. That final resurrection which is analogous to Christ's own is not to be understood as the dreadful summons from the grave to meet the eternal Judge. It is the reward of justification, the gift of fulness of life, as we read in the parable of Sheep and Goats: 'These shall depart (from before their Judge) into eternal punishment: but the righteous into eternal life.' It does not precede but follow the judgement. The righteous clad with immortality are nothing else but the Bride, the City of living stones. She begins to descend during the seventh vision of the sixth day, she is founded and displayed in an eighth vision, the appendix (XXI, 9 ff.).

Does St John consciously intend his book to end with an octave-day rather than a Sabbath? Perhaps it is right to answer that the sabbath is for him almost a point without magnitude. God rests from his completed work, but in so resting he initiates a new act which is the eighth-and-first day. We may compare the Gospel once more. On the sixth day Christ conquered, and achieved his rest from the labours of his flesh. But the sabbath-day which follows is in itself nothing, it has no content: it is simply the restful sepulchre out of which, with the eighth and first day, the resurrection springs.

Such a line of interpretation is suggested for the Apocalypse by the form of the 'intrusive visions' in VII, which offer a close parallel to the end of the whole work.[1] The anticipatory conclusion to which they bring us is an unnumbered *eighth* vision. Out of the sabbath of the sealing springs the octave of the great multitude, the vision of final bliss. Surely, then, St John means us to understand that the end, when it comes, is the octave to which the last sabbath of all gives birth.[2]

The first Sunday (Apoc. I) and the Friday (Apoc. XIX) are Christophanies: should not the octave-Sunday (XXI, 9 ff.) be a Christophany too? It is interesting that the last little sabbath-vision (XX, 1–8) is empty of Christ, as is the sabbath of holy week in the Gospel. The Bride is descending, but the Husband is not named: he that sitteth on the throne declares the finishing of the work, but there is no mention of the Lamb. In the final vision it is

---

[1] See below, pp. 80 f., 84.

[2] If we view XXI, ff. as part of the final apocalypse (XIX–XXII) it is formally an octave. If we view it as part of the whole apocalypse (I–XXII) it is formally a Friday evening (appendix of the sixth 'day') and therefore a Sabbath Eve. (There is no distinct Sabbath morning; eternity is timeless). The two ways of viewing XXI, ff. balance the Christian week against that of Genesis.

otherwise. The interpreter-angel promises a vision of 'the Bride, the Lamb's wife', and St John sees her, bright with the glory of God, and with her luminary which is Christ. In all things God and the Lamb are now as one. They are jointly the temple of the holy city, and together her light. The throne that stands there is the throne of God and of the Lamb, whom worshipping, the saints will serve one God: 'they shall see *his* face, and *his* Name shall be upon their foreheads' (XXII, 3–4).

There has been hitherto a certain tension between the unity of the Lamb with God and his unity with us. The Lamb is 'in the midst of the Throne,' yet the Throne is never said simply to be God's and his: he has his place in the midst of the Throne, but he stands also among the seven Churches, or on Mt Zion with the twelve times twelve thousand: he comes forth as God's harvester, riding on the white cloud, or as his champion on the white horse. He reigns as God's Anointed on earth in the Millennium, while the Great Throne remains above the firmament. But in the consummation of the end, the Great Throne is set in the heart of the redeemed creature, and the heart of the redeemed creature is the manhood of Christ. The presences of Christ's manhood with God and with us are no longer distinct. 'We are in him that is True, even in his Son Jesus Christ. This is the true God, and life everlasting.'

The last vision of the Apocalypse fulfils the revelation of the deity of Jesus, and so becomes a Christ-vision worthy to stand with the Christophanies of the previous Sunday (Apoc. I) and the Friday (Apoc. XIX). There is not, indeed, a formal Christophany, and yet Christ is made almost more present here than in either of the Christophanies. We have seen above that the vision of the Bride is written in careful parallel to the vision of the Whore, and the parallel is nowhere more strikingly enforced than in the conclusion. The visions of Babylon run out into heavenly exultation over the fall of the harlot, but still more over the coming marriage of the Bride. The visions of Jerusalem have shewn us the Bride in her marriage glory, and carried us to the heights of heavenly exultation. The visions of Babylon proceed from the exultation to an Amen, first spoken by the heavenly host, then paraphrased by the angel of St John's inspiration. 'These', says he, 'are true words of God.' St John falls to worship the angel, but the angel forbids idolatry: let him keep his worship for God. Immediately the heavens open, and he appears in whom God must be worshipped, riding the white horse, and called Faithful and True. (St John still had this scene in mind when he wrote the words we have just quoted from his First Epistle. 'We are in him that is True, even in his Son Jesus Christ. This is the true God, and life everlasting. *Little children, keep yourselves from idols*'.) The vision of the white-horsed rider is the Friday Christophany.

After the final exultation in the vision of the Bride (xxii, 3–5) St John draws out the parallel with the previous vision, to the very brink of the Christophany: and there he changes direction. Once more the angel of inspiration is heard to say, 'These words are faithful and true.' Once more St John falls to worship, is forbidden, and told to worship God. He listens to the voice which proceeds from the angel's lips: it is the voice of Jesus. 'Behold, I come quickly', he says: 'and my reward is with me, to render to each man according as his work is; I the A and the Ω, the first and the last, the beginning and the end . . . I Jesus have sent mine angel to testify unto you these things for the churches. I AM the root and child of David, the bright and morning star. And the Spirit and the Bride say, Come. And let him that heareth say, Come. And let him that is athirst come: let him that will take the water of life freely. . . . He which testifieth these things saith: Yea, I come quickly. Amen; come, Lord Jesus.'

The Christophany on St John's last page, then, is this: the angel speaks with the voice of Jesus. To appreciate the meaning of this, we must recall the relation between the figure of Christ and the figure of the angel throughout the Apocalypse. It is not every appearance of Christ or every angel-vision that we have to consider; but only the interventions of either figure in the role of principal revealer. The whole apocalypse is to be understood as mediated to St John by five acts of revelation. (1) Christ himself appears, and gives the messages to the Churches. (2) The Lamb is seen in heaven unsealing the book. Through the act of unsealing two 'weeks' of visions are opened. The seal-visions *accompany* the Lamb's act, the trumpet-visions *result* from it when it is completed. (3) A glorious angel brings St John an open scroll, which he digests. The result is that he sees two more 'weeks' of visions, the beast-visions and the vials. (4) One of the vial-angels steps forward, as it were, out of the frame of the vision in which he has just been seen, to show St John further visions. He shows the seer the visions of Babylon. When he comes to the heavenly liturgy of Alleluias (XIX, 1–10) the angel speaks words so divine that St John falls to worship him. The angel forbids him, and the figure of the glorious Christ is manifested as though to claim the misdirected worship. Christ does not, however, replace the angel in his capacity of revealer: he and his acts are still what the angel reveals. (5) After the 'week' of last things is complete, one of the vial-angels comes forward once more to show the vision of Jerusalem. After the vision the angel begins again to say things so divine that St John attempts to worship him afresh. He is again reproved: but this time the worship is not directed away from the angel to a visionary Christ whom the angel shows; it is directed as it were inwards to the living Christ in the angel's soul, out of which the Saviour speaks with his own voice.

We might give a superficial and exterior account of this series of revelatory acts as follows. It is a pattern, first contrasting, then uniting, two figures. (a) In (1) and (2) Christ the revealer is presented, and in (3) the angel-revealer: so far they have been brought into no sort of relation with one another. (b) In (4) they are related, but the relation is negative: the angel is shown to be something very different from the Christ he reveals. (c) In (5) the negation is overcome: the angel is not, indeed, Christ, but Christ reveals himself through the angel, so that the person of the angel can be, in a sense, discounted, and Christ heard through and in him.

This is a merely formal account of the matter, for it does not explain the reason for the introduction of the angel or the importance of the reconciliation of his mediatorship with the higher mediatorship of Christ. A more substantial account might run somewhat as follows. In the Candlestick-vision (1) Christ the revealer is seen on earth. In the vision of the Lamb and the Book (2) he is seen in heaven, and this appears to give a climax when compared with (1). But the climax is achieved at the price of increased *distance*. We are further from this Christ than from the

74

Christ of the Candlestick-vision. And so, paradoxically enough, we feel that there is a further stage of climax when the glorious angel of (3) brings the book down to earth, and actually gives the seer to eat and digest what he had merely contemplated in heaven. We see, then, that the stress on the heavenliness of Christ the revealer brings in his angel as a compensation, so that Christ may be utterly in heaven, and yet may fully reveal himself on earth— how? Through his angel. Now it becomes vital that we should perceive the relation between the angel and Christ. The angel speaks the words of God, but he *is* not the Word of God (4). Nevertheless, the Word of God speaks in him (5); Christ is absolutely present to us here, but, so long as this world lasts, always in his angel. The unmediated presence of Christ awaits the Advent. And so he who speaks in the angel speaks of the day when he will cast the angel off: 'Behold,' he says, 'I come quickly.' In myself I come: in my angel I am here already. Looking back over the Apocalypse, we are now to understand that the angel was already present though unseen in the Candlestick-vision, mediating Christ. Did not St John preface the Candlestick-vision with the title: 'Apocalypse of Jesus Christ . . . which he signified through the sending of his angel to his servant John'?

The Christ-voice of XXII recalls the Christ-vision of I, the only other place where Christ names himself the First and the Last (I, 17). In XXII he declares himself the bright and morning star: in the Candlestick-vision his countenance shone as the sun shines in his strength, and he was master of the stars. For the first day is the Day of Light, not the light of the created sun or moon, but light itself. Because Christ, and the Father in Christ, are this light, the city of the final vision has no need of the lights which were created on the fourth day: 'no need of the sun, neither of the moon, to shine on her; for the glory of God hath lightened her and the lamp thereof is the Lamb.' 'They shall see his face, and his Name shall be on their foreheads, and there shall be night no more; and they need no light of lamp, neither light of sun, for the Lord God shall give them light, and they shall reign for ever and ever.'

Does St John's eighth day stand in any detailed relation to the scheme provided by Genesis? One might think not, since the

75

creation-work was completed in the six days. The sabbath finds in Genesis no more detailed type than the bare statement that there was rest. The eighth day, as such, has no type in Genesis at all. It is, among other things, another and higher antitype to the *first* day of creation than that provided by Apocalypse I–III: it is a new FIAT LUX: and that, we might think, is all the relation it bears to the Genesis scheme.

On the other hand we have to reckon with that feature of Genesis which, as we know from the case of Philo, intrigued the Jewish mystical interpreter—the apparent double account of creation. No doubt that age was aware that, in the literal sense, the same history narrated in I was to be understood as recapitulated in II, but why had the Holy Ghost inspired the recapitulation, if not to suggest some mystery? For Philo, with his Platonic bent, the first creation is the more divine; for St John's eschatological mind, it is the other way about.

After the account of the sabbath in Genesis, we read: These are the generations of the heaven and earth when they were created, in the day that the Lord God made earth and heaven. [Here, then, is the *one-day* creation of the world to come contrasted with the six-day creation of this world.] . . . And the Lord God formed man of the dust of the ground and breathed into his nostrils the breath of life. [This is clearly the second creation which is the resurrection: the former creation simply made man by a word *ex nihilo*, but here he is being remade from his dust. The interpretation is suggested by the resurrection-vision in Ezekiel XXXVII, 'Come from the four winds, O breath', etc.] And the Lord God planted a garden eastward in Eden, and there he put the man whom he had formed. And out of the ground made the Lord God to grow every tree that is pleasant to the sight and good for food: and the tree of life also in the midst of the garden. . . . And a river went out of Eden to water the garden, and from thence it was parted and became four heads: the name of the first is Pishon: that is it which compasses the whole land of Havilah where there is gold . . . anthrax and beryl-stone. [Here we have the Paradise of the last vision, with the Tree of Life, the river, the precious stones and the gold.] And the Lord God said, It is not good that the man should be alone: I will make him an help meet for him. . . . And he

76

took one of his ribs . . . and made it a woman and brought her unto the man. And the man said: This is now bone of my bones and flesh of my flesh: she shall be called woman, because she was taken out of man. Therefore shall a man leave his father and his mother and shall cleave unto his wife, and the twain shall be one flesh. [Here is the 'great mystery' which St Paul had already referred to Christ and the Church, and which receives abundant expression on the eighth day of the Apocalypse: the Bride being identified with the city of living stones, itself identified with Paradise.]

(2)

The Apocalypse is an octave, according to what is perhaps the prevalent symbolism. But this symbolism is extracted by emphasising the relation of the last vision (the Bride) to the last little week (XIX-XXI, 8), to which it stands as octave-day. In the great week of the whole book, the last vision is Friday evening, or Sabbath Eve. There are no more than six complete sevenfold days, and it appears that St John saw them in three parallel pairs. So much light is thrown by this arrangement upon the rhythm of his image-sequences, that it seems worth while to set it out. In each of the three columns we will place two 'evenings' and two 'mornings'.

1st Evening.		
The Son of Man among the candlesticks.	Sealing of 144,000 and Great Multitude.	Beast-visions (II)[1]: The Sealed 144,000, and the Son of Man.
1st Morning.		
Messages to seven Church-angels.	Blasts of seven trumpet-angels.	Plagues of seven vial-angels.
2nd Evening.		
The Glory, the Book and the Lamb.	The Angel, the Book and the Reed.	Interpreter-angel, and visions of Babylon.
2nd Morning.		
Seven seals.	Seven Beast-visions (I).	Seven Last Things.
		Vision of Zion.

[1] For different purposes we find ourselves dividing the Beast-Visions before and after the vision of the Lamb with the 144,000. This is no scandal: the vision is in fact a watershed.

77

We observe certain things at a glance. In the first evening, the third column draws together the themes of the other two. In the first column is the Son of Man, in the second the 144,000 sealed, in the third the 144,000 sealed and the Son of Man. In the first morning, we find counted sevens of angels in all three columns, the match between the last two being particularly close. In the second evening, the first two columns have a common feature in the book of divine revelation, both visions being drawn from the first vision of Ezekiel, as we shall show in due place. In the second column it is an angel of inspiration who brings the book, and this person has his antitype in the interpreter-angel of the third column. In the second morning we have sevens throughout. But in contrast with the first morning, they are not sevens of angels, nor are they counted, except in the first column, and even there the seven things are not a uniform series, like the messages, trumpets or vials: there is a uniform four (the horsemen) *plus* a vision of the souls of the martyrs, and another of the portents of the Last Judgement.

The form of the Genesis-works will permit a division of the week into pairs of days. For the first two days witnessed the creation of heavenly things (light; the firmament), the second two the creation of our world (land and sea; the luminaries[1]), the third two the creation of life (fishes and birds; beasts and men).

In the scheme of the Apocalypse, as we have set it out above, the final vision, that of Jerusalem, is a seventh eve, so it falls outside the six days. But it does not hang in the air, without a type in the preceding visions. On the contrary, as we have seen, the type of the Jerusalem-Vision is the Babylon-Vision. But the Babylon-Vision is not in the proper place to act as type to the Jerusalem-Vision; it is much too far advanced, being halfway down the third column, not last in the second. Well, what of it? Why should not St John take the Babylon-Vision quite out of its turn when he uses it as a type to the Jerusalem-Vision? Why should not he simply skip all that intervenes between the Beast-Visions and

[1] St John does in fact treat the works of these two days as making up the frame of the world. By subdividing water he makes it a list of four (land, sea, fresh waters, luminaries). These four occupy a place of great importance in his symbolism; see below, p. 198.

78

the Babylon-Visions? There is no reason in the world why he should not, but in fact he does not. He prefers to condense, rather than skip. As far as the last day in the last column, everything is regular, but then he begins taking two units of type to each unit of antitype. The antitype thus uses up the type so fast, that the vision of Jerusalem ends level with the vision of Babylon. In order to represent this in a diagram we must write the first three elements of the third column twice.

The Son of Man among the candlesticks.	Sealing of 144,000 and Great Multitude.	Beast-visions II: the sealing of 144,000, and Son of Man.
Messages to seven Church-angels.	Blast of seven trumpet-angels.	Plagues of seven vial-angels.
The Glory, the Book, and the Lamb.	The Angel, the Book, and the Reed.	Interpreter-angel, and Babylon-visions.
Seven Seals.	Seven Beast-visions I	
	Beast-visions II *Seven Vials*	Seven Last Things.
	Babylon-visions.	Jerusalem-vision.

The irregularity only concerns the second set of types taken up in the last day. The first set of types, those from the first column, are used with perfect regularity in the third. The correspondence (for example) between the Seals and Last Things is especially close, and especially important. Both begin with a vision of a white-horsed conqueror.

The whole detail of the correspondences of the sequel to the vials with the sequel to the messages on the one hand and the sequel to the trumpets on the other, can best be exhibited in a three-column table, with the vial-sequel in the middle, although it comes last in the book.

Seven messages.	Seven Egyptian plagues (vials).	Seven Egyptian plagues (trumpets).
Angel's summons, and spiritual rapture into heaven.	First angel's summons, and spiritual rapture into wilderness. Vision of the Woman and the Beast.	Vision of the Woman and Dragon, and of the Beast. First angel with gospel.

79

	Second angel crying, Fallen, fallen is Babylon the great . . . for all the nations have fallen through the wine of her adulterous wrath.	Second angel crying, Fallen, fallen is Babylon the great, who made all nations drink of the wine of her adulterous wrath.
Vision of Glory,		
culminating	Third angel confirms by the cast of a mill-stone a heavenly voice: . . . In the cup that she mingled mingle her the double . . . The kings of the earth shall weep and lament, when they see the smoke of her burning, standing afar for the fear of her tor-ment.	Third angel crying: If any worship the Beast . . . he shall drink of the wine of God's wrath, mingled unmixed in the cup of his anger, and shall be tormented with fire . . . and the smoke of their torment goes up for ever and ever.
in		
heavenly liturgy: (a) the Elders and Cheru-bim fall and worship, (b) the universal choir takes up the praise. Amen.	Voices in heavenly lit-urgy: (a) the Elders and Cherubim fall and wor-ship, (b) the universal choir takes up the Alle-luia.	
	A beatitude. These words are true words of God, says the self-confessed angel of pro-phetic Spirit.	Heavenly voice pro-nounces a beatitude. Yea, saith the Spirit . . .
Rider on the White Horse appears when Christ opens the first seal.	Rider on the White Horse, crowned with many diadems, springs through the opened heaven.	Rider on the White Cloud, crowned with a golden crown.
	Angel summons the kites to the field of death.	Angel summons the sickle-bearer to the vintage of death.
II–IV Further plagues of horsemen.	III Carnage of horsemen, effected by him who treads the vintage of wrath.	Treading of vintage described as a carnage of horsemen.
	IV Another angel with the key of the abyss.	Seven angels with the last plagues.

80

v Deliverance of the souls of those slaughtered for the word of God and testimony they held.	v Enthronement of the souls of those beheaded for the testimony of Jesus and the word of God, and that worshipped not the Beast nor his image.	Heavenly triumph of those victorious over the Beast and his image.
	Muster of Gog and Magog: their destruction by fall of fire from heaven.	Sixfold outpouring of fire from heaven: the Armageddon muster.
vi Rolling up of heaven and signs of the last judgement.	vi Flight of earth and heaven: the last judgement.	Flight of mountains and islands, as effect of
Sealing of saints and final bliss of the redeemed. He that sitteth on the throne shall tabernacle over them. They shall hunger no more, nor thirst any more: the Lamb shall guide them unto fountains of waters of life: and God shall wipe away all tears from their eyes.	vii Jerusalem revealed for restoration to earth. A great voice out of the throne: 'The tabernacle of God is with men, and he shall wipe away all tears from their eyes, and death shall be no more, nor shall there be mourning nor crying nor pain any more' ... And he said: 'They are done' ... 'I will give to the thirsty of the fountain of water of life.'	great voice from the throne, 'It is done': Babylon remembered for destruction.
	One of the vial-angels shews the vision of the bride.	One of the vial-angels shews the vision of the harlot.

In turning to comment on the three-column table, let us take the second of the two parallels first. After the visions belonging to the seventh trumpet, the next substantial episode is the drama of the woman persecuted by the red dragon. After the vision belonging to the seventh vial, the next episode is the woman leagued with the scarlet beast. The second woman is a parody of the first, just as antichrist is the parody of Christ: the episodes of the two women are in evident and contrasted parallel. Their beginnings are in line, but their ends are not; for the one vision of xvii covers the substance not only of the one vision in xii, but of the further three visions in xiii, 1–xiv, 5 as well. For it contains an elaborate account of the great Beast, who first appears in XIII; and it fore-shadows his defeat by the Lamb, who appears in XIV, 1–5.

To conclude: XVII condenses into one long interpretative vision a parallel to the whole dramatic vision-sequence of XII–XIV, 5, the first and principal part of 'the Beast-Visions'. Where, then, does the form of XVIII–XIX come from? The first line of it unmistakably directs us: 'Fallen, fallen, is Babylon the Great.' We have had that already in XIV. What St John does is to write the whole new series in XVII–XIX to the form of XIV, 6–14, substituting the *angelus interpres* with his shewing of the harlot's overthrow for the flying angel with his good news of divine judgement. That is to say that whereas in XII–XIV the series of the three angels *follows* the visions of the woman and the beasts, in XVII–XVIII the series of three angels *embraces* the vision of the woman on the beast, the first angel being put in charge of the vision. The second angels in the two series correspond exactly, in the substance and the very words of their message, 'Fallen, fallen is Babylon the great.' But as for the third angels, St John desires so much to amplify in XVIII what he had written in XIV that the form would be utterly spoiled if the third angel of XVIII were allowed to make as long a speech as St John's matter requires. The angel must make a short and dramatic appearance, in parallel with the cry, 'Fallen, fallen is Baby-lon. . . .' St John gives the long amplification to a voice from heaven, which elaborates in a poem of three stanzas what the third angel of XIV had far more briefly said. The third angel of XVIII comes in with a dramatic confirmation of the heavenly voice, plunging his millstone into the sea whence it shall rise again no more, and pronouncing a sixfold 'no more' over fallen Babylon.

The transition from the fifth to the sixth of the beast-visions, from the angel-cries, that is, to the harvest-vision, is contrived with perfect art, and it is plainly the model for the transition from the evening visions of XVII–XIX, 10 to the morning visions of XIX, 11 ff. The last angel-cry announces torment for the wicked who consent to worship the Beast and his image. 'Here', the angel concludes, 'is the endurance of the saints, who keep the command-ments of God and the faith of Jesus'—here (that is to say, in the divine judgement) the martyrs and confessors find their vindica-tion. This truth is immediately confirmed by a beatitude which

82

falls from the sky: 'Write, Blessed are the dead that die in the Lord, and that presently[1].' The voice of inspiration says Amen to the voice of heaven: 'Yea, saith the Spirit, let them rest from their labours, for their works accompany them.' That is to say, that since the martyrs carry their merits with them, they may be happy to rest from their struggles, because they are assured of a speedy reward. The Yea of the Spirit has the effect of breaking up the continuous façade of conventional images which have furnished the previous visions: it brings us back to the mysterious point of personal inspiration out of which all vision springs. What follows comes with the force of a new revelation, in which the promise of the Spirit becomes flesh and blood. 'Their works accompany them.' The picture of work and its reward is more constantly associated with the figure of harvest than with any other. Behold, then, the Son of Man, sitting on a white cloud, with a sickle in his hand to harvest the earth. He reaps the field of holiness; his angels vintage the grapes of sin; and in the next vision we see the gathered saints exultant above the Sea of Glass (xv).

We have to compare with this transition the transition in xix. From the angels crying vengeance on the wicked we pass to the joy of the expectant saints, now visibly revealed in heavenly exultation. There is the same mysterious emergence of the voice of inspiration—without being clearly told so, we become aware that the voice which speaks is that of the angel through whom St John sees the heavenly vision, and who declares himself to be the minister of the prophetic spirit. The angel says Amen, and gives his beatitude, 'Blessed are they that are bidden to the marriage-supper of the Lamb.' And thereupon the beatitude and the Amen become flesh and blood. Jesus, the Word of God Faithful and True, the Bridegroom of the White-robed Church, breaks through the opening skies. The vintage of wrath follows, then the millennial thrones of the saints.

The irregularity of parallel between the middle and right-hand

---

[1] ἄπαρτι. This word so closely preceding the appearance of the Son of Man on clouds, sounds like an echo of Matthew XXVI, 64, where the prototype of all martyrs makes his profession before the court, and adds, 'Presently (ἄπαρτι) shall you see the Son of Man sitting at the right hand of Power and coming with clouds.'

83

columns of our table helps to explain the form of the week of Last Things. This week appears to have two climaxes, at the fifth (millennial thrones), and again in the seventh (the World to Come). Some light is cast on this by the parallel. For since the end of the eve of vials (Rider on the Cloud) is matched by the beginning of the advent morning (Rider on the Horse), the glory out of which the morning of vials opens (exultant saints by the Sea of Glass) finds a match at the beginning of the second half of the week of last things, viz. at the fifth vision (enthroned saints in the millennial kingdom). The purely formal and very brief vial-plagues (1–5) receive no separate recognition, and so the substance of the vial-series (Armageddon muster, and 'It is done' pronounced over Babylon) find their fulfilment in the rebellion of Gog, and in the 'It is done' pronounced over Jerusalem. Then we come to the Whore-Vision in the one column and the Bride-Vision in the other.

Let us look at the other set of comparisons presented by our long three-column table. There is no detailed parallel at all (how could there be?) between the seven messages and the seven vials: but the parallel between the seven unsealings and the seven last things is of crucial importance. When the first seal was opened and the first Cherub cried Maranatha, the white-horsed rider appeared who was not what the saints were longing for, but only a first scout in front of the Advent-host; and therefore the martyr-souls under the fifth seal cried, 'How long?', and were commanded to wait until their number was fulfilled by the great tribulation. The tribulation has now passed: he who appears on the white horse in XIX leads the hosts of Advent, and with the fifth vision the martyr-souls receive their thrones at last. In these two fifth visions and no-where else have we visions of the *souls* of martyrs.

The seal-visions conclude (to all practical purposes) in the two extra visions following the sixth. Those visions are cancelled in their place, and allowed to stand only as an anticipation of the conclusion to the whole book. But in XX–XXI the final conclusion arrives and the cancelled conclusion is reinstated. Those who 'came out of the great tribulation' receive their reward when Jerusalem is revealed. And here we will leave the comparison between the three columns.

84

We may naturally ask ourselves about a system of parallels both so complicated and so irregular, whether it was the effect of conscious construction on St John's part, or whether he got caught up in the rhythms of his own previous thought-processes, and composed a sort of mental music by direct inspiration, varying and combining earlier phrases in the later movements of his melody, realizing, certainly, that he was moving in cycles of varied echo, but not aware in detail how the echo went. We may raise questions of this kind: I do not know that we can answer them. But whether it is hard reason or whether it is mental music, this is how it goes, and if we wish to appreciate it, we must observe the rhythms.

(3)

There is one further rhythmic pattern which we will examine here, a pattern perhaps as important as any in the building-up of the poem.

When we were establishing in the previous chapter the principal divisions of the Apocalypse, we naturally paid first attention to the hard formal elements, about which there could be least mistake. Here were, anyhow, six regular series of seven visions each, each seven forming the core of a section which (in all cases but one) included other material besides. What we have now to observe is that there is a more flexible repetitive rhythm in the sections, a rhythm not identical with the sevenfold rhythm, but interplaying variously with it.

When we were looking at the 'intrusive visions' or 'premature conclusions' in the seals and trumpets (VII and X–XI) we observed that they had the effect of rounding off the sections in which they stand into something like complete apocalypses on their own. There is no single remark one can make which more illuminates the character of the Apocalypse, than the statement that it is in perpetual tension between the claims of the part and the claims of the whole: each section being almost allowed, but never quite allowed, to become an apocalypse whole in itself. One cannot illustrate it better than by comparison with the Biblical and primitive vision of the Church. The Church, the Bride of Christ, was so effectively present in every local ecclesia, that it was, in that place,

85

the Church of Christ, whole and undiminished: and yet, because what was present there was the universal Church, it was but a partial manifestation, and the whole Church could be seen only in the whole company before the throne of God on the mystical Zion. In some such way, the spirit of apocalypse is so effectively present in each part of St John's book, that each is an apocalypse, and lives with a life of its own; and yet no part can contain the whole, or if any, then only the last part, because it gathers up the substance of all the preceding parts in a final consummation.

In so far as the sections are themselves apocalypses, they have a common rhythm, and it is this we are considering. We set aside the first section, which is in any case not an apocalypse. The eschatological movement begins in the Seals, where we have the sequence: (1) repetitive series of judgements (four horsemen), (2) vision of the martyr-souls awaiting their reward, (3) great earthquake, the portent of final judgement, forcing the heathen to acknowledge God, (4) the saints exultant before the throne in their blessedness (second intrusive vision). If we reduce this series to its bare elements, what does it say? (1) Repeated hammer-blows of judgement fall upon the world, (2) but they do not produce the penitence or the overthrow of oppressive heathendom, nor do they visibly vindicate the martyrs. (3) The dreadful day is coming, however, which will do this, and (4) thereafter the full number of the saints will exult in the Kingdom of God.

What prevents this from becoming a complete apocalypse? Two things chiefly. (a) We have been told from the start that there are seven seals to be broken, and one still remains. When this is broken in a vision which we will number (5), it reveals a heavenly liturgy out of which fresh judgement opens. (b) Between (3), the vision of the dreadful Day, and (4) the vision of ultimate bliss, is inserted the vision of the 144,000, in which the Saints are sealed against woes yet to come. By this we know that (3) cannot have been the full revelation of the Last Judgement, nor can (4) be more than an anticipatory glimpse of ultimate bliss. The woes against which the saints are sealed have yet to run their course.

Let us now follow this rhythm into the trumpets. We find (1) repetitive series of judgements (all six trumpets), (2) vision of the martyrs under Antichrist (the two witnesses), (3) great earth-

86

quake, forcing the heathen to 'give God the glory' (conclusion of same vision), (4) exultation before the throne of God, because his Kingdom has come (seventh trumpet), and (5) liturgical exposition of the Ark (end of same vision). The plot of the story is the same here as in the previous series—the hammer-blows of judgement do not break the wicked power; on the contrary, the martyrdom under antichrist (the 'great tribulation') follows. Only after that does judgement become so manifest as to make mankind 'give God the glory'. Then we hear exultation in heaven, because the Kingdom has come.

What are the features which prevent us from taking the trumpet-apocalypse as complete? It is not that, when the end has apparently come, the seventh trumpet has still to blow. On the contrary, the seemingly final moment is that which the seventh trumpet introduces: and if this apocalypse is ambiguous, it is because the vision of the seventh trumpet is itself ambiguous—it is not clear whether the exultation heralds or celebrates the last act. If there were no other features to suggest incompleteness, we should presumably suppose that it celebrates it. Is the sign of incompleteness to be found in the feature which corresponds here to the sealing of the saints in the seals—the beginning of the intrusion after the sixth numbered vision? To the sealing of the saints closely corresponds the measuring of the temple, whereby the elect of God are made inviolable. But since this scene comes much earlier in the rhythm here, between (1) and (2), not between (3) and (4), before the vision of martyrs, not after, it can be supposed that the saints are being protected against what follows in (2), the persecution of Antichrist; and so they are, in fact. The measuring is, however, introduced by the angel's oath and the digestion of the scroll. The oath says that in the days of the seventh trumpet-angel, when he shall sound, the secret purpose of God is accomplished; a saying as ambiguous as the seventh trumpet-vision itself. If we insist on 'the days of', a considerable period introduced by the trumpet is suggested: if we insist on 'when he shall sound', we get the impression of immediate fulfilment. The saying which accompanies the gift of the scroll is more to our purpose. The seer is to digest it, because he must 'prophesy anew over many peoples, nations, tongues and kings'. This suggests a longer perspective

87

than the couple of pages which still remain of the trumpet-apocalypse: it suggests that St John is, in fact, no more than half through his prophetic task. But a clearer indication still is provided by the scheme of the three woes threatened by the eagle after the first four trumpets. The fifth trumpet is declared to have been the first of these woes. But the sixth trumpet is not, by itself, the second, but only the sixth trumpet with the addition of the intrusive visions following it. Immediately before the seventh trumpet we read 'the second woe is past: lo, the third woe cometh quickly.' Since it is obvious that the seventh trumpet-vision does not contain the third woe, we are left looking for more. The hymnody at the seventh trumpet must herald, not celebrate, the judgement and the kingdom.

To pass now to the next series. We have (1) three uniform animal figures, expressing the persecutions of antichrist, (2) a vision of the Lamb's martyrs, and voices culminating in a declaration of the bliss of those who die in the Lord, because their works accompany them: so let them rest. Then the Son of Man on clouds begins their reward. All this closely recalls (2) in the seals, the martyrs beneath the altar, the beginning of their reward, and the word about their rest. (3) Advent-judgement, the dreadful vintage, (4) Exultation of the saints in heaven, above the sea of glass, (5) Liturgy of the Glory entering the temple. We will not waste words in pointing out that the plan here is the same. Nothing makes it clear that this apocalypse is incomplete, until we reach the beginning of (4). Before we hear the exultation of the saints, the seven angels are introduced 'who hold the seven plagues, the last, for in them is accomplished the wrath of God'. Evidently, then, an apocalypse of seven angel-plagues like those of the trumpets has yet to run its course. The appearance of the angels is the first *clear* sign that the preceding visions of final advent were anticipatory shadows. But, after the experience of the seal- and trumpet-apocalypses, we might be wise enough to infer it from the very slightness of these advent-visions, compared with the solidity and weight of the beast-visions preceding them.

The vial-apocalypse begins with (1) five uniform strokes of judgement (first five vials); then we have (2) assembly of the kings and the ungodly to meet their doom at 'the Battle of the Day of

God Almighty ; (3) great earthquake, overthrowing the gentile city (cf. the earthquake at XI, 13: there only a tenth of the city fell). There follows a huge exposition of this theme in the Babylon visions. (4) Exultation of saints over the fall of Babylon and the marriage of the Bride; (5) voice out of the temple, and liturgical hymnody. (4 and 5 are intermingled in XIX, 1-10.) What most convinces us that this cannot be the whole story is that the host assembled at Armageddon has not been given its antagonist. Moreover the great earthquake of the seventh seal has left alive blasphemers of God still unhumbled (XVI, 21).

The last visions have, of course, no signs of incompleteness; they exhibit the common rhythm with no qualifications attached: (1) four visions of the Great Battle, (2) the martyrs' interim reward (millennial thrones), (3) cosmic earthquake and Last Judgement, and (4) New Jerusalem and bliss of the Saints.

One last remark about the interior rhythm of creation-works shall conclude this chapter. This rhythm first appears in the trumpets. The fifth and sixth trumpets get us as far as living things from the abyss (sea) and land, i.e. as far as the fifth and sixth Genesis days, or perhaps only as far as the fifth day divided into two: for the hosts at the sixth trumpet come from the earth indeed, as contrasted with the abyss, but it is more explicitly said that they come from the great river Euphrates. Perhaps, then, St John is dividing the creatures of 'the waters' into creatures of (a) the abyss, (b) the river. But whether this is so, or whether the sixth trumpet brings us to the sixth day with land-beasts, it still leave the crowning work of the sixth day, the Image of God, the Dominion of the Son of Man, without mention. The rhythm of creation cannot end without it. We must recognise it at the seventh trumpet, of which the immediate effect is the heavenly voice, 'The Kingdom of the World is become our Lord's and his Anointed's, and he shall reign for ever and ever.'

In the Beast-Visions the series of creation runs through to the Son of Man (XIV, 14) and the sabbath (XV). As to the Vials, the sixth of them brings us no further than the creatures of the river (demon-frogs, hosts from Euphrates): the seventh seal does not advance us: the vision of Babylon shows the city seated on many waters. The Kingdom is proclaimed in the visions of exultation

89

which conclude the section (XIX, 5), and the new Eve and her Husband are named (XIX, 7–9). With the beginning of the next section (XIX, 11) the New Adam appears.

The immediate and evident relation of this Royal Bridegroom to the preceding voices may rightly suggest to us the solidity of another apparent sequence. The vial-section is in many ways analogous to the trumpet-section. The trumpet-section concludes with the hymning of the Messianic kingdom at XI, 15 ff., the vial-section with the similar hymnody in XIX, 1–10. As the latter has its direct sequel in the Royal Bridegroom, so has the former in the birth of the Man Child: each being the first vision of a new series. In XIX, it would therefore seem, we have reached the point of blessed consummation at which the manifestation of Adam, the Son of Man, is complete; here is that world-dominion of God's Image which is the proper purpose of man's creation. But in XI–XII we are not yet so far advanced. We recall that Genesis tells how Adam failed to establish his dominion, and left to the world no hope but the child-bearing of Eve: she should one day bear the seed who bruises the serpent's head. Here then she is, in blessed Mary, the woman crowned with stars, with her old adversary the serpent set over against her, to prosecute his feud. But her Son is snatched away to heaven: when will he return? Meanwhile the serpent and his allies are persecuting on earth the woman and the rest of her seed.

And so St John, by following the Genesis-sequence on from the sixth day of creation-week into the history of the Fall, achieves his transition from the apparent finality of the messianic kingdom in XI, 15 to the fresh series of apocalypse in XII ff.

90

CHAPTER IV

The task upon which we are engaged is not a simple one. The Apocalypse is, as we believe, threaded upon several strands of continuous symbolism. The first thing to be done was to sketch the shape of the poem. Next the several strands of symbolism would have to be examined one by one. But it has not, in fact, proved convenient to set forth the shape of the structure without working out one of the continuous symbolisms at the same time: and so, in sketching the architecture, we have already given some account of the symbolism of the week. What we have now to do is to go over the ground again, weaving in a second symbolical strand. After that there are others still.

St John's book is a 'week' of weeks, that is, six weeks (*plus* a sabbath-eve). A 'week' of weeks, is, of course, an artificial period: we do not count weeks by sixes or sevens, but by fours: four weeks are a month. The Jews of St John's time were still fully conscious of the astronomical basis of their calendar. Their months were strictly lunar. Now the lunar month naturally divides itself into four weeks. We observe the night in which there is no moon, the night in which there is full moon, and the two intermediate nights at which the bright half of the circle exactly equals the dark. There are no other points in the lunar period which can be readily judged with the eye. You can see a half-moon, you cannot see a quarter-moon. The blank moon, the full moon, and the two half-moons divide the $29\frac{1}{2}$ days of the lunar month into periods which, strictly speaking, are each of $7\frac{3}{8}$ days. There must have been a time, we do not know how far back, when the week had kept in step with the month—when the new moon always began a week. One had, let us say, three seven-day weeks, and then waited for the change of the moon. This meant letting the fourth week stretch out to eight and nine days respectively in alternate months: or perhaps one might have one eight-day week in the first month, and two in the second. Anyhow, by the first century

91

the Jews had long run their weeks on as we do in disregard of the moon: 'In six days the Lord made heaven and earth, and rested the seventh day' had now become more important to them than the moon's phases. Yet the natural relation of a seven-day week to the four quarters of the lunar month remained too obvious to be missed. Weeks demanded to be grouped in fours, and not (for example) in sixes.

Now of the six 'days' in his working 'week' of weeks, we have seen that St John glorifies the Sunday and Friday, the first and the last, as festivals of Christ. This leaves four plain 'days' in the middle. If we make the translation, therefore, out of 'days' into weeks, we have a week *plus* a month *plus* a week as the scheme of the Apocalypse.

The whole of our calendar is ultimately based on the interrelation of three astronomical cycles: the great and little cycles of the sun (day and year), and the cycle of the moon (month). It was a natural tendency of the imagination to see analogies between them. Because the actual cycle of the moon divides the great cycle of the sun into twelve parts, men had artificially divided the little cycle of daylight into twelve hours (but not the night: our twenty-four hour day-and-night was unknown to the ancients). Between the lunar cycle and the great solar cycle, the analogy is especially easy: for both have a natural division into four parts. Just as the blank moon, the full moon and the half-moons are notable, so are the shortest day of the year, the longest day, and the two days which exactly equal their nights. The year is a 'month' whose four 'weeks' are the quarters.

Such analogies as these are in themselves inevitable, and they were particularly at home in the apocalyptic tradition—one has only to recall Daniel IX–XII with its 'weeks' of years. It is not in any way surprising, therefore, that St John should make his middle month of four weeks (Apoc. IV–XVIII) do duty also as a year of four quarters. So his whole scheme of six weeks becomes a scheme of six quarters; in one aspect it is a week *plus* a month *plus* a week, in the other it is a quarter *plus* a year *plus* a quarter. Since the Jews counted their years from the Spring equinox (Lady Day), this will mean a winter quarter, *plus* a year from spring to winter inclusive, *plus* a spring quarter. And this arrangement has its own merit, for while such a cycle embraces a whole year within itself, it also runs from the bottom of the sun's course (midwinter) to his height (midsummer). So it agrees with what we observed when we were examining the apocalyptic week—that the book runs from Christ the birth of light (Apoc. i) to Christ the fulness of light (Apoc. xxii).

On the way, however, it runs through all the quarters of the year, and this brings within St John's scheme all the symbolical riches of the Jewish sacred calendar. The detailed exposition of them will be our task presently. What we have now to do is to lay out the general plan.

The Jewish sacred calendar was and is lunar: a year consists of twelve months of 29 and 30 days alternately. Such a year is many days short of the solar cycle. Things have to be kept straight by intercalating an extra month about every three years. All the dates of the Jewish calendar wander up and down the year as our Easter does: but the effect of intercalation is to make their *average* positions right: by average position the first day of the first month is at the spring equinox, the first of the fourth at the summer solstice, the first of the seventh at the autumn equinox, the first of the tenth at the winter solstice: but of course only one of these dates can have its *actual* correct solar position in any given year. It is obvious that the only thing to do if one is making a symbolical use of the calendar is to neglect the whole business of intercalation, to give all the lunar dates their average solar positions, and equate three months with each quarter-year.

Let the Jewish year, then, consist of four regular quarters of three months each. What does the sacred calendar put into each of the quarters? It is natural to begin with the first and the third, because they balance one another. The first moon of the first quarter is the Paschal moon, and Passover is at the full of it. Exactly opposite to it in the circle of the year is the full of the first moon of the third quarter, the moon of the seventh month; and that brings Tabernacles. Passover and Tabernacles are the two great feasts of the Jewish year, and we shall naturally think of the first quarter as the three moons beginning with the Passover moon, and the third quarter as the three moons beginning with the Tabernacles moon.

So much for the equinoxes. Now what can we do for the solstices? There are no great feasts at the full moons following either solstice: but the feast of Dedication is an octave which firmly bestrides the winter solstice, beginning five days before it: and so the fourth quarter may be reckoned as the moon which rises in Dedication, together with the two moons following it. About the second quarter nothing can be done. There is no great feast which touches its first moon. The only great feast in that region is Pentecost, but Pentecost is irrevocably enclosed within the first quarter. It is a one-day feast on the sixth of the third month, and it is tied to Passover, the great feast of the first quarter, by very close bonds.

St John must do something to balance his scheme. He has so far a Passover-and-onwards quarter, a blank quarter, a Tabernacles-and-onwards quarter, a Dedication-and-onwards quarter. How is the blank quarter to be filled? The answer is found by borrowing from the overladen third quarter. We said that the first and seventh months balanced, because their full moons brought with them the two great feasts of the Jewish year. This is true in so far as it goes, but it is not the whole truth, and the balance is not complete. For the first day of the seventh month is also a major feast, whereas the first of the first month is not. Just as the Jews reckoned the beginning of the day from the eve, not the morning, so they kept New Year in autumn, not spring, at the new moon of the seventh month, not of the first. So St John can fill his blank quarter by reckoning it as the towards-New-Year quarter. So the quarters are:

(1) Passover and Pentecost
(2) Towards New Year
(3) Tabernacles and onwards
(4) Dedication and onwards.

Such is the year. But the year of St John's scheme has an extra fourth quarter in front of it, and an extra first quarter after it. So we begin with Dedication (4). Dedication is otherwise called the feast of lamps, and its symbol is the seven-branched golden candlestick. St John's first section (I–III) begins with the vision of the seven golden candlesticks, which give form also to the Messages. The symbol of Passover (1) is the Lamb, and of Pentecost (since it was kept as the feast of Lawgiving) the Book. In St John's second

94

section (IV–VII) the Lamb opens the Book, and this gives its form to the Seals. The symbols of New Year (2) were the trumpets, 'Trumpets' being an alternative name for the feast. St John's third section (VIII–XI) is the blowing of trumpets. Tabernacles (3) celebrates the safe keeping of Israel in the 'tabernacles' of the wilderness: St John's fourth section (XII–XIV) begins with the escape of the woman into her divinely prepared place in the wilderness, and proceeds to develop the theme of spiritual safe-keeping under persecution through the days of Antichrist.

Let this suffice for a preliminary verification of our hypothesis. We will not pursue it into the second Dedication-quarter (Apoc. XV–XVIII) and the second Passover-Pentecost quarter (XIX–XXII). We will merely observe that the Christ of Advent, the second Rider on the White Horse (XIX, 11) turns out to be a new Paschal Deliverer from 'Egypt', as he must be; and that the first Rider on the White Horse (VI, 2) was also the beginning of a paschal series. We may add that the great vision of the Son of Man (Apoc. 1) is in the eve of the first Dedication, and the lesser vision of the Son of Man (XIV, 14) is in the eve of the second.

We ought further at this point to note that the anomalous character of the second quarter is permitted to appear in St John's handling of his imagery. The sevenfold series belonging to the other quarters spring out of great festal scenes, liturgies of jubilant worship in heaven. The second quarter begins with no feast, and the trumpet-series accordingly has its rise out of a half-hour's silence in heaven. There is also, admittedly, an incense-offering there, but the incense-offering was not characteristic of any feast, it was made twice every day. The six trumpets are simply preliminary to the great seventh trumpet, which marks the actual Feast of Trumpets (New Year). And it immediately introduces the visions of the next quarter, which New Year initiates. So much for the preliminary sketch. The detail is more interesting.

In the chapters which follow, three tasks have been attempted concurrently: (a) to set out those features of the Apocalypse which may be said to demand the hypothesis of the festal calendar; (b) to show that, even where the calendar-hypothesis is not positively required, what St John writes is nevertheless perfectly natural, on the supposition of the hypothesis; (c) to show that, if

95

we assume that St John is writing from the festal scheme, the features of his visions which cannot arise out of it directly may do so indirectly through intelligible lines of association. It would be exceedingly vexatious to the reader if these three undertakings were to be rigorously separated. What he will find is a continuous exposition, working from the hypothesis. If he feels at a given point, 'This is no more than possible, it is not proved,' he may rest assured that he has the author in agreement with him. If he will read on, he will be able to decide in the end whether enough has been proved, or not—proved with such proof as the subject-matter allows: we are not doing geometry here.

(1)

The week of Seven Messages is to represent the quarter extending from Dedication towards Passover. The introductory Christophany stands outside the week, and therefore outside the quarter, and is, strictly, anomalous. In the 'week' of sevenfold 'days' it had its part to play as eve to the first 'day'. Here in the calendar of feasts it has no such part. It must simply be reckoned as a poetical prelude. It is not a prelude to Dedication simply, but to the 'week', i.e. quarter, which extends from Dedication towards Passover, and in fact it combines the themes of the two feasts: of Dedication primarily, and Passover secondarily.

Dedication is not a feast to be found in the Old Testament. The institution is recorded in the Books of the Maccabees. The 25th day of Chislev, roughly speaking our Christmas Day, was consecrated as the anniversary of the rededication of the temple by Judas. But Israel commemorated on that day the dedication of the sanctuary simply, and not only the particular Maccabaean event. The Torah-lesson used was the history of the dedication-festivity for Moses's Tabernacle, according to Numbers VII–VIII, 4,[1] special emphasis being laid on the lighting of the sevenfold candlestick, with which the narrative concludes; and in parallel to it the vision of the candlestick in Zechariah IV was read as a prophetical lesson. Since the feast fell about the winter solstice, it is likely that some Gentile feast of light lay behind it; Judas was careful to rededicate on the day on which the Gentiles had inaugurated their

[1] As to the starting-point in VII, usage differs.

96

'abomination'; presumably they had chosen an existing holy day of their own. However that may be, the actual Jewish feast, with its emphasis on the lighting of the great candlestick, could not fail to suggest the triumph of light over darkness, the beginning of a new era of light when the shortest day of winter should have passed. Dedication, therefore, forms a perfect pair to the FIAT LUX which inaugurated the Genesis: and St John appropriates it to his first day, writing his vision of the Resurrection-Christ into the forms of Zechariah's vision of the candlestick.

For Zechariah the candlestick of the Lord burns in Israel, while priesthood and principality are the two anointed stocks on either hand, whose oil feeds the light. This is good Jewish theology. For the Christian, Christ is the candlestick of the Lord and holds the middle place: the seven candles of the Churches burn before him with borrowed light. The text both of Numbers and of Zechariah appears to hold suggestions of such a transformation. The divine voice thus directed Aaron: 'When thou settest on the candles, on the side before the face of the candlestick shall the seven candles burn. And Aaron did accordingly: on the one side before the face of the candlestick he lighted the seven candles thereof' (Num. VIII, 2–3). This can be read to mean that the seven candles are planted not on, but before, the candlestick, which has some other more glorious light of its own.

The suggestion contained in Zechariah is more material. In the Candlestick vision Jesus Son of Josadek, the High Priest, and Zerubbabel Son of Salathiel, the Prince, stand on either side like heraldic supporters of the sevenfold light. But in the previous vision of the High Priest (III) and in the subsequent Oracle of the Crown (VI, 9–15) things are said about Jesus which seem to give him an unrivalled eminence and to set him in the midst. The Christian reader would naturally conclude that the Candlestick-vision assigns Jesus his place in so far as he is simply the Son of Josadek and the colleague of Zerubbabel, while the other visions hint at where he stands considered as a type of Jesus the Son of God. It is for St John to reinterpret the Candlestick-vision itself in such a way that it, too, makes room for the divine Jesus.

Zechariah's vision of the High Priest thus begins. 'Be silent, all flesh, before the Lord' (said the angel) 'for he is waked up out of his holy clouds. And he shewed me Jesus. . . .' We see him clad in the pure new vestments of a priest, in token that he is a brand plucked from the burning, that Israel is justified before God in the person of Jesus, and that their accuser is put to rebuke in his presence. Who can this be, the Christian rabbi will ask, but the Jesus of the resurrection, who, in token of victory over Satan and the fires of his passion, exchanges the soiled raiment of Adam's flesh for the white raiment of his own glory? Zechariah's Jesus, with his companions, receives the oracle: 'Behold, I bring forth my Servant RISING. For behold the stone that I have set before Jesus, on the one stone seven eyes.' It may not seem clear either who my Servant RISING is, or what the stone cut to seven eyes or facets means: but as we read on we seem to get the needful comments. The Oracle of the Crown reads as follows: 'Take crowns and set them on the head of Jesus, saying: Thus saith the Lord of Hosts: Behold the Man, RISING his name: and he shall rise from beneath Him and build the temple of the Lord, and he shall receive excellency and sit and rule on His throne, and shall be the priest at His right hand, and counsel of peace shall be between them twain.' 'My servant RISING' is therefore no other than Jesus, the Jesus of the Resurrection, springing up from beneath, building the mystical sanctuary of the Church, and sitting in the throne of God at his right hand.

The name RISING is, in the Greek,[1] ambiguous, describing either the rising of the sun or that of vegetable growth: in the former sense it is conventionally translated Dayspring, in the latter Branch: in the Hebrew it certainly has the latter sense, and is Jeremiah's and Zechariah's synonym for the title, 'Root, or Shoot, from Jesse,' given to Messiah in Isaiah XI (cf. Jer. XXIII, 5, XXXIII, 15). The sense 'Dayspring' is appropriate enough to St John's purpose in Apocalypse 1, which is to reveal Christ, the Master of the candles, as the Light of the World. But it is the other

---

[1] 'Did St John know the O.T. in Hebrew or Greek?' is not a question. He obviously knew much of the Hebrew, presumably from a synagogue education: he had to preach in Asia from the Greek, and probably had no access to a Hebrew text. Those who used both regarded the Greek as an *inspired* exposition, and so did not have a scientific preference for the original, as we should expect them to have.

98

sense of which St John makes evident and particular use, as we shall see as we turn to examine the riddle of 'the stone with seven eyes'.

It seems plain enough that the seven-'eyed' stone is a jewel, its eyes being facets; and that its presentation to Jesus authenticates his priesthood, whereby iniquity is banished from the land and felicity secured. A jewel which authenticates office is no doubt a signet; Pharaoh's signet given to Joseph made him lord of Egypt. Here it is the Lord God who gives his signet. To the primitive Christian the seal or signet of God was the Holy Ghost: this is the seal wherewith Christ is marked out by the Father, and with which Christ marks the saints. The Spirit of the Father is a seal: but why a seal with seven 'eyes'? The sevenfold character of the Spirit is set forth by Isaiah in precisely that oracle in which the Shoot or Root of Jesse is named: it is upon him that the seven spirits rest, just as it is the Branch here to whom the seven-eyed signet is presented. Christ is authenticated with the sevenfold Spirit.

So far we have met nothing which should lead us to press the metaphor of the stone's seven 'eyes': we can be content to understand them simply as facets: the sevenfold Spirit is a seven-faceted seal. But Zechariah's next vision, the Candlestick, takes up the phrase 'seven eyes' and makes us see them as actual eyes. As the seven-eyed signet was seen as the assurance of Jesus' priesthood, so the seven-flamed candlestick is now seen as the assurance of Zerubbabel's success: he will complete the temple he is building. Why does the sevenfold candlestick give this assurance? The sense must be plain to every Jew. Only after Moses' tabernacle was finished and dedicated was Aaron commanded to light the seven candles. Zechariah sees the candles already burning: it is a sign that the work is complete in the predestinating thought of God.

Because God's candlestick burns already, the seven candles of wax will one day be lighted by Jesus Son of Josadek. But God's candlestick burns already, not a mere ritual candlestick, but the candlestick of his favouring presence, already shining in the land of Israel. Because this candlestick burns now, the ritual candlestick will burn soon. On that day the seven flames of the divine candlestick will watch with joy Zerubbabel, plummet in hand, passing the work as finished and truly set: for these seven are 'the eyes of the Lord which run to and fro over all the land'.

Seven eyes of the signet set before the Branch, seven Spirits of the Lord resting on the Root from David's stock, seven candles which are seven eyes of the Lord, running to and fro over all the earth—St John fused all three together, as the images in the fourth and fifth chapters plainly shew. First, 'seven lamps of fire burning before the throne, which are the seven spirits of God': then 'the Root of David . . . a Lamb . . . having seven eyes, which are the seven spirits of God, sent forth into all the earth'.

The seven candles are the seven eyes of the Lord. Surely, then, the candlestick is the Lord himself, the mystical Lamb, whose eyes the seven are. The end of Zechariah's vision appears to support this conclusion: for two olive-plants seen standing beside the candlestick, to the right and the left, are interpreted as the two anointed heads which stand beside *the Lord of all the earth.*

The seven candles then, have a double sense. There are the candles of the temple, lighted on earth by Jesus the High Priest, that is to say, there are the seven Churches. But then again there are the seven Spirits of God, burning as a sevenfold fire not on earth but in the temple of heaven before his throne, and shining in the head of the mystical Lamb as his eyes, penetrating into every corner of the earth.

In the vision of i, both the candles of the Churches appear, and also the divine candlestick, the Lord of all the earth, the mystical Lamb. The seven flames should, by strict logic, appear as his eyes, but this the conventions of the vision forbid. Christ appears not as an emblematic Lamb, nor as a symbolic candlestick, but in his proper nature as the Son of Man. St John can go no further than to describe his (two) eyes as like to burning flame. Yet the correspondence between the seven flames of the divine candlestick and the seven earthly candles cannot be allowed to disappear: it must receive alternative expression. In his right hand Christ holds seven stars, the angels of the Churches, to whose heavenly existence the earthly existence of the Churches is bound to correspond.

The conventions of the Son-of-Man vision exclude direct representation of the seven lamps of the Spirit which are the eyes of the Lamb. But in the messages to the Churches St John is not thus confined. In the first message he speaks who holds the seven stars and walks among the seven candles: in the fifth message, the

100

candles are reinterpreted, and we read, 'who has *the seven spirits of God* and the seven stars.' Our minds pass back over the Candle-stick-vision to the introductory Blessings: 'From the IS, WAS and COMETH, and from the seven Spirits before his throne, and from Jesus Christ' the Lamb 'who redeemed us by his blood'. According to the Blessing, the Seven Spirits belong to the Father, but now according to the fifth message the Son has them. The vision of glory in IV–V draws together the two attributions of the Sevenfold Spirit: the Seven Spirits are both seven lamps of fire before the Father's Throne, and also seven eyes of the redeeming Lamb.

We have, perhaps, run into rather more detail than the present occasion requires, but it may serve to show in general how St John's mind worked upon the ancient texts. To return to the principal theme: Jesus the High Priest is the new Aaron who lights the seven candles: but being the Dayspring he bears in him-self the sevenfold flame of the Holy Ghost, and kindles them from no other source: he is, indeed, the candlestick of the Lord, and they are lighted to burn before his face, the face that shines as the sun shines in his strength. That is what St John collected out of Numbers and Zechariah.

So much for the theme of Dedication in the Vision of the Son of Man. Now what of the Passover theme? Is it necessary to say any more about this than that the Passover appears here in its Christian form? Who does not know that the Vision is an Easter vision? It is on the Lord's Day, and every Sunday is an Easter. He who appears declares himself 'the Living that was dead, and, lo, am alive for ever more and hold the keys of death and hell'. St John takes the conventional image of the visionary who falls as though dead before his celestial visitant, and makes it express the re-enactment of the Lord's Passion in the believer. St John falls as dead before Christ, and Christ at a touch revives him, in virtue of his own saving death and resurrection, using the words we have just quoted.

The combination of Dedication and Passover goes further back —it appears already in St John's greeting to the Churches. This greeting (*a*) blesses through the mystery of the ineffable Name, the IS, WAS, and COMETH, the Father, Sevenfold Spirit, and Son; (*b*) runs on into a doxology to Christ, 'Who loveth us, and loosed us from our sins by his blood, and made us a kingdom, priests unto God his Father.' As to (a) we shall have more to say in its place, for St John's use of the divine Name requires separate treatment. It is enough to say here that the priestly blessing with the ineffable Name receives its prescribed form in Numbers VI, 22, a text immediately preceding the history of Moses's Dedication-festivity, as read at the Dedication-feast. When St John returns to the Dedication-themes on his last page, he draws together the 'putting of the Name upon the sons of Israel' by means of the Aaronic blessing, and the shining upon them of that divine light which the sevenfold candlestick symbolized. 'And they shall see his face, and his Name shall be upon their foreheads, and night shall be no more. And they have no more need of candlelight or sunlight, for the Lord God shall shine upon them, and they shall reign for ever and ever.'

The doxology to Christ (b) is evidently paschal. He has 'ransomed us from our sins by his blood', as God ransomed Israel out of Egypt by the paschal blood. By so doing God brought them away free to Sinai, where he said to them, 'Ye shall be unto me a kingdom and priests.' So the paschal Christ has made us a kingdom and priesthood to his Father. No less paschal is the title of Christ in the Trinitarian blessing, 'Firstborn from the dead.' Because Israel was 'God's son, his firstborn', and Pharaoh would not let him go, God slew Pharaoh's son and firstborn. And for this cause all firstborn animals were to be sacrificed according to the Law, and the firstborn of man redeemed by the death of a beast, as Israel had been by the paschal blood. Christ, God's Firstborn, is the new paschal victim, by whom God's children are redeemed; yet he lives too, the first-begotten from the dead.

About the seven messages to the Churches there is obviously little to be said in the present connexion. In St John's formal design they represent the 'week' from Dedication to Passover, but it is plain that the matter with which they are filled is not specially connected with one season of the year more than another. We have been told in the introductory vision that the Seven Churches represent the seven candles, therefore the messages are formally connected with the principal Dedication-image. The Lord who utters them entitles himself in each by one of the attributes of the

102

Resurrection-Christ in the introductory vision: therefore the messages are formally connected with the principal Easter symbol. With these formalities we must be content.

(2)

The seven unsealings are to represent the quarter with Passover in its first month and Pentecost in its third, just as the seven messages represented the quarter stretching from Dedication towards Passover. There is an important difference between the two sevenfold images, however. The form of the unsealings of itself expresses climax, the form of the messages does not. There are seven messages to be delivered: one is not of greater weight than another, and the movement on from the first to the last does not of itself bring us nearer to anything except the end of the messages. It is otherwise with the unsealings. The breaking of each seal brings us nearer to the point at which the book will be open: and when the seventh seal is broken, then and then only, the book is actually unsealed. So the unsealings represent a revelation which, having its root in Passover, is fulfilled at Pentecost.

This is just as it should be, for (a) Pentecost is related to Passover as harvest to firstfruit, (b) Pentecost, when it comes, is celebrated as the festival of divine revelation.

(a) The day of Firstfruits, from which the Israelite was to count his seven weeks to Pentecost, had come to be fixed at the second day of the Unleavened Bread, the second morning after the killing and eating of the Passover. The Christian was unlikely to forget this, for on the Day of Firstfruits Christ arose, to be both the fulfilment of the paschal victory, and the firstfruit of the harvest of souls. So that Easter, the Christian Passover, is no other than Firstfruits Day, and stands at an exact interval of seven weeks from Pentecost.

(b) Pentecost, originally a harvest-home pure and simple, had come to be celebrated as the anniversary of the Law-Giving, because the Exodus story places arrival before Mount Sinai at about the season of Pentecost. Thus no symbol could more happily express Pentecost than the unsealing of the book in the hand of God. The voice from the mountain, in revealing the Ten Commandments, thus began: 'I am the Lord thy God which brought thee up

103

out of the Land of Egypt.' The revelation begun in Egypt was completed at Sinai, the pact initiated with paschal blood in Egypt was confirmed with covenant blood under the mountain, the unsealing which begins at Firstfruits is fulfilled on the day of Pentecost.

The week of seals, like the week of messages, has its prelude in a theophanic vision (IV–V). This vision, like that in I, is anomalously related to the week which springs from it. It is not Firstfruits Day, for Firstfruits Day is contained in the quarter which is represented by the week, whereas this is a prelude standing outside the week. If we wish to make the vision of IV–V serially continuous with any part of its context, it is more reasonable to join it with what precedes, and to consider it as an eighth added to the seven messages. It is probable that St John felt this, anyhow, to be significant. The Christian Firstfruits Day is the octave day of Holy Week, and Pentecost, again, is the seventh octave day after it. For that reason we observe Pentecost on a Sunday. IV–V represent a prelude to the Passover-Pentecost week, and accordingly they contain a fusion of the Passover and Pentecost themes; Passover and Pentecost are both octaves, and these chapters form the octave to the messages.

We have seen that the image of unsealing is primarily pentecostal, not paschal. Since the great vision of IV–V has to provide the setting for the drama of the unsealing, it is bound to be itself pentecostal in its principal outlines. But as we shall see, there is no lack of paschal filling.

The torah-reading for Pentecost was the giving of the Decalogue by God, revealed in storm and fire on the mountain-top (Ex. XIX). The prophetical reading which inevitably accompanied it was God revealed in fire and storm to Ezekiel, to give him a message and the scroll of a book (Ezek. I): it was natural that the dreadful appearance of the Lord to Isaiah in the Temple (VI) should also be read, for Isaiah, too, received his message there. Ezekiel's vision supplies St John with the mystical cherubim, the Throne above the firmament, the rainbow aureole, and the book seen in the divine hand, from which it has to be taken. Ezekiel, in taking the book, is shown to be a type of Christ the sole revealer by the words in which he is addressed, 'Son of Man.' Isaiah supplies St John with the temple-setting, manifest in the temple-

104

ornaments, the sevenfold candlestick and the great 'sea' or laver of glass, which in St. John's vision stand before the Throne. Isaiah's seraphim give the cherubim of St John their *six* wings each, and lay the 'Holy, holy, holy' on their lips. Perhaps Isaiah's distress at his worthlessness, and his hearing of the voice, 'Whom shall we send, and who shall go for us?' may have something to do with the loud proclamation heard by St John, 'Who is worthy to open the book and loose the seals thereof?' and with St John's much weeping, because none worthy was found.

The lesson from Exodus is no less influential. It provides the mysterious trumpet of summons, the lightnings, voices, and thunders, and the mediator who is alone able to look upon the theophany or to receive the scripture written by God. It provides also the great assembly or 'Church' of all Israel before the presence of God. It is probable that we have greatly underestimated the part played by this 'Church in the wilderness'[1] in fixing what the primitive Christians meant by 'church'. The Author to the Hebrews may open our eyes—as he had very likely opened St John's. 'Ye are come not unto what might be touched, and that burned with fire, and unto blackness and darkness and tempest and the sound of a trumpet and the voice of words, whereof the hearers intreated that no word more might be spoken to them . . . but ye are come unto Mount Zion . . . and to myriads of angels, to the general assembly and church of the firstborn who are enrolled in heaven, and to God the judge of all and to the spirits of just men made perfect and to Jesus the mediator of a new covenant, and to the blood of sprinkling that speaketh better words than Abel's' (Heb. XII, 18–24). Here we have that great congregation of the universe of which we read in Apocalypse IV–V, including its head who is both sacrifice and mediator, the recipient of the book and the slaughtered Lamb, the Abel or prototypic martyr of the New Covenant. This is the 'Church' in which all Christians really worship, whether the walls that close them round are in the house of Prisca or in the house of Stephanas. The walls melt, and leave them in the one congregation before the great Throne. Yet as their vision clears to behold the heavenly things, these begin to take on familiar contours: the presiding throne, on which in their weekly

[1] Acts VII, 38.

105

eucharist the bishop sits: the thrones of the elders placed around in support of it: the inspired Man, whose sufferings for the Name make him worthy to take the book of scripture and open it by God-given exposition, in heaven Jesus, at Ephesus his servant John.

Pentecost is the feast of divine revelation. The Christian Pentecost which St John describes took place in heaven, but had its effect on earth. The Lamb, by virtue of the sevenfold Spirit which is his seven horns of strength, his seven eyes of knowledge, opened all revelation, and when the day of Pentecost was fully come, he poured it on his servants in prophetic Spirit. The pentecostal gift is constantly renewed, as in this 'apocalypse of Jesus Christ, which God gave him to shew his servants what must quickly be, and which he signified by the message of his angel to his servant John'. Yet the first Whit-Sunday is not cast into the shade by such renewals, but kept all the more lively in mind.

He who opened revelation on Whit-Sunday is he who entered heaven new from his resurrection at the Easter noon (so St John teaches in his Gospel; see xx, 17, 27), that is, the noon of the first-fruits-day of which Whit-Sunday is the jubilee and harvest-home. It is the Christ of Passover, the paschal Lamb 'standing as slaughtered', who by his sacrificial merit has attained to take the book and loose the seven seals thereof. And so while Pentecost provides the frame of Apocalypse IV–V, it is inlaid with the principal of all paschal emblems.

Wherever the sacrificial Lamb is mentioned by Christians, the lamb or ram which God himself provided to redeem Isaac is not long out of mind (Gen. XXII, 13). In Genesis the only and beloved son of a human father (though, according to ancient Jewish interpretation, as bravely willing to die as was Jephthah's daughter) was refused or reprieved, and the ram caught in the thicket substituted. But what can the ram avail? Nothing, unless he is a shadow and emblem of the Heavenly Father's only and beloved Isaac, who both dies and is reprieved, who stands, yet as slaughtered, and whose life through death redeems indeed. 'Where is the lamb of offering?' Isaac had said, and Abraham, 'God will provide himself the lamb, my son,' not knowing how, and at his wits' end. But presently, called by an angel's voice, he withheld the knife, and

106

lifted up his eyes and looked, and lo, behind, a ram caught in the thicket by his horns. Compare the pathos of St John's vision: 'And I saw a strong angel proclaiming with a great voice, Who is worthy to open the book and to loose the seals thereof? And no one in heaven or earth or under the earth was able to open the book, or to look thereon. And I wept much, because none was found worthy. . . . And one of the elders said to me, Weep not: behold, the Lion that is of the Tribe of Judah, the Root of David, hath prevailed to open the book and the seven seals thereof. And I saw in the midst of the throne and of the four cherubim . . . a Lamb standing as slaughtered, having seven horns and seven eyes. . . .'

The first hymn addressed to the Lamb contains paschal and pentecostal echoes. 'Thou wast slain, and didst purchase unto God with thy blood men of every tribe, tongue, people and nation, and madest them unto our God a kingdom and priests.' 'Didst purchase with thy blood'—that is the paschal redemption. 'Unto our God a kingdom and priests'—that is the first voice from the mountain, which thus spoke with Moses: 'Ye have seen what I did unto the Egyptians, and how I lifted you on eagle's pinions, and brought you to myself. Now therefore if ye will obey my voice indeed and keep my covenant, then ye shall be a peculiar treasure unto me from among all peoples. For all the earth is mine, but ye shall be to me a kingdom of priests, a holy nation' (Exod. XIX, 4–6).

It is time that we turned to the examination of the seven unsealings. They are to cover the quarters from the paschal month on to midsummer. Midsummer is not a feast, as we have seen: St John's way of representing it is to make it the beginning of what leads to the great trumpet of New Year. The seventh seal should unseal midsummer: what it unseals in fact is a half-hour's silence, out of which opens the series of seven trumpets, the New Year trumpet being the seventh. The first six are preliminary only, yet all are trumpets of judgement, a foretaste of New Year which is the season of judgement.

That is what the seventh seal brings when it is at length broken. In front of it St John inserts the long 'intrusion' of VII. This means that the first six seals are cut off from the seventh, and have a sort

107

of completeness of their own; and in point of fact St John covers the whole ground in the six. The sixth advances to the same point as the seventh, and opens up the summer quarter. That is to say, it presents the shadow of the coming Judgement Day. The kings and the mighty, the captains, the rich and the strong and every man free or bond, hide themselves in the caves and call on the mountains to cover them from the face of enthroned majesty and from the Lamb's wrath: for, they say, the great Day of Wrath is come. The finality of the scene in the scheme of unsealing could not be more strongly emphasised than it is. The unsealing is to effect the unrolling of the scroll of revelation. The sixth seal presents us with the alternative image of the rolling back of the scroll of obscuration, the withdrawal of the firmament which hides the face of God.

Because of the apparent finality of the sixth seal, St John passes on to the vision of ultimate bliss in the intrusive ch. VII, for no other sequel seems adequate to it. Once the veil of the firmament has been withdrawn in judgement, what remains, but the World to Come? Yet in fact the end is not yet; the sixth seal brought but the shadow of New Year; we must still have the fallow time of the midsummer 'sabbath', before the New Year is reached, and the work of God can proceed. The fallow time, when it comes, could scarcely be more fallow than it is, a half-hour's silence in heaven. Why half an hour? St John is not thinking of the calendar, but of the incense-ritual, which introduced a pause into the progress of the animal sacrifice. But how much time does it stand for in the calendar? Probably the whole summer quarter. For whereas St John fills the space allotted to the quarter with anticipatory trumpets, he knows that the trumpet does not really sound until New Year. His seven trumpets are a subdivision of the one trumpet. The 'half-hour's silence' is a recognition of this fact: there is a gap in the calendar between the Book of Pentecost and the Trumpets of New Year.

The ritual he assigns to midsummer is the ritual of the incense, twice offered on every day of the year: it is as undistinguished as the summer solstice is in the Jewish Calendar. It manages, for all that, to pick up certain features which reveal it (a) as the sequel of the prelude to the spring quarter, which is very proper since it is prelude to the summer quarter itself: (b) as the sequel of the six seals. (a) We are to see that what began in the Lamb's taking of the book is fulfilled when the last seal has been broken, for then the book is open. St John was summoned to the heavenly vision by the voice of a trumpet. The midsummer ritual begins with the vision of seven trumpets. When in the heavenly vision the Lamb took the book to open it, the elders and Cherubim fell before the Lamb, having golden vials full of incense, which are the prayers of the saints. Now that the Lamb has opened the book, an angel with a golden censer makes liturgical offering of the incense before God. 'There was given him much incense that he might put it to the prayers of all the saints on the golden altar before the throne. And there went up the smoke of the incense at the prayers of the saints from the hand of the angel before God.' The acceptance of the prayers is then expressed in two things. The incense-angel tosses the charcoal out of his censer on to the earth, and the trumpet-angels take up positions to blow. The coals of fire will fall on the persecutors of the saints, and the trumpets will sound their doom. (b) Now as to the relation of the incense-ritual to the six seals. The angel with the censer takes his stand by the altar, i.e. that previously mentioned (VI, 9), the brazen altar of slaughter, there to receive the incense he should offer at the prayers of all the saints: he carries it into the holy place and offers it on the golden altar, the altar of incense, before the Presence. According to Leviticus XVI, 9–13 the bloody sacrifice is followed by Aaron's taking a censer full of burning charcoal from off the altar before the Lord, and his hands full of sweet incense beaten small. Then, coming within the veil, he puts the incense on the fire before the Lord. St John's angel presumably has his fire from the altar of slaughter, and there receives the incense in his hands, to put on the fire at the golden altar. Thus the virtue of the bloody sacrifice is carried in, and presented before the very face of God.

And what was the bloody sacrifice? It has been revealed to us at the fifth unsealing: beneath the altar the souls of the slaughtered for God's word and the testimony they held, crying, 'How long?' This is the virtue which the angel takes from the altar, and to which he adds the incense of heaven when he offers it on the altar of gold. The prayers of the slaughtered saints, crying, 'How long?'

109

are the charcoal, the motive power which causes the incense to steam up 'at the prayers of all saints'. So at the fifth seal the bloody offering, and at the seventh the offering of incense.

The souls of the slaughtered saints are under the altar, because there were perforations permitting the sacrificial blood to run down under the altar, and 'the blood is the soul'. St John's age was not the least inclined to employ, for general purposes, the equation between soul and blood: the soul is breath and mind. But in one connexion the old equation was inescapable. The chapter of Leviticus following that which we have just quoted for the incense-offering declares: 'The soul of all flesh is the blood thereof, and I have given it to you upon the altar to make atonement for your souls: for the blood thereof shall make atonement instead of the soul' (Lev. XVII, 11, cf. 14). The lives of the martyrs are offered as atoning sacrifices. St John was, in fact, not a Protestant. He does regard the death of the martyrs as meritorious and atoning, and as giving force to their prayers. He does not regard this merit and atoning force as underivative, but as grounded in the work of Christ, because he is in the highest sense *the firstfruit* from the dead. This is the position of the Catholic Church. St John's doctrine is perfectly plain to anyone who will trouble to compare the Lamb standing as slaughtered in Apocalypse V with the slaughtered saints of VI, or who will read XII, 11: 'They overcame (the dragon) because of the blood of the Lamb and because of the word of their testimony and for that they loved not their life, even to the death.' The blood of Christ both atones and cries, uttering better words than Abel's: here the blood of the martyrs cries, as Enoch says of Abel,[1] for the extirpation of the race of Cain: it also atones for saints on the altar of sacrifice.

At Passover the slaughtered Lamb: at the fifth vision of the paschal series the slaughtered saints, who, to quote St Paul, 'make up in their own bodies what was still to be supplied of the passion of Christ' (Col. I, 24). They are still 'firstfruits', waiting for the fulfilment of the harvest of souls, the Pentecost when their number will be accomplished and their cry heard. Meanwhile they receive an earnest of ultimate glory in the white stole, and a reminder that the pentecostal waiting is only 'a little while', as Jesus said to the

[1] I Enoch XXII, 5–7, cf. XLVII, 1, and Genesis IV, 10.

110

disciples at the supper (John XVI, 16). Christ is their firstfruit, they are the firstfruits of the Church. Presently the whole harvest of martyrs will be gathered in: and then the harvest-home.

The vision of the martyrs is placed at the fifth seal because the pattern requires it: in reality it describes the state of affairs any time before the sixth. The martyrs have had their Good Friday, and in the white stole they receive their Easter: they are awaiting Pentecost. What of the four seals previous? They lead up to the fifth and are there for the sake of it.

The martyrs' cry, 'How long?' is several times heard in Scripture, nowhere more insistently than in the first chapter of Zechariah: 'How long, O Lord, dost thou not shew mercy on Zion, whom thou hast overlooked these seventy years?' (Here again is a fated period, the period of exile). So says the angel-advocate of Israel, and, like the martyrs of the fifth seal, he receives an answer in 'fair and comfortable words', purporting imminent salvation and the overthrow of enemies.[1] The Angel's cry, 'How long?' is occasioned by the return of the four riders on horses red, bay, dappled and white, from their ride through the four quarters of earth. The Lord's scouts report that all is quiet, and this is the cause of the angel's disappointment: whether because there is little hope of Israel's shaking off the yoke if there is nothing stirring among the nations, or because it is discouraging to see peace for every land except the land of Israel. St John adapts the four riders to his own use: the discouragement of the martyr-souls arises from the cause, that they thought to see in four grievous plagues the immediate signs of advent, and were four times disappointed. Thus for St John the four horsemen become the bearers of the four grievous plagues, not the scouts of the four quarters of the earth. The martyrs are represented as having failed sufficiently to lay to heart the warning of their Lord: 'When ye hear of wars and

___
[1] The gift of the white stole makes St John's martyrs the promised companions of Jesus the High Priest, Zechariah III, 3–5, Apocalypse III, 4–5 and III, 18. 'They shall walk with me in white.' In Zechariah III Jesus, himself newly clothed, receives the promise: 'Walk in my ways . . . and I will give thee men who shall pass up and down among those that stand here' (i.e. the angels?). 'Hear, O Jesus and thy companions that sit before thee, for they are men that look for a sign—Lo, I bring forth my servant Dayspring.'

rumours of wars, be not moved; they must come, but the end is not yet. For nation shall rise against nation (in conquest) and dynasty against dynasty (in civil war), there shall be earthquakes in places, there shall be famines: these are but the beginning-pains of travail.'[1] These words are followed in the synoptic apocalypse by the warning of martyrdom.

There is nothing in Zechariah I to recommend the four riders for the function which St John assigns to them: the four chariots of Zechariah VI would indeed be far more suitable. We cannot understand his interpretation of the Zechariah vision on any other ground but his starting from the cry, 'How long?' This shews that the martyrs are the centre and pivot of the six seal-visions. For as to the sixth seal, it simply shews in earthquake and terrors from the sky the more effective judgement which New Year will bring.

The third horseman is dearth; he carries a scale in sign of rationing, for in the siege, Ezekiel had said, they shall eat their bread by weight. He puts a grievous price on wheat and barley, but is forbidden to hurt oil or wine. We have here the familiar triad, 'corn, wine and oil.' The essential element, the staff of life, is broken here and now. The oil and wine are reserved, no doubt, for future judgement; but St John's restless wit does not allow anything so tame as a mere catalogue of agricultural disasters. A disaster on the fig appears in the sixth seal, but with an astonishing transformation of sense. 'The stars of heaven fell to earth as a fig casteth her unripe fruit under the shaking of a great wind,' as she may do in Pentecost-season. The cosmic winds are curbed in the next vision, for the sealing of the saints. When they break loose in the trumpets to ravage land, sea, and trees the disaster to the trees is indeed mentioned in the first plague, but the principal matter of the

[1] So St Mark (XIII, 7–8). St Luke adds 'pestilences' after 'famines', and 'terrors and signs from the sky'. St John has conquest (the bow), civil war (the sword, or dagger, rather), famine (the scales) and pestilence (the death): he saves up earthquake and terror in the sky for the sixth seal, and squares his four with the four grievous plagues of Ezekiel XIV by dropping, in the conclusion to the four horsemen, the distinction between bow and sword, and adding the plague of noisesome beasts: 'There was given them power over the quarter of the earth to kill with sabre' (not dagger) 'famine, pestilence, and by the wild beasts of earth'.

112

plagues is something very different. And the plagues of the olive and vine, when they distinctly appear, are not locust or caterpillar —the locusts of the fifth trumpet are demons forbidden to touch herb or tree, they have more important business with mankind. The olive-trees cut down by the folly of Antichrist are the prophets of God, whose fall brings ruin on the city (XI): the vines, not locust-eaten but all too fruitful, fill the vats of divine judgement, from which flows out a river of blood to sixteen hundred furlongs (XIV, 17–20): and the perfect product of that vintage is the sevenfold libation of fiery wine, in which is accomplished the wrath of God (XV–XVI).

Let us now take up the 'intrusive visions' of VII. We have said that in them St John runs straight on from the apparent manifestation of the Last Judgement at the sixth seal. That was the shadow of *New Year*. He does not run quite straight on from this point; he inserts first a warning not to be misled, by this merely anticipatory glimpse, into the supposition that we have reached the consummation which it foreshadows; he allows us to see a set of plagues still in store for the world, but for the present held in check, while the saints are sealed; their sealing is a new *Dedication,* as we will show in a moment. And then we proceed to the *Paschal*-vision of the triumphant saints, having flown round all the four corners of the year—from midsummer we slipped forward to New Year, from New Year we advance to Dedication, and from Dedication to Passover.

We have seen already that the imposition of the divine Name by means of the Aaronic blessing directly preceded the Torah-lesson for Dedication-Day (Num. VI, 22 ff.). The imposition of the Name is a magnificent conclusion to the numbering of the tribes which occupies the preceding part of the book and gives it its title. First the twelve lay-tribes are numbered, and arranged in a four-square camp (I–II). The numbering of the Levitical families follows (III–IV). Then Moses is directed to put out of the camp all that are unclean (V, 1–4), and there follows an appendix on uncleannesses and 'separations' (V, 5–VI, 21). Then the Aaronic blessing is given, to 'put the Lord's Name upon the children of Israel', now that the Lord's host had been numbered, ranged and purified.

113

In Apocalypse VII, 1–8 the foursquare camp[1] is threatened from the four corners of the earth. An angel with the seal of God approaches from the East, where the standard of Judah stands according to Numbers II, 3, and seals the tribes in order with the seal of the Living God, beginning at Judah. The seal prints their foreheads with the Name of God, as is perfectly evident from XIV, 1. The numbers of those sealed are given tribe by tribe, in the solemn repetitive style of Numbers I. Alongside the Torah-lesson St John uses two lessons, one from the Prophets (Ezek. IX) and one from the Writings (I Chron. XXVII). The text of Chronicles tells us how, when a second dedication was projected, David summoned the numbered heads of the people, and gave the plans of the temple to Solomon in a great assembly. The text contributes to St John the 12 courses of the 12 thousands each—though in Chronicles the figure is doubled (12 courses of 24 thousands). Ezekiel supplies the image of the angel who prints the mark on the forehead, and the threat of imminent divine vengeance from which the mark exempts.

All the particular features of VII, 1–8 send us to the Aaronic Blessing, and the Feast of Dedication. At the same time it is to be noticed that St John has handled the Dedication-theme in a manner which peculiarly fits it for being the prelude to Passover. For paschal deliverance was effected by the visitation of wrath upon the Egyptian firstborn, and this act had its own immediate prelude—the marking of the tents of Israel with the paschal blood, to exempt them from the sword of the destroyer. So we can read straight on from the vision of the sealing in VII, 1–8 to the vision of the thanksgiving for paschal deliverance in VII, 9 ff., and hardly notice that we have passed from one feast to another.

That VII, 9–17 is a paschal vision can hardly be disputed. The initial object of vision is a numberless multitude praising God and the Lamb, and dressed in white robes. It is explained that the white robes are white because they are washed in the blood of the Lamb, and that these are men who have come out of the great oppression, the new Egyptian bondage. There can be no hesitation about the predominantly paschal character of the vision, and yet St John can-

---

[1] The camp is not actually named, but when the threat from the four corners reappears in XX, 8–9, we hear of 'the camp of the saints'.

not restrain himself from looking beyond Passover to the feast of Tabernacles. The saints carry palm branches, a characteristic Tabernacles ceremony. More explicit still are the words, 'Therefore are they before the throne of God, and serve him day and night in his temple, and he that sitteth upon the throne shall *tabernacle over them*', as when they were in the wilderness-tabernacles and he spread his cloudy tabernacle over their heads. So canopied, and supplied with spring-water and manna, 'they shall hunger no more, neither thirst any more, nor shall the sun strike them, nor any heat: for the Lamb in the midst of the throne shall shepherd them and lead them to water-springs of life'—the waters of life are a promise especially recalled and invoked at the tabernacles feast.

The vision of the great multitude is an extra eighth, and an anticipated conclusion: if we forget that the seventh seal has still to be opened, we can read IV–VII as a complete apocalypse. In such a view, the Passover-Tabernacles of VII, 9–17 balances and fulfils the Passover-Pentecost of IV–V. Again we see the great assembly worshipping before the Throne. But where previously the Lamb stood alone as firstfruit of mankind, while the saints were represented in absence by the incense of their prayers, now the numberless host is seen, drawn from every nation, tribe, people and tongue. So the angelic hymn of the previous vision has exact fulfilment. 'Worthy art thou', they sang, 'for thou wast slain and didst purchase to God by thy blood men of every tribe, tongue, people and nation, and didst make them to our God a kingdom and priests, and they shall reign on the earth' (v, 9–10). They have come out of Egyptian oppression: they have washed their robes and whitened them in redeeming blood. They are sealed with the mark of a divine covenant. God tabernacles upon them, and every tear is wiped from their eyes.

The fusion of Tabernacles with Passover which we read in VII, 9–17 is not surprising in St John. It is part of his doctrine that Tabernacles is not a Christian feast: it has its fulfilment in the Christian Passover. Perhaps not even the Passover is a yearly feast for him; there is nothing but the weekly resurrection-feast of Sunday. However that may be, Tabernacles has its fulfilment in the Christian Passover, whether Passover is commemorated in Sunday or in Easter. And so, in his Gospel, St John says that Christ was urged to make an ascent to Tabernacles, but refused, saying, 'I ascend not to this feast.' He went there secretly, and made no public appearance until the feast was half done. The Sanhedrin would have brought about his passion at Tabernacles, but they could not, for his hour was not yet. When Passover came, his public ascent was made in the triumphal entry. About St John's treatment of the entry two things are remarkable. He attaches it firmly to Passover-tide, which the previous gospel-tradition had not done: and he makes explicit the implicit Tabernacles-features of it. For it is he and he alone who says that the branches carried by the people were branches of palm; and the carrying of palm branches was a characteristic Tabernacles-ceremony. In the other gospels greenery is used to pave the road; in St John the palms are carried, as in the Tabernacles processions. So Tabernacles is fulfilled at Passover, just as it is in Apocalypse VII. Here too are the palm branches, and the hosannas. The saints are clad in white robes, and hold palms in their hands, and they cry, 'Salvation' (i.e. hosanna) 'to our God and to the Lamb.' For the form of salutation, compare 'Hosanna to the Son of David' (Matt. XXI, 9, 15).

So the section which is principally concerned with the Passover quarter (IV–VII) ends with a glorious feast in which Passover embodies the ceremonies of Tabernacles. The section principally concerned with Tabernacles (XI, 15–XIV) contains many allusions to the Tabernacles-symbols, but no glorious Tabernacles feast. A second paschal section (XIX–XXII) ends in a glorious Tabernacles (XXI, 2–8). Thus the Apocalypse always either fuses Tabernacles with Passover, or makes it a pendant to Passover. It is allowed no glory of its own.

116

CHAPTER V

(1)

The feast of New Year, the first of the seventh month, is the beginning of a ten-day period of which Atonement Day is the tenth. This period is a sort of Lent in preparation for the Easter (as it were) of Tabernacles. Lent finds its climax on Good Friday, and so did the ten days on Atonement. There is one day's gap between Good Friday and Easter: there are four days between Atonement and Tabernacles. Though Atonement is nearer to Tabernacles than to New Year, yet it forms one with New Year, not with Tabernacles. New Year is a feast, Atonement is a fast. Thus in a catalogue of Feasts we may count New Year and Tabernacles each as one, annexing the Atonement Fast to New Year. Again, to a more cursory view, all three solemnities form a single holy season.

The peculiar liturgy of New Year is the blowing of trumpets, an obvious ceremony to mark a period of time. The liturgy of Atonement is the purification or re-hallowing of the temple, the purging of the channel of grace which the holy place represents, from the accumulated defilements of another year. This purging is carried out by the High Priest, with atonement blood taken from the altar of slaughter and smeared on all the parts of the sanctuary, including the mercy-seat in the Holy of Holies, the veiled shrine never beheld by human eyes on any other day, nor then without enveloping fumes of incense-smoke.

St John stretches back the distinctive symbols of New Year, the trumpets, over the whole period from midsummer to New Year, just as he stretches the pentecostal symbol of unsealing back over the weeks from Firstfruits to Pentecost. Once midsummer is over, every week that passes is a milestone on the road to the Feast of Trumpets. This means that the seventh trumpet, and it alone, marks the New Year feast. The trumpets are assigned to the 'seven angels of the presence', a synonym for the archangels, of whom Michael is chief. The seventh trumpet will therefore be his,

117

and in the vision following it, there and there only, his name appears (XII, 7). It was Jewish belief that Michael would sound a trumpet to initiate the supreme New Year of the Great Judgement: and to this St Paul refers when he says: 'The Lord himself shall descend from heaven with a signal-note, the blast of the archangel, the trump of God' (I Thess. IV, 16). The seventh trumpet is alone the trumpet of New Year, the former six are previous; they fill the second quarter, it initiates the third.

The angel of the incense-liturgy (VIII, 2 ff.) empties the charcoal of his censer upon earth, and the seven trumpet-angels put themselves in posture to blow. In the succeeding week we have the several blasts, in which we see the effect of the falling coals of fire. The first trumpeting brought down fire, mingled with hail and bloody dew, to burn up earth, trees and herbs. At the second a flaming volcano vomited itself into the sea: at the third a blazing comet swept down to poison the waters by its baleful influence: at the fourth the fires of heaven itself were darkened: at the fifth a falling star released the demons of the pit. All these portents of fire and darkness are the fire and smoke from the incense, presented at the golden altar of the midsummer liturgy. At the next trumpet, the golden altar himself utters a voice from his four horns, to invoke the supreme fulfilment of the liturgy. At his voice the sixth trumpet-angel looses with his own hands the four angels of pestilence who principally inflict what the saints were sealed against at the time when four angels restrained the four winds of destruction (VII, 1). We see, then, that all the six trumpet-plagues express the fulfilment of the midsummer liturgy.

The plagues are plagues of Egypt. They are selected and rearranged to fit the scheme of the six creative works. The plague on earth is that of hail and lightning: the plague on the sea is that of Nile-water turned to blood: that on fresh waters has to be supplied by an inversion of the miracle at Marah.[1] At Marah Moses

_____

[1] The latter part of the book of Wisdom is a homily based on a comparison and contrast between the plagues in Egypt and the mercies in the wilderness: the sweetening of Marah is the opposed antitype to the corruption of the Nile. The Author of Wisdom also says that the plagues show the Creator armed with all the creatures against the wicked, which is the underlying principle of St John's list. The same Author sees the punishment shaped to fit the crime, and this idea appears in St John's *second* treatment of the plagues, in the third vial: 'They have shed blood . . . and thou hast given them blood to drink.'

sweetened the waters with a wholesome shrub, here they are embittered by an influence named wormwood. The plague on luminaries is that of darkness, the plague of living things from the abyss is that of locusts, but here the locusts are demons and inflict with their stings what is probably to be taken as the antitype to yet another plague, the plague of boils. The plague of living things from the land is roughly the same so far as its ministers go, for the demon-cavalry are but another version of the locust army of Joel's prophecy: but they differ in what they inflict, the plague not of boils but of death, the last and decisive stroke of Moses's rod.

The analysis of the six trumpets presents many fascinations to the student of the inspired imagination, but this is not perhaps the place to pursue it. It is, however, worth making the remark that at the end of the vision of the countless multitude St John has just shewn the righteous enjoying the mercies in the wilderness which are the opposites of the plagues in Egypt. 'He that sitteth on the throne shall spread his tabernacle over them: they shall hunger no more, neither thirst any more, neither shall the sun strike upon them nor any heat. For the Lamb that is in the midst of the throne shall feed them, and guide them unto fountains of waters of life, and God shall wipe away all tears from their eyes.'

What is the point of the occurrence of Egyptian plagues at this stage of St John's vision? The reader is likely to object that he is being carried back behind Passover: the plagues, if they belong anywhere, should stand in the space actually occupied by the messages to the Churches. And indeed, when St John comes to tread over again the journey from Dedication to Passover in xvi, the plagues of Egypt return in the seven vials. What are they doing in the trumpets here?

For an answer to this question we have to recover the Jewish manner of reading the Bible. The Jew sees three texts in evident parallel, a lesson from the Law, a lesson from the 'former prophets' and a lesson from the 'latter prophets'. In Exodus we read how the ten plagues overthrow Egypt, while Israel (we are again and again told) is exempted from the evils; and when it comes to the worst and last stroke, Israel is sealed against it by the mark of paschal blood. In Joshua we read how the seven encompassings of

Jericho overthrow the city, by trumpet-blasts and shouting: but not until believing Rahab and her house have been sealed for salvation with a blood-red cord. In Ezekiel we read how six angels of slaughter overthrow old Jerusalem, after a seventh has sealed the righteous against destruction by a mark on the forehead.

St John, on any shewing, combines the three parallels. The plagues of VIII–IX are plagues of Egypt. They are occasioned, however, not by strokes of Moses's rod, but by blasts of Joshua's trumpets. The saving mark of VII is in the form neither of Exodus nor of Joshua but of Ezekiel, and to Ezekiel also belongs the symbolical scattering of coals which, precedes the smiting of the wicked. Evidently the three parallels are woven together in St John's mind, and this is evidenced by what happens when the theme returns in XV–XVI. There we have (a) a closer and more elaborate version of the Ezekielian scene of the scattering of fire, (b) a fresh version of the Egyptian plagues, (c) the fall of the heathen city by earthquake, as Jericho fell, this being the climax of the whole work.

So, then, since the threefold scheme is one for St John, what we have to ask about its occurrence in VII–IX is, which of the three strands belongs to the context here. The answer which we have to give is that two of the strands are appropriate, but that they fasten into different parts of the context. St John's threefold scheme of Moses, Joshua and Ezekiel extends over two separate passages of his vision, joining them like a bridge: the sealing of the saints in VII, 1–8 is one, the scattering of fire and the plagues in VIII, 3–IX, 21 make up the other. The situations at the two ends of the bridge are different. In VII the scene is pre-paschal, the sequel to it being the thanksgiving for the deliverance at Passover (VII, 9 ff.). So, of the three strands, the paschal or Mosaic strand ties in here. The setting of VIII–IX is the blowing of the New Year trumpets, and so here the Joshua theme is uppermost. The blasts of the trumpet against Jericho are the beginning of a New Year indeed, the possession of the Kingdom of God by the Twelve Tribes. At New Year we may remember the trumpets which levelled the city of the wicked, and at Tabernacles the consequence, the possession of the land of corn, wine and oil.

After the vision of the sixth trumpet the extra visions (X–XI, 13) are intercalated. These visions, especially the latter part of them, are generally accounted the most difficult in the book, so it behoves us to approach them warily. Let us make the best of the guidance which is offered to us by the parallel in the corresponding part of the seals.

We have seen that the distribution of material in the two series is comparable, but that it is not the same. Dislocation starts with the disparity between the two series of plagues, the four horsemen and the six plagues of Egypt. The six play essentially the same part in the trumpets as the four in the seals, and St John underlines the comparison with much emphasis in the framing of the sixth trumpet-vision. It is the *sixth* angel who, with his own hands, looses the angels of death, but their number is *four,* and it is in obedience to a voice from the (*four*) horns of the incense-altar that he looses them. Their work is carefully compared with the work of the last horseman and his companion: 'To them was given authority over the fourth part of earth, to kill with sword, famine, pestilence, and by the wild beasts of earth' (VI, 8). 'By these three plagues was killed the third part of men, through the fire, smoke, and brimstone proceeding from their mouths' (IX, 18). The sixth trumpet, then, matches the fourth seal, and so the themes of the fifth and sixth seals cannot appear in the fifth and sixth trumpets: they have to be pushed down into the extra visions (X–XI, 13). So the theme of the martyrs and of the great earthquake which appear as the fifth and sixth seal-visions both appear after the sixth trumpet-vision. It is in XI that we see the martyrdom of the two witnesses and their vindication by the great earthquake.

The extra visions after the sixth seal began with a sealing, whereby the saints were protected against the six trumpet-plagues. Since then we have witnessed the six trumpet-plagues, and a new mark of divine protection is now given, the measuring-off of the sanctuary which contains the true worshippers of God (XI, 1–3). Does this sign, like the sign of the sealing, protect against the evils which will be manifested in the next quarter (there the trumpet-plagues, here the beasts of XII–XIII)? It does, but there is a difference. In VII only the protection was anticipated; we had to wait until the next quarter for the plagues. In XI the plagues as well as the protection are anticipated: the 'Beast from the Abyss' who attacks the witnesses in XI is no other than the 'Beast from the Sea' who makes war on the woman's seed in XIII.

Since in XI the protection receives immediately its natural consequence, the attack, there is nothing to emphasize its intrusiveness, its prematurity. But it is important that these things should be emphasized. St John wishes here to insert into the context, before our eyes, the seed from which the next little apocalypse will develop, just as he did in VII, 1–8. He gets the effect he desires by developing the person of the protecting angel. In VII the angel himself carried the seal and himself bestowed the mark. Here the angel (or another acting in connexion with him?) gives the measuring-reed to St John: but before he does that, he gives him a book, and before he gives him the book, he swears an oath. The oath and the book are made vehicles of revelation looking beyond the present scene, and so St John achieves the effect of anticipation which he requires.

We may observe how the angel of VII is developed in x.

I saw an angel ascending from the rising sun	I saw another strong angel descending from heaven . . . his face like the sun . . .
having the seal of the Living God	having in his hand an open scroll . . .
and he cried with a great voice . . . Hurt not the earth, sea or trees until we have sealed the servants of our God. (And then at the seventh unsealing, the plagues will break loose on the wicked).	and he cried with a great voice . . . and sware by the Everliving Maker of heaven . . . earth . . . and sea that there shall be no more delay, but in the days of the seventh angel when he shall sound, the hidden counsel is accomplished. (But until then it is not, and there is delay).

One angel ascends, the other descends, one from the rising of the sun, the other himself as the sun among clouds. One carries the seal of the Living God, the supreme authentication: the other carries the book, to which we have lately seen the seal attached sevenfold, and authenticates its message with an oath by the Living God. Both cry aloud, the first to interpose delay before the judgement can break loose, the second to measure the delay that there will be. St John then takes and digests the book, so that he may prophesy of what will so certainly come into force when the seventh angel has trumpeted.

A special device is used to impress upon us that the whole vision of the martyrdom and vindication of the witnesses is anticipatory merely of what the seventh trumpet will unleash. We are shewn no *vision* of the two witnesses. The visionary situation is all the time that of St John's receiving the book and the reed, with instructions. The instructions about the reed are drawn out into a prediction of the effect to be obtained: 'Measure the temple of God and the altar . . . and I will grant to my two witnesses that they may prophesy. . . .' The effect has still to be obtained. St John, we may take it, obeys the instructions about the reed, as we are told he has done about the book. But the predicted effect of his action will become visible in subsequent visions.

When St John takes and eats the book, the Apocalypse seems to make a fresh beginning: the seer is given a new draught of inspiration, as though for a second task. The scheme of the liturgical year makes this perfectly intelligible. The year has two beginnings: for while the months are counted from the paschal month, New Year is kept at Michaelmas. The Jewish hesitation between two beginnings for the year is like the Jewish hesitation between two beginnings for the day: is it sunrise or sundown? The first month and Passover mark the morning, the seventh and Tabernacles the evening of the year.

St John has both beginnings, and the October beginning closely matches the April beginning. In the vision of IV–V the book of revelation is received and opened by the Lamb, and this is the antitype to Ezekiel's vision, when he was visited by the Glory and received the book (Ezek. I–III). Ezekiel, in so far as he is named 'Son of Man' is the type of Christ, but in so far as he is the son of Buzi he is the type of the Christian prophet. There is one type, therefore, the vision of Ezekiel, and two antitypes, Jesus Christ and his servant John. The Apocalypse gives the divine antitype in the Firstfruits-Pentecost vision and the human antitype in this

123

New Year's Eve vision. The various features of the type are carefully sorted out between the two antitypes. Ezekiel is visited on earth by the vision (b), and sees the divine glory enthroned over the firmament (a). A book being seen in the hand of his visitant (a, b), is opened by heavenly power (a) and received wide open (b) by the recipient, who is told to eat it (b); it is sweet as honey in the mouth, but carries a bitter message to digest (b).

In Apocalypse IV–V, (a), there is no visitation on earth, the Glory is seen above the firmament, and the recipient of the book, himself divine, takes over the divine work of opening the book. In Apocalypse X, (b), the seer is visited on earth, not by the divine Glory but by a glorious angel, the book is already wide open in the angel's hand, having been opened already by Christ in heaven; and eating it, as he is commanded to do, St John finds it sweet in the mouth but bitter to the stomach. The two visions, taken in conjunction, express the whole mystery of revelation: 'the revelation which God gave to Jesus Christ, to shew his servants what must shortly come to pass; and he signified it by the message of an angel to his servant John.'

Ezekiel's vision, as we noted, when it appeared in Apocalypse IV–V, appeared as the prophetical reading attached to the torah-reading for Pentecost, which was the giving of the decalogue according to Exodus. The giving of the decalogue according to Deuteronomy (v) was read at New Year, a fact which St John can express by the re-use of Ezekiel. According to the lectionary, then, Pentecost and New Year are in parallel with one another. St John, as we saw, carries the image of the pentecostal lawgiving back into a prelude for the Passover-Pentecost 'week', while he assigns the New Year lawgiving to a prelude for the New-Year-and-onwards 'week'. And so the 'eves' of his two half-years are brought into parallel. In Exodus the revelation of the tables is made in overwhelming awe and majesty on the mountain, in Deuteronomy it is brought down into the plain to be digested and reflected on, for this is the meaning of the Deuteronomy, or second giving of the law.[1]

[1] St John uses the same topic in his epistles, I John II, 7–11, II John 5. The Deuteronomic law of love is simply the old commandment with fresh light breaking upon it.

124

St John gives further expression to this contrast by attaching the two halves into which he has split the Ezekiel vision to the two members of a pair of Daniel-visions. Daniel's visions may be divided into apocalyptic dreams and angelic visitations. The crowning apocalyptic dream is that of the Son of Man in VII, and the crowning visitation is that of the glorious angel in X–XII. In the apocalyptic dream Daniel's spirit is taken up to penetrate a heavenly mystery, at the angel's visitation he is 'in the body' and heavenly power comes down to earth. Apocalypse IV–V makes plain allusion to Daniel VII, the vision of the court of heaven with its many thrones among which the one is pre-eminent, the thousand thousands of ministers and the myriad myriads of celestial guards, the solemn opening of the heavenly books, the sudden mysterious advent of the Son of Man, to be acknowledged the possessor of eternal dominion, glory, and kingdom over all peoples, nations and languages. Even closer is the allusion of Apocalypse X to Daniel X–XII, and in particular to XII, as a glance at that chapter will suffice to shew: 'I heard the man clothed in linen which was above the waters of the river, when he held up his right hand and his left hand to heaven and sware that it shall be for a time, times and a half and . . . all things shall be accomplished. I heard, but I understood not. Then said I, O my Lord, what shall be the latter end of these things? And he said: Go thy way, Daniel, for the words are shut up and sealed till the time of the end.' St John's angel stands to swear with one foot only on water, so that, placing the other on land, and lifting a hand to heaven, he may attest the creator of earth, sea and sky. He does not bring 'words shut up and sealed' but a scroll wide open, because it is now that 'time of the end' of which Daniel wrote. The parables which were once dark, sealed up, are now open and interpreted. The angel's oath is accompanied by the overpowering utterance of the seven thunders. Their voices are to be 'sealed up' and left unwritten by St John, not because the time is yet unripe for attending to them, but because the time for doing so is already past. They are but introductory portents, like the seven seals or the seven trumpets, and the last introductory portent, the seventh trumpet, is now upon us. By digesting the scroll, St John will see the days of the seventh trumpet-blast. The vision of the oath, we observe,

125

has an intimate relation with Daniel XII, even in what it adds or alters.[1]

The function of Daniel's swearing angel was to mark a period. He was to declare on oath that the oppression of Antichrist would last for a time, times and a half. St John's angel does not declare exactly this, because the reader knows it anyhow from Daniel's pages, and St John does not love stale repetitions. He tells us not that the first part of redemption, the overthrow of Antichrist, will befall within half a 'week', but that the whole of redemption will be accomplished within the days of the seventh angel's trump, presumably, that is to say, within the liturgical year inaugurated by his trumpet-blast. We shall see that this promise is exactly fulfilled.

Though St John does not put the 'time, times and a half' into the mouth of the angel, he introduces it in parallel to the angel's message. The angel gives St John a scroll, and an unnamed hand presents him with a reed, commanding him to measure the sanctuary for protection through the 'half-week of years' (42 months) during which the heathen will trample the holy city, as Daniel had said they would (Dan. VIII, 13–14). Under the protection of the measuring two witnesses prophesy for the same period, and when they are martyred at last, they lie dead not, like 'their Lord that was crucified', until the third day only, but for a full half-week, in symmetry with the period of their prophecy. The mysterious period reappears in XII and XIII as the duration of the woman's protection from the dragon, which is also the period of the tyranny of Antichrist.

St John is as exact in his arithmetic as we should expect him to

[1] Daniel X–XII and VII as types of revelation on earth and in heaven respectively are used to contrast also the Son of Man vision of I with the Glory vision of IV–V. As Daniel XII is exploited in Apocalypse X, so is Daniel X in Apocalypse I, as we see from the features of the heavenly visitant; clothed in linen, his loins girded with pure gold, his eyes as lamps of fire, his feet like in colour to burnished brass, himself as the similitude of the sons of men. The seer falls paralysed before him: the heavenly visitant touches him with the words, 'Fear not.'—Daniel VII and Daniel X–XII appear, indeed, to alternate throughout the Apocalypse: I, 7 and I, 9–20; IV–V and X; XI–XIV and XVII–XIX, 16; XIX, 17–XX and XXI–XXII. The second members of the pairs make an interesting sequence of their own; see above, pp. 73 ff.

be. According to the scheme of the great week (of weeks), the Angel of the Oath appears at the beginning of the eve of the third day, and the whole of God's secret purpose, his sixfold work, is completed with the close of the sixth, exactly three days and a half from the swearing of the oath.

This is to see the Angel of the Oath in the context of the whole Apocalypse. But he has also to find his place in a smaller field, since the trumpets can be read as an apocalypse by themselves. In this view the period of Antichrist is simply the gap (XI, 1–13), the forty-two months of the two witnesses, and the secret purpose of God is fulfilled when the New Year trumpet sounds (XI, 15–19). So that the angel's oath is, after all, ambiguous. 'There shall be no more delay, but in the days of the seventh angel's blast, when he shall sound, the secret purpose of God is accomplished.' If we emphasize 'in the days of' we have the suggestion of a period inaugurated by the trumpet, as the time within which the accomplishment takes place. If we emphasize 'when he shall sound' we have the suggestion of fulfillment immediately upon the trumpet blast.

We must look now into the gap between the oath and the trumpet, the passage which has caused the interpreters such agony. We have from the start some idea of what it must contain. First, there will be a parallel to the sealing in VII, 1–8. Second, there will be an account of the days of Antichrist. Third, there will be a vision of the martyrs, in parallel with the fifth seal, and an earthquake to vindicate them, in parallel with the sixth. It is, happily, possible to effect one simplification here. The story of Antichrist *is* the story of the persecution and vindication of the martyrs, so we can reduce our three to two. Let us now attend to the parallel our text affords to the sealing of the saints in VII.

The sealing of the numbered saints with the Name of God we saw to be a dedication-vision, for the numbering of the holy people is the prelude both to Moses's dedication and to Solomon's; and in the Mosaic history the putting of the Name upon the Children of Israel follows the counting of the host and precedes the dedication of the sanctuary. If the numbering and blessing of the people is a part of the dedication it only is so by the analogy it bears to the measuring and hallowing of the shrine. God numbers

127

the people, the temple of flesh and blood, and puts his Name upon them: he measures the temple of wood and stone, and says of it, 'My Name shall be therein' (Deut. xii, 5, etc., I Kings viii, 29). The counting defines the number on whom the Name rests, the measuring defines the area wherein the Name dwells. In the Christian dispensation the two things are one: the only temple is the living temple; whether we describe it as a temple or a camp, we mean the same thing. When St John is commanded to take the reed and measure the sanctuary, including the shrine and altar-court but excluding the outer court which is unconsecrated, we understand perfectly well that the mystery of the Dedication is being re-enacted, with a new stress on the exclusion of the un-hallowed.

The equation between the temple and the camp or city is taken for granted by St John in the use he makes of his symbols. 'Measure off the inner sanctuary from the outer court' means 'Exempt the dwellings of the faithful, and abandon the *city* as a whole to be trampled by the Gentiles for the three and a half years which Daniel predicted'. The fact that the outer court of the temple had always been unconsecrated and left open to the Gentiles becomes a token of the fact that the city as a whole will be overrun by the heathen and only the dwellings of the faithful respected: and this again is still only a token. St John is not saying that when Jerusalem falls the Gentiles will trample over the greater part of it; but that in the days of Antichrist a great part of the visible people of God will be perverted to apostasy. The fall of Jerusalem had happened a quarter of a century ago when St John wrote, and no part of the city had been exempted from Gentile 'trampling'. In the days of Antichrist which were presently to come, no earthly power would be able to touch the spirits of the predestinate, while as for the rest, they had never been within the measures of the hallowed ground, or on the muster-roll of God's elect. Whether the visible people of God who apostatize to Antichrist are faithless Christians or unchristianized Jews, it is impossible to judge from St John's text.

The first step in understanding xi, 1–13 is to appreciate its relation to the Dedication-Feast; the second is to appreciate its relation to the visions of Zechariah. St John seems to make a continuous

128

use of these visions, so twisting yet another strand into his rope. The first Zechariah vision is the vision of the Four Horsemen, and this has appeared in the seals. The second vision is the vision of the Four Horns which scatter Israel and Judah. St John has worked this symbol in too, with his unfailing resource. For just as Zechariah's Four Horns are the serial successors of his Four Horsemen, so St John's trumpet-plagues are the serial successors of his seal-plagues. In the seal-plagues he shows us the Four Horsemen, and in the trumpet-plagues the Four Horns. We have already seen how St John forces the parallel between the four horsemen and the six trumpets, and in particular how he drives it home in the sixth trumpet, when a voice *out of the horns* of the incense-altar directs the sixth angel to unbind the four leaders of the armies of death. 'From the (four) horns,' with which the four leaders are matched, is part of the parallel with the four horsemen; for the third rider is directed by a voice *from among the four cherubim,* with whom the four riders are matched. The connexion of the sixth trumpet with the altar of incense is especially stressed, because the sixth trumpet is the last. But the whole trumpet-series expresses the fall of the coals from the incense-liturgy, and what is made explicit in the sixth trumpet applies to all. They all reveal the incense-altar putting forth the horns of its strength against the enemies of the saints. That is to say, they show the power of intercession to bring vindication, for the incense-liturgy expresses the prayers of the saints presented before God.

So much for the first two visions of Zechariah. It is clear that St John makes the first vision a material part of his symbolism, while the second is worked in for the sake of working it in. It has no real effect on what he has to say. If the voice directing the sixth trumpet-angel had proceeded from the incense-altar rather than from its horns, the reference to Zechariah's second vision would have been effaced, but the sense of St John's poem would have remained the same.

The next three visions of Zechariah are those of the Measuring of Jerusalem, the High Priest and Satan, and the Candlestick. What is remarkable is that while hitherto St John has assigned one Zechariah-vision to each of his own weeks of visions, he suddenly starts to compress three of Zechariah's visions into one of his own, for all the three we have just named afford material to Apocalypse XI, 1–13. Having once started to compress like this, he continues to do it: all that remain of Zechariah's visions are used in the Beast-Visions.[1]

If we look at the three visions in Zechariah II–IV we can guess why St John lumps them together as he does. The first and the third are obvious Dedication-visions, and it falls to him here to write of Dedication, in parallel with what he wrote in VII, 1–8. The Measuring of Jerusalem we have already related to Dedication, while as for the Candlestick, it was an actual Dedication-lesson, and St John had already used it in that sense in Apocalypse I. Let us imagine St John arrived at Apocalypse XI. His own scheme requires a Dedication-vision, and the next vision in Zechariah's series after his vision of the Horns (which St John has just used) is the measuring-vision. It fits his purpose excellently; but just ahead in the Zechariah list is the Candlestick-vision, which absolutely demands to be brought in where Dedication is the theme. There is nothing for it but to condense the two visions into one: and if two, then three, since there is a third (Zechariah III) intervening between the two.

Zechariah II is a symbolic measuring of Jerusalem, not to be walled with human hands, but so that God may be a wall of fire round about, and the Glory in the midst of her.[2] St John combines Zechariah's measuring of the city with Ezekiel's measuring of the

[1] The remaining Zechariah visions are (1) the flying sickle of judgement ('sickle' in the Greek, 'scroll' in the Hebrew) (2) the bushel measure and the women with storks' wings (3) the four chariots of the winds (4) Jesus crowned with gold—though this is not strictly a *vision*. (3) is the close antitype of the four riders, which St John has used in Apocalypse VI: he makes no fresh use of the four chariots. (1) and (4) are combined in the vision of Jesus crowned with gold and riding the sky armed with a sickle (XIV, 14). (2) may be seen in the woman furnished with eagle's wings (XII, 14) and in the flying angels (XIV, 6–12). The visions of Zechariah (Zech. I–VI) extend from Apocalypse VI to XIV. Zechariah's concluding oracles (XII–XIV) refer to the Last Things: St John applies XII, 11 to Armageddon (Apoc. XVI, 16) and XIV, 6–11 to the World to Come (XXI, 23–XXII, 5). And so the applicable parts of Zechariah stretch through St John's whole vision of the future (Apoc. VI–XXII) in some sort of order.

[2] I Enoch XLI makes a use of this passage which very likely directs St John. Enoch remains closer to Zechariah. For him as for St John the symbol signifies predestination.

130

temple (Ezek. XL, ff.), thus producing the double symbol in which temple and city are made equivalents, as we saw above. Ezekiel's angel does what St John is commanded to do, he measures the limit of the inner court to make a separation between the holy and the common (XLII, 15–20). The limits of the outer court he leaves unmeasured.

By glossing Zechariah II with Ezekiel XL–XLII, St John has adapted it for fusion with Zechariah III and IV. For by narrowing the measured area from city to sanctuary he comes to grips with the High Priest and the Candlestick. The Lord is to be a 'wall of fire round about', not the whole city, but only so much of it as corresponds to the inner court of the temple. He is to be 'a Glory in the midst' that is to say, a flame of presence in the sanctuary of the temple, a luminous indwelling, that of which the temple-candlesticks are the symbol. The candlesticks of the Christian temple are the apostolic witnesses to the Light of the World, but as Zechariah III shows us, the Light of the World and his witnesses or companions are at present doing battle with the demonic Adversary, and while the battle lasts they wear 'soiled raiment' or 'sackcloth'—it does not matter which we say, for both are the expression of fasting and penitence.[1]

St John had already fused Zechariah III and IV in the first scene of his whole book. The vision before us bears the same relation to the Candlestick-vision of Apocalypse I as the vision of the oath bears to that of the Enthroned Glory in IV–V. In the vision of the Glory St John supplies an antitype to the heavenly aspect of Ezekiel I–III, in the vision of the oath an antitype to the earthly aspect: in the Candlestick-vision he supplies an antitype to the diviner aspect of Zechariah III–IV, and in the vision of the reed an antitype to the more human aspect. When we were treating of the Candlestick-vision of St John we observed that the Candlestick-vision of Zechariah must appear in Christian eyes to treat of the High Priest Jesus simply in so far as he is the Son of Josadek, while the preceding vision of the clothing of the High Priest

1 St John says 'sackcloth' to remind us that in XI, 1–13 Dedication is being seen from the point of view of the season of the yearly fast, New Year—Atonement: for the whole context of X–XI remains dominated by the image of the Great Trumpet.

131

treats of him in so far as he is the type of the Son of God. In his own Candlestick-vision St John made the diviner aspect of Zechariah's double oracle his canon of interpretation. This left no place for a human Jesus and Zerubbabel who stand on either hand supplying oil to the mystical lamp-stand: there is only the divine Jesus in the midst, who is himself the great Candlestick as well as the lamp-lighter. But now in XI the shift onto a more human plane permits Zerubbabel and Jesus to come into their own. These are the Lord's two witnesses, the two oil-trees which stand before the Lord of all the earth, that is, to St John's mind, before the divine Jesus, the great candlestick in their midst. The form established in Apocalypse I persists: as the seven candles were there made to be derivative candlesticks burning in the presence of the source of light, so here the two oil-trees are secondary candlesticks as well as trees. Witnesses who shine with a derived light in testimony to the Light of the world are a Johannine commonplace, as readers of St John's Gospel will recognise (I, 8–9, V, 33–39, VIII, 12–18).

Christ sent his apostles two by two, to witness of him in every place, in symbol (St John will think) of the double anointing, the oil of principality and the oil of high-priesthood, which redounds from him to them. Because they have this, they are the candlesticks of the sanctuary. At this point St. John is overwhelmed by the wider connexions of the commonplace about 'witnesses', of whom there must be two 'to establish every word'. The Fourth Gospel, in the passages we have cited, discusses the matter with theological subtlety: Are the witnesses Moses and Elias (i.e. scripture and John Baptist), are they the Father of Jesus and the Works of Jesus, or the Father and Jesus himself? The topic is discussed again in the First Epistle.[1] Here in the Apocalypse the mere image-types of tradition overwhelm the seer. The Son of Man in the midst has a figure on either hand—these are surely the two mysterious witnesses to the oath in Daniel XII, 'one on this side, the other on that' of the swearing angel. Or again, we see Jesus the great Candlestick, shining with the glory of God, and on either hand—who but Moses and Elias, as in his Transfiguration? So the two witnesses develop the powers of these two, able to call down fire on their enemies, to shut the heaven from giving rain, to smite the

[1] I John v, 7–12.

132

earth with every plague: for the prophetic ministers of the new covenant are no less mighty in the word of the Lord than were the prophets of the old. So the place where they prophesy is, as it was for Elias, the Israelite land that slays the prophets, the land 'wherein their Lord was crucified', and it is also the 'Egypt' where Moses preached; but then it is also the 'Sodom' where the Lord's two angel-apostles would have suffered outrage in the street, but for the hospitality of Lot.[1]

The 'two olive-trees' are dressed in raiment of mourning, for they participate in the High Priestly Jesus in all things: they are engaged, as is the Jesus of Zechariah's High-Priest vision, in a conflict with Satan: or more exactly, Satan is the opposite of Jesus; they are matched against Satan's 'seed', the Beast from the Abyss. They also receive their dramatic vindication: like 'their Lord that was crucified' they undergo martyrdom. They lie dead three days and a half, but after that they rise up on their feet and manifestly ascend into heaven in the cloud-chariot: an exaltation which reminds us of what is recorded of Elias and was believed of Moses also.

Their passion is three-and-a-half days, their ministry had been three-and-a-half years, or forty-two months. For Elias had 'shut the heaven' against rain for three-and-a-half years by the power of his word, according to the tradition reproduced by St Luke (IV, 25) and St James (V, 17), and during that time God kept him in safe keeping, first in the wilderness, then at Sarepta. Moses's ministry in the wilderness lasted not forty-two months only, but forty-two years, for it was already the second year when Israel incurred the penalty of forty years' wandering because of their faithlessness on receiving the report of the spies.

If we pass our eye back over XI, 1–13 we can now see the use which St John has made of the Zechariah vision of the High Priest and Satan. The vision appeared to be irrelevant to Dedication. The Dedication-theme demanded the visions on either side of it, and so we thought of St John as working it in as best he could for the sake of its companions. If in doing so he yielded to necessity, he has certainly made of necessity a virtue. For in developing

[1] The comparison between disciples sent two by two, and the Lord's two angels sent into Sodom, appears in Luke X, 12; c.f. Matt. X, 15.

133

this Zechariah-vision he has accomplished two purposes which we saw to belong to his own structural plan. He has given the theme of the martyrs a place in the trumpets parallel to that which it holds in the seals: and he has worked forward from Dedication to Passover, as he does also in the extra visions of the seals, where the intercalated eighth day becomes a true Sunday, a commemoration of Easter. Let us consider these two matters in order.

The martyrs under the fifth seal have a close attachment to the plagues of the first four. In those plagues they had looked in vain for their own vindication, and therefore they cried to God. Their cry united with the prayers of the militant church, and of the heavenly host, and was presented before God in the liturgy of the incense, out of which the trumpet-plagues were born. These plagues are the offspring of the prayers of the saints: and so, when the figures of the witnesses appear in XI, they are credited with the power to inflict the plagues of the trumpets. The fact that they are living confessors, not dead martyrs, makes no difference. Their word is fire against their enemies, as was that of Moses and Elias. We recall that the first effect of the incense-liturgy was the fall of fire. They turn the waters into blood, as happened at the second trumpet: they smite the land with every stroke of Moses's rod, that is, with those same Egyptian plagues which the trumpets occasion. In fact, the pagan reader, if he could decipher this chapter, might find in it a justification for the famous charge against the Christians: 'Detestation of mankind.' Is there earthquake, dearth or pestilence? The Christians are attacked as the authors of it. Yes, says St John, and so they are, just in such a sense as the Israelites were authors of the Pharaoh's calamities. If you persecute the saints, they will cry to God, and their cry will return on you in a rain of fire. Antichrist arises, and determines to make short work of these evil magicians by organized extermination. It does him little good. The saints ascend into heaven, and earthquake decimates the city of earth. The heathen world should have heeded Gamaliel: 'Beware of fighting against God' (Acts v, 39).

When the Antichrist appears and the witnesses are martyred, St John proceeds from Dedication to Passover by way of the Passion of the Lord. St John says almost in so many words that the witnesses re-enact the passion of 'their Lord that was crucified'.

It was he who visited Jerusalem as God's angels had visited Sodom, to see what entertainment he would receive: it was he first who suffered outrage in the streets, who died, rose, and ascended; and that was Easter. The witnesses 'fill up in their own bodies what was still to be accomplished of the sufferings of Christ', and are made partakers also of his resurrection. Presently in XII St John supplies the divine parallel. The Woman's Son, in the face of Satan's assault, is 'caught away to God and to his throne'. St John's intercalary vision (XI, 1–13), though it begins in Dedication, reaches Passover in the saints' resurrection, and hints at New Year in the vindicating earthquake. We are ready to pass to the next part of the calendar, the trumpet of New Year.

The seventh trumpet sounds at last. Since the trumpet-blowing is the actual ceremony of New Year, there can be no half-hour's silence, as at the seventh seal; this is New Year itself. The trumpet sounds the New Year and the trumpet receives its proper greeting, voices in heaven hailing the establishment of the divine kingdom. For every New Year was kept as a regnant year of the Kingdom of God, and the New Year of Apocalypse initiates a fresh stage of the coming of that Kingdom into its own on earth. No sooner have the shoutings died away, than Atonement Day receives its proper symbol too, the unveiling of the sacred ark: in the ritual, only to the eyes of the High Priest, but here in the apocalypse, an unveiling simply, for Christ our High Priest opens to us the Holy of Holies.

What may well surprise the reader of St John is that the Holy of Holies should be found to contain a symbolical ark, rather than the Enthroned Glory himself. It cannot be denied that a shift takes place in the temple-symbolism at this point. In the vision of IV–V the ornaments of the temple, the sevenfold candlestick and the great 'sea', stand before the Throne, which is what the Mercy-Seat of the Ark merely represents; in heaven the reality displaces the symbol. When the angel of the midsummer-vision (VIII, 3–5) carries the incense from the great altar to the incense-altar within the shrine, he offers it not before any symbolical ark, but before the presence of God himself. In the first nine chapters the heavenly temple and the divine presence might be taken as synonymous. The sixth Message promises the faithful Philadelphian a place in the eternal temple of God (III, 12): the vision of the countless

135

multitude says, 'Therefore are they before the throne of God, and they serve him day and night in his temple, and he that sitteth upon the throne shall spread his tabernacle over them' (vii, 15). In contrast with all this, the central mystery of the heavenly temple in the Atonement-vision here is the Ark of the Covenant, and when in the Dedication-vision of xv God's glory enters the shrine, this is an exceptional marvel, as at the dedication of Moses's Tabernacle or Solomon's Temple; the visible presence does not take the primary form of the Enthroned Glory, but the secondary form of the terrible shekinah-cloud by which God manifested his presence on earth; and the service of the temple is disturbed and suspended by the portent. And when we come to the final visions of the book, we find that this temple, this vessel which will hardly contain the Glory of God, is superseded. In the New Jerusalem no temple is seen, for the whole city is the Holy of Holies which God indwells.

The transition from the symbolism of i–ix to that of xi–xxii is effected by the measuring-vision of xi. The temple which simply is the divine presence cannot be protected with a ring of divine fire, nor can the divine presence be brought to become the glory in the midst of it. A temple of which such things can be said must be or represent the still incomplete 'Israel' of the present age. This is plain enough in the case of the temple which St John is to measure with his pen in the vision of the reed. This temple is the Church: the profane part of it is abandoned to heathendom, only the sanctuary of the predestinate is hallowed by the Atonement. The Candles of the Sanctuary, the two witnesses, strive with Antichrist on earth, and only in their last scene ascend into heaven.

Nevertheless, if we ask whether the temple of the reed-vision is in heaven or earth, the answer is that it is not said to be in either, and that it is in both. The saints have an earthly existence 'in the body', wherein they do battle with Antichrist. But in so far as they are the temple, or its candlesticks, or its ministering priests, they are 'in heavenly places with Christ Jesus'. When the battle with the Antichrist comes to be more fully set out in xiii, we read: 'He opened his mouth in blasphemies against God, to blaspheme his Name and his Tabernacle, them that tabernacle in heaven: and it was given him to make war with the saints and to vanquish them.'

136

The Tabernacle which Antichrist blasphemes is nothing but the Church he assails, 'even them that tabernacle in heaven,' whose bodies he tortures on earth. The description 'dwellers upon earth' is wholly reserved by St. John for the wicked, whose spirits know no better habitation.

So, when in XI, 19 the liturgical pattern of his book brings St John back to the unequivocal mention of the heavenly temple, this temple is found to be the celestial existence of the militant saints. And who does not know that this existence, in heaven though it is, needs to be purged with blood, to be hallowed and protected, and to be more fully indwelt by the divine presence? At the heart of it is the true Mercy-Seat, which every Christian may find by lifting up his heart, and on the Mercy-Seat the Lord is, his Spirit and his Name, and not in the golden shrine of Solomon. We may all be High Priests, to appear before that indwelling God; and yet this is not to enjoy the Beatific Vision. A day will be when there is no longer a temple for God to visit according to the limiting capacity of the creature, in divers manners and degrees; for there will be a new creation, when the creature will be simply placed under the radiance of the divine Countenance, and made such a habitation of God as full illumination will make it. And this is the city of which it is said, 'I saw no temple therein, for the Lord God Almighty and the Lamb are the temple thereof. And the city hath no need of sun or moon to shine on her, for the Glory of God hath lightened her, and the lamp thereof is the Lamb.'

(2)

The Beast-visions (XII–XV) cover the third quarter. The quarter begins on the day of the New Year trumpet, passes through Tabernacles and runs on to Dedication. Let us say that it begins in Holy Season (New Year—Tabernacles) and ends in Dedication. St John's visionary sequence in XII–XV begins where it ought, and ends where it ought; but its total course is far longer than the single quarter: it begins in Holy Season, runs on through Dedication and right round the year through Holy Season into Dedication again. A comparison with the two previous sections of the Apocalypse will show us that there is nothing strange in this. It was the business of the seals to cover the first quarter. By the sixth

137

seal they had more than covered it, they were looking towards *New Year*. The first extra vision provided a *Dedication*-scene (the sealing): the second extra vision brought us to *Passover* and the first quarter once more: with the seventh regular vision we went on from the beginning of the second quarter. Or take the trumpets. The six plagues carry us through the second quarter, and the angel of the oath prophesies about the things to come in the third, when the New Year trumpet has sounded. The temple-measuring is a theme of Dedication, which stands at the beginning of the fourth quarter; the resurrection of the saints, being paschal, carries us into the first quarter; thence we go on again into the region of trumpets, and the seventh trumpet sounds the New Year.

In both seals and trumpets the six straight visions carry us to the end of the quarter with which the section of St John we are reading is properly concerned. Then the extra visions shoot away round the circle of the year, so that we are ready to pass into the next quarter with the seventh vision, just as though there had been no 'intrusive visions' at all.

In XII–XIV there are no 'intrusive visions', and yet, as we saw, the straight visions in XIV have much the same character as the intrusive visions in VII or X–XI, 13. This being so, it will not be surprising if XII–XIII carry us through the quarter with which the section is concerned, while XIV takes us flying round the year, so that we are ready to pass to the next quarter at XV.

What is the point at which the visions of XII–XIV should be divided? The first part is to be parallel to the six straight visions in VI or VIII–IX, the second part is to match the extra visions of VII or X–XI, 13. Well and good: but where does the first part end, and the second begin? Two divisions recommend themselves on different principles. If we count the regular sequence of animal figures, we shall have four visions in the first part, the Dragon, the Beast, the False Lamb, the True Lamb. If we count plagues as constituting the first part, we shall finish before the fourth: with the vision of the Lamb the good news begins. Which division does St John adopt for the purpose of his scheme of feasts? He does not come down clearly on either side of the argument, or, to speak more sensibly, he does justice to both aspects, with his unfailing subtlety: the fourth vision is neither before nor after the transition, but

138

within it the transition takes place. So, then, in XII we are at Holy Season, in XIII at Dedication. In the vision of the Lamb on Mt. Zion (XIV, 1–5) Dedication and Passover are plainly combined. With the Son of Man on Clouds we reach Pentecost, and with the Ghastly Vintage, Tabernacles: and so we are ready to pass through Dedication in XV on into the next quarter, the quarter dominated by the vials.

The images of XII belong to Holy Season; they fuse the themes of New Year and of Tabernacles in the most marvellous way. With the birth of the Man Child we are at New Year: with the woman's escape into the wilderness we are at Tabernacles.

The connexion of New Year with the delivery of the woman appears to have been in origin fortuitous. The first of the three years in which the Law was read through according to the synagogue usage of those days reached the birth of Joseph at the New Year feast, and a connexion was made between the Biblical description of the New Year's trumpets as 'a trumpet-*memorial*' and the verse: 'God *remembered* Rachel and hearkened unto her and opened her womb.' Trumpets of *memorial* may seem to awaken the divine ear to hearken, and to call God's covenant into remembrance. In the past he had remembered the barren woman and given her a son to be the saviour or father of his people, as was Joseph, or as Isaac was: and so the story of the birth of Isaac was also read as a special lesson at New Year. In the future the prophets foretold how Zion herself would be like a woman in seemingly vain travail of birth, whom God would in his own good time compassionate, and give her delivery: and it was easy to think of this as coinciding with the birth of King Messiah. One cannot help divining that the more subtle and profound reason for the conversion of a liturgical accident into a principal feature of the New Year's feast was the connexion between a new era and a birth, rather than the suggestion lying in the word 'memorial'. Anyone who wishes to refresh his memory about the inevitableness of the birth–new era association in the first century and before, may take a glance at Virgil's Fourth Eclogue. The newness of the New Year found alternative expressions in the enthronement of the king and the birth of the child. St John is able to combine them: the prince is born and rapt to the Throne. In Psalm II, which St John's

139

quotation (XII, 5) shows him to be using, the enthronization of the anointed king is real, his 'begetting' by the Lord on that very day is metaphorical. The liberty of symbolism enables St John to treat both fathering and enthroning as equally real, and still to place both on the same day. From the point of view of symbolical perfection, it may seem a pity that the birth should fall at the *seventh* month, and this is so, if we are simply speaking of the Jewish calendar: but since St John begins his whole book not at the first month but with the Feast of Dedication in the very end of the ninth, his vision has travailed for the due period of nine moons when it brings forth the Child.[1]

The mother in St John's vision is Rachel, and as all mothers are, she is Eve,[2] cursed in the pain of her travail, and blessed in the messianic hope of seed that shall rise to crush the serpent's head. St John uses the Rachel-attributes to express that heavenly existence of the Israel of God which he has just expressed otherwise in the heavenly temple and the Ark. Rachel's son, in his second childish dream, saw his parents as the sun and moon, and his brethren and himself as the twelve zodiacal signs: his own sign being exalted to such a height and glory, that the sun and moon and the other eleven fall to worship it. The new Rachel of St John's vision is in her existence heavenly, standing on the moon as in her own station, clothed with the dignity of her husband the sun, and crowned with the glory of her children, the twelve stars. But what she now travails with, once born, is exalted above all height and placed in the all-worshipful Throne. The mystery of Christ's birth, in so far as it is the object of Satanic ambush, is altogether in the heavenly sphere. The attack that alone could touch him is not Herod's malice misdirected against his infancy, but Satan's temptation, a spiritual, not an earthly thing, though sharpened with hunger and tipped with the nails of the cross. 'The prince of this world cometh, but he hath no part in me,' says the Johannine Christ, as he goes to face his passion. In Christ's heavenly existence, he remains untouched. The birth and the rapture are heavenly: the pursuit of the woman is in her earthly

[1] In St John's Christian calendar, if he can be said to have such a thing, our Christmas becomes Lady-Day, and our Michaelmas becomes Christmas.

[2] She is also the Mother of Emmanuel (Is. VII, 14).

140

existence, in so far as the Israel of God can be subject to physical persecution: and so we see her on earth, in flight into the wilderness.

Just as the Beast from the Abyss cannot touch the souls of those within the sanctuary, but those that are in the outer court, he can: so the Serpent cannot pull down any of the stars in the Woman's coronet, but other of the stars, indeed a third of all, he can. With a swing of his tail he sweeps up a third of 'those who tabernacle in heaven', and casts them down to become mere dwellers upon earth. The ruin of a third of the visible Israel is the Dragon's reply to the plagues of the trumpets, which destroyed a third of all earthly things and especially of ungodly men.

It is this detail of the pulling down of the stars which offers the best point of connexion between the birth of the Man Child and the war in heaven. For one thing, it demands exposition. What does it mean? It means that Satan, by temptation to sin and by the irrefutable accusation based on its success, obtains the condemnation of souls in the court of heaven. Here, then, is the court, here is the contest between Michael and the Dragon. The image is appropriate to the season: it is a Rabbinic doctrine that in the days from New Year to Atonement, the world is judged. The accuser has ruined all the souls he can: as for the elect, they have now a sure support: their merits are grounded in, and upheld by, the prevailing sacrifice of the atoning Lamb. When the Man Child reached the Throne, Satan's battle was already lost. Having no more standing-ground in the court where he had indicted Job, Lucifer himself follows the downward ruin of the falling stars. On his belly he shall go, and the dust of earth shall he eat: he has received a blow on the head of his uplifted pride, and falling prone must be content to strike at the earth-treading heels of those whose tabernacle is roofed in heaven. Having great wrath at the loss of his spiritual prey, he will wreak it on their bodies, and in vain. The woman, the Church, is not to be destroyed; she shall be preserved by the virtue of atoning blood throughout the dreadful half-week of years. But her children will be slaughtered in great number. Against them, with the aid of new allies, the Dragon turns. We will not, however, run on into XIII yet: we will turn back to observe the emergence of Tabernacles themes in XII.

The Feast of Tabernacles, more sensibly translated the Feast of the Booths, celebrated the 'ingathering of fruits' in the same way as Pentecost celebrated the harvest of corn. The principal fruit was the grape, and the booths are simply enough understood as the grape-pickers' huts in the vineyards. But this basis of simple nature was made to carry much supernatural weight: the Israelite, camping in his booth, was to remember the days of the camp in the wilderness with all its attendant blessings. Passover, Pentecost and Tabernacles were all made to commemorate the Exodus, but from various angles. Tabernacles gave to the dwelling in tents the aspect of a blessing; it had been a time of safe-keeping from enemies in the hand of God.

The woman escapes from the dragon, as Israel from Pharaoh, and this is the beginning of a period of safe-keeping in the wilderness which has as many months as the wilderness-sojourn had years. (A time, times and a half, i.e. $3\frac{1}{2}$ years, counted as 42 months in XI, 2. Israel had been two years in the wilderness when they incurred the penalty of the additional forty years' wandering, so they had 42 years in all). It is from this point, i.e. from the episode of the woman's escape, that the period of preservation begins. That is, XIII must begin the history of the $3\frac{1}{2}$ years, and so it does, for everyone knows that the $3\frac{1}{2}$ years are the reign of Antichrist, and in XIII, 1 up he comes out of the sea. It is, of course, St John's own Christian paradox that the period of blessed preservation is the period of acute persecution. It has been explained for us in the vision of the fall of Satan. It is precisely when Satan has lost the battle for the souls of the saints in heaven that he begins the fruitless persecution of their bodies on earth.

We may observe how well the story of the woman fits the theme of the Exodus in all its details. The birth of the Child, we have said, expresses the birth of Joseph. But Joseph, as the discerning reader of St Stephen's speech may perceive (Acts VII, 9–36), is himself a type of Moses. Leviathan lay in wait to devour the man child of Israel when Moses was born, for Leviathan, the dragon or crocodile of Nile, is according to Ezekiel (XXIX, 3) a type of Pharaoh and Egypt. But when the mother of Moses 'brought forth a man child', he was providentially rapt away into the protection of the throne, to become the saviour of his brethren.

142

Leviathan pursued after the escaping Church of Israel, and would have caught her entrammelled in the waters, had not the waters been miraculously swallowed up to allow her passage dry shod. And so she reached her 'tabernacles', where God also vouchsafed to spread his cloudy tabernacle over her, and declared at the mountain that he had, as St John's vision describes, 'lifted her on eagles' pinions' to bring her to himself (Exod. XIX, 4).

It seems right to mention a prophetical text which so exactly fits here that it is hard to believe St John did not have it in mind. The preservation of the people in their wilderness-booths is an inevitable echo in the mind which reads Isaiah XXVI, 20, 'Come my people, enter into thy chambers, lock thy door; hide thyself a little while, until the wrath of the Lord be past. For lo, the Lord out of his holy place brings the wrath on the dwellers upon earth, and the earth shall reveal her blood and not conceal the slain. In that day shall God bring his sword holy, great and strong on the Dragon (Hebr. Leviathan) the fleeing serpent, the Dragon the crooked Serpent, and the Dragon shall he slay. In that day, a fair vine, a longing to break into song over her.' God had called Israel away into the safety of the booths in the wilderness and overthrown that old Leviathan, Pharaoh, by his own might and power without Israel's aid in the waters of the Red Sea. Israel breaks forth into song, a vintage-song, in that day, for it is the day of Tabernacles, the vintage-feast. As it had been in the Exodus, so it will be in the last redemption. The booths of Tabernacles-time foreshadow the booths in which the Israelites will be protected while the Lord breaks their last enemy.

This prophecy will bear a very detailed comparison with what St John writes. The woman is secured in the wilderness, the Dragon is smitten in the head by Michael, and God 'brings the wrath upon the dwellers upon earth' in the succeeding vial-plagues, 'wherein is accomplished the wrath of God'; he sends his wrath visibly 'out of his holy place', entering the temple in cloud and smoke for the very purpose; and all this happens in a setting of vintage, as we shall presently see. But no less exact, no less surprising, is the applicability of the preceding text in Isaiah to the preceding text in St John. Here is Isaiah's prelude: 'Lord, in oppression have I remembered thee, in a short oppression is thy chasten-

143

ing upon us. And as the travailing woman draws near her child-bearing and cries out at her travail, so have we been for thy Beloved (Son), because of thy fear, O Lord. We have conceived and travailed and brought forth, we have wrought the spirit of thy salvation upon earth; but the dwellers upon earth shall fall. The dead shall arise, those in the tombs shall awake and those in the ground shall rejoice, for the dew from thee is their healing; but the land of the ungodly shall fall.' So for Isaiah, as for St John, the prelude to the preservation in booths and the fall of Leviathan is a mystical travailing of Israel to bring forth Messiah. His birth is equivalent to the defeat of the enemy, and it brings with it the resurrection of the dead. St John does not enlarge on the latter point, though he might have done. The snatching of the Man Child to the Throne is actually the resurrection and ascension of Christ, and St John has provided us a model by which to interpret, in the preceding vision of the two witnesses. Their rapture into heaven under the very eyes of the serpent's seed is their resurrection from the dead, and it is both the image and the effect of what was done in 'their Lord who had been crucified'.

We may now turn to the visions in XIII. They contain the manifestation of Antichrist. That this is a Dedication-theme is evident. The Dedication was instituted to celebrate the Maccabean restoration of the temple, after its desecration by Antiochus Epiphanes: and Antiochus is the Antichrist-beast of those Daniel-visions which St John principally uses here. The day of Dedication, Chislev 25, not only commemorated the restoration after the desecration: it commemorated the desecration itself, for, as I Maccabees tells us with solemn emphasis, Judas was careful to reconsecrate the temple on the same day of the year as had seen the inauguration of the pagan cult there. When the theme of Antichrist's attack on the temple appeared previously in XI, 1–13, we saw that it appeared as part and parcel of a Dedication-oracle, the Temple-measuring.

The synagogue-liturgy made the link between the themes of dedication and profanation especially in relation to the Name of God. Antiochus blasphemed the Name, the Maccabean martyrs hallowed it by their deaths. God had said that he would put his Name in the temple. The principal Dedication-lesson, as we saw above, was Numbers VII, which directly follows the Aaronic Blessing and the imposition of the Name, and itself contains the dedication of Moses's Tabernacle. Another Torah-lesson belonging to the feast was the stoning of the Israelite who blasphemed the Name (Levit. XXIV: the chapter begins with a law about the great Dedication emblem, the golden candlestick[1]). At Dedication in St John's Gospel, Christ is falsely accused of blasphemy and threatened with stoning, because he has united the Father's Name with his own. Here in the Apocalypse the first Beast wears on his head names of blasphemy, he is given a mouth speaking boasts and blasphemies, and he opens it in blasphemy of God, his Name and his tabernacle. The second Beast organises the worship of the first, and makes all men accomplices in the irremissible sin, by taking the blasphemous name of the Beast upon them as the Name of God. Then in defiance of him the Lamb is seen, standing on Mt. Zion with his flock of the 144,000 predestinate, having his own Name and the Name of his Father on their foreheads. Compare the Christ of the Johannine Gospel, standing on Mt. Zion (in Solomon's Porch) on Dedication Day, and saying: Ye believe not, because ye are not of my sheep. My sheep hear my voice and they follow me (These are they that follow the Lamb whithersoever he goeth) and I give unto them eternal life, and none shall snatch them out of my hand. My Father, which hath given them unto me, is greater than all, and none is able to snatch them out of the Father's hand; I and the Father are one. (Having his Name, which is his Father's Name, on their foreheads, they are inviolate.)

In composing the description of the Beasts St John has got two schemes in mind. (1) The Lord's own prophecy had warned against 'false Christs and false prophets, showing signs and wonders, to lead away, if it were possible, the elect' (Mark XIII, 22). Here the accent seems to fall, if anything, on the false prophets, for the description of activity following the two titles, though

---

[1] Here is a surprising liturgical accident. Leviticus XXIII is a law of feasts, and its appropriate paragraphs were read at Passover, Pentecost, New Year, Atonement and Tabernacles. There is no paragraph for Dedication, since it is a post-Biblical feast. But it is natural to read the next section (Levit. XXIV) at Dedication, simply to keep up the sequence. And in that section are the Candlestick and the Blasphemy of the Name!

grammatically applicable to both, is in point of fact the special crime of the false prophet according to Deuteronomy XIII, 1–5 and all subsequent tradition. (2) Daniel's prophecy laid all stress on the false Messiah, the self-deifying heathen tyrant, supremely revealed in the Fourth Beast of Daniel VII and the last King of the North in Daniel XI, who are the same person in fact. St John reconciles the representations in Daniel and in the Gospel by a free and masterful treatment of the Daniel images. The Antichrist to come is the summing-up or epitome of all the four 'beasts' of Daniel VII, all the heathen tyrannies from Nebuchadnezzar to Epiphanes: he has all the heads and all the horns and all the animal kinds that they share between them somehow featured in himself, and like all four of them he comes up out of the sea. For the model of the false prophet St John simply seizes the next beast-figure to appear in Daniel, the horned ram seen on *terra firma* in VIII; and this he does in defiance of the plain statements in that chapter which make the ram the equivalent of one of the four from VII, the Medo-Persian power. St John follows out the suggestion in the Lord's prophecy by giving the more drastic activities to the second beast, though the greater dignity and power belongs to the first. Yet in this there is no incongruity, for the first still acts through the second. After all, the Dragon is greatest of all three, yet the Dragon requires the first Beast: he can accomplish more with such an instrument than without him. So with the first Beast in turn: his power is the ground of all that the second Beast does, yet without the second Beast he cannot do so much. Pharaoh needs his magicians, and Balak his Balaam. Things are at their worst when the diabolical trinity is complete, when Satan has his Antichrist and Antichrist his false prophet.

In the traditional imagery Antichrist set himself or his image in the temple of God; but in St John's picture such a form of representation can scarcely stand. The temple is not a place, but the true church of God existing in heaven, and it is meaningless to say that Antichrist sets himself or his image there. Satan, his master, has just been flung out of heaven once for all: Antichrist's dominion is wholly of the earth. So St John simply says that the Beast blasphemes 'God, his Name and his Tabernacle, them that tabernacle in heaven', and then goes on to tell how he himself becomes

146

a rival object of worship on earth, worship which the second Beast develops in the form of organized and enforced idolatry. He sets up the image of the first Beast: in this we are to see the antitype to 'the abomination of desolation' which Antiochus had placed in the temple at Jerusalem.

The vision of the Lamb on Mt. Zion is, to begin with, a dedication-vision (as the paraphrase in John x should suffice to convince us). It shows the sacrificial martyrs, of whom Jesus is the first, by whom the Name is honoured, and who are therefore the true spiritual temple on the true Zion, whatever may be happening to the physical temple-site. The Name on their foreheads is in direct contrast to the blasphemous name first revealed on the Beast's heads, and now multiplied on the foreheads of his worshippers.

The Zion where they stand is to be mystically interpreted, like the temple which is measured in the reed-vision. It is not heaven, still less is it the site of old Jerusalem. The required comment may be found in St John's Gospel: 'The hour cometh when neither in this Mount' (Gerizim) 'nor yet in Jerusalem shall ye worship the Father'. (If in either place, then rather in Jerusalem, for) 'ye worship what ye know not, we know what we worship. For salvation is from the Jews. But the hour cometh and now is, when the true worshippers shall worship the Father in Spirit and Truth'. That will be, says the Samaritaness, as Messiah shall direct. 'Jesus saith unto her, I AM that speak unto thee' (John IV, 21–26). The ancient law enjoins worship on Mt. Zion, there God has given tryst to meet the people of his covenant. In the new dispensation what is the tryst that he has given? Zechariah had anticipated Christ in answering the Samaritans concerning worship at Jerusalem (Zech. VII–VIII). 'Thus saith the Lord' the prophet had replied, 'I am returned unto Zion and will dwell in the midst of Jerusalem, and Jerusalem shall be called the city of truth. . . . They shall dwell in Jerusalem, and I will be their God in truth. . . . Therefore love truth. . . . In those days ten men shall take hold of the skirt of him that is a Jew, saying, We will go with you, for we have heard that God is with you.' Where is this Zion which is otherwise called 'the city of truth'? The true worshippers shall worship *in spirit and in truth,* that is, in Christ and in the Paraclete. Where he who says, 'I am the truth' (or, in the phrase of the

147

Apocalypse, 'Thus saith the Amen') is present by the Spirit, there is Jerusalem.

There is Jerusalem, even in the day of Antichrist; when it is death to withhold incense from the image of the Beast, the true worshippers are gathered round the Lamb: when none can buy or sell without the mark of the Beast, the hundred and forty four thousands wear the Name of the Father, which is also the Son's Name, to shew that he has bought them: while all the world adores a lie, no lie is found on the lips that pray in truth; they are without blemish.

The Dedication-theme is unmistakable in the vision of the Lamb and the twelve times twelve thousand: yet the Passover image is scarcely less forcible. The vision is a vision of the Lamb. And whereas 'the Lamb' is constantly used by St John as an equivalent for the Name of Jesus, nowhere but here and in the Passover of IV–V is the Lamb presented as a direct object of vision. Elsewhere we see Christ as the Son of Man, or as the Warrior King. The adoration of the Lamb in v is carefully reproduced here. '*The four cherubim and the twenty-four elders* fall before *the Lamb,* having each a *harp.* . . . And they *sing a new song,* saying, "Worthy art thou . . . for thou wast slain, and *didst purchase* to God by thy blood of every tribe and tongue and people and nation." (v, 8–9). 'And I saw the *Lamb* . . . and I heard a voice from heaven . . . as of harpers harping on their *harps,* and they *sing a new song* before the throne and the *four cherubim and the elders.* And none could understand the song except the twelve times twelve thousand, the *purchased* from the earth' (XIV, 1–3). In the vision of v we are in heaven, we see and hear the angelic host celebrating the Lamb's purchase of a universal Israel by paschal blood. In XIV we are beneath, on Mt Zion, where the Lamb is mystically present among his worshippers. The angels' new song rings down from the clouds: none can comprehend their hymn to the Redeeming Blood except the twelve times twelve thousand who have been purchased by it. For a voice from heaven heard by others but understood only by the sacrificial Lamb, compare John XII, 28. Jesus, in a passage equivalent to the Gethsemane scene of the other gospels, makes the sacrifice of his life to his Father's will, and adds 'If any will serve me let him follow me, and where I am, there

148

shall my servant be.' (These are they that follow the Lamb whithersoever he goeth). A voice from heaven sanctions his resolve. The crowd say that it has thundered, or that an angel has spoken to him (the angel-voices of XIV are heard as a sound of many waters, or a great thunder). Jesus says that the voice has come not for him, but for them. His death, his victory over Satan, his 'elevation' from the earth, will draw all men unto him. (Purchased out of the earth, to stand with him in Zion and understand the heavenly voice, which descends not for his sake, but for that of man).

The scene of John XII, 28 is Jesus's going up to Mt. Zion for the Passover. We have just read the verse, 'Fear not, Daughter of Zion: Lo, thy king cometh unto thee. . . .' It is to be noticed that the Zechariah-oracle about the King riding on the ass (IX, 9) has been blended in these words with the similar oracle in Zephaniah III. Zechariah has: 'Rejoice greatly, daughter of Zion, shout, daughter of Jerusalem: behold thy king cometh unto thee.' Zephaniah has: 'Rejoice greatly, daughter of Zion, shout, daughter of Jerusalem. . . . The King of Israel is in the midst of thee. . . . Fear not, Zion . . . the Lord thy God is in thee' (III, 14–17). If St John remembered the Zephaniah oracle when he came in his Gospel to the Lamb's ascent of Zion at Passover, it is not surprising, for he had had it in his mind when he wrote of the Lamb's Passover on Mt Zion in Apocalypse XIV. It is worth while to quote the whole prophecy:

'In that day thou shalt not be ashamed for all the practices wherein thou hast offended against me, for then I will strip from thee the basenesses of thy lust (or pride), and thou shalt no more exalt thyself *upon my holy mountain.* And I will leave in thee a people meek and humble, and they shall *reverence the Name of the Lord* that remain of Israel, and they shall do no iniquity and speak no vanity, and *there shall not be found in their mouth a tongue of guile.* For they shall *graze and lie down* and there shall be none to affray them. Rejoice greatly, *daughter of Zion,* shout, daughter of Jerusalem, joy and be glad with all thy heart. For the Lord hath stripped away thine iniquities, *he hath redeemed thee* from the hand of thine enemies, *the King of Israel in the midst of thee:* thou shalt see evils no more. At that time shall the Lord say to Jerusalem, Fear not, Zion, let not thy hands hang down. *The Lord thy God is in thee,* the Mighty will save thee, he will bring upon thee rejoicing and renew thee in his loving-kindness and delight over thee with joy, *as in feast-day.*' (Zeph. III, 11–17). Here St John can recognise the flock which follows its Lamb-Shepherd, hallowing the divine Name; the redeemed in whose mouth is found no guile; the festal joy on Zion, the Lord's holy mountain, when the divine King stands in their midst.

The twelve times twelve thousand bearing the divine mark carry us back unmistakably to the sealing-vision in VII—indeed we may say that XIV, 1–5 fuses into one the two visions of that chapter, the sealing and the Passover of the saints. In VII we are emphatically told that the twelve twelve thousands express the Church as a twelve-fold Israel, twelve thousand for each tribe. And so, when we see them standing on Mt Zion, we are put in mind of the law which commanded the whole of Israel to appear at Jerusalem for the three yearly feasts, of which Passover was the first. 'In all things that I have said unto you take ye heed, and make no mention of the names of other gods, neither let it be heard out of thy mouth. Three times thou shalt keep a feast unto me in the year. The feast of unleavened bread shalt thou keep . . . in the month Abib, for in it thou camest out of Egypt . . . and the feast of harvest . . . and the feast of ingathering at the year's end. . . . Three times in the year all thy males shall appear before the Lord God' (Exod. XXIII, 13–17, cf. XXXIV, 17–23). In the ancient laws the feasts appear in their primitive character, as feasts of agriculture. For the most part St John overlays this elementary basis with the theology which Judaism had erected upon it: but in XIV he gives us a series of the three compulsory feasts quite in the spirit of Exodus: the Lamb of Passover, the harvest of Pentecost, the vintage of Tabernacles (XIV, 1–5, 14–16, 17–20).

The law of festival commanded the attendance of all males, and this aspect of things might be especially prominent at Passover, where the firstborn males remembered their redemption by the paschal lambs. The lambs were sacrificed, the worshippers lived, the lambs being accepted in place of them. The lambs must be without blemish, the worshippers of the old covenant could not be. But in the new dispensation all the Christians, for all are firstborn, partake in the merits of the spotless Lamb; 'they are without blemish.' That is St John's last word in the vision. He is so far swayed by the imagery of the ancient feast as to write of the new congregation as an assembly of males. 'These are they that have not defiled themselves in companying with women, for they are virgins.'[1] They are he-lambs 'without blemish': they are also 'firstfruits', for the Christian Passover is Firstfruits Day.

The threefold vision of the flying angels inserts a pause between the vision of Passover and the vision of Pentecost. Pentecost brings the Son of Man on clouds, equipped as a harvester. At this point St John comes very close to a central image of the synoptic tradition, and we should be wise to interpret him by St Mark and St Matthew. According to St Mark, the Lord says in his parable: 'When the fruit is ripe, straightway he' (the sower) 'sendeth forth the sickle, because the harvest is come' (IV, 29). The context of the parable, and especially the sentence in IV, 14, 'The sower soweth the word,' will lead the Christian readers to identify the sower, who is also the harvester, with Christ. Later in his Gospel St Mark tells us how the Lord described the supreme moment of his own Advent in these words: 'Then shall they see the Son of Man coming in clouds with great power and glory: and then shall he

[1] There is nothing here about celibacy, either for or against. St John does not write 'defiled with women' as we might say 'defiled with pitch', as though all women defile. He writes: 'These are they who, with women, have not performed acts of self-defilement.' This gives no ground for any opinion as to the writer's doctrine of marriage. Nor does any clearer conclusion follow from the next clause, 'for they are virgins.' According to St Paul's doctrine, the married man is honouring his loyal 'marriage' or his virginal 'betrothal' to Christ, the fornicator is not. The word translated 'virgin' is the ordinary Greek for an adolescent girl, with extended use to cover all women who have not known men. The application to males is a violent metaphor, and has no need to mean 'having never used their virility'. It is just as likely to mean 'standing in relation to someone (e.g. a betrothed spouse) as a virgin does'. In the absence of other indications, we ought to interpret St John in line with St Paul and the rest of the New Testament. St Paul uses 'virgin' in the special sense, 'a chaste betrothed woman,' in connexion with that risky development of Corinthian religiosity, the perpetual betrothal which never became a marriage. St John writes: 'For they are virgins: these are they that follow the Lamb whithersoever he goeth.' Compare the virgins who enter with the bridegroom to the marriage-supper in the Matthaean parable, or the pure bride who is the equivalent of those bidden to the marriage-supper of the Lamb in Apocalypse XIX, 7-9.

151

send forth his angels and *gather* his elect. . . . From the fig tree learn her parable: when her branch is tender and she puts forth leaves, ye know that the harvest season is near' (XIII, 27–28). The combination of the two Marcan texts is natural in itself, and was anyhow made by St Matthew. He gives an expanded version of the Marcan harvest-parable, and adds an interpretation of it, in which occur the words: 'The Son of Man shall send forth his angels, and they shall gather out of his kingdom all offences and all workers of lawlessness' (XIII, 41). He is actually speaking of the harvest of weeds, which, in his parable, precedes that of the wheat: the conclusion is that the corn is gathered into the garner, and the righteous shine forth in their Father's kingdom.

The harvest of the wheat has uniformly a favourable sense in the New Testament: it is so in St John's gospel too; see especially the text which most closely echoes Apocalypse XIV, 14, 'Behold the fields white already for harvest' (John IV, 35). The firstfruits have just been mentioned in the Passover-vision, and there they stand for the saints (XIV, 4). Now that Pentecost brings the full harvest, the corn must surely retain the same sense: Christ harvests the elect. His advent is prefaced by the heavenly voice: 'Blessed are the dead that die in the Lord, and that presently. Yea, saith the Spirit, let them rest from their labours, for their works accompany them.' The Son of Man immediately appears, sickle in hand: what for, if not to harvest the saints, heavy with the fruit of their good works?

St Matthew's parable places a sinister harvest of tares alongside the harvest of wheat. For the purpose, perhaps, of keeping in tune with the facts of the harvest field, he puts the burning of the weeds before the garnering of the corn; this involves interpreting the judgement as the uprooting of offences from a holy kingdom. Once the wicked are disposed of, the righteous shine forth in the Kingdom like the sun. If we forced St Matthew's words, we should arrive at a contradiction of the general tradition of primitive Christendom: the Lord's first act is to snatch away the righteous; then the fires of wrath fall on the wicked. This is St Paul's doctrine. As soon as the Lord appears, the Christian dead will be caught up to meet him in mid-air (Blessed, therefore, are the dead which die in the Lord). Christians alive on earth will directly follow their ascent. Then before the saints' admiring eyes Messiah will over-

152

throw the wicked in flames of fire (I Thess. IV, 16–17, II Thess. I, 7–10). St Matthew himself conforms to this order of events in other texts, e.g. III, 12, 'He will gather the wheat into his garner, and the chaff he will burn with fire unquenchable,' or XXIV, 40–41, 'The one shall be taken, the other left'—the *parabolic* context being the image of Noah's ark, which takes some on board and abandons others to their fate, and the *real* context the Son of Man's harvest: 'He shall send forth his angels and they shall gather his elect' (XXIV, 31).

St John accepts, perhaps, from St Matthew the picture of the sinister harvest alongside the blessed harvest, but he does not fall in with his reversal of the expected order of events. The sinister harvest shall follow: it shall be the harvest of grapes which follows the harvest of wheat, the Tabernacles which follows Pentecost. The sinister interpretation of the vintage was ready to hand in a famous oracle, Isaiah LXIII, 1–6, where the Lord as a bloodstained warrior trampling his enemies is compared to a vintager splashed with the red juice. But St John finds Joel III, 13 more to his purpose: 'Put in the sickle, for the harvest is ripe; come, tread, for the winepress is full; the vats overflow, for their wickedness is great.' The 'harvest' of Joel is very likely no other than the grapes: in any case it is to be taken in an equally sinister sense. But St John chooses (*a*) to insist on the antithesis 'harvest'—'winepress', (*b*) to give to the harvest the favourable sense which the Christian tradition demanded. The harvest is the Son of Man's Pentecost, the vintage is the Angel's act of judgement at Tabernacles-season.

In the symbols of the three feasts of obligation St John has set forth the whole economy of judgement. First there is martyrdom, represented by the Lamb-slaying of Passover (XIV, 1–5). The flying angels insert a pause, the time of waiting in which the saints must be content with voices, mere portents of the martyrs' coming reward. With Pentecost it comes: the harvest of merit is gathered (XIV, 14–16). Tabernacles follows, completing the vindication of the martyrs by the punishment of their oppressors (XIV, 17–20).

The Son of Man himself gathers the righteous, the angel gathers the wicked. It is only the gathering which St John brings before us here. We do not see the *reward* of the righteous at all. We do see

153

the penalty of the wicked under the figure of the grape-treading: we are not told that the treading is the work of the angel who gathers, indeed we should infer that it is not, for the winepress is the winepress of the wrath *of God*. The impression is confirmed when we come to XIX. Jesus is the bloodstained warrior of Isaiah's prophecy: he treads himself 'the press of the wine of the fury of the wrath of God Almighty' (XIX, 13–15). This means that he destroys the Beast's armies. But as for the *gathering* of the armies 'into the winepress', that is the work of the angels: the vials, especially the sixth, drive the wicked to Armageddon, and the vials fall from angelic hands.

The angels gather the wicked, but not until the Son of Man has gathered the righteous. This 'gathering' is, one would think, one of the greatest events of the Apocalypse, and it occupied anyhow the centre of primitive Christian expectation. The Lord's own Apocalypse in the Synoptic Gospels works up to this point, and there breaks off. Once the saints are in the hands of Christ, there is nothing more they need to know. It is all the more surprising that St John devotes so few lines to the matter. The vintage of wrath is fully amplified in the sequel, but no more is said of the harvesting of the saints. One way to explain this is to suppose that St John means us to take the universality of martyrdom under Antichrist with absolute rigour: there is no one alive for Christ to rescue, and the Son of Man's harvest becomes no more than a traditional way of saying that the dead live in him and will participate his triumph at the Great Battle, and his reign in the Millennial Kingdom. When the kingdom comes, St John speaks of those who enjoy it as partakers in 'the first resurrection'. Perhaps the first resurrection is to be dated from the Son of Man's harvest, and the harvest is in fact nothing but the resurrection.

There are difficulties about this way out of our perplexity. In the days of the Beast, 'he who is for captivity goes to captivity, he who is to be slain is slain.' The language suggests a destiny to be fulfilled in each man, and it will hardly do to say, 'But when the second Beast appears, he has all captives put to the sword.' The second Beast decrees death to all the recalcitrant, which means, no doubt, that any Christian can be killed for refusing worship, but if he were proposing immediate and systematic extermination, he

154

would hardly add the provision that those who refuse to receive the Beast's mark should be excluded from the markets. And it is hard in any case to believe that St John would have felt free so completely to abandon the Lord's own teaching as given in the synoptic apocalypse. The Lord taught that the persecution of Antichrist should be met by flight into the wilds, and that the days were shortened so that some 'flesh' might be saved.

It seems useless to pursue this question further. The Son of Man harvests the Elect, and we do not know why St John is so brief in his mention of it. The event, however briefly mentioned, does not remain barren of consequences. In xv for the first time[1] we see the saints exultant above the heavenly firmament: they have been harvested, and when the plagues of the vials fall on earth, there is nothing but the chaff of wickedness for them to burn. Against the trumpets and the woes of Antichrist the saints were protected, sealed against the first, 'measured' against the second. If no similar provision is made against the vials, it is because the saints are on earth no longer.[2] They will descend again in the train of the White-horsed Rider.

Enough of the pentecostal vision. Let us make one remark about the vintage which follows it. Tabernacles was the feast of wine; it was also the feast of water-pouring. The ceremony was an intercession for rain, and special prominence was given to a promise contained in the Tabernacles prophecy *par excellence,* Zechariah xiv, that living waters should go forth from Jerusalem. They would become rivers, reaching the Dead Sea before and the Mediterranean behind. A more elaborate vision of the living waters from Zion could be read in Ezekiel xlvii. There the stream is measured by a double test. A distance from the source is given in figures, and the depth for fording, wading or swimming is given at the point so defined. St John measures the flow of blood from the ghastly vintage in the same style: at sixteen hundred stades it is so deep that the horses wade to the bridles. The measuring suggests

[1] Always excluding the anticipatory vision in vii, 9 ff.
[2] 'Come forth, my people, out of her' (xviii, 4) cannot be quoted against this interpretation. The Heavenly Voice, like the Vision of the Harlot (xvii) begins with the present time. 'Come out of Babylon, that you may not share her plagues when they come, for her sins cry to heaven.'

Ezekiel XLVII, the horses' bridles recall Zechariah XIV, where we read in the Greek version, '*Holy to the Lord* on the bridles of the horses.' It seems likely that St John is aware of these allusions, and that he is treating the ghastly vintage as a twofold symbol. The blood is vintage, for wine is 'the blood of the grape'. The blood is a river, for 'blood of the dead' is the opposite of living waters, as we see in the first plague of Egypt, or in the third vial. The ghastly vintage is also the river of death. The river of life will be manifested in XXII, 1–2, in a context of quotations both from Ezekiel XLVII and Zechariah XIV (Apoc. XXII, 3, Zech. XIV, 11).

CHAPTER VI

(1)

We have seen in Apocalypse XIV a series of the three obligatory feasts, Passover, Pentecost and Tabernacles. With XV we run straight on into the additional great feast, Dedication. Though this is, in theory at least, a lesser feast than the three, it is treated here on a more ample scale, because St John begins at this point a new series of visions, the series belonging to the quarter which starts from Dedication. In entering on this quarter we tread for the first time over old ground, for this is the quarter with which St John began. The themes of the Dedication-festivity have been used already once, and this may impair their force. But if they are in this way weakened from behind they are still more overshadowed from in front. For we are drawing near the great consummation, and nothing short of the advent of Christ itself can now wear even the semblance of a joyful feast. Our eyes are fixed on the Passover of our redemption. At this Dedication the divine glory enters the temple, as the meaning of the feast prescribes. The presence of the glory might be the manifestation of the Name in the temple by incarnate God, as it is in St John's Gospel, 'I and the Father are one . . . I whom the Father dedicated and sent into the world' (X, 30 ff.). Or it might be the indwelling of the City by Father and Son in the World to Come: 'The Lord God Almighty and the Lamb are the temple thereof.' It is, at this stage, neither: God visits, but he visits to judge, to 'bring the wrath on the dwellers upon earth'. Yet even so, what are the fiery libations of the vials outpoured on the wicked, compared with that ultimate annihilation soon to follow, 'They were thrown into the lake of fire'?

The previous Dedication in I has used up the lessons proper to the feast, which describe the *celebration* of the Dedication: St John now falls back on texts which describe an earlier stage, the actual setting up and hallowing of the Holy Place. The text from the

157

Law is to be found in Exodus XL, 17–35. We read how Moses sets up the Tabernacle and its ornaments (17–28), then the altar of sacrifice (29), and after that the laver, filling it with water, and himself and the priests washing hands and feet in it (30–32). The screening round of the court finished the work, and without more delay 'the Cloud covered the tent of meeting, and the Glory of the Lord filled the Tabernacle. And Moses was not able to enter the tent of meeting, because the Cloud abode thereon' (33–35).

The corresponding 'prophetical' text is I Kings VI, 1–VIII, 11 with its parallel, II Chronicles III–V. Chronicles is to be preferred, for it is in closer conformity with Exodus XL, it excludes irrelevances, and it adds impressive features to the liturgical climax of the narrative. It tells us in turn of the making of the temple (III) and the altar (IV, 1) of the brazen 'sea' and the lesser lavers, the 'sea' being for the priests to wash in (IV, 2–6, 10). After the account of the sacrificial vessels we read of the carrying of the Ark into the most holy place under the wings of the Cherubim, and then: 'It came to pass, when the priests were come out of the Holy Place— for all the priests that were present had sanctified themselves, and did not restrict themselves to their turns of duty: the Levites also which were the singers, all of them . . . arrayed in fine linen, with cymbals, psalteries and harps, stood at the east end of the altar, and with them an hundred and twenty priests sounding with trumpets —it came even to pass, when the trumpeters and singers were as one, to make one sound to be heard in praising and thanking the Lord; and when they lifted up their voice with the trumpets and cymbals and instruments of music, and praised the Lord, 'for that he is good, for his mercy endureth for ever;' that then the house was filled with a cloud, even the Lord's house, so that the priests could not stand to minister by reason of the cloud; for the Glory of the Lord filled the house of God.'

The common pattern in Exodus and Chronicles is easy to discern. (1) The temple or tabernacle is set up; (2) then the altar; (3) then the laver or 'sea', a vessel for the priests to wash in: Moses and the priests do so there and then, while of Solomon's priests it is said that they have all performed their ritual purification to be fit for the ceremonies; (4) then the Glory-cloud fills the sanctuary, in such wise that the ministers cannot enter till it departs. To this common pattern Chronicles adds two circumstances. The priests who had put the Ark in place had come out again before the Glory entered; and the entry of the Glory seemed to be in response to the hymnody of Levitical choirs with harps and all sorts of music.

St John follows the pattern we have described, including the two additional features from Chronicles. He cannot use it without modification, because he is not describing the building of a new temple but the last dedication anniversary in an old one. He cannot show the setting up of one part after another, but he can shew divine power manifested through one part after another of the temple, with a climax at the visible appearance of Glory in the house of God. Such a method of treatment will be in conformity with what we have already seen: when the sixth trumpet sounded, *the altar of incense uttered a voice,* directing the trumpet-angel to loose the angels of pestilence, because it was the hour and day and month and year to kill the third of men.

St John begins to introduce the Dedication-symbols in the preceding vision. There is the divine Harvester on the White Cloud; but what is his hour? An angel issuing from the *temple* gives it to him,[1] crying with a loud voice 'Send forth thy sickle and reap; for the hour to reap is come; for the harvest of the earth is dry.' It is no sooner reaped than a vintager issues from the temple, and the angel of fire, issuing from the *altar,* gives him his hour in similar words. The succeeding seventh vision reveals not one, but seven ministers with instruments of judgement, for in them is accomplished the wrath of God. Every circumstance is heightened for their appearance. They do not come until the *great 'sea'* has been manifested, filled with a fiery mixture[2] and surmounted by the Levitical choirs, in token that they have been purified in it. They sing a hymn to the sound of their instruments. In response, as it were, to this, the doors of the heavenly temple are opened

[1] How can the Son of Man require such instruction through God's messenger? He says himself, 'Of that day and hour knoweth none, not the angels in heaven nor the Son, but the Father alone' (Mark XIII, 32).

[2] There is no emphasis on the 'mixing'. Because the ancients put water in their wine, to 'mix' means to fill for drinking: in XIV, 10 St John actually says 'mixed unmixed' for 'prepared neat'. 'Filled with liquid fire' is what he means here.

159

wide, and the seven angels come forth and receive libation bowls full of divine wrath. The temple which they have just left fills with smoke from the divine Glory and Might, so that none can enter, and out of the Glory comes a voice to give the seven their hour: 'Go and pour the seven vials of the wrath of God upon the earth.'

The Levitical choir whose hymn opens the temple is made up of such as have triumphed over 'the Beast and his image and the number of his name'. It is most natural to interpret this to mean those who have been put to the full rigour of the test described in XIII, 15–18, that is to say, the martyrs. We have lately seen the 144,000 on Mt Zion, alone privileged to understand a heavenly music of harping which rang down to them from the sky. What we now see is the martyrs, in the white robes they received at the fifth seal, released from beneath the altar whence they cried, and themselves singing to heavenly harps. The laver of their purification, above which they stand, is 'filled with fiery mixture', for their hallowing has been the ordeal of fire, and what is to be poured upon the wicked they have first endured. When the third vial is poured the angel of the smitten waters, and the altar from beneath which the martyr-blood cried before, conspire to say: 'Righteous art thou, the IS and WAS, the Holy, in judging so. For they shed the blood of saints and prophets, and blood hast thou given them to drink; they have their desert. Yea, Lord God Almighty, thy judgements are righteous and true.'

Standing above the sea of glass the martyrs sing a hymn thus described: (a) 'the song of Moses the Servant of God and the song of the Lamb (that is, of Jesus); (b) saying: Great and marvellous are thy works, Lord God the Almighty; righteous and true are thy ways, thou King of the Ages. Who will not fear, O Lord, and glorify thy Name? For thou only art holy; (c) For all the nations shall come and worship before thee, for thy righteous judgements have been manifested.' This description asks for comparison with the Song of Moses in Deuteronomy XXXII. We make the comparison, and find (b) to be the beginning and (c) the end of the song, while the title (a) is founded on the epilogue.

After the singers' own exordium, the body of Moses's poem thus begins: (b) 'Give greatness to our God: God, true are his

160

works, and all his ways are judgement: a faithful God, and there is no unrighteousness with him, righteous and holy is the Lord'. And here is the conclusion: (c) [Let all the sons of God worship him[1]:] rejoice, ye nations, with his people, [and in him let all the angels of God be strong[1]:] for the blood of his sons he avengeth, and will avenge and recompense righteousness to his enemies. . . .' And this is the epilogue: (a) 'And Moses came and spoke all the words of this law (Hebr. 'song') in the ears of all the people, *even he*' (*Moses*), '*and Jesus* the Son of Nave'.

It is to be concluded, then, that Deuteronomy XXXII is referred to, even though St John composes his own hymn quite freely, with echoes of Psalm LXXXVI, 9, and other texts. What was in the Old Covenant the song of Moses (and Jesus), has become in the New Covenant the Song of (Moses and) Jesus. The Song of Moses was both a declaration and an invocation of the victorious judgements of God. He composed it just before his death, leaving to Jesus the Son of Nave the work of judgement and victory. The work of that Jesus was not finally effective, but now the greater Jesus declares, invokes and executes divine vindication. The Song of Moses and the death of Moses were celebrated in the end of the year, after the feast of Dedication. So with the ending of the year 'It is done' was pronounced over the ministry of Moses, and yet the spirit and principality of Moses rose from death in Jesus the Son of Nave, the triumphant warrior who fought the battle of the Lord and brought Israel into his inheritance. In the seventh vial St John records the divine 'It is done' pronounced over the end of the liturgical year, and over all the five weeks since the Apocalypse began. There has been much of Moses in them. Here, in the Vials, the strokes of his rod are to be recalled for the last time. It is done: the five books of Moses end with Deuteronomy. The sixth is the book of Jesus (Joshua): and with the beginning of St John's sixth week Jesus rides forth, the Resurrection and the Life, the triumphant warrior, the victor of the last battle, the conqueror of Paradise.

The Song of Moses contains the following passage, which St John perhaps only refrains from quoting because he has visibly expressed it in the action of the liturgy: 'Our enemies are without

[1] Not in the Hebrew.

understanding. For of the vine of Sodom is their vine, and their tendrils of Gomorrah: their grape is a grape of gall, a cluster of bitterness unto them: wrath of dragons is their wine, and wrath of vipers immedicable. Lo, is not this considered with me, and sealed up in my treasuries? In the day of vengeance I will repay it, in the time when their foot is caught.' (31–35). What we witness in Apocalypse xv is the bringing forth of the vintage of Sodom and Gomorrah, fire, that is, and brimstone, which the enemies of God have grown on the soil of their folly, and God has sealed up in his treasuries against the day of their recompense. Now is the day, and the seven angels pour it on their heads.[1]

We have been studying the conversion of a joyful dedication into a liturgy of judgement, but we have neglected so far the text which does more than any other to pave the way for so violent an alteration. This is without doubt Ezekiel x, 4–7. Ezekiel has his vision of a blessed Dedication, but that is his final vision, when he sees the New Jerusalem, and the Glory of the God of Israel returns to dwell for ever in it. This blessed Dedication is written by the prophet in careful and contrasting parallel with a previous and dreadful visitation for the overthrow of old Jerusalem. As in the new city all will be holiness, so in the old all is defilement, and God's Glory occupies for the last time the Mercy-Seat of Solomon's temple, to make of it the seat of his wrath. Fire and sword desolate the city, and the Glory relinquishes it, not to return until the times of the end. Ezekiel spares us none of the dismaying antithesis: the temple is filled with the Cloud as when Moses dedicated the Tabernacle or Solomon the temple. Then at the divine command a man clothed in linen receives from one of the cherubim fiery coals to scatter over the city. The identical part played by the cherub in Apocalypse xv, 7 is enough to show that St John is using Ezekiel.

St John's vision is not a repetition of Ezekiel's. What he sees is not the overthrow of Old Jerusalem: that happened in the nine-

[1] The song of Moses and the Lamb must be primarily Deuteronomy xxxii, and yet, as so often, St John brings in a secondary reference besides. The singers are above the 'sea' of their purification, as Israel rising from their Red-Sea baptism, and singing with Moses the victory achieved over Pharaoh by the redemption of the Paschal Lamb (Exod. xv).

teenth year of King Nebuchadnezzar. Neither is it the return of the Glory to New Jerusalem: he will treat of that on his final page. It is something in between, and belonging to the age of the persecuted Church. The temple which is visited is a pure temple visited in mercy, not in wrath, yet the visitation is for wrath on the wicked city in which the temple stands, 'the city where the Lord was crucified'. The temple is in the city, and yet it is in heaven. The line which was measured round the sanctuary by the inspired seer may be invisible to human eyes, but to angelic vision it marks the top of a cliff of sheer descent from heaven to earth. The inhabitants of earth may think that the surface of the hallowed enclosure is level and continuous with the ground on which they walk. They do not know that on that day everything outside the fatal line fell an immeasurable depth, or else that everything within it rose an immeasurable height. The divine Glory visits the temple, and thence the fire is poured which falls upon the world, and the air above it, and the sun that warms it. It falls on the sun, and it is quickened with intolerable fire: it falls into the air, and the thunder becomes earthquake to shake down the cities of the earth.

There is an ambiguity about St John's image which can hardly be resolved. In Moses's dedication, and in Solomon's, the Throne of God remained above the firmament, only the glorious cloud descended. Yet as the day of doom approached, the prophets saw the throne in the temple as well as the cloud. In the year that King Uzziah died Isaiah saw the Lord sitting upon the throne, high and lifted up, his skirts filling the temple; at the voice of his seraphim the lintel moved and the house was filled with smoke. ('With smoke' not 'cloud' says St John also, remembering Isaiah's vision). Ezekiel, caught up in the spirit from Babylonian exile, was swept behind the chariot which bore on a mysterious firmament the throne of God. The throne and chariot descended on Jerusalem, for the scene of judgement: while the cherub gave the coals of fire to the angel of vengeance, the chariot with its attendant cherubim stood in the inner court of the temple, but the Glory, that is, it would seem, all that was above the flying firmament, including the throne, left the chariot and went up the steps over the vestibule of the house. The house was filled with the cloud, and all the inner court shone with rays of the Glory. It is not clear whether the

163

Glory remains throned on the threshold, or is to be understood to have passed right through to the place of the symbolic throne, the mercy-seat of the Ark. Perhaps St John would interpret so.

In St John's vision the cherub apparently stands in the court outside the temple: and this suggests the visitation of the Enthroned Glory, who leaves his attendant ministers outside the shrine. But we are told nothing of a visible divine entry. We are told simply that the temple was filled with smoke from the 'glory and power of God', and we do not know whether, after all, to interpret by Ezekiel, or by Exodus and Chronicles: whether the presence is displayed simply in the glorious cloud and smoke, or whether these are emanations from the Throne: or supposing that the Throne is there, whether, after all, it has entered from without—perhaps the Throne has become mysteriously present at the mercy-seat, as we may suppose to have happened in Isaiah's vision, and the smoke has spread outwards from it to fill the rest of the house. When we reach the great voice, 'It is done,' we do hear of the Throne as being in the temple, for the voice is 'out of the temple from the Throne'. The Throne is within the smoking glory: it is not said to be seen, only the voice proceeding from it is heard.

It is easier to find St John's allusions than to reconstruct his picture. Perhaps there was no picture for the eyes. Suffice it to say that he is speaking of an imperfect temple, a temple of this age, the spiritual existence of the militant Church, which can be visited or filled in various degree by the divine presence, and is here filled with more of the power and glory than it can well sustain.

The seven vials cover the space between Dedication and Passover, and they weave together the themes of the two feasts. The liturgical frame belongs to Dedication, the material part of the seven plagues leads up to Passover. For the plagues are plagues of Egypt, and everyone knows that the strokes of Moses' rod are the preludes to the paschal deliverance.

A comparison between the Egyptian plagues of VIII–IX and of XVI is inevitable; and there is one fact about it which is especially striking in the present connexion. The trumpet plagues were, as a series of plagues, self-contained, and they found their climax in what must seem the inevitable culmination, Moses' last stroke, the stroke of death. By contrast, the tenth and greatest of the Exodus

164

plagues finds no place in the vials: the seventh vial inflicts no more than a plague of thunder and hail. This is because the stroke of death is the act of the paschal deliverance itself; the Israelites had already eaten the Passover when death fell on the Egyptian first-born; St John must therefore reserve that stroke for the Rider on the White Horse. Scripture sometimes attributes the blow to the Lord's own hand, sometimes to the destroying angel. The Book of Wisdom assigns it to the Word of God, leaping down from the sky as a stern warrior, and this is the form St John follows in xix. The heaven opens, and there appears the armed rider, whose name is called 'the Word of God'. In ix the work of slaughter was given to the destroying angels. Thus St John obtains a climax in viii–ix, xvi–xix, in proportion as the Word of God is greater than any angel.

The effect of the climax is only seen if we can look far enough to appreciate the continuity between xvi and xix. Otherwise we shall see xvi as no more than a stale repetition of viii–ix, and indeed a weaker and less emphatic repetition. A distinguished pioneer in the modern interpretation of the Apocalypse was so disturbed by this, that he proposed drastic remedies to correct it: he got rid of the first four trumpet-plagues entirely, condemning them as un-intelligent interpolations. But St John meant us to read his book as a whole. The six trumpet-visions were to set up in our minds the standard of an Egyptian plague series culminating in the stroke of death: we were then presently to read the vial-plagues, and we were to feel the due degree of mental discontent, when not merely six, but the whole seven ran out without bringing the required climax. The long and leisurely interlude of xvii–xviii was to in-crease the tension, so that when the stern warrior with the death-dealing sword leapt out of heaven at last, bearing the title of the Word of God, the effect was to be all the greater.

There is, in fact, as we noted in a previous chapter, absolute continuity of the history between xvi and xix. The sixth vial brings the wicked hosts to Armageddon, and there they are left, awaiting the Rider on the White Horse. The victims are prepared, but where is the knife? The seventh vial brings little more than portents—the divine declaration 'It has come to pass', the thunder, earthquake, and hail. The earthquake brings the cities down, but

165

not even the physical ruin of Babylon can sound like finality, while the Armageddon host is still awaiting its antagonist.

The substance, then, of the vial-plagues looks towards Passover and the Rider on the Horse. But the liturgical frame looks back to Dedication. We must compare the trumpet plagues once more. The trumpets themselves were a festal emblem, belonging unmistakeably to New Year. 'Vials', i.e. libation-bowls, are not of themselves proper to any feast: the drink-offering was poured upon every major sacrifice. Since the pouring completed the ceremony, there may be felt to be a special appropriateness in mentioning the vials of Dedication, since Dedication completes the year of major festivals. But there is more than this. The wine which is poured out in St John's vision is 'the vintage of Sodom and Gomorrah', that is, sulphurous fire. Now at the Dedication a glory-cloud fills the sanctuary, and the fire of heaven falls upon the altar to consume the sacrifice: this happens both when Moses dedicates the Tabernacle, and when Solomon hallows the Temple.[1] St John has shown us the glory-cloud filling the 'Temple of the Tabernacle' (xv, 5–8), and it seems probable that the pouring of the vials has something to do with the fall of the heavenly fire. The fire ought, one might object, to fall on the altar of the heavenly temple, since it is the shrine of this temple that the cloud fills. It may be so. But perhaps St John has varied his symbolism, under the influence of the Old Testament image of the Lord's ghastly sacrifice (Zephaniah I, 7, Ezekiel xxxix, 17, etc.). He certainly takes that image up presently, when he bids the birds to the sacrificial banquet (xix, 17). The Lord confirms the consecration of the Church by filling her with his glory, and by making a burnt-offering of her enemies with the outpoured fire of heaven.

The trumpet-plagues also expressed the fall of heavenly fire, for they followed upon the act of the incense-angel, when, once his perfume had ascended at the golden altar, he refilled his censer with burning coals and scattered them over the earth. And the connexion between the incense-liturgy and the trumpet-blasts

[1] Also when Elijah sets up the altar on Carmel, after summoning thither the priests of Baal to their doom, a scene which is in any case worked into the symbolism of the sixth vial.

166

was reinforced at the sixth trumpet: it was the voice from the four horns of the golden altar which gave the sixth trumpet-angel his orders, so that he let loose the four angels of death. In the vials the relation between the outpouring of fire and the fall of the plagues is more direct—the angels receive in the liturgy the command to pour the fire of wrath, and the pouring of it is the seven plagues. Nevertheless St John takes pains to keep before our eyes the liturgical situation out of which the vial-pouring has arisen. We remember how the utterance of voices from the temple, then from the altar, then out of the Glory, gave signals for the work of judgement in the *introduction* to the vials. The temple-angel gave a sign to the harvester, the altar-angel to the reaper; the voice from the smoking Glory, answering voices round the Sea of Glass, commanded the seven angels of the vials to pour. They have received their commission, then, and require no more signal-voices, yet voices from the holy place accompany this work, not by way of signal but by way of comment.

After the third vial-plague the angel of the waters justifies God for turning both sea and fresh water into blood. The angel of the *altar* makes reply, not, of course, the angel of the altar-fire, but of the altar as the recipient of sacrificial blood. The heavenly altar drank the blood-souls of the martyrs (VI, 9); he now justifies God for making their enemies a sacrifice of vindication. At the seventh vial a great voice speaks out of the *temple*. It is not a comment on the work of the seventh angel alone, but on the sixfold preceding work. The wicked have been brought to Armageddon, there to encounter him who comes as a thief on the great day of God Almighty. The angels have done their part. When the seventh vial is poured the great voice says, 'It is come to pass,' and this voice is the principal substance of the vision: its mere accompanying portents, the lightnings, voices, and thunders, the earthquake and the hail, destroy the cities of the world, shake mountains and islands out of their places, and beat to earth the blasphemers of God.

It may be that in the fall of the cities, especially Babylon, we are to see the theme of Dedication revived at the seventh vial. For the overthrow of Babylon is the building of Jerusalem: Ezekiel's vision of the new city is in careful parallel to his vision of the overthrow of the old (VIII–XI, XL–XLVIII). St John balances with equal

167

care the judgement of the harlot-city and the restoration of the bride (XVII; XXI, 9–XXII), and, as we saw above, he uses Ezekiel's vision of overthrow as a principal source for the symbolism of Dedication in Apocalypse XV.

St John treats the Dedication as the last feast of the year, and Passover, the first of the next year, immediately follows it: the interval between them is not distinguished by any feast which can hold a place in the numbered series of feasts. Yet St John may allude to the minor commemoration of Purim in his Passover Eve (XVII–XIX, 10), just as he alludes to the minor commemoration of Moses's Death in his Dedication-morning (XV, 3), without altering the fixed lines of his scheme. Purim is the next full-moon before Passover, and may naturally be felt to be the 'eve' to it.

Purim commemorates the events described in the Book of Esther. We recall how in a setting of pagan ostentation, the rebellious woman Vashti is deprived of her royalty, because she is the corruptress of all wives throughout the empire, and how the Israelite girl, Esther, is made queen in her place, being 'purified' and given the adornments proper for her nuptials. Esther's replacing of Vashti is already a portent of the triumph of Israel over heathen rivals. These rivals, especially Haman, are plotting the destruction of Israel, but when, for reasons which the story explains, Mordecai, Haman's Jewish enemy, is made to ride in triumph on the king's horse in the king's raiment, the fall of Haman is prefigured. It is completed in the banquet-scene— Haman thought himself blessed to be bidden to the table of the King and his bride, but the banquet led to the salvation of Esther and her kindred and the death of Haman, and the Jews enjoyed two days of vengeance and exultation.

The elements of this history, broken up, certainly, and re-arranged, can be found in Apocalypse XVII–XIX. The wicked rebellious 'woman', Babylon, the corruptress of all the world, is dethroned, she that had said, 'I sit as a queen and am no widow and shall never see grief.' She loses all the splendours of pagan luxury paraded by the merchants in their lament for her. She is replaced by the pure Bride, the spiritual Zion, who is given glistening clean linen to wear, and the voice is heard, 'Blessed are

168

they that are bidden to the marriage-supper of the Lamb.' There is exultation of the saints over the fall of their persecuting enemies, and the victory becomes certain when their champion rides forth on a royal horse in royal raiment to be worshipped as the Heavenly King himself. In the Esther-story worship is refused to Haman by the pious Israelite, who explains (in the Greek addition to Esther) that his refusal is refusal to worship a creature. Mordecai is sent out on the horse to be worshipped by royal command, because he is clothed with the majesty of the King on whom God has conferred the dominion of the earth. In St John's vision the angel is not to be worshipped, because he is only a creature, but the champion of Israel, Messiah, is to be worshipped, because God has bestowed the divine royalty upon him.

The most striking of St John's divergences from the pattern of Purim is that the Rider on the Horse has become the royal bridegroom, not merely the servant whom the bridegroom delights to honour. This alteration transfers us from Purim to Passover. For at Passover the Canticles were read, where the bridegroom is Solomon: Solomon who, like Mordecai, had triumphed over conspiracy by the sign of a state ride on the King's (his father's) beast. This assured to him the succession: his rival feared and took hold of the horns of the altar. (I Kings 1.)

There is no need to labour here the generally admitted use of Canticles at Passover. In XIX, 1–10 St John associates the theme of the sacred marriage with the Alleluia-psalmody. The Alleluia-psalms were used at Passover and have been appropriated to the Christian Easter.

If we are thinking of the Solomon-theme in Canticles we can hardly fail to draw Psalm XLV into the pattern. 'At thy right hand doth stand the queen in the gold of Ophir. Hearken, daughter, incline thine ear . . . forget thy people and thy father's house. So shall the king desire thy beauty: for he is thy Lord, and worship thou him[1] (9–11). My heart overfloweth with a goodly word, I utter my works to the king. . . . Gird thy sword upon thy thigh, most Mighty, thy glory and thy majesty; and in thy majesty ride on prosperously, for truth, meekness and righteousness. . . . Thine

[1] The Greek transfers the worshipping from the bride to the daughters of Tyre, who appear in the next verse.

169

arrows are sharp, the peoples fall under thee. . . . Thy throne, O God, is for ever and ever' (1–6).

Compare with this Apocalypse XIX, 7–16: the fair array of the bride, the command to worship the Lord in no angel but in Christ; Christ riding forth to make war in righteousness, called Word of God, with a sharp sword proceeding from his mouth wherewith to smite the peoples, and on his garment and his thigh a name written, King of Kings, and Lord of Lords: followed by the white-robed host who are but another expression of the white-robed bride.

(2)

The appearance of the warrior Word of God is, as we have said above, the sign of the paschal advent, because Wisdom XVIII, 15–16 thus describes the destroyer of the firstborn on Passover night: 'Thine almighty word from heaven out of the kingly throne leapt, a stern warrior, into the land of destruction, as a sharp sword bearing thine unfeigned commandment; and alighting he filled all things with death, and touched the heaven, though he bestrode the earth.' The work was begun upon the firstborn, and completed upon Pharaoh's host at the Red Sea. 'The Lord is a man of war,' sang Moses and Israel, as they watched the Egyptians drown. St John has no occasion to distinguish between the heavenly warrior's smiting of the firstborn and his smiting of the Egyptian host. At the great battle the Armageddon-host is slain, like the firstborn, by the sword proceeding from the mouth of the Word of God, which is no other than 'God's unfeigned commandment'. The leaders of the host are flung into the lake of fire, as it is written of Pharaoh's fate: 'Sing unto the Lord, for he hath triumphed gloriously: the horse and his rider hath he flung into the sea.' St John's battle also is seen as a battle of horsemen. The victors are mounted, so are the vanquished, for the birds are summoned to eat the flesh of horses and their riders.

We need carry no further the mere collection of Passover-features. Obviously this is Passover, and the Rider on the Horse is the Easter Christ. Let us proceed to a more important work, the comparison of this Passover and its sequel (XIX, 11–XXI, 8) with the previous Passover and its sequel (IV–VIII, 6). It would be hard

170

to exaggerate the value of this comparison for an understanding of the whole Apocalypse.

The first Passover was introduced by three 'openings', of which the third was a climax, a door opened in heaven, so that St John might enter there, and see the great theophany. And this he could do, because the Lamb had triumphed and himself entered heaven, and revealed 'all the secrets of the hidden things'. The second Passover begins with an opening—'I saw the heaven opened', but this is for an opposite journey: 'That same Jesus which was received up from us into heaven, shall so come in like manner as we beheld him go into heaven.' In the first Passover there was a distinction between revelation and action. The revelation was perfect, and made by Christ, but the consequent action was partial, the work of the rider on the white horse. In the second Passover there is no such distinction. There is no revelation other than the action, and the agent is Christ, and the act is perfect. He is the Rider on the White Horse. In the first Passover it is 'I saw an open door in heaven . . . and I saw a Lamb standing . . . and he taketh the book. . . . And I saw when the Lamb opened the first of the seven seals . . . and behold, a white horse. . . .' In the second Passover the opening of the book is swallowed up in the opening of heaven: 'I saw the heaven opened, and behold, a white horse. . . .'

The four riders headed by the rider on the white horse invade the earth in partial judgement; the many riders following their white-horsed captain win the total victory. Because the four riders were but the beginning of judgement, the souls slaughtered for the word of God, and the testimony which they held, had to hear the lesson of patience, 'that they should rest a little while, until their brethren which should be killed even as they should be fulfilled in number.' Because the Rider on the White Horse has brought the fulness of judgement, the number of the martyrs is full, and now the souls beheaded for the testimony of Jesus and for the word of God live and reign with Christ a thousand years.

The position occupied by this millennial reign is one of subtle balance. On the one hand it contrasts with the corresponding vision in the former pentecostal period. Those who then were commanded to wait no longer wait but reign. On the other hand what we have in xx is still a pre-pentecostal vision, contrasting with complete consummation. The thousand-year reign is of this age, all things have still to be made new after the final Pentecost. It is hedged about with incompleteness: the last enemy, the Devil, who has the power of death, has not yet been destroyed, but merely bound, and he is destined to break prison after the thousand years. A sleeping volcano overhangs the millennial kingdom. Truly, they now have thrones who were bidden to wait before. Yet the waiting was not the whole of the fifth seal-vision. They were bidden to wait, but they were also in part rewarded, and their condition was relieved. They were no longer to be naked souls, run down beneath the altar: they were to wear the white robes of immortal being. The white robes are not a full reward, but neither are the thrones of the millennium. The millennium is the antitype of the fifty days from Firstfruits to Pentecost. The martyrs of the Christian dispensation who undergo the first resurrection and fill the millennial thrones are themselves but firstfruits to the great harvest of all the righteous dead, which is gathered when the millennium ends.

It is in the context of the comparison we are making that the image of the millennium has to be understood. The last consummation approaches through a rhythm of ordered stages, and in this rhythm the millennium has its place. Looked at from the point of view of this majestic process, it is a pentecostal period worthy of the Passover and Harvest-home of the Universe, between which it stands. Looked at from the point of view of the martyrs, it is a privileged alleviation of the lot of the soul between death and the general resurrection. They have already been given their white robes: they are now given a foretaste of resurrection itself. So the millennium takes its place beside the later catholic doctrines exempting martyrs and other canonized saints from the general interim-state of the Christian dead, whether called purgatory or by some other name. Such are the emphases which appear in St John's picture. If we press for answers to questions which he does not pose, we shall no doubt get strange results. Over whom do the martyrs reign? Presumably over Christian people remaining alive at the advent of the Rider on the White Horse, or subsequently converted from among those who had not gone to Armageddon. There are still unconverted tribes, it would seem, in the four corners of the earth, Gog and Magog, whom Satan later uses for his mischief. But those in the centre of the earth, over whom the martyrs exercise a blessed reign as assessors to the throne of Christ—are they immortal, or are only the martyrs? Do they die after their three-score years and ten, and go to swell the multitude awaiting the general resurrection? The more we ask such questions as these, the further we shall get from what the image of the millennium means to St John. If we wish to know that, we must attend to the use he makes of it. Whether or no he ought to be called a 'millennarian' in the sense afterwards so much disliked by the orthodox is a problem which we will leave to the curious in heresy.

The millennium is not an inspiration of St John's, but a rabbinic commonplace. We hear of it in connexion with scholarly debates the detail of which need not be inflicted on the reader, but which attach it to a verse in Psalm XC, 'A thousand years in thy sight are but as yesterday.' As II Peter III, 8 may show the Christian student, this verse was taken to establish the equivalence between a thousand years and a 'day of the Lord'. The reign of Messiah must surely have the completeness of a 'day of the Lord', and so it must be a millennium. The doctrine of the millennium, therefore, was part and parcel of the rabbinic distinction between the days of Messiah and the World to Come. This is not a distinction which a Christian mind would have been likely to have invented, but as it is ready to his hand, St John can convert it to his own uses with his unfailing dexterity. The rabbi opposed the throne of the Son of David to the throne of God. The former belongs to this world, and is not the fulness of the divine Kingdom. In the World to Come 'the Lord alone will be king over all the earth; in that day shall the Lord be One, and his Name One' (Zech. XIV, 9): and Messiah will have nothing more than a titular precedence over other Israelites. Now Christianity begins at the place where the distinction between the two Thrones is overcome.

The Lamb is in the midst of the (great) Throne, the Son is in the bosom of the Father, and this is precisely the meaning of the Unity of the Lord, or of his Name, in the World to Come. Judaism did not understand the *distribution* of the Name JHVH between Father and Son, and so did not understand the significance of the asserted unity: it was a barren tautology. But in the Christian vision of the World to Come the mystery is revealed: 'The throne of God and of the Lamb shall be therein, and *his* (not their) servants shall do *him* service; and they shall see *his* face, and *his Name* shall be upon their foreheads. . . . The Lord God shall shine upon them, and they shall reign for ever and ever.' (XXII, 3–5).

There is, then, no opposition between the throne of Messiah and the Throne of God, nor does St John permit such an opposition to appear. He substitutes another. 'I saw thrones'; that is the millennium. 'I saw a great white throne'; that is the eve of the World to Come. In the millennium Christ reigns humanly, as the Apostle of God on earth, in such fashion that the martyrs can sit with him, much as the Twelve sat with him at the Supper, when he promised them thrones. In the World to Come he sits in the great Throne, and that Throne being made immediately present to the creatures excludes plurality of thrones, and yet makes the dethroned saints a thousand times more kingly than they were before—'the Lord God shall shine upon them, and they shall reign for ever and ever,' by communion with eternal and unoriginate dominion.

The pentecostal period is the Millennial Kingdom of the saints; their participation in the everlasting Kingdom begins at Tabernacles. Between the two is the Great Judgement which the New-Year trumpet proclaims. For before the everlasting Throne can extend a tabernacle over the saints, it must dissolve and drive away the impure fabric of the old creation: it must reveal who are saints and who are not. New Year and Tabernacles are all one Holy Season, the manifestation of the everlasting Throne is all one thing. The countenance of terror which the creatures cannot sustain is the face of mercy turned upon the people of the covenant. The light and terror fall together on the Israel of this world, where wheat and tares grow inextricable until the day of harvest. But when the last New Year has fully unveiled the terror and consumed the tares, the light shines steadily on those who inherit the Tabernacles of the World to Come.

At New Year a great white throne is seen, and he that sits thereon, before whose face *earth and heaven* fled, but the dead, small and great, could not: they stood before the throne. And *the*

174

sea gave up the dead in her, and so did those other demonic regions, hades and death, to be themselves consigned with all the damned to the waters of ultimate destruction, the lake burning with fire and brimstone. After that there is revealed a *new heaven* and a *new earth,* for the old *heaven and earth* have departed, and the *sea* is no more; and he who sits upon the throne himself declares: I will give to him that thirsteth of the *fountain of the waters of life*; but all the false, their portion is the lake that burns with fire and brimstone, which is the second death.

The dissolution of the first creation is simply effected by the revelation of the great throne. As by the breath of him who sits on it, all the creatures in which the souls have wrapped themselves are blown away, as it might have been the leaves under which Adam hid himself, and they are left naked before the face of him who is. Earth and heaven cannot stand before that countenance; the veil of the firmament being withdrawn, everything dissolves. The visions of the throne which St John has seen since that of the fourth chapter have been seen, and not seen: in the Spirit he found himself above the firmament, and yet 'No man hath ascended into heaven, save him that from heaven descended, the Son of Man that is in heaven' (John III, 13), and all the seer sees is a visionary shewing through the mediation of an angel. The necessary correction is afforded by the Dedication-visions. Even the heavenly temple can scarcely endure the Enthroned Glory veiled within a cloud of smoke: the overflow of fire falls from angelic hands on all the world. What will it be, then, when not the temple but the polluted frame of nature beholds the Throne without a veil?

The old creation has departed, the new appears. The New Year of the world dawns with a New Year sign which St John has taught us to recognise, 'a great sign in heaven, a woman adorned with the sun and the moon beneath her feet, and on her head a crown of twelve stars'—'The holy city, new Jerusalem, coming down out of heaven from God, prepared as a bride adorned for her husband'. We go straight on from New Year into Tabernacles: the woman now needs no flight into the wilderness that she may reach them.

The New Year terrors of the sixth seal (Apoc. VI) were followed by a scene of joyful feast in the World to Come. There, according

175

to St John's scheme of recapitulations, the feast was viewed not as Tabernacles, but as Passover: and yet images belonging to Tabernacles forced their way into the conclusion of it. It was written there of the white-robed host: 'They are before the throne of God and serve him day and night in his temple, and he that sitteth upon the throne shall spread his tabernacle over them. They shall hunger no more nor thirst any more, nor shall the sun light on them nor any heat. For the Lamb that is in the midst of the throne shall shepherd them, and lead them to living fountains of waters, and God shall wipe away every tear from their eyes.' Such was the anticipation, and this is the fulfilment on the last sabbath day: 'Behold the tabernacle of God is with men, and he will tabernacle with them; and they shall be his peoples, and GOD-WITH-THEM[1] himself shall be their God, and shall wipe away every tear from their eyes. . . . And he saith . . . I will give to him that thirsteth of the fountain of living waters freely.'

With Midsummer the last week, to reckon strictly, ends: there are no more *weeks* of visions. Yet it is not possible for the consummation of all things to be Midsummer, or the Pentecost before it, or the Judgement-Trumpet after it. St John hastens on to review the whole year of feasts. The last working day is the judgement-aspect of New Year, the sabbath is Tabernacles: the appended vision of the Bride is, plainly enough, Dedication, for it shows us the frame of that city which is itself to be God's Holy of Holies. The vision stands in parallel to XVII, the appendix to a previous Dedication. It recalls three times the symbol of the candlestick (XXI, 11, 23, XXII, 5), on the third occasion equating the lamp-lighting with the imposition of the Name, according to the Dedication-lesson, which begins from Aaron's blessing and ends with his lighting of the lamps. 'God's servants shall do his liturgy, and his Name shall be on their foreheads, and there shall be night no more; and they need no light of lamp nor light of sun, for the Lord God shall lighten them, and they shall reign for ever and ever.'

Pentecost, New Year and Tabernacles, Dedication—and now,

---

[1] At the previous Tabernacles (XII) the Virgin of Isaiah's prophecy brought forth Emmanuel. At this final Tabernacles the promise of the name, 'God-with-us,' is actualized.

last of all, on into Passover again. For the incident of the angel refusing worship wakes the echoes of XIX. We turn from the angel to look for the Rider on the White Horse. He is not yet to be seen; the world of vision fades, and we find ourselves in the congregation at Ephesus, listening to the last phrases of the letter from Patmos, and imploring our Saviour that, as he himself testifies, he will come quickly.

*   *   *   *

What follows here is an appendix to the whole theme of the festal calendar as our three chapters IV–VI have set it forth. For it has to be confessed that a further complication must be admitted before the imagery of the festal liturgies can be fully understood. St John, we have said, compares the Dedication-feast with the drink-offering, because the feast occupies in the yearly calendar the place which the offering occupies in the daily sacrifice. The libation ends the service of the altar, as the Dedication completes the calendar of great feasts. Now this comparison is of a type which St John especially favours. He loves to compare the structure of the part with the structure of the whole. As the six hours in the working morning, so the six mornings in the working week. As the four seven-day weeks in the month, so the four three-month quarters in the year. As the successive sacred acts in the daily liturgy, so the successive day-liturgies in the yearly calendar. We have so far noted only the comparison between the last act of the liturgy and the last liturgy of the calendar. We have now to extend the comparison over the whole field.

The Mishnah-tractate *Tamid* gives an account of the daily liturgy in the temple, as it was recalled and discussed in the century after the destruction of the city, during the period, that is to say, in the beginning of which St John wrote. This gives us just what we need. We do not want to know what happened in the temple before 70 A.D., we want to know what the synagogues afterwards supposed to have happened there, for there is every likelihood that what they supposed is what St John supposed. Comparing the tractate with the Apocalypse, we reach the following conclusions.

St John divides the liturgy into four acts to correspond with the four quarters of the year.

177

(1) At dawn the lamb of the daily offering is slaughtered, flayed and dismembered, and the *blood-offering* is made against the base of the altar.

(2) The liturgy of the altar is suspended while the *incense-offering* is carried into the temple and made on the golden altar within.

(3) The reappearance of the priests from the temple is the sign for the *burnt-offering* to be made. The dismembered lamb is thrown into the altar-fire, and consumed to the accompaniment of trumpet-blasts.

(4) After the pieces have been flung into the fire, the *drink-offering* is poured upon them, just after the first trumpet is blown.

St John applies the lamb-slaying and blood-offering to Passover, the incense-offering to Midsummer, the burnt-offering with its trumpets to New Year, and the drink-offering to Dedication. How does he interpret the four sacrificial acts, and how does he make them appropriate to the four seasons?

(1) The slaying of the lamb and the offering of its blood is obviously appropriate to Passover. At Passover a lamb was sacrificed not for the whole house of Israel only, but for each several household: at no other time were so many lambs slain. And especial significance attached to the lamb's blood: it was the blood of Passover, the redeeming mark by which Israel was delivered. St John is concerned also to relate this moment of the liturgy to Pentecost, because Pentecost falls in the Passover quarter. We may deduce from Philo's writings and elsewhere that there was a tendency to interpret the daily offering in accordance with the ritual of Atonement Day. On Atonement Day the High Priest carried the sacrificial blood into the temple with the incense, right to the Holy of Holies. It was natural, then, to think of the blood-offering as the price at which the entry of the holiest place was made[1], even on the days when no blood was carried in with the incense, and when the priest went no further than past the first veil. Every incense-offering was a symbol of Atonement Day. Every blood-offering opens to us the secrets. The secret of Solomon's temple was the Ark of the Covenant, containing the tables of the Decalogue. The secret of every Synagogue was the Ark of the Law,

[1] See Hebrews IX, 11, X, 19.

178

containing the sacred scriptures: the opening of the Ark and the bringing forth of the scripture was the most august ceremony of the synagogal sabbath-liturgy.

The blood of Passover brought Israel to Sinai and the tables of the law, and that was Pentecost. The Blood of Atonement carried the High Priest in to the shrine where those very tables lay, hidden in the Ark. By virtue of the blood of the Covenant the Israelite can approach and draw forth the scroll from the synagogal Ark and unfold sacred truth to his people. The Lamb is worthy to take the book and open the seals thereof, for he was slain, and purchased multitudes for God with his blood (v, 9). Those who sing this hymn have incense in their hands, to remind us that the opening of the Book in the Synagogue is equivalent to the penetration of the Holy Place in the temple, for this took place at the incense-offering.

We have suggested that Apocalypse IV–V equates synagogal ceremonies with temple-ceremonies. The fact is, in truth, evident. For the setting of the vision is a fusion of Temple and Synagogue. Here are the laver, the candlestick and the cherubim of the temple: and here is the sacrificial lamb. But the throne which the cherubim flank is the seat of a head of synagogue, with his twenty-four elders sitting about him: and here is the book of the law.

(2) What we have been shewn in IV–V is the blood-offering viewed as the price by which the way to the incense-offering is opened. At the Midsummer vision (VIII, 1–6) we pass to the incense-offering itself, and view it in turn as a ceremony which opens the way to the burnt-offering with its trumpets. We stand with the congregation in the open court about the altar. We see the priestly trumpeters standing by. They are given their trumpets: when will they be able to blow? Not until an angel-priest has gone to the altar of slaughter and received charcoal from its undying fire, and incense besides in a separate vessel. Not until he has entered the temple, spread the charcoal over the top of the golden altar there, and scattered the incense upon it. When he comes out again the burning of the lamb may begin. When all the pieces are in the fire, the trumpets will sound, the half hour's silence will end.

For St John's purposes the next stage after the incense-offering must begin with the trumpet, because the New Year trumpet

179

opens Holy Season. There is a difficulty here: for the trumpet did not directly follow the incense-ritual. The sacrificial portions must first go into the fire. St John overcomes this difficulty by incorporating the ritual of burning into the incense-liturgy under a symbolical form. The incense-angel does not stand still on the temple steps as he should do while the pieces are thrown into the altar-fire. He himself approaches the altar, refills his censer with fire, and throws it to earth. When the firing of the victim has taken place under this symbolical form, the trumpets can blow. But why should the throwing of fire to earth symbolize the firing of the victim? Because in St John's *application* of the liturgy the burnt sacrifice is a holocaust of the wicked: the earth is the victim of the sacrificial fire.

The meaning of the incense-liturgy itself is made plain. The angel receives his incense by that altar from beneath which the martyrs' blood has just been heard to cry. He is given incense of heaven to 'put to' the prayers of the saints, and at or by the prayers of the saints it steams up before God. It seems clear that the prayers are the charcoal. The death of the Lamb and his martyrs gives their prayers access to the holy place, and the addition of the angels' ministry, the incense, makes them a prevailing intercession. We have here a complication of the simpler symbol in v, 8, where the incense is just the prayers of the saints, and the angels merely present it.

(3) There are two ways of looking at the burnt-offering. The original and most natural view regards it as the second stage of the altar-liturgy. The blood has been offered: now the portions are burnt. Both are pure, holy and acceptable offerings to God. The incense-liturgy is simply a pause between the two. On the other hand, one might regard the incense-liturgy rather than the burnt-offering as the fulfilment of the blood-sacrifice. The blood opens the way into the temple: the incense goes into the temple itself and is accepted before God. Approach to God, the propitiation of God, has gone as far as it can go. When we turn our backs on the Ark and come out of the shrine again it must be for some other purpose. We have gone to God: now we are coming from God, commissioned to execute that for which we prayed. Since the prayer was for vindication, the burnt sacrifice is the execu-

180

tion of it: the holocaust is no longer seen as the pure lamb of the blood-offering, but as the dwellers upon earth, the destined to Gehenna.

We have seen St John constrained to give the firing of the portions under symbolical form to the incense-angel, so that the New Year's act might begin with the trumpet-blowing. But while the trumpets blew, the portions continued to burn, and so the plagues which accompany St John's trumpets are plagues of fire and smoke. St John makes seven blasts, to accord with his scheme of weeks. There were three in fact at the ordinary sacrifice, and indeed his seven are probably to be viewed as the sevenfold subdivision of the first of these. For St John's trumpets carry us over from silence to psalmody (VIII, 1, XI, 15), and it was the first trumpet which effected this transition: the other two divided between the psalms.

Just as the half-hour's pause for the liturgy of incense well expresses the empty time of Midsummer, so the burnt-offering as St John interprets it expresses well enough the quality of New Year. The New Year Trumpet is the preface of Gehenna, and the trumpets of the sacrifice accompany the burning.

(4) As St John shows the blood-offering to pave the way for the incense and the incense to pave the way for the trumpets and the burning, so he would presumably wish to show the trumpets as paving the way to the drink-offering: but facts are against him. The drink-offering followed, certainly, the throwing of the victim into the fire, but it did not follow the trumpet, or if so, only by the fraction of a second: the trumpeter took his cue from the gesture of the priest who stooped forward to pour the wine. The drink-offering is not something which can be shown to arise out of the trumpet-blowing by a solemn liturgical progression. St John resigns himself to recapitulation. He goes back to the incense-offering, and derives the libation from there.

Just as the incense was prefigured at the lamb-slaying (v, 8) and the trumpet-blowing at the incense (VIII, 1), so St John prefigures his next step at the blowing of the great trumpet. The step is in fact a step backwards: the temple is opened (XI, 19), as for the incense. Symbolically this means, as we saw, the uncovering of the Ark. The Ark could never, in fact, be seen through the temple

181

door at Jerusalem.[1] The opening of the shrine is the first step, the second is the filling of it with incense-smoke. This takes place in xv. The temple is opened once more, this time for the priestly angels to come out: they leave the temple full of smoke behind them. St John does not make a flat repetition of the previous incense-liturgy. There the smoke represented a Godward act, the presentation of prayers: here a manward act, God's entry into the temple in the smoking cloud of his glory. Both symbolisms belonged equally to the liturgical incense. The second is obviously appropriate to Dedication.

On certain occasions, when the High Priest himself ministered, the minister of the incense and of the libation was the same. St John's seven angels come out of the temple, as from the incense-offering, and receive the libation-bowls. There should be one bowl and one pourer: St John has multiplied the High Priest sevenfold as he multiplied the trumpet sevenfold. The seven angels, however multiplied, retain the distinctive High Priestly ornaments: they are, if we may trust the usually preferred reading, 'vested in stone bright and pure,' i.e. the High Priestly jewels.

The drink-offering was poured once: St John makes it fall sevenfold on the burnt-offering of wrath. When it has been fully poured, the action of liturgy is completed, and a voice from the temple pronounces that it is done.

The fourfold sacrifice fulfils the liturgical year, but St John's scheme extends beyond the year in both directions: there is a first quarter of Dedication before, and a second quarter of Passover after it. These quarters are fitly covered by the prelude and the epilogue to the sacrifice.

The first ceremony of any note to be completed in the day's ritual was the dressing of the lamps. We say, 'to be *completed*,' for it began simultaneously with the blood-offering. When the sacrificing priest heard the temple door move on its ponderous hinges, opened by those who went in to trim the lamps, he cut the lamb's throat. But the whole business of the cutting up of the lamb and the presentation of its blood was obviously more

---

[1] Among other reasons, because there was no Ark in the second temple. But it was deemed to be there and the ritual went on as though it were. The place of the Ark did duty for the Ark.

lengthy than the trimming of the seven lamps, so the ritual of the lamps may be reckoned the first ceremony of the day. (We may observe here that just as the opening of the door was the sign for the lamb-slaying, so the emphatic sign of the door, thrice repeated in III, 7, 20, and IV, 1, introduces the vision of the Lamb.)

The duty of the lamp-dresser was to trim the lamps after their all-night burning, and to leave three only well alight for the day. This gives exactly the suggestion we require for the Candlestick-vision of I–III. Christ is there not to light the lamps but to see how they burn and to admonish the guardian angels who watch over their burning. This is to trim the wicks. He judges between lamp and lamp. Some are at least threatened with extinction. St John cannot actually say that four are put out and only three left to burn, for that is not the word of Christ to the Seven Churches.

So much for the prologue to the sacrifice. Now as to the epilogue. The drink-offering completed the action, but it did not complete the worship. One of the chief glories was the hymnody and harping of the Levitical choir, which began at the drink-offering, and continued while the smoke of the acceptable sacrifice went up to heaven. If St John were maintaining strict liturgical accuracy, which it is obviously no part of his purpose to do, he would have to restrict all harping and hymnody to this single point. We might allow the 'great voices' which follow the trumpet in XI, 15, and when the same point has been reached again with the pouring of the vials, we could have hymnody to our hearts' content: all other singing and liturgical shouting would have to be deleted, above all the 'song of Moses and the Lamb' with which the choir breaks out while (it would appear) the incense is still being offered (XV, 2–4).

But although St John inserts much hymnody which lacks liturgical warrant, there is only one of his great liturgical 'Sabbaths' which consists of psalmody and psalmody alone, and that is XIX, 1–10, the Alleluias. It is to be observed that here alone the liturgical form of the singing is emphasized; the choir-leader's 'Praise ye the Lord' which introduces the fresh psalm of the Hallel, and the solemnity of the Amens. St John also lays emphasis on the continued ascent of the smoke of the sacrifice during the singing. In the previous chapter we have had a tremendous

183

revelation of the sacrifice of wrath and 'the smoke of her burning':
now the choir itself sings 'Alleluia: and her smoke goes up for ever
and ever.'

It was done, the sacrificial action was done, when the vials had
been poured. But they are done, the words of God are done, only
when the holy sentences of the psalms have been fully chanted, and
the last Amen has been pronounced. The last Amen comes alive in
the flesh of the Advent Christ, the Word Faithful and True (XIX,
11 ff.). No sooner is the heavenly liturgy finished, than all those
things begin to be fulfilled for which the liturgy had prayed.
There is no need to say the last Amen, for here is Christ coming,
the living Amen to all the promises of God. And when his coming
has been fulfilled in the marriage of the Bride, then we hear 'The
words of God are done' from the lips of him who sits upon the
throne (XXI, 6).

CHAPTER VII

We have now to call attention to some very remarkable structural peculiarities of the Apocalypse, and to deduce from them, if we can, how St John went to work in composing his poem.

We have remarked already that each of the six sections of which the Apocalypse is composed mirrors in little the form of the whole, and is for that reason on the way to becoming a small-scale Apocalypse on its own account. This is as true of the first section (I–III) as of any other, though not in the same manner. I–III is not a systematic prediction of the Last Things, and so it cannot have the shape of the whole work, which is such a prediction. On the other hand, the contents of the several messages in II–III bear a special relation to the contents of the corresponding sections of the whole Apocalypse. One would have to suppose either that St John used II–III as a model for the rest of his book, or that he composed IV–XXII first and then made II–III as an epitome of it. The former hypothesis is, in fact, preferable.

The first message stands for the first section, of which, of course, it forms a part. For Christ is characterized in it as he who holds the seven stars and walks among the seven candlesticks, i.e. as the Christ of the Candlestick-vision. His threat to Ephesus corresponds: 'I come to thee, and will remove thy candlestick out of its place, except thou repent.'

The second message stands in a very important relation to IV–VII and especially to the six seals, but the reader must take this on trust for the moment: it will be convenient to exhibit it presently as part of another exposition.

The third message contains the reference to a particular martyr, Antipas, Christ's faithful witness, who died at Pergamum, where Satan's throne is. Most of the Church is stalwart, but some have been seduced by a teaching of Balaam, 'who taught Balak to ensnare the Israelites into idolatry and fornication.' The reader of the

Apocalypse of course sees the figures of the False Prophet and the Beast in Balaam and Balak. Now the third section of the whole Apocalypse, VIII–XI, contains as its most striking feature the martyrdom of Christ's 'two witnesses' in a 'spiritual Sodom or Egypt' where Christ himself was crucified before them. The Beast makes his first appearance in the same passage, to be their tormentor. Some part of the 'temple', i.e. the Church, is measured off in token that it will stand fast: the rest is to be overrun by heathendom.

In the fourth message the theme of false prophecy and of seduction into heathenish laxity runs on: but now it is epitomized in the person of 'the woman Jezebel', who is threatened with punishment for her fornication. The fourth part of the Apocalypse (XII–XIV) introduces the figure of 'the woman' Eve, and her opposed type, 'Babylon the Great, who of the wine-of-wrath of her fornication has made all nations drink' (XIV, 8). The theme of Antichrist is continued in XII–XIV from the previous section: now the false prophet appears (Jezebel 'calls herself a prophetess'). Deep Satanic mysteries are hinted at in the Beast's smitten head and his mysterious number, over which the faithful triumph. There are faithful men at Thyatira who 'have not known *the deep things of Satan*, as the saying goes'. The promise to them is authority over the nations, and to shepherd them with a rod of iron, as a potter's vessels are broken, even as Christ received from his Father. He will, moreover, give them the morning star. The vision of XII is placed wholly among the stars, from which Satan and his accomplices are cast down, while the faithful keep their places, through the victory of the Man Child, him 'who is to shepherd all the nations with a rod of iron' and is therefore caught up into his Father's throne (XII, 5).

The section of the vials, one might think, can have little in common with the fifth message, for it is almost wholly taken up with two things—a repetitive series of plagues, and a huge expansion of the theme of the wicked 'woman', continued from the previous section. This is true enough, but it is counterbalanced by one very striking fact. The climax of action in the vials is the gathering of the Armageddon-hosts 'for the battle of the great day of God Almighty'. The words which we have just transcribed are fol-

186

lowed by the astonishing parenthesis: 'Lo, I come as a thief. Blessed is he that watches and keeps his garments, that he walk not naked and his shame be not seen.' It is as though the Christ of the Seven Messages had suddenly torn aside the veil of apocalyptic images to speak in his own voice. The Christ of the seven messages —but of which message among the seven? The fifth: 'If then thou watch not, I will come as a thief, and thou shalt not know what hour I will come upon thee. But thou hast a few souls in Sardis, who have not defiled their garments. . . .'

The sixth message continues the theme of Advent: 'I come quickly' it says. The sixth section (XIX–XXI, 8) is, of course, the Advent itself. It begins with the final 'opening' of the whole vision, when the new David, the warrior Messiah, called Faithful and True, breaks through the opened skies; and it ends with the descent of New Jerusalem. The sixth message begins: 'Thus saith the holy, the true, that hath the key of David, that opens and none can shut . . . I have set before thee an open door.' And thus it ends: 'I will write on him the Name of my God and the name of the city of my God, the New Jerusalem, which descends out of heaven from my God, and my own new Name.' The new Name of Christ is also a theme of XIX, as we will shew in its place.

There are seven messages in II–III, but the Apocalypse as a whole is a six days' work. Thus there is no complete section to correspond with the seventh message. The seventh is the Sabbath, and the Sabbath of the whole work must be found in what follows, when the sixth day's work is done. The seventh message, in fact, strikes the note which is echoed by the concluding words of the book, XXII, 6–7, 10–21. In the message Christ is 'the Amen, the witness faithful and true, the beginning of the creation-work of God'. In XXII he testifies that the words are 'faithful and true', and he is himself 'the A and Ω, the first and last, the beginning and the end . . . he that witnesses these things'. A sharp contrast of severity and tenderness side by side is equally prominent in both texts: and we should further compare the two passages which so strangely equate the advent-hope with the presence of Christ in the eucharist of the ecclesia:

'Behold, I stand at the door and knock. If any hear my voice and open the door, I will come in to him and sup with him, and he

187

with me. He that overcometh, I will grant him to sit with me in my seat, as I overcame, and sat with my Father in his seat.' 'Behold, I come quickly, and my reward is with me, to pay every man as his work is. . . . I am the root and child of David, the bright and morning star. And the Spirit and the Bride say, "Come," and let the hearer say, "Come," and let the thirsty come; let him that will take living water free.'

The whole system of comparisons which we have sketched cannot be put aside as fortuitous. The two conclusions in I–III and I–XXII may match simply because they are conclusions, but the other parallels are not to be explained in any such simple way. Either, we said, St John formed the Messages on the Sections, or *vice versa*. In fact he must have formed the sections on the messages. For the verse 'I come as a thief' breaks into the fifth section from its home in the fifth message: we cannot plausibly invert the relationship. And throughout the Apocalypse we find St John making formal elaborations in what follows upon what has preceded. The messages themselves are an example, for they are built up, as everyone knows, by taking titles of Christ out of the preceding Candlestick-vision, and then drawing spiritual divinations out of the titles, such as the conditions of the several churches demand.

But now, if the sections are formed upon the messages, how is it that the messages supply, in order, just what the sections seem to require? For the sections have also to conform to the themes of

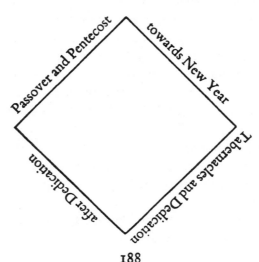

188

the calendar-feasts. May it be that the messages themselves follow the rhythm of the calendar-feasts? May St John have had the rhythm in his head already, as he wrote the messages?

The calendar-system of the Apocalypse as a whole we have seen to be based upon the four quarters, which we may represent by the diagram of a simple square[1] (see opposite page): Since the seven messages start from Dedication (the candlestick), we may represent their suggested relation to the calendar like this:

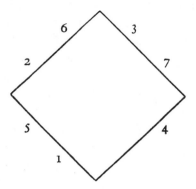

1 and 5 will run forward from Dedication, 2 and 6 will be concerned with the paschal season, 3 and 7 will look towards New Year, and 4 will run from New Year through Tabernacles. Let us see whether the contents of the messages appear to bear out such an arrangement.

1 and 5, we are amazed to observe from the start, are a consciously arranged pair, anyhow. 'He that holds the seven stars in his right hand, that walks among the seven golden candlesticks' addresses the Ephesians: 'He that hath the seven Spirits of God and the seven stars' addresses the Sardians: and we know that 'Seven Spirits of God' is an alternative interpretation of Zechariah's 'Seven candles'; cf. 'Seven candles of fire . . . which are the Seven Spirits of God' (IV, 5). Thus both messages begin from the seven candles which are the principal emblem of the Dedication. The first message continues to play with the image of the candlestick ('I will remove thy candlestick except thou repent'). The fifth, on the other hand, is devoted to the development of the image of

1 We set the square cornerwise, to correspond with the solar cycle. The sun is at his *height* at midsummer, at his *depth* at midwinter.

189

death, with its opposites life and wakefulness, or the book of life. Now the season after Dedication is winter, which is constantly to St John the season of death.

2 and 6 are even more closely paired than 1 and 5: for they are paired in the body of the messages as well as in the titles. The titles of 2 and 6 are formed upon the self-description of Christ in the Candlestick-vision. 'I am the first and the last, the Living that was dead, and lo, am alive for ever and ever, and have the keys of death and hell.' The message to Smyrna paraphrases the first part of this self-description, 'the first and the last, who was dead and lived,' the message to Philadelphia the second part, 'the holy, the true, that hath the key of David.' The shadow of the key is over the Smyrnaeans too: 'Lo, the Accuser is about to cast some of you into prison.' The accuser is Satan, but he speaks through the lips of the Jewish delator: 'I know the slander of self-styled Jews who are none, but a synagogue of Satan.' The message to Philadelphia takes up the very phrase: 'They of the synagogue of Satan, who say they are Jews and are none, but do lie—I will make them come and worship before thy feet.' To the Smyrneans it is said, 'Be faithful to death, and I will give thee the crown of life', and to the Philadelphians, 'Hold what thou hast, that none may take thy crown.'[1] So much for the parallel between the two messages. But now, what have they to do in particular with the paschal season? They fasten on the very feature of the Candlestick-vision in which Christ's Easter-triumph is most clearly displayed, 'the Living who was dead and lo, is alive for ever, and holds the keys of death and hell.'

The third and seventh messages are not so close a pair, because the seventh is occupied with its own function of being seventh, of presenting Christ as the Amen who comes with the sabbath feast. There is a connexion, however. The message to Pergamus fastens on the phrase in the Candlestick-vision, 'Out of his mouth a sharp two-edged sword proceeding.' 'Thus saith he who hath the sharp

---

[1] The fresh turn of phrase is determined by the image of 'the key-bearer of the house of David' (Isa. XXII, 22). In that passage the unworthy Shebna loses his crown ($\sigma\tau\acute{\epsilon}\phi\alpha\nu\sigma\varsigma$) to the faithful Eliakim, and Eliakim is fixed in a sure place: cf. the promise to the faithful Philadelphian: 'I will make him a pillar in the house of my God, and he shall go forth no more.'

two-edged sword. . . . Thou hast some who hold the teaching of Balaam . . . to eat idolatrous meat. . . . I will make war on them with the sword of my mouth. . . . To him that overcomes I will give of the hidden manna.' In the message to Laodicea we read: 'Because thou art luke-warm . . . I will spue thee out of my mouth. . . . If any open the door, I will come in to him and sup with him, and he with me.' Although there is no direct relation between the titles of Christ in the two messages, there is a close relation between the title of the Laodicean message and a phrase in the body of the Pergamene. 'Antipas, my faithful witness' is worthy to prefigure Christ's self-description, 'the witness faithful and true.' Now what of the relation of these messages to the quarter which runs towards New Year? The New Year trumpet represents, as we have seen, two things: the throne of God's kingdom, and the last judgement. In the message to Pergamus St John starts with that attribute of Christ in the Candlestick-vision which above all displays the Judge, the Sword of the Lips; this alludes without doubt to Isaiah XI, where it is said of him on whom the Seven Spirits of the Lord rest that he is a judge, 'smiting the earth with the rod of his mouth, and with the breath of his lips slaying the wicked.' So much for judgement: the message then proceeds direct to the throne of kingdom: 'I know where thou dwellest, where Satan's throne is.' It is the Satanic judge there enthroned who kills Antipas the faithful martyr by the breath of *his* lips. The message to Laodicea is full of the threat of immediate judgement, and it concludes: 'He that overcomes shall receive from me to sit with me in my throne.' But the image of the blessed feast (III, 20) looks beyond New Year to Tabernacles, and suitably enough. For the message to Laodicea, being the seventh and last, looks forward to the consummation in the seventh month; then the greatest feast of the year is celebrated at the full of the 'sabbath' (seventh) moon of the year.

There remains only the fourth message, which has no pair. What has this to do with the Tabernacles-season? It is engrossed by the image of the woman. Has that image anything particularly to do with the season? We refer the reader back to our examination of the connexion between the season and the woman in Apocalypse XII (p. 139 above). We shall have more to say about it presently.

191

So far, then, the evidence suggests the following conclusion. In the Messages St John was, as it were, proceeding straight round the four sides of a square, representing the four quarters of the year: and by this procedure he in fact fitted the seven messages to become the models for the six sections of his whole work *plus* its conclusion, whether or no he had it in mind so to use them when he was composing them.

We will now call attention to a curious feature of the messages which shows how consciously St John went over a four-piece series and then began to repeat it. The titles of the messages are, as we have seen, derived from the Candlestick-vision out of which the messages spring. And they are not taken haphazard. In the first four messages St John covers the whole Candlestick-vision, proceeding in order through it, *backwards*: in the last three he begins to go over the same steps again in the same order as before. He does not take the whole vision; he selects, but the freedom of his selection is limited by this condition: what he takes, he takes in order.

The last sentence of the Candlestick-vision (1, 20) is Christ's own exposition of the candlesticks and stars, and it is from this that the first message proceeds: 'He that holds the seven stars in his right hand, that walks in the midst of the seven candlesticks of gold.' The second message goes back to Christ's self-description (1, 17–18,) 'The first and the last, the living that was dead,' etc. The third goes back to 1, 16, the sword proceeding from the mouth, and the fourth to 13–15: 'Son of Man' (in the message, 'Son of God') . . . 'his eyes as flame of fire, and his feet like bronze-hued incense.' Going back behind 'Son of Man' in 13*b* St John meets the seven golden candlesticks once more in 13*a*, and so rejoins his starting-point: the title of the fifth message becomes a second version of the title of the first, and in the sixth, as we have seen, he proceeds to make a fresh use of the passage from which he had drawn the title of the second.

What do these facts prove? They prove that St John chose to stride backwards across the Candlestick-vision in four steps, and then to go over the same ground: and this in spite of the fact that the vision abounds in attributes of Christ, and could easily have furnished him with separate texts for all the seven titles he re-

192

quired: he could have made seven steps of his backward journey just as easily as four, if he had wished to do so. Why did he make four? Because he was working on the square of the year.

We will now leave the seven messages, and go on to the seven seals. Let us suppose that St John's procedure is the same here. Let the four horsemen go round the four quarters, and the remaining seals run straight on. But the point of departure will be different: in the messages we were starting with the winter quarter: here we start with the spring quarter. So the figure should be this:

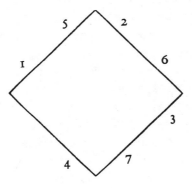

Before we do anything else, let us observe how closely the seals correspond with the equivalent messages, that is to say, with the messages which belong to the same sides of the square. It is as though the square had taken colour from the messages, so that St John finds all the message-images embedded in it when he goes over it again for the seals. We promised to show that the second message stood in a peculiar relation to the seals. The relation is this: the seals follow the messages one by one, starting from the second.

Both messages of the spring quarter spoke of the victor's crown: we need quote only the words to Smyrna, 'Be faithful to death, and I will give thee the crown of life. . . . The conqueror shall not be hurt by the second death.' The first horseman is 'given a crown, and rides forth conquering and to conquer.' The image is the same, but it is completely different in application: this is the spring, when kings go forth to war. The second horseman receives power to take away peace and to make men slaughter each other: and he is given a great sword ($\mu\acute{\alpha}\chi\alpha\iota\rho\alpha$). Compare the former of the messages in the summer quarter: 'That hath the sharp two-edged sabre ($\dot{\rho}o\mu\phi\alpha\acute{\iota}\alpha$). . . . Antipas my witness, my faithful, who was slain among you.' In case we should attach too much importance to the different word used for the weapon in VI, 4, we have the old word $\dot{\rho}o\mu\phi\alpha\acute{\iota}\alpha$ in the summary just below, 'to slay with sabre and hunger,' etc. (VI, 8.)

The third horseman, we must admit, has no correspondence with the fourth message; we need not be ashamed of the admission, for we shall presently see that the material he receives from another source completely engrosses him. We may notice that the two first horsemen derived from the corresponding messages the emblems which they were said to be *given*: the crown, the sword. This horseman derives nothing from the corresponding message: and he is *given* no emblem. He appears already carrying the balances, as the first rider appeared carrying the bow. Whatever the bearings of this may be, with the fourth horseman we return to a message-association, and perhaps the most striking of all. The message involved is the fifth, as it ought to be.

No one can fail to be moved by the sudden change of style in the last horseman. He neither bears nor receives any emblem: no riddle is presented to us, and all the preceding riddles seem only to be there so as to throw into relief the terrible directness of 'He that sat thereon, his name was Death'. St John derives his inspiration from the fifth message, which is wholly made up of a play upon the two words 'name' and 'death'. 'Thou hast a *name* for being *alive,* and thou art *dead.* Awake, and strengthen the rest that was about to *die.* . . . If thou wake not, I come as a thief. . . . But thou hast a few *names* in Sardis who have not defiled their garments: they shall walk with me in white, for they are worthy. He that overcometh . . . I will not blot his *name* from the book of *life,* but confess his *name* before my Father.' 'Thou hast a name for being alive, and art dead'—'His *name* is death.' The image in both applications alludes to the death of winter, but the applications are completely different. The message speaks of spiritual death, which is the same thing as spiritual slumber: the seal speaks of the (black) death, deadly pestilence.

In the fifth seal we are back at the spring quarter again. As in the former of the spring messages, those who are faithful unto death

194

are in prison for a short time (a little while, ten days) assured of ultimate deliverance and reward (the crown of life, the white stole of immortal being). The prisons are in different places, in Smyrna, under the heavenly altar ('the treasury of souls'). He that has the keys of Death and Hell is master of both. Since it is a spring vision, we must set the martyr-souls on the background of Christ's own Easter Sepulchre.

The sixth seal has no special relation either to the summer messages or to the second horseman, but it does justice clearly enough to the summer quarter, which is the approach to the trump of judgement: the heaven departs as a scroll, and mankind trembles before the coming day of wrath. With the seventh seal the new-year trumpets are manifested.

We have been arguing for the relation of the four horsemen to the four quarters from their correspondence with the messages. Such an order of argument suits our exposition, for we wish to follow St John's working mind forward from the beginning. But considered on its merits, it is preposterous, it puts the cart before the horse. For the relation of the four horsemen to the four quarters is far more evident in itself than any correspondence to the quarters which we can find in the messages.

The four horses of several colours in Zechariah I are closely parallel to the four chariot-teams of several colours in Zechariah VI. The chariots are explicitly said to signify the four winds of heaven: the chariots and the horsemen have the same function, to patrol the earth. The reader may have formed the opinion by now that St John was sensitive to parallels, and that such as strike us were not likely to be lost on him. If he used the four horsemen in VI it is probable that he was thinking of the four winds which blow from the four quarters, especially as the vision of sealing in Apocalypse VII (a) carefully balances the visions of unsealing in VI, and (b) opens with the image of the four winds restrained at the four corners of the earth.

But what, it may be asked, have the four quarters of the heaven from which the winds blow to do with the four quarters of the year? To the ancient mind there would not be a moment's hesitation. The four quarters of the year are made by the sun's journey round the circle of twelve zodiacal signs, three to each quarter.

195

The four quarters of the year *are* the four sides of the heaven, from which the winds blow.

But, you may ask, if so, why does St John talk about the four winds, rather than (let us say) the middle signs of the four heavenly quarters, since he is not writing of the winds but of the seasons? If he had had to choose, perhaps St John would have agreed with you, but he did not have to choose: he did both. Each of the horsemen (winds) sets forth at the cry of one of the four cherubim: and the four cherubim are the middle signs of the four quarters.

St John takes the list of the cherub-faces from Ezekiel, but he alters the place of the man-face. Ezekiel has man, lion, bull, eagle, St John lion, bull, man, eagle. Why should he make the alteration? It is the least change he could make if he was to bring Ezekiel's list into conformity with astronomical fact; and even so, it involves going backwards instead of forwards round the ecliptic. The Lion is the middle of the summer quarter, the Bull of the spring, the Man with the Pitcher of winter. The constellation of the Eagle is not a zodiacal sign, but from St John's place of observation it rose together with the Scorpion, and the Scorpion is the middle sign of the autumn quarter. The usual way of counting would be forward from the spring, Bull, Lion, Eagle (= Scorpion), Man (Aquarius). St John does not tell us in what order the Cherubim cry when the first four seals are opened. But as he is in fact going through the quarters forwards from spring in the horsemen, the order will be this.[1]

Let us see what light the astrology casts on the imagery of the four horsemen. Why does the first carry a bow? The bow of Orion, the giant archer of the sky, is right against the breast of the Bull. In the second horseman we have nothing left to explain, but at least we may observe the natural congruity between the Lion and the sword of the mouth, especially to a Hebrew. The lion is pre-eminently the beast which slays with the mouth: the sorcerers

---

[1] By giving the cherubim one order in the introductory vision (IV–V) and the reverse order in the elaboration (VI) St John proceeds just as he did in I and II–III, where, having given the attributes of Christ in one order, he founds the titles of the Messages on them in the reverse order. There is something of the same kind in VIII–IX; c.f. note on p. 200 below. C.f. also X, 2–3 (book, voice, thunders) and 4–11 (thunders, voice, book).

prayed against in the psalms are called lions, and have swords in their lips, because their breath kills: the sword, in Biblical speech, has a 'mouth' and 'devours': in that section of the whole Apocalypse which belongs to the lion's quarter, the culmination of judgement is found in monsters with lions' heads, whose breath slays, for it is fire, smoke and brimstone (IX, 17–18).

The third horseman carries a balance in his right hand. Now the constellation of the Balances is in the quarter of the Scorpion (= Eagle), and it is to his right, always supposing that the sign is facing us out of the sky. The Balances are the sign which presides over the feast of Tabernacles, both according to the conventional reckoning and according to astronomical fact in St John's day. Now Tabernacles was the feast of the ingathering of all fruits. They are weighed in the balances, and the corn is found short— not the wine or oil. Why the corn only? We are, I believe, in a position now to give a firm answer to this venerable problem. In VI all the quarters of the year, including the autumn quarter, are being viewed from the point of view of the spring quarter. It is a Jewish saying, recorded in the Mishnah-Tractate Rosh-ha-Shanah, that at Passover we are judged through corn, at Pentecost through fruits of the tree, and personally at New Year, when all the living file like soldiers before the seat of God's judgement. So in the third seal we see an ingathering at autumn time at which the *corn* is found to be short, because it was damaged at the critical season for corn, the very beginning of harvest (Passover). Presently, when Pentecost has passed, we shall see judgement by the fruits of the tree (VII, 1, 3, VIII, 7).

The fourth horseman owes nothing to astrology in particular. Death is winter, and winter is death, and 'the death' is the mortal pestilence. The fifth seal is only astrological in so far as the picture of sacrificial slaughter which it presents may remind us that the two principal altar-victims, the ram or lamb and the bull, are the first and second signs of the spring quarter. St John does not pay any special attention to the bull, but the Ram or Lamb ($\check{\alpha}\rho\nu\iota\sigma\nu$) presides over the paschal month, and is the standing image for Christ as Paschal Victim. The martyrs are paschal lambs too, participating in his sacrifice. The sixth seal derives nothing from the stars of its own quarter in particular: the stars in general fall earth-

197

wards when this seal is broken, the sun is darkened and the moon turned to blood. We have here, perhaps, a general summing-up of stellar judgements in the last vision of the unbroken series (the seventh seal being nothing but the beginning of something else).

We will, for the present, neglect the visions intermediary between the seals and trumpets (VII). Some of the most interesting astrological matter is to be found in them, but we are not yet in a position to deal with it. From the seven seals, then, we proceed direct to the seven trumpets. Here we are immediately met by a difficulty. The trumpets actually sound for New Year's Day, that is, at the very corner of the square, at the point where the summer side joins the autumn side. If the visions of the trumpets are to go on from the Trumpet of New Year, as the visions of the candlestick go on from the candlestick of Dedication or those of the Seal-breaking Lamb from the Lamb of Passover, they will begin with the autumn quarter. But if they do so, they will not, it would seem, conform to their purpose in the whole scheme, which is to fill the midsummer quarter and work *towards* the New Year's trumpet. Never mind: may not the six trumpets proceed from the New Year trumpet and make a circuit of the square, so as to end up just short of the New Year? So the seventh trumpet shall be the actual New Year's Feast, and the six will have acted as a preparation for it.

We begin therefore with the autumn quarter. Because the whole section of the trumpets represents the creation-day on which land, sea and waters were made, St John enriches the figure of the square with a new symbolism: its sides are to represent the four elements of the world. The heavenly bodies will naturally be on one of the upper sides, earth and sea at the bottom:

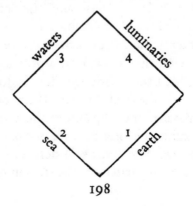

198

It is to be noted that the summer quarter has already been dedicated to the luminaries by the sixth seal, in which we saw the quaking of the sky, stars falling, sun blackened, and moon turned to blood; all this in the summer quarter. The autumn quarter has also been marked out as earth by the third seal. Of the fruits of the earth, we there saw the corn alone smitten, not the trees: but when the first angel blows his trumpet, destruction falls on earth, trees and pasture. The second angel corrupts the sea, the third the waters; the fourth darkens sun, moon, and stars.

As we leave the fourth vision for the fifth, a flying eagle appears in mid-heaven,[1] just to remind us that the scheme of the four cherubim has not fallen quite out of sight: we are re-entering the eagle's quarter (autumn, the earth). The eagle, we remember, is an equivalent for the scorpion, forced on St John by Ezekiel's list. St John has a chance to do the scorpion justice here, in spite of Ezekiel; for when the locusts of the fifth trumpet-plague appear, they turn out not to be locusts really at all, but scorpions. 'There was given them power as the scorpions of earth have power. They were bidden not (as locusts would) to hurt the grass of the earth, or any green, or any tree, but only (as scorpions do) the men that have not the seal of God in their foreheads. . . . Their torment is as the torment of a scorpion striking a man. . . . They have tails like scorpions, with stings, and in their tails is their power to hurt' (and not in any of the impressive locust-like features which St John also assigns to them).

The falling star who lets loose this plague falls, as he ought, upon the *earth*, which belongs to the eagle's quarter according to the arrangement of the four previous trumpets. The plague must be seen as properly belonging to earth and eagle: and yet at the same time St John takes pains to make it an epitome of all the four previous plagues on the four quarters. It is the plague of earth, so the star falls upon the earth; and the plague effects '*not* grass, or any green, or any tree'. (The plague of the first trumpet struck earth, trees, and green grass.) It is the plague of the sea, for the

---

[1] St John is in difficulties; the eagle's quarter is the earth, but the eagle must fly in heaven, beneath the stars. So he is introduced as an appendix to the sign of the stars, giving warning of what will follow from the moment when the next plague swoops down on earth.

falling star has a key to open the pit of the *abyss*, which is an equivalent for *sea*. (As we have seen, 'the Beast from the Abyss,' 'the Beast from the Sea' are alternatives.) It is the plague of the waters, for it was a falling star which smote the waters before, and it is a falling star that opens the abyss now. It is the plague of the luminaries, for by the smoke of the abyss the sun and air are darkened.

St John has certainly taken great pains to make the fifth plague a summary of the four preceding it: and yet the third and fourth of them are no more than touched: primarily it is a plague upon *earth* by means of the demons of the *abyss* (equivalent for sea). We need not be surprised, then, if St John considers this plague to have covered both earth and sea, both autumn and winter. It is firmly fixed to autumn by the scorpion-features, almost as firmly to winter by the naming of the demon-king, 'the Angel of the Abyss, his name in Hebrew Abaddon, and in Greek hath he the name of Destruction.' Compare the horseman of the winter quarter: 'His name is Death, and Hades (= the Abyss) accompanies him.' Autumn and winter have been covered. And so, when the sixth trumpet sounds, it is at the spring quarter, at rivers and wells, that we find ourselves, loosing 'the four angels bound at the great river, the Euphrates'. This is the spring, the season 'when kings go forth to war': and the conquering cavalry rides out from behind the river, as the Assyrians and Chaldeans had done, as the Parthians were expected to do, as the white-horsed rider did at the first seal of St John's vision.

St John is careful to make this plague also an epitome of all its five predecessors, but with his usual fertility of wit, he finds a new way of contriving it. It is a voice from the (four) corners of the incense-altar which bids the sixth trumpet-angel loose the four angels at Euphrates. The liturgy at the incense-altar had set the whole trumpet-series in motion, and we have now reached the climax of it; so it is natural that the incense-altar should be heard of again. The elements of the incense-liturgy were incense (VIII, 3), smoke (4), and fire (5). The plagues of the trumpets fall in fire, smoke, and—not incense,[1] naturally, for what is incense in the

---

[1] Incense, smoke, fire in the introductory vision, fire, smoke (incense) in the elaboration. For this reversal of order see note on p. 196 above.

200

liturgy of peace will be brimstone in the sacrifice of wrath. The first three plagues are fire: fire to burn up earth and vegetation, a mountain of fire to corrupt the sea, a blazing comet to bewitch the waters. Then two plagues of smoke: the luminaries are darkened; the smoke of the pit darkens sun and air, and spreads in locusts over the earth. Last the plague of brimstone: the cavalry of the sixth trumpet shoot brimstone out of their mouths, but with it fire and smoke too, so that they carry with their own distinctive plague an epitome of the others. 'They have breastplates fiery, hyacinthine, and sulphurous: and the heads of the horses as the heads of lions, and out of their mouths proceed fire, and smoke, and sulphur; and by these three plagues the third of men were killed, by the fire, smoke and brimstone proceeding from their mouths.' (Fiery, hyacinthine, sulphurous'—'fire, smoke, and sulphur.' Why *hyacinthine* for *smoky*? We shall be able to answer this question when we have seen the position of the hyacinth in St John's list of precious stones. To let the cat out of the bag—the twelve stones are assigned to the twelve constellations, and the hyacinth to Scorpio. The plague of smoke explicitly so described is the plague of locust-scorpions under the scorpion-sign. No doubt St John regarded the stone he called jacinth as more or less of a smoke-blue.) The epitome of all trumpet-plagues in the sixth trumpet is modelled on the epitome of all horsemen-plagues in the last horseman: 'To them' (Death and Hades) 'was given power over the fourth part of earth, to kill with sword and famine and the death, and by the wild beasts of earth.'

The glorious angel who succeeds the sixth trumpet-plague comes from the next side of the square, where the sun and stars belong. He descends from the sky, clothed with cloud, crowned with the rainbow, his face as the sun, and he takes hold of all the elements: since he faces us, his right foot is in the *sea*, and his left upon the *earth*. He lifts his hand to heaven, and attests the maker of all three, the ever-living God. The *waters* have to be omitted, because they conflict with the diagrammatic symbolism of the vision. The top of the cornerwise square is being treated as heaven, the bottom as earth-and-sea. What business have the waters up there in the sky, on a level with sun, moon and stars? Perhaps they are to be seen in the *cloud* wherewith the *sun*faced angel is shrouded.

201

The next time an angel invokes the Creator, it is as maker of heaven, earth, sea *and the fountains of waters* (XIV, 7).

The glorious angel, like the two last trumpet-angels, makes an epitome of the quarters, and yet like them, he belongs specially to one place; he belongs to the sky and the sun. Therefore he belongs to the Lion's quarter, and therefore with the Lion's voice he speaks (X, 3). He carries in his hand a scroll—the last time we heard the word was in the summer vision of the sixth seal, when the sky departed like a rolled-up scroll. He stands in the summer quarter, before the great trumpet of New Year, and his message is a prediction of what the trumpet will bring when it sounds.

The oracle of the reed is in one piece with the visions of the glorious angel, and it continues the same form of representation, that in which the upper half of the square (as heaven) is set over against the lower half (as earth and sea). St John, armed with a measuring-rod, is called upon to draw the horizontal line of division. Beneath it will lie the region to be given over to the tyranny of Antichrist: above it 'the temple and the altar'. The spring quarter has been identified as the place of the altar, ever since we saw the souls of the martyrs there in the fifth seal: it is the place of the sacrificial Lamb. The temple of the sky is naturally to be found in the other half of the top of the square—the region of the summer and the stars. The sanctuary being thus measured off, Christ's two witnesses prophesy under supernatural protection—they are the two candlesticks of the holy place. But at length the Beast arising from the abyss puts out the candle of worship for 'a time, times and a half'—the candles lie dead for half a week on the street of the city.

The Beast arises from the abyss. We saw how, in the fifth trumpet, 'abyss' was made to cover earth and sea, that is, the whole bottom half of the square. So it is symbolically perfect, when St John opposes to the two witnesses for temple and altar the Beast from the abyss alone. He kills them, and their bodies fall upon the street of the wicked city beneath the horizontal line. But after the half-week a heavenly voice summons them, and they go up again into heaven. An earthquake shakes the city of earth, and her inhabitants fear and give glory to the God of heaven.

The trumpet sounds and St John's mind rises into heaven in the wake of the witnesses: he sees and hears the New Year hymnody.

A vision of the temple (not the altar) carries him to the side of the summer quarter, over against the place of the trumpet: the place of the trumpet which is also the place of the heavenly woman. For the understanding of the astrology here we must pause and consider some astrological facts. The conventional arrangement of the zodiacal signs places three in each quarter, with the result that the points of transition from one quarter to the next—the solstices and equinoxes, represented in our figure by the corners of the square— are under no sign, but at the point of division between one sign and another. So the New Year trumpet ought to sound when the Sun leaves Virgo to enter Libra. But the conventional arrangement had been mapped out about 400 B.C., and by St John's time the shift called 'the procession of the equinoxes' had (so to speak) shifted all the signs a fifth of a place to the right relatively to the sun's circuit. At the autumnal equinox the sun was still six days short of passing out of Virgo into Libra, by the end of the first century A.D. We may conveniently represent the astrological facts of St John's time by the following diagram.

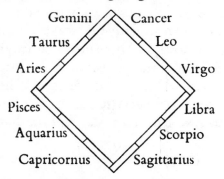

We need not be surprised, then, to observe that the blowing of the New Year trumpet discloses the sign of the Virgin, a sign which properly belongs to the summer quarter. Summer being the quarter of luminaries, she is clothed with the sun, established on the moon, and crowned with the twelve stars.

If St. John had no symbolical interest in doing otherwise, he might well have been content to follow the conventional astrology, and treat the equinox as the beginning of Libra. But in fact, as we have seen, he is deeply interested in the connexion between New Year and the woman's child-bearing: and so he prefers the

203

actual astrology to the conventional astrology, and places New Year in Virgo.

The drama of the woman and the dragon in XII partly turns, it would seem, on the ambiguous position of the woman at the hinge between 'heaven' and 'earth'. Her proper place is heaven (summer): yet she belongs to earth and autumn too. The vision is going to describe how the dragon falls from heaven upon the earth and sea. (XII, 12.) This reminds us of the glorious angel in X who descended from heaven on earth and sea. It is natural to suppose that we are going to have another vision in which the whole square is used at once, as a setting for an action embracing heaven and earth.

The woman's position, anyhow, is known: she is the last sign of the summer quarter. Her Son, when he is born, must be the messianic Lion, just above her: by the equivalence established in V, the Lion is no other than the Lamb. The dragon, set over against her in the heavens, will be in the spring quarter, the region of waters. We have seen Euphrates as the place from which the worst demons come (IX, 13 ff.): the Dragon is Leviathan, the Nile-monster, the type of Pharaoh, and he is especially this in XII, where the woman's escape into the wilderness is so manifestly the escape of Israel from Egypt, after the man-child (Moses) had been providentially snatched out of the jaws of persecution to the protection of the throne. Moreover Satan as accuser ($\delta\iota\acute{\alpha}\beta o\lambda o s$) is firmly associated with the spring quarter by the second and sixth Messages[1] (II, 9, III, 9). We can without more ado draw the square which sets the stage for the drama in XII–XIII.

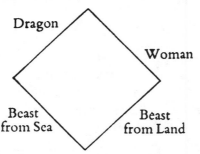

[1] The servants of Satan appear in these Messages as falsely messianic: they say they are Judah, but are not: they are a synagogue of Satan. Now Satan himself appears as a parody of Judah himself, i.e. of Christ, the Lamb. The seven heads and ten horns are a distortion of the seven horns and seven eyes. The parody of the Lamb is inherited by the other two Beasts, but it starts in the Dragon.

The Dragon attacks: the messianic child is caught up into the Throne, and the woman escapes into the wilderness, which is, of course, on *earth*. The angels (stars) of the summer quarter take up the battle against the Dragon, and he falls on the earth and sea. Moving up through the earth against the woman, he casts a river after her, which reminds us that he is native to the region of rivers. But the earth rescues the woman by swallowing the river. It is the region of earth, it is also the quarter of the eagle through which he crawls: the eagle's wings are given to the woman, and she makes good her escape. Baffled, the Dragon turns back to the verge of the *sea*, whence the first Beast emerges. He is presently supported by the second Beast who rises out of the *earth*.

Since the astrological character of the Woman and Dragon is so much emphasized by St John, it seems reasonable to look for astral features in the detail of the vision. Up behind the middle sign of the spring quarter the constellation of the Great River (Eridanus) lies, and just to one side of Eridanus is Cetus, the water-monster, his head turned upward against Aries, that is, against Christ, the Paschal Lamb. It is, in fact, not the woman but her Son for whom Leviathan lies in wait. You may object that Christ as woman's Son must be no Lamb, but the Lion who adjoins the woman. St John has forestalled this objection by the unforgettable and emphatic equation of the Lion and the Lamb in v, 5–6.

We will next observe that at the Dragon's fall the equivalent name 'Serpent' is introduced for him, and that this name is twice used in the story of the Dragon's pursuit of the woman. The constellation of the Serpent trails along that part of the ecliptic which makes up 'earth', the autumn quarter. The tip of his tail touches Sagittarius, his great glittering head is uplifted over Libra as though to strike at the woman. In vain, for the Eagle who soars over the Serpent's tail, and is the snake's hereditary foe, gives the woman his wings, to make good her escape.

The visions of XIII have not the same astral character as XII and we will not decode them by poring over the celestial globe. But we have to remark that the great and blasphemous mystery of the first Beast, his head smitten to death and the death-stroke healed, is in agreement with his emergence from the sea, the quarter of winter and of death. He is, in fact, both dead and damned, and those who worship him take death upon themselves. We have nothing to remark about the other Beast, the False Prophet, except that the only other false prophet actually called prophet by St John is the prophetess Jezebel, who also belongs to the autumn quarter.

The visions we have just been examining cannot be regarded as a procession through the calendar. Perhaps because they represent the demonic counter-attack, they go backwards round the square, against the direction of the sun. First we see the Virgin (summer), then the Dragon (spring), then the first Beast (winter), then the second (autumn). But the backwards working does not prevent the individual positions of the figures from being seasonally appropriate. The appearance of the woman, as we know, marks theNew Year trumpet: she escapes into 'earth' (the beginning of the autumn quarter) to find her 'tabernacles in the wilderness' (Feast of Tabernacles on the fifteenth of the seventh month). Leviathan is manifested in the region of Passover, attacking the Lamb, because the Pharaoh's attack on the male children belongs to the story of the paschal deliverance. The two Beasts are disposed on either side of the bottom corner which represents Dedication, for the Feast of Dedication celebrated both the setting up of the Abomination of Desolation, and the supplanting of it by a newly purified temple.

The Kingdom of Antichrist, according to the measuring-vision (XI, 1–13), conquers the outer court only, the downward-pointing triangle in the square: even for the 'time, times and a half' of Antichrist's tyranny, the upward and heavenly part of the mystical Zion is inviolable: here is the 'tabernacle' in which their spirits dwell, whose bodies he afflicts on earth. At the cleansing and rededication of the temple, the whole square top of Mount Zion is hallowed anew and possessed by the saints. So, after the visions of the Beasts, St John hastens to show us the four-square spiritual temple of God's elect, the twelve tribes of twelve thousand each, corresponding to the twelve zodiacal signs, embracing the whole circuit of the square Zion. The Lamb with his own tribe of Judah stands in the place of the Lamb, the other tribes each in their own places: but all equally bear the seal of the divine Name, and all equally stand upon Mount Zion.

The vision of the Lamb and the 144 thousands embraces the whole square, but it is centred in the Lamb, and therefore in the spring quarter, and in heaven. It sets the heavenly kingdom over against the earthly kingdom of the Beast, it balances light against darkness. From this point onwards movement begins again to take the direction of the conquering sun. The invasion of darkness took the contrary direction (summer, spring, winter, autumn). We are now to witness reconquest by the forces of light. First of all it is a mere advance of heralds proclaiming war: invasion will follow. The Lamb on Zion having been manifested in the spring, the first angelic herald is seen flying in the summer quarter. The description of the first flying angel, we have said, is carefully modelled upon the description of the flying eagle in VIII, 13. The eagle is an appendix to the fourth trumpet, which plagued sun, moon, and stars; when we see him we have had one round of plagues on the four elements, and he warns us of a far worse series to come with a second round: a plague from earth-and-sea (locusts), a plague from the great river (horsemen), a plague from the stars (Lucifer, the Dragon). The eagle, himself flying 'in mid-heaven', beneath the stars, points forward to these things. His pair, the flying angel of XIV, 6, is also 'in mid-heaven', beneath the stars, and he calls upon those in the next quarter, 'the inhabitants of earth,' to fear God and worship the maker of heaven, earth, sea, and water-springs. His theme is the theme proper to the summer quarter which faces towards the trumpets of New Year: 'Fear God, for the hour of his judgement is come.' Now is the last opportunity of penitence.

The second angel, for the autumn, declares that judgement has fallen: Babylon is overthrown. The theme of achieved judgement is not the only seasonable feature of the episode. No less so is the theme of the vintage, alluded to in the description of Babylon as of one who has made all nations drink the wine-of-wrath of her fornication. The third angel, for the winter quarter which springs out of Dedication, tells of the torment in store for those who adhere to the throne of the Beast, of him, that is, who arose from the winter sea, and fixed his throne between sea and earth. The theme of the vintage runs on from the previous angelic message, just as, in St John's grand architecture, the vintage of Tabernacles runs on in the drink-offering of Dedication. When the vials are poured on earth it will mean that the world is made to drink of the wine of

207

God's wrath; and that is exactly what this angel says: 'He who worships the Beast shall drink of the wine of the wrath of God, prepared unmixed in the cup of his anger.' This means, in fact, that the downward point of the square where the Beast's throne is will open for them in a gulf of fire and brimstone, and the smoke of their gehenna will go up for ever under the over-arching sky where stand the Lamb, his angels and his saints. This is the vindication of the martyrs' suffering, which they endured under the shadow of the throne of the Beast.

A voice from heaven, proclaiming the bliss of the dead who die in the Lord, lifts us from the winter of their martyrdom to the spring of their hope, from earth and sea into the sky. The sign of the winter quarter is the Man with the Water Jar: the hope of the martyrs is the Son of Man who rides the rain-cloud: we must lift our eyes from sea to sky, from winter to spring, if we are to see him come. St John looks up, and he is there, crowned with gold.

There follows a second and even more rapid flight round the four quarters: the voices of proclamation are succeeded by the shadows of action. St John has really only two things to tell of in this movement, not four. In the spring, the Son of Man's harvest of souls, in the autumn, the angelic vintage of wrath. But he contrives to conform to the scheme of the four seasons all the same. In the two previous movements of the Beast-visions, one anti-clockwise (XII–XIII) and one clockwise (XIV, 1–12), a common form may be seen: a series of four, the first being a Christophany, the remaining three of a different quality from it, but uniform with

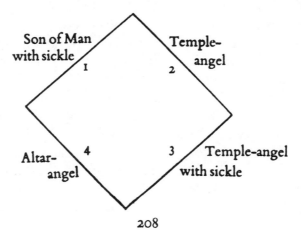

one another. First we had Christ in the womb, and three monsters; then the Lamb on Mt Zion, and three angels. Now we have the Son of Man on clouds, and again three angels. If we write straight round the square, we get the result which the accompanying figure describes. We know that the place of the Lamb is the altar. If the Son of Man appears in the spring quarter, he must be in the place of the Lamb, especially since the Lamb marks Passover, when the corn-harvest begins, and the Son of Man comes to reap. The altar, then, belongs to him, and the temple is at the opposite side. But what business has the angel of the fourth quarter with the altar? It seems as though St John is using a simple vertical division, everything to the one side being 'altar' and everything to the other being 'temple'. If we draw both this vertical division and the customary horizontal division as well, we seem to understand the vision excellently.

The corn-harvest, being in the spring quarter, is heavenly: the spring, and therefore the altar, does the harvesting; the part of the summer (first temple-angel) is limited to telling the harvester his

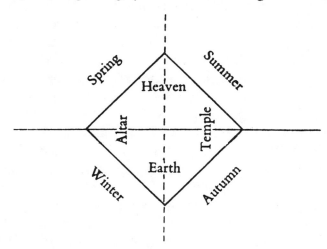

hour. The vintage, being in the autumn quarter, is earthly: the autumn angel, who is therefore a second temple-angel, does the vintaging: the part of the winter (altar angel) is simply to give the signal. The heavenly harvest is of the blessed: the vintage of earth is a vintage of wrath.

St John does not say simply, 'an angel issuing from the altar,'

209

he adds, 'he that has power over fire.' The domain of the altar has to be divided horizontally. The upper part is the Son of Man = the Lamb, the acceptable victim *upon* the altar: the lower part is the altar-fire.

Throughout the Apocalypse fire is uniformly the symbol of judgement. We never see the righteous offered as a holocaust. Even in the incense-offering of VIII, 2–5, the fire is not explicitly mentioned except as that which the offering angel throws back in judgement on the heads of the wicked, after his offering to God has been made. Here too the altar-fire is the symbol of the holocaust of the wicked. The third flying angel said that to drink the wine of God's wrath was to be tormented with fire: now the angel who performs the ghastly vintaging takes his signal from the angel of fire; and he is himself the third of his company.

The beginning of XV is modelled on the beginning of VIII. In VIII we had first the mention of the trumpet-angels, who must be found in the region of angels, stars and summer: then we moved back to the spring-quarter and the altar of slaughter: thence back into summer again for the incense-offering in the heavenly place, and so on into earth and autumn and right round the square, in the successive plagues on the elements. XV begins with the mention of the seven vial-angels, who must be found in the region of the summer: then moves back into the spring, to contemplate the levitical choir of saints standing by the altar (2–4): then forward again into the summer and the temple for the visit of the glory-cloud (5–8): and thence on round the square in the successive plagues (XVI). When we were examining XIV, 14–20 we were confronted with a square divided by a vertical line into temple and altar, and by a horizontal line into heaven and earth. The horizontal line turned out to be the firmer: the two heavenly quarters were paired in the heavenly harvest, the two earthly in the earthly harvest. In XV it is the vertical line which is firmer. The whole side of the altar stands for the salvation of the saints, the whole side of the temple for the angels' vengeance. On the side of the altar there is upward movement, on the side of the temple movement downwards. On the one side we begin with the 'sea' of glass below, filled with fiery liquid: we lift our eyes to behold the saints as risen from the ordeal of their baptism, singing hymns of praise.

210

On the other side we begin with the temple and the angels: we see them receive bowls of fiery wrath to pour down upon the earth below.

St John has varied his image. The martyrs will be standing in their accustomed place, which is also the place of the Lamb. If St John had put the altar-fire in the quarter beneath them, where it stands in xIV, 18, he would have produced the unacceptable image of the saints as a holocaust, burning in the flames which are the proper punishment of the wicked. It is, on the contrary, St John's custom to contrast the once-for-all slaughter of the blood-offering with the slow burning of the holocaust. The martyrs triumph in a moment, and put death behind them: the wicked are a holocaust which burns and burns, the smoke of their torment goes up for ever, they have rest neither day nor night. St John avoids the picture of the saints as a holocaust, by transforming the altar-fire into the sea of glass, for this occasion filled with fire. The martyrs have put their fiery baptism behind them. The image of the 'sea' of glass agrees perfectly with the usual association between the winter quarter and the sea.

The series of seven vials, which we have now to consider, presents us with few novelties, so closely is it modelled upon the series of trumpets. Since it goes forward from Dedication, we might expect it to begin with the winter quarter. But Dedication is an octave dated from Chislev 25, a date five days within the autumn quarter. So it is possible to begin a Dedication-and-onwards series with autumn, and St John will prefer to do so, for then he can keep the vials in exact correspondence with the trumpets.

The four elements, earth, sea, waters and luminaries, are smitten once more in turn. We notice that the smiting of the *waters* in the spring quarter is made to recall the blood of the martyrs seen beneath the *altar* in the spring quarter once before (vi, 9). The *water*-angel justifies God for giving them blood to drink who had 'poured out the blood of saints and prophets'; and the *altar* answers: 'Yes, Lord God Almighty, true and righteous are thy judgements.' So much for the first four vials.

The fifth vial follows the fifth trumpet in bracketing together earth and sea. In the fifth trumpet this was effected with a good deal of elaboration. Going over the course again in the vials, St John takes it more easily. The vial falls neither on sea nor land, but on 'the throne of the Beast'. Where is the throne of the Beast? He came up out of the sea, to meet the Dragon, who had taken his stand on the sea-sand, and there, we are told, the Dragon gave him 'his power and throne, and great authority'. We must suppose, then, that the throne of the Beast is at the point where earth and sea join. The vial falls between sea and land. St John takes notice that he is beginning a second round in this vial by recalling the plague on the land under the first vial. The first vial brought 'a noisome and grievous sore upon men'. After the fifth 'they blasphemed the God of heaven for their pains and their sores, and repented not of their works'.

The sixth vial, like the sixth trumpet, falls on Euphrates. When we reach the region of rivers we complete the list of the three regions from which the False Prophet, the Beast, and now finally the Dragon, first arose: earth and sea under the fifth vial, and now the rivers under the sixth. We have traced demonic malice back again to its fountain. When the vial falls on Euphrates the Dragon, the Beast and the False Prophet each vomit from their mouths an unclean child of the water, a demon in the form of a frog. These demons collect a new manifestation of that host of invasion which always marches from behind the river and out of the spring of the year.

With the seventh vial the vial-series runs out beyond the number of the continuous six trumpets which are its model, but the orderly movement round the square goes on unbroken. The seventh vial falls upon the air. The region of the air is the region of the luminaries. The fourth trumpet described the region as sun, moon and stars. In the fifth trumpet it was referred to as 'the sun and the air'. The fourth vial has smitten the sun, and here is the seventh smiting the air. The portents which follow belong to the summer quarter, for they express the threat of judgement at the coming trumpet. As in the sixth seal, which fell in the same quarter, there is a mighty earthquake; the mountains and the islands are again removed (VI, 14, XVI, 20).

The visions of Babylon which follow (XVII–XVIII) play essentially the same part in the vial-section (XV–XVIII) as do the visions of

212

the glorious angel (x–xi, 13) in the trumpet-section (viii–xi). The glorious angel himself as good as reappears. 'Another mighty angel descending from heaven, arrayed with cloud, and a rainbow over his head, and his face as the sun, and his feet as pillars of fire . . . and he cried with a loud voice, as a lion roareth' (x, 1–3). 'Another angel descending from heaven, having great power, and the earth shone with his glory, and he cried with a mighty voice, "Fallen, fallen is Babylon. . . ." ' (xviii, 1–2). The same interpretation of the square is used in the two passages: the two upper sides are treated simply as heaven, arched over earth and sea below.

Let us take up the Babylon-visions in order. At the last vial we were in the quarter of summer and of the luminaries. One of the vial-angels now steps forward, and carries the prophet away by the Spirit into a wilderness. We remember from the adventures of the Woman and the Serpent that the wilderness is earth, the autumn quarter. He is carried into the wilderness to see the great whore sitting upon, or beside, many waters, that is, where earth joins sea, the bottom point of the square, where the Beast's throne is. And in fact she is seen as enthroned upon the Beast himself. We must remember that the downward point of the square marks the Feast of Dedication, and that it was the anniversary both of the dedication of the Abomination of Desolation in the Temple, and of the rededication of the temple to God. Babylon is the parody of Zion: her golden cup is full of abominations, and her written name declares her the mother of them (xvii, 4–5).

It is beside our purpose here to go into the detail of the allegories in xvii. We proceed to xviii, and behold the glorious angel descending from heaven. He inclines to his left; it is the *earth* that shines with his glory. He tells how the kings of the earth and the merchants of earth have been corrupted by Babylon. A voice from heaven takes up the tale; she had thought herself a queen for ever, and wantoned with the kings of the earth: the kings of the earth lament her, the merchants of the earth weep and wail over her fall. Then the voice passes on from earth to sea, relating the laments of 'shipmasters, coasters, mariners, and as many as work the sea'. The voice is silent; and 'a strong angel took up a stone, as it had been a great millstone, and cast it into the *sea*': such should the fall of Babylon be.

The next scene is of great jubilation in *heaven* (XIX, 1–10). Heaven still means what it did in the Babylon-visions, the two upper sides of the square taken together. It over-arches the ruin of Babylon, the seat of the Beast: it receives the smoke which rises endless from her burning. On the one side it displays the sign of the Lamb, on the other the sign of the Virgin: they stand to the right and the left, like the bridegroom and bride in every wedding-ceremony, and their coming nuptials are sung by the heavenly host.

From the bridegroom's side, out of the spring quarter, rides the warrior-Lamb, sprinkled with sacrificial blood. This is the beginning of a second paschal series: like the spring rider in the first, he comes mounted on a white horse. Two armies have marched out of the spring in the interval, one of demons and another of ungodly men: now comes the host which is to win the last battle of all.

Moving into the quarter of the luminaries, we see an angel standing in the sun. He looks forward into the next quarter,[1] the quarter of the eagle, to summon all the birds that fly in heaven to devour the slain of earth. We move on into the eagle's quarter, the slaughter is accomplished, and the birds are satisfied with flesh. So the battle takes place, as is but reasonable, in the quarter of the *earth,* which is also that of the eagle. Whilst the multitude of slain glut the vultures, the two Beasts are taken alive and flung into Gehenna. Gehenna, it must be remembered, is a gulf of fire which has not yet opened, it belongs to the last days. In the Apocalypse it makes its first actual appearance after the Great Battle. It is to be located at that fatal point where earth and sea join, the most downward part of the square: the point at which the Beast's throne stood, at which Babylon, burning in smoke towards heaven, has already foreshadowed the lake of fire and brimstone.

The next vision shows an angel armed with the key of the *abyss,* an equivalent for the sea: we move on into the winter quarter. Here Satan is imprisoned and sealed down for a thousand years. And so we come to spring and the millennial thrones. The millenium represents a pentecostal period, the fifty counted days

---

[1] His position is the same as that of the flying eagle in VIII, 13, or the flying angel in XIV, 6.

from Passover to Pentecost. The souls of the martyrs, who waited beneath the altar during the pentecostal period in the seals, now live and reign on earth with Christ. This is Easter, and it is the first resurrection. When the millennium is over, but still within the bounds of the same quarter and the same vision, the last of all the spring armies marches against the camp of the saints. Gog and Magog are destroyed by fire from heaven.

All the summer premonitions of Judgement Day are at length fulfilled: we move into summer to await the last trumpet: mountains and islands moved before, but now both earth and heaven have fled.

The trumpet and the judgement being past, we turn the corner into a new quarter and a new world, we see the Bride descend, and hear the Tabernacle of God promised to mankind. So we proceed to Dedication, and the measures of the city.

One general reflection may be allowed to conclude the chapter. The rhythm we have been examining introduces considerable complication into St John's festal symbolism. Each section of his book represents the feasts of a single quarter, and yet (we now discover) within each section he flies round all four quarters not only once, but twice or three times. Thus there is a tension between the symbolism of the whole section which requires that a single quarter should dominate, and the symbolism of its detail which runs round all the quarters. The body of the Apocalypse digests this tension, as it does so many others. The movement of each section flies round and round the year: yet the symbolism of its own quarter predominates. So far so good; but from the expositor's point of view things are made difficult. How is he to be sure whether a certain detail of symbolism belongs to the calendar-position of the section as a whole, or to the calendar-position of a point on its interior movement through the quarters of the year? Or whether St John has achieved a double reference to both at once?

CHAPTER VIII

We have followed the plan of the four quarters through the Apocalypse: and as we have proceeded, it has gradually assumed more shape and detail. When we come to the last vision of all, we learn that the Jerusalem of the World to Come is a four-square city embracing the whole zodiac: we learn, moreover, that the jewels of Aaron's breastplate and the names of the tribes go round the walls. The combination is not surprising, for the jewels of the breastplate carried the names of the tribes, 'engraved like the graving of a signet': by bearing them 'on his heart' Aaron was to bear the children of Israel on his heart before the Lord. Moreover in the second dream of Joseph, the patriarch saw himself and his eleven brethren as the 'twelve stars', i.e. constellations of the zodiac. The blessings of Jacob on the twelve tribes (Gen. XLIX) is a zodiacal poem, although it is not probable that St John knew it to be so.

Since we have seen St John's use of the diagram to be so careful and systematic, it is no absurdity to suppose that he actually constructed the diagram threefold—that he wrote the jewels round the ring of stars, and the patriarchs round the jewels, and drew symbolical inferences from the result. You may not wish to assume that he did anything so elaborate: but you will admit that it would be great carelessness on our part, having reached the present point in the argument, not to make the construction, and see whether it assists interpretation or not.

We will now simply draw the zodiacal square. The line on which the twelve signs lie is, of course, not a square but a circle. But the square diagram has its advantages, because it makes the four points—the spring and autumn equinoxes and the summer and winter solstices—stand out so clearly. We have set it corner-wise with the summer solstice at the top, because it is the highest point to which the sun climbs. Here is the figure round which the Aaronic jewels are to be writen. Exodus XXVIII tells us that the

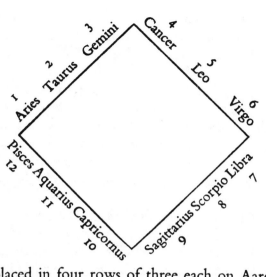

jewels are placed in four rows of three each on Aaron's breast-plate, and proceeds to name for us the stones in their rows. It does not tell us that they go round the four sides of a square in the order given: it is more natural to suppose that they run horizontally one under the other. If we are putting them round the square, we shall naturally take the rows in the Exodus order and go straight round, assigning one to each side. But nothing obliges us to put ourselves to the pain of writing upside down. If we spare ourselves this, the result is as follows:

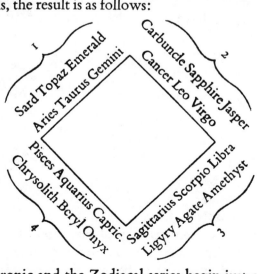

Both the Aaronic and the Zodiacal series begin just over the left-

217

hand corner, and go round clockwise. But when St John comes to write out the list of jewels, he begins just over the right-hand corner and goes round anti-clockwise. This gives us the order: jasper, sapphire, *carbuncle,* emerald, *topaz,* sard, chrysolith, beryl, *onyx, ligyry, agate,* amethyst. This is not quite St John's list; all the Exodus-stones he retains at all he keeps in these positions, except topaz and onyx, which he interchanges; but for carbuncle, ligyry and agate he simply substitutes other stones not named in Exodus anywhere. It was to be expected: St John never copies anything as it stands, he always exercises his wit upon it. We shall examine his alterations presently.

In the passage which gives us the list of stones we are also told that the names of the twelve tribes go round the city, three to a side, but the list of tribes is not given there; it has already been given in VII. There is the list, but how are we to fit it to the city? Where are we to start? And which way round are we to go?

St John gives us certain indications. When we reach VII, the city has not yet been heard of. The chapter presents us with the figure of a square world, of which the corners are the four cardinal points, North, East, South and West, from which the traditional 'four winds' blow. In the almost immediately preceding Four Horsemen, we have seen the four winds (the riders) associated with the four quarters of the year (the Cherubim). Before we can get any further, we have got to determine the relation between the two figures:

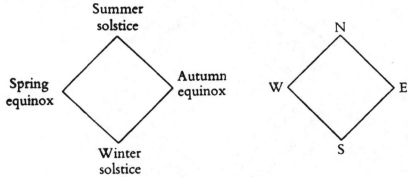

'But,' we may say, 'there is no problem here. The summer solstice is the top of the first figure, because it is the highest point of the sun's path: and the North is the top of the second figure—that

218

goes without saying.' Does it go without saying? We draw our maps that way up, because the North is the most important point to the map-user. He can find where he is by laying his map towards the Pole Star. St John is not drawing a map in the ordinary sense, and the North is of no particular use to him. He is more likely to fix his orientation by the analogy between the great and little solar cycles, the year and the day. The summer solstice is the noon of the year: the noon of the day is the moment at which the sun stands directly south. The winter solstice is the year's midnight: the day's midnight is the moment when the sun, to us invisible, is directly north. The spring is the morning of the year, the autumn its evening: the sun rises in the east, and sets in the west. So we should be well advised to draw the combined figure thus:

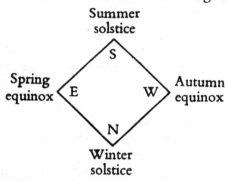

St John's standing symbolism confirms this construction. The quarter between the spring equinox and midsummer is for him the region of the Euphrates. From Ephesus the Euphrates is certainly to the east, and somewhat to the south-east. And when in the sixth vial the river is dried, it is to permit the passage of kings 'from the rising of the sun'. We may add a slight confirmation from the position of the Beast's Throne. As we have drawn the diagram, it will stand at the northern point. The Antichrist king of Daniel's prophecies is 'the King of the North' and the Biblical Babylon is 'the North-Country'. The self-deifying King of Babylon in Isaiah XIV makes it his boast, that he will exalt his throne above the stars of God, and sit upon the mount of congregation in the uttermost parts of the North (Isa. XIV, 13-14). In Apocalypse XII we read of Lucifer's attempt to tyrannize over the stars: in XIII the Beast's throne is erected in the uttermost North.

We may now return to Apocalypse VII. After sketching the figure of the four-square world with the winds at its corners, St John shows us an angel approaching from the sunrise with the seal of the Living God. That is to say, he approaches on the side of the spring equinox and, since St John calls the spring *quarter* 'sunrise' in XVI, if anything on the upper rather than the lower side of it.

Let us say, then, that the angel with the seal appears in the spring quarter. The series of visions in the previous chapter had carried us into the summer quarter. If the angel with the seal recalls us to the spring quarter, we are beginning to move backwards. It may be natural to suppose, then, that as he goes round the four-square Israel sealing the tribes, he will continue to go in the same direction, i.e. anticlockwise.

He starts with Judah, which is the Lamb's own tribe. He also starts from the east, and the Lamb is the most easterly sign of the south-east quarter. So let us write the names round anticlockwise, taking Aries for Judah.

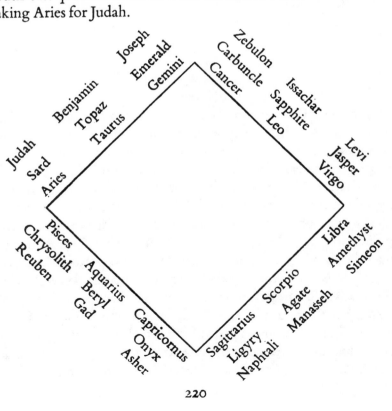

Before we proceed any further, a great light breaks upon us here. St John says in IV that he who sits upon the throne is as a jasper and a sard to look upon, and that his throne is ringed with a rainbow like an emerald. Ezekiel indeed saw God as amber from the loins and upward, as fire from the loins and downward, and it is no doubt true that the jasper St John has in mind is of a very clear amber (crystal-clear, he says in XXI), while his sard is a clear red. It is equally true that an emerald, if it is cut, will shine with rainbow-colours. But so will other stones: the ancients write of the emerald simply as green. The one jewel which Ezekiel does mention, the sapphire of the throne itself, St John omits, while he supplies tolerable but by no means inevitable jewel-equivalents for other parts of the prophet's visionary picture. It seems pretty plain that his procedure is not to be explained by reference to Ezekiel alone.

We cast our eye on the diagram, and what do we see? The jasper is the stone of Levi, the sard of Judah, and the emerald of Joseph. Now these are the three glorious tribes. God gave the throne to Joseph for his own lifetime, he was the prince among his brethren, they came and bowed down to the soles of his feet: so the throne is ringed with emerald. But Joseph was not destined to sit upon the throne for ever. It was to be occupied by the two anointed houses, Judah for the principality, Levi for the priesthood: so he who sits upon the throne is as a jasper and a sard. For whatever royalty God bestowed upon the tribes was but a reflection of his own glory; the throne of Joseph, the kingdom of Judah, the priesthood of Levi, all are his.

The piece of Jewish theology which we have just put down is not an inference which we draw from the scriptures; there is no need to ask whether St John was familiar with it. It was written out for him at great length and with rich elaboration in a very well-known work, of which the impress is to be seen all over the face of the New Testament, the 'Testaments of the XII Patriarchs'.

We may observe also the appropriateness of the astrological signs belonging to these three patriarchs. Joseph's is Gemini. The throne of Joseph is essentially the throne which he shares with the King (Pharaoh), and the divine throne is the throne in which the Son reigns with the Father, it is 'the Throne of God and of the Lamb'. The starry woman of XII bears the unmistakable traits of the mother of Joseph: her Son, once born, is caught away from the lying-in-wait of his enemies into the throne of God. Joseph's escape from all his perils on to the steps of Pharaoh's throne signifies Christ's ascension to the right hand of God, to his place in the throne of the Heavenly Twins, the Father and the Son. Gemini is the top of the Zodiac, there the sun is enthroned in his midsummer splendour. Then as to the colour of the stone. St John gives Joseph's emerald the hues of the rainbow. Joseph's many-coloured coat is well-known: it was the badge of his father's love.

Judah is the Lamb. According to the Old Testament tradition, he is the Lion. St John makes a virtue of the discrepancy and enforces the paradox. 'Weep not: the Lion of the Tribe of Judah, has conquered' . . . 'And I saw . . . a Lamb standing as slaughtered.' (v, 5–6). His stone is the sardius, which was red. It is the hue of sacrificial blood.

Levi is the virgin. The priesthood is a pure virgin, to whom it is given to wear white linen raiment. Ritual purity is the chief requirement of the old priestly condition. Moreover the priesthood possess the sanctuary of Zion, and Zion, the virgin daughter of Zion, is once more an evident sense of the sign Virgo. And so, while Judah as the slaughtered Lamb has the altar for his place, Levi's place is the temple. There is, perhaps, no special appropriateness in the amber-coloured stone, but St John insists on the brightness, the purity of it, 'a stone most precious, a jasper, sparkling as crystal,' so that a heavenly luminary can be compared with it (xxi, 11).

Encouraged by these happy equivalences, let us proceed with the construction of St John's mystical diagram. Returning to the principal text, the frame of the city (xxi), we observe that there are three gates to each side of the square, and that the twelve jewels

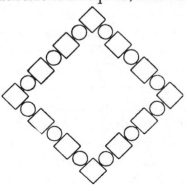

222

are the blocks of continuous wall-foundation between the gaps made by the gates. The openings are closed each by a pearl. And so we get the figure shown on page 222: St John places the names of the tribes on the pearls, the jewels bear those of the twelve apostles. This expresses the dignity of the apostles as new patriarchs, enthroned over the twelve tribes of Israel, one to each tribe. The names of the apostles play no part in the Apocalypse: we have not to find where we should put Peter, James, and John, but we require to know to which side of each tribal gate lies the apostolic stone belonging to that tribe. This is not difficult to decide. For we know that in astronomical fact the signs were pushing round clockwise, so that, for example, the domain of Virgo (i.e. Levi), the pearl just above the right-hand corner, extended to the corner.

Since the pearls are uniform all round, and the names of the apostles are blanks, we shall naturally omit both pearls and apostles, and the figure will be as follows—we give two forms, one with the Exodus stones, the other with St John's alterations to them:

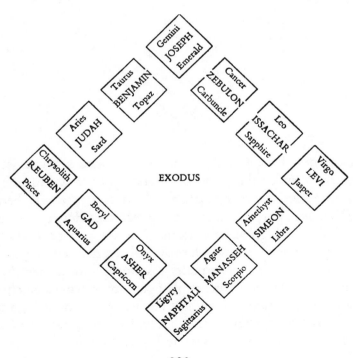

By a simple inspection of these figures we can see immediately the sense of all St John's alterations in the Exodus stones, except one. Zebulon cannot be allowed to retain the carbuncle (anthrax), because it is a better red than the sard, and the sard of the Lamb and of Judah must be without rival as the sign of sacrificial blood. Why St John substituted the chalcedony in particular must remain obscure to us, since we do not know what sort or colour of stone

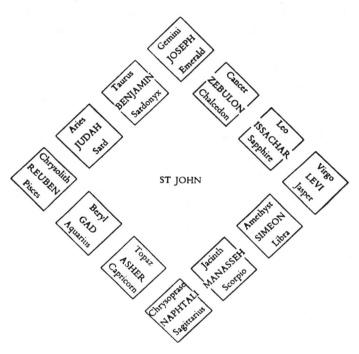

the name describes. On the face of it, it means bronze-stone. Immediately under the jewel of Levi St John rewrites 'Ligyry, agate, amethyst' as 'chrysoprase, hyacinth, amethyst' because 'gold, hyacinth, purple' is a constantly recurring description of the materials for the high priest's vestments in the very context of the breastplate-passage from which the jewels are derived. 'Hyacinth', anyhow, is 'hyacinth', and amethyst is purple—the ancients spoke of 'amethystine robes'. The simplest *gold*-stone would be chrysolith, but that is already somewhere else in the list, so St John takes another gold-stone, chrysoprase. 'Gold, hyacinth, purple' is made immediately to follow Levi's stone (upon the hint of the 'purple'

224

already there) because Levi is the High Priest and these are the High Priestly colours.[1]

There remains only the interchange of topaz and (sard-)onyx to be explained. The most obvious conjecture to form at first sight is that St John wrote 'sard, sardonyx' for 'sard, topaz' because he wished to express an affinity between Aries and Taurus: and that then, when he came to the simple onyx in its own place, he substituted the topaz, which he had discarded to make room for sardonyx. Sardonyx and onyx could not stand in the same list, sardonyx being simply one not especially important variety of onyx. If sardonyx has been used, onyx has been used up.

So far, so good: but we are left with the question, what affinity between Aries and Taurus St John meant to express. It will hardly be the affinity between Judah and Benjamin. It is true that these are the two principal lay-tribes which remained faithful to the throne of David,[2] but everybody knew that; it seems unnecessary to make a sacred mystery of it, and it is irrelevant in any case to St John's concerns. A more hopeful starting-point may be found in the position of Taurus between Aries and Gemini. Aries is the Lamb, and Gemini is the Divine Throne. Sometimes the Lamb is viewed as 'in the midst of the Throne', but more often as distinct and standing in Aries to the right of it. When he is in the second position, great interest must of necessity attach to what is even more immediately to the right of the throne in Taurus, mediating, as it were, between the Father and the Son.

In the Glory-vision of IV St John tells us that the Seven Spirits of God are (a) lamps of fire burning before the throne (b) the seven eyes and seven horns of the Lamb. Now Taurus, viewed from the throne, is below and before it: viewed from the place of the Lamb, it is upon his head. And Taurus contains the Seven Stars, the most famous cluster in the sky, the Pleiads. Since they may be interpreted either as a sevenfold candlestick before the

[1] It is possible to form a conjecture about the way in which St John came by this idea. If his Septuagint had the text common to our Mss., the list of Aaronic jewels was repeated for him in Ezekiel xxviii, 13, with the evident corruption *chrysium argyrium* ligyrium agate amethyst', where only 'ligyrium', etc., is required. Here, then, he saw 'Gold . . . purple', said to himself, 'Gold, hyacinth, purple,' felt its appropriateness, and wrote it.

[2] There was Simeon besides, but Simeon hardly existed as distinct from Judah.

throne, or as the 'Seven Spirits of the Lord' resting upon the Root of David, the Lion-Lamb of the tribe of Judah, they show how the Spirit is the bond of the Trinity. And it is, in fact, the Trinity expressed in the unfamiliar figures of St John's astrology which meets us in the opening of his book. He sends grace and peace not from God the Father, the Lord Jesus Christ, and the Holy Ghost, but from the IS, WAS and COMETH, from the Seven Spirits which are before his throne, and from Jesus Christ, the faithful martyr. We learn presently that Jesus Christ also 'has the Seven Spirits of God'. It is the plenary indwelling of the Son by the Spirit that St John wishes to emphasize. All things, especially the Spirit of God, evidently belong to God. But it is new and saving knowledge that the Spirit in full sevenfold power is the Spirit of the Son, the eyes of his discernment, the horns of his strength; that the sardonyx belongs to the sard.

At this point a fresh light breaks upon us. The text in which St John speaks of the sevenfold Spirit indwelling the Lamb (v, 6) is, as we have said more than once, based upon the Jesus-visions of Zechariah. Now those visions appear to symbolize the sevenfold Spirit in the seven facets (eyes) of a signet, as well as in the seven flames of the great candlestick. 'Behold the stone that I have set before Jesus: on the one stone are seven eyes'. Once we see things in terms of St John's diagram, we say, 'Stone? Yes, of course—the sardonyx. This is the stone cut to seven eyes. It is the seven-faceted signet on the right hand of God, which is set before Jesus (the Lamb, the sardius). It authenticates him, as Pharaoh's signet authenticated Joseph.' But the Christian understands that this seven-faceted seal is no mere emblem of office; it is the gift of the sevenfold Spirit.

Very well, then; when we see an angel arising from the east with the seal of the Living God (VII, 2) we know immediately that he holds the sardonyx. He proceeds to impress it on the forehead of the Lamb, Judah; whose else? For the Lamb stands ready, just beneath the Seven Stars. He brings the seal down to the Lamb of Judah, and then continues in the same direction, from Judah to Reuben, from Reuben to Gad, and so on round the circle, to end in Benjamin.

Without any further attempt to determine the special significance of the several tribes, we can now understand the arrangement of the tribal list. It is not a list anywhere to be found in Scripture, but it is the most elegant and symmetrical arrangement possible, if Judah is to be fixed at Passover (Aries) and Levi at the other great Feast-Season (New Year–Tabernacles: Virgo). That is really all we need to presuppose; we can also presuppose if we like that Joseph is to be put at the top, in the throne; but we can just as well regard his appearance there as a happy by-product of the arrangement based on Judah and Levi.

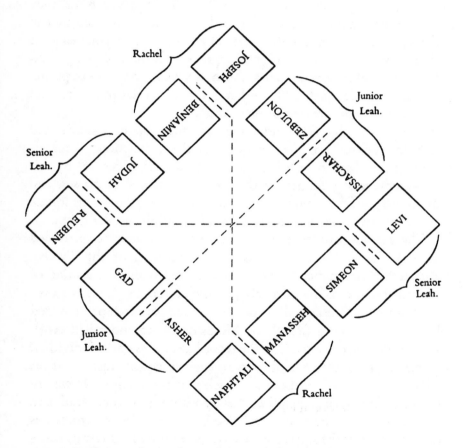

St John begins by making the usual division between the eight tribes of the house of Leah and the four of the house of Rachel: he then divides the house of Leah into four senior and four junior tribes, so that he has three equal lists:

227

Senior Leah	Junior Leah	Rachel
Reuben	Issachar	Joseph
Simeon	Zebulon	Benjamin
Levi	Gad	Naphtali
Judah	Asher	Dan (Manasseh)

Dan is an ill-omened name, because of the Golden Calf. St John substitutes Manasseh, the secondary branch of the double tribe of Joseph.[1] 'Joseph' itself can stand for Ephraim, Joseph's primary inheritor.

If Levi and Judah are going to fall upon Virgo and Aries, they have got to stand *almost* diametrically opposite to one another in the square. St John makes a virtue of necessity; he pairs each of them with one of the senior Leah tribes, (Simeon-Levi, Judah-Reuben) and makes the pairs, taken as wholes, *perfectly* opposite. He then divides each of his other lists into its natural pairs, and places them opposite one another too.

If we ask why Gad and Asher are not above, Issachar and Zebulon below, we may answer (a) the connexion 'Reuben-Gad' is familiar, these being the transjordanian tribes, (b) by this arrangement St John gets all the secondary tribes, Manasseh and the children of the handmaids, in the 'earthly' regions of his square (land and sea). 'Heaven' is wholly made up of the nobler tribes.

The various privileges and merits of the twelve tribes provided a stock theme for homily, as the 'Testaments of the Twelve Patriarchs' may suffice to show. One started with the meaning of the tribal name, as the birth story of the patriarchs (Genesis XXIX–XXX) gives it. One added the oracle on each patriarch pronounced by Jacob in Genesis (XLIX), by Moses in Deuteronomy (XXXIII). One made what one could of the recorded actions of the individual patriarch, and drew analogies with the subsequent history of his tribe, or of its principal heroes. Such was the method. If we are going to find such material in the Apocalypse, we shall find it in the messages to the Churches. We have seen that the messages take the sides of the square one by one. There are four tribal names on each side, if we include both corners. This is *embarras de richesse*. Of course St John selects his matter.

---

[1] That Joseph is in fact two tribes (Ephraim and Manasseh) gives an added appropriateness to the Twins as zodiacal sign for Joseph.

228

The first and fifth messages take the side which contains Reuben, Gad, Asher (and Naphtali). Reuben, Jacob's firstborn, is the most interesting name here. It would appear that the first message is composed on Reuben and Asher, the fifth on Reuben and Gad. The first message seems to play round the text of Reuben's birth-story. 'The Lord saw that Leah was *hated,* and opened her womb. . . . And she called her child's name Reuben, saying, "Because the Lord hath *seen my humiliation*; now will my husband *love* me." ' The Lord has 'seen the humiliation' of Ephesus; 'I know', he says, 'thy works and trouble and endurance.' (This or an equivalent phrase becomes common form in the messages, but that does not affect the fact that it is minted in the first of them.) 'But', he says, 'I have it against thee that thou hast lost thy first *love*. . . . But this thou hast; thou *hatest* the works of the Nicolaitans which I hate also.' Reuben fell away from his father's love and offended grievously against him, so that his father deprived him of his birthright. But he became a model of penitence, so it was taught. 'Repent', it is said to Ephesus, 'and do the first[1] works: else I come to thee and will remove thy candlestick out of its place.' To the faithful Christ promises what Jacob promised to Asher. 'Asher's bread is fat, he shall yield dainties for princes.' Since 'dainties' is used by the LXX as a translation of 'Eden', it is natural to see this as a promise of the fruits of paradise. 'God made Adam to dwell outside the paradise of dainties,' we read; 'and he appointed the cherubim and the brandished sword of flame to keep the way to the tree of life.' Christ's promise takes away the brandished sword: 'He shall eat of the tree of life, which is in the paradise of God.'

The first message, we may agree, neither weakens nor confirms our case. St John may have been thinking of Reuben and Asher, or again he may not. The fifth gives us more solid support. Reuben's ultimate repentance was inferred from Moses's oracle upon him: 'Let Reuben live and not die, but be few in number.' 'I know thy works,' the fifth message runs, 'that thou hast a name for being alive, but art dead. . . . But thou hast a few names in Sardis who

---

[1] The harping on 'first' reminds us how Jacob calls Reuben 'the firstfruit of my strength' and complains that he does not fulfil the promise of his birthright.

229

have not defiled their raiment. . . . He that overcometh, I will not blot his name from the book of life.' This, surely, is as good as we could fairly demand. We add, for what it is worth, the possible reference to Jacob's oracle on Gad: 'Stealers steal upon him, but he steals on them at last'—'I come as a thief, and thou shalt not know what hour I come upon thee.'

Now the second and sixth messages. (Reuben), Judah, Benjamin and Joseph are the names on the side which they take. Much space in the 'Twelve Testaments' is devoted to the relations between each of the other patriarchs and Joseph, naturally enough, for the story of the sons of Jacob is substantially the story of their dealings with Joseph. The second message sets Judah over against Joseph. Jewish tradition did its best to whitewash Judah, but Christian interpretation was bound to fix on one fact. It was Judah who persuaded the brethren to sell Joseph. For Judas sold Christ to his enemies, and Jewry sells the Church to hers. 'I know thy oppression and poverty', says Christ to the new Joseph, 'though thou art rich' (How rich? Rich enough to feed the world with bread?) 'and the delations of those that call themselves the sons of Judah and are not, but are a synagogue of Satan. . . . Behold, the slanderer will cast some of you into prison' (like Joseph, slandered by Potiphar's wife) 'to be tried'. Joseph is the very type of the acceptable man tried in the furnace of adversity. Faithful to the death, he receives the garland of life.

The sixth message continues the theme of Joseph and the wicked Judah. Those who say they are Judaeans and are not, but a synagogue of Satan, shall come worshipping before Joseph's feet. It was Judah who led the last and most abject embassy of the brethren to entreat Joseph's favour. He was forced to see in him the son of his father's love and the man of Pharaoh's regard: and so it is said here: 'They shall acknowledge that I have loved thee.' But alongside of the wicked Judah this message introduces the true messianic Judah, 'the house of David,' for which Christ himself speaks. It is interesting that of all Davidic figures that which appears here is the faithful and all-powerful vizir Eliakim, on whose shoulder is the key of the house of David, who opens and shuts and none can gainsay him (Isa. xxii). It is interesting, for Joseph was the all-powerful vizir of Egypt, able to open and shut every granary door

230

in the land, once the Lord had opened the door for him out of prison into princely power.

We come to the third and seventh messages, for which the patriarchal names (Joseph), Zebulon, Issachar and Levi are available. Both messages, as we should expect, concentrate upon the important name of Levi. It may be that the exordium of the third plays on Zebulon: 'I know where thou dwellest' (Zebulon's birth-story derives his name from 'dwelling') 'where Satan's throne is' ('*Lord* of the dwelling', Beelzebul, is a name of Satan). The rest of the message is devoted to Levi. Levi was held to owe his priestly privileges to his ferocious zeal. Levi's sword avenged the defilement of his sister on the men of Shechem; the Levites unsheathed the sword to vindicate the honour of God against fornication and idolatry in the service of the Golden Calf; Phineas, the head of the house of Levi, intervened when the same abominations began at Beelpeor; he spitted an offending Israelite and a Moabite harlot on one spear. Levi's action against Shechem obtained the sacred predestination of his tribe, the day of the Calf secured the Levirate, and the zeal of Phineas secured the High Priesthood. St John takes up the story of Beelpeor, because (it may well be) he has just been playing on Beelzebul, 'Where Satan's throne is.' Satan's throne was at Beelpeor too, but Phineas, God's faithful witness, was not lacking to the occasion. As we are about to see, Judah and Levi are the types of the 'two witnesses' in XI. In the ferocity of their zeal the two are well abreast of Phineas. Unlike him, they suffer martyrdom. Antipas, the faithful witness, had died at Pergamus, and the Church had stood by him. How strange, then, that they are so slow to show the zeal of Phineas against idolatrous feasting and fornication among their own members. It was Balaam ('Smiter of the Folk') who showed the king of Moab how to entrap Israel by means of the women: it is Nicolaus ('Conqueror of the People') whose teaching has seduced the Pergamenes to eat idolatrous feasts and to fornicate. Phineas's spear was only just in time: the sword of God's pestilence hung over the people's necks when Phineas struck. 'Repent therefore,' it is said to Pergamus, 'or I come quickly upon thee and will make war on the sinners with the sword of my mouth.' The concluding promises appear to be Levitical also. The faithful shall receive what was granted to the

231

intercession of Moses, the manna. The people gathered white round flakes of manna, and called it by that name, not knowing what it was. Christ will also give the faithful something else round and mysterious, a white pebble with a name on it which none knows but he who receives it. This reads like an allusion to the lots which were cast for the various priestly duties in the temple.

The seventh message introduces Christ himself as the Faithful Witness, and he passes judgement on Levi. Levi is now seen as the sacrificing priest. Quite in the spirit of the Lord of Israel rejecting unworthy sacrifices in some oracle of the Old Testament, Christ declares that he will spue out of his mouth what Laodicea sets upon his table. (The ancient sacrifices represented the worshippers: in the new covenant they are identical with them.) With the penitent it shall be otherwise; the Lord will come and feast with them at their table. Laodicea is rebuked for saying, 'I am rich, and have enriched myself, and have need of nothing,' not knowing that she is a wretched, pitiable beggar. Levi was a landless tribe, fattened by the Lord on his offerings, but how often the priesthood forgot it! Perhaps, however, the turn of phrase owes something to Moses's oracle on Issachar and Zebulon: 'You shall call (on God) there and sacrifice a sacrifice of righteousness, for the riches of the sea shall nourish thee and the traffic of dwellers by the strand.' When the Lord counsels Laodicea to *buy* of him all she needs, we may suspect the influence of the fourth name, Joseph, from whom his destitute brethren came to buy what alone could save them from starvation, and who in fact 'sold' them forgiveness, peace and plenty, and their gold, which they had brought to 'buy' with, he threw in besides.

(Levi), Simeon, Manasseh and Naphtali are the names which fall to the lot of the fourth message. In the third St John was handling the theme of the Levite hero Phineas at Beelpeor. In the fourth message the name of Levi is still before him, and the name of Simeon is added to it. This is an invitation to continue with the matter of Beelpeor, because it was a Simeonite whom Phineas made an example of his zeal. The case of the Simeonite leads St John to reverse the emphasis as between idolatry and fornication: and leads him to replace the villainy of Balaam with the villainy of the seductress. Cosbi the Moabitess is a poor pair for Balaam: it is better to substitute Jezebel, the mistress of whoredoms and idolatries and the patroness of false prophets: especially in view of the fact that the otherwise undistinguished name of the Simeonite offender, Zimri, was immortalized by Jezebel's defiance to Jehu: 'Is it peace, thou Zimri, murderer of thy master?' (The link is purely associative: it was not of the same Zimri that she spoke.) The detail of the message is largely moulded on the history of Ahab and Jezebel and their children. We do not know from what tribe Ahab and his father Omri came. *Manasseh,* St John may have supposed, since they built their capital on Manassite land. Omri was the founder of Samaria.

The title of the message has a levitical flavour: 'the Son of God whose eyes are as flame of fire and his feet like bronze-hued incense.' Whatever does or does not belong to Levi, incense does. On the other hand the promises are stubbornly Judaean and Davidic. 'I will give' (the faithful) 'power over the nations, and he shall shepherd them with a rod of iron, as I received from my Father: and I will give him the morning star' (i.e. a share in the dominion of David). What have these Judaean symbols to do here? Are we simply to see in them the balancing of Judah against Levi—the priest is offered a share in the throne of the king? Or are we to recall the very important part played by the name of *Simeon* in the Christian story? Who is made vizir of the kingdom of heaven, to whom are given the keys of the house of David?

Any attempt to interpret the messages from the tribal names is bound to lead us into many such vain conjectures. We cannot hope, in the nature of the case, to follow every turn of inspired association. But we should be unwise to reject the evidence for Reuben in the fifth message, for Judah and Joseph in the second and sixth, and for Levi in the third and seventh. Let us leave the matter here, and return to the frame of the city which the tribal names adorn.

If we take the figure of the city as it appears in XXI, we can get two slightly different patterns from it, according as we take the positions of the gates (pearls) or foundation-blocks (jewels). If we are thinking of the four corners of the square, we shall look at the foundation-blocks, for the corners are blocks, not gates. But if we are thinking of the four quarters and the four cherubim, we shall

233

take the position of the gates, because the cherubim are the middles of the sides, and the middles are gates, not blocks. Here are two figures for comparison:

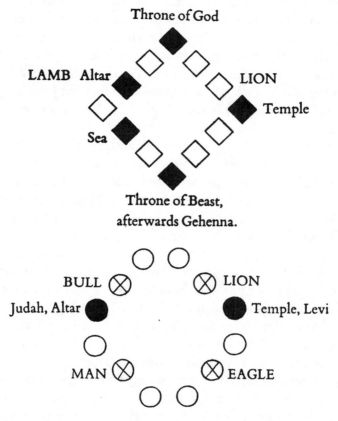

Each figure has its merit. The second balances Judah and Levi, temple and altar, as the two foundations of the upper part of the figure, that is to say, of 'heaven': the first balances the Lamb and the Lion, and gives expression to the opposite positions of the two thrones at top and bottom, and to the cornerstone-position of the temple. But it displaces the altar, which ought to lie directly east of the temple. (We can, indeed, balance the geometrical pattern by marking the 'sea' or great laver in aquarius: but the balancing of altar against sea does not appear except in xiv, 14–xv.) In fact St John uses the two figures indifferently, taking either point of view from moment to moment, as it suits him to do.

234

We have spoken of the qualities of the stones representing altar, throne, and temple: we will look at the 'sea' and the throne of the Beast. The 'sea' is the pitcher of aquarius, and his stone is beryl, which (if we know anything of the ancient stone) is probably a pale bluish-green, a good colour for water. The diametrical opposite to the throne of God is sagittarius, not in himself perhaps significant; but his stone is chrysoprase, and in this St John seems to have achieved a double hit. If we lean upon the 'gold', the first part of the name, then chrysoprase enters into the 'gold-hyacinth-purple' of the High-Priestly vesture. But if we give equal emphasis to the two parts, 'golden-green', we have the colour of brimstone, as near as the name of any precious stone can suggest it. So here is 'the lake of fire that burns with brimstone', the diametrical opposite of the divine throne.

The double sense of the chrysoprase proceeds to infect its neighbour. If we read 'brimstone, blue, purple' for 'golden, blue, purple' the blue may be seen as the smoke which rises from the brimstone. And so, in the fifth trumpet-plague, the blue jacinth of the scorpion is given this sinister sense: it is the smoke of the pit, out of which the scorpion-locusts swarm. In the sixth plague St John carries symbolical elaboration to a further point. He will combine the two symbols: Aaronic breastplate (gold, hyacinth, purple), and stench of Gehenna (brimstone, smoke. . . .). The hosts of destruction appear armed with breastplates fiery (for purple), *hyacinthine,* and sulphurous, riding horses which breathe fire, smoke and sulphur (brimstone), by which three plagues are killed the destined number of mankind. The astonishing elaboration of imagery, revealed in the otherwise inexplicable use of the word *hyacinthine,* is not a meaningless vagary. St John wishes to show us how God, represented by the ministers of his wrath, has put on 'righteousness for a breastplate, and garments of vengeance for clothing' in the day when he repays fury to his adversaries (Isa. LIX, 17). Even so, why is the breastplate a priestly breastplate? The whole of the 'fire, smoke, and brimstone' of the trumpet-plagues are the expression (as we shewed above) of the 'incense, smoke and fire' of the liturgy in heaven out of which they arise. We saw how carefully St John works out the parallel. The liturgy is the acceptance of the saints' prayers for vindication, and the

235

very stuff of the liturgy becomes the stuff of the vengeance exacted. It is part and parcel of the parallel that the priestly garments of the incense-angel should become garments of vengeance clothing the destroyers.

One of St John's most important divisions of the square is the division between heaven and earth, the kingdom of light and the kingdom of darkness. This division illustrates perfectly what we said above about St John's continual oscillation between the two ways of regarding the square. For the division between heaven and earth seems at first sight to be bound up with the cornerwise, foundation-block view, since it expresses the vertical opposition between the two corners which are the thrones of God and of the Beast. And yet, when we come to draw the horizontal line which divides the two kingdoms, we are forced to adopt the side and gate view, for otherwise we should cut our two central units in half. If we take the second figure and draw the line, we get an interesting result: the 'heavenly' tribes are the tribes which stand for the blessing on Mt Gerizim, the 'earthly' tribes those which stand for the cursing on Mt Ebal, in the twenty-seventh chapter of

Deuteronomy—very nearly, but not quite. We have to allow here as elsewhere for St John's substitution of Manasseh for Dan: that goes without saying. But we have also to admit that Zebulon and Simeon have exchanged places. Still, we must not be ungrateful: St John has so many different symbolisms to reconcile in one figure, that so approximately perfect a result is surprising enough.

The horizontal line is actually drawn, before our very eyes as it were, with reed and ink, when St John is given a reed and told to measure the temple of God and the altar and those who worship in the area, and to rule out the exterior court. The temple is Levi, the altar Judah, those who worship in the enclosure are the other tribes of the blessing, the outer court is made up from the tribes of the curse.

With the figure before our eyes, we can understand St John's abrupt transition in XI, 1–3. 'Measure the *temple* of God and the *altar,* and the worshippers therein; but the court without the temple leave thou out and measure it not, for it is given to the gentiles, and they shall trample the holy city for forty-two months. And I will give to *my two witnesses,* and they shall prophesy a thousand two hundred and sixty days, girt with sackcloth.' St John's words are arranged in careful parallel, to the following effect:

(a) Put the temple and altar within the line
(b) Rule the outer court outside it:
$\qquad$ for
(b) The outer court is given to the heathen for $3\frac{1}{2}$ years
(a) To my two witnesses it is given to prophesy for $3\frac{1}{2}$ years.

The parallelism requires that 'my two witnesses' should be (in some sense) the temple and the altar. Well, but they are: they are Judah and Levi, as becomes perfectly plain when St John proceeds. 'These are the two olive trees and the two lampstands that stand before the Lord of the earth.' St John is quoting Zechariah's Candlestick-vision. It is perfectly plain in Zechariah, and Jewish commentators agreed upon it, that the two olive trees are the two oil-bearing (i.e. anointed) stocks of Judah and Levi, David and Zadok. So long as they are planted and living before the face of God, Israel exists. In Zechariah's vision they are the prince Zerubbabel and the priest Jeshua. Thus Judah and Levi, principality and priesthood, supply the *first* sense to be attached to the figures of the two witnesses. St John proceeds to lavish upon them several senses beside: the two-foldness of apostolic witness to Christ is not only royalty and priesthood, it is also law and prophecy,[1] and so on. We need not go further: it is the first step only that concerns us.

Levi and Judah 'stand before the Lord of the earth'. Although

[1] How do you get from 'Kingdom and Priesthood' to 'Law and Prophecy'? Probably by thinking about the Jewish Bible. Priesthood, Levi, Moses, is the Law: the books of the Kingdoms are part of the canon of prophets and the setting for the work of the prophets. Elijah is the chief hero of the latter part of 'Kingdoms'.

237

Levi is the temple, the throne of God is seen at the head of the figure, not in Levi but in Joseph. Judah and Levi are the two witnesses, equally standing before him to the right and left. It is only in the vision of the vials that the divine glory enters the temple, so that 'a great voice' can 'issue out of the temple from the throne'. And this is the prelude to what happens in the last visions, when the throne of God and of the Lamb is planted in the Virgin, and the temple which is the Virgin expands to embrace the whole city.

In the previous phase, when the temple and altar stand equally before the presence of God, it is very natural that the parallel should be completed by the interpretation of 'temple' as 'incense-altar'. The altar of slaughter and the altar of incense both stand before God: the altar of slaughter is open to Judah, the altar of incense is the preserve of Levi who can alone enter the temple to behold it. The two altars, in fact, appear before we even hear of 'the temple and the altar'. In VIII, 3–5 we have the ritual procession from the slaughter-altar, where the fire ever burns, to the golden altar, on which the charcoal is spread at the time of the incense-offering only; and then the incense is put to the charcoal and goes up in smoke. The charcoal is 'the prayers of all saints': the incense of angelic worship, 'being put to them' by the angel, goes up in smoke 'at the prayers of the saints', as the incense goes up by reason of the burning charcoal.[1]

[1] It is possible that we have here the answer to two puzzles. (a) Why, we have asked, when constrained to expel 'carbuncle' from its place among the jewels, did St John substitute 'bronze-stone' (chalcedon)? (b) Why, everyone asks, did St John alter the simple language of Ezekiel, 'feet like sparkling bronze,' to 'feet like bronze-coloured incense, as of incense which has been melted in the oven'? (I, 15.) Solution: the reason for expelling carbuncle from its place on Levi's side is that it rivals the red of the fire and blood on Judah's altar. But something fiery does belong to Levi—the incense-offering. So instead of carbuncle (Greek anthrax=charcoal) let us write bronze-stone, and also make mention of bronze-coloured incense (chalcolibanus). Just as the Glory of the Father combines Judah's sard and Levi's jasper, so the person of the Son of Man combines Judah's fire and Levi's incense: 'His eyes as flame of fire, and his feet as chalcolibanus' (I, 14–15, repeated II, 18). The eyes of fire are specially Judaean (see IV, 5, V, 5–6), so let the incense-coloured feet be Levitical: and let the (in itself needless) remark 'as fired in the oven' help to couple the 'eyes of fire' with the incense-coloured feet, and remind us that Levi's incense cannot ascend except by borrowing Judah's fire.

238

The saints who are being thought of here are especially the martyrs whom we saw making their prayer from beneath the altar of slaughter a few pages back. And so at this point of the book, 'altar of slaughter and altar of incense' appears to stand for Christ the victim and his martyr-church on the one hand, and the angelic ministers on the other. When the sacrifice of the saints is carried with the incense of heaven into the heavenly temple which the angels serve, that is the perfection of liturgy. St John elaborates a little here. Before he introduced the picture of the saints beneath the altar as a bloody sacrifice, he said more simply that the angels offer before God the incense of the saints' prayers (v, 8).

Perhaps it will be best at this point to trace the gradual appearance and progressive definition of the heavenly temple and its appurtenances. In the Candlestick-vision St John is on earth—to be more exact, he is in the sea, on the island of Patmos: and so he is in the quarter of sea and winter, between Dedication and Passover, which is the quarter to which the Seven Messages specially belong, and out of which they start. When the Messages have finished, he is summoned by a heavenly voice to pass on into the spring quarter for the paschal visions. The theme of the spring quarter was last touched in the sixth message, addressed by 'the key-bearer of the house of David, who opens and none shall shut' to the Philadelphians. 'I have set before you', he said, 'an open door.' Now that the messages are done, St John sees the open door, and passes from the winter quarter to the spring quarter, from the lower to the upper half of the square, from earth to heaven. Being arrived he sees a view of heaven which embraces, in fact, the whole square.

The throne stands in the midst of the heavenly city, as it will do in the midst of the New Jerusalem. It is in the middle, for the periphery of the square, made up of the twelve jewels and the twelve pearls, is interpreted as a ring of twenty-four thrones round about it. It is probably to be taken as orientated like the temple, facing east: it may be an indication of this that the jasper of Levi is mentioned before the sard of Judah in connexion with the divine Glory, for the throne stands templewise. If it faces East, we can see why the seven lamps of fire (the Pleiads in Taurus) and the 'sea' of glass (the pitcher of Aquarius) are said to be in front of it, being the middles of the south-east and north-east sides. No sooner has

239

St John mentioned them, than he proceeds to reinterpret them with the other two middles in a complete list of the four cherubim. The cherubim are 'in the throne, on its circumference'—by a sudden shift of interpretation the throne now expands to cover the whole area. The cherubim are counted symmetrically, beginning from behind the right hand of the throne and ending behind the left hand:

Their bodies and wings form a living fence about the throne, a fence studded with eyes 'both on its outward and its inward sides' (IV, 8), for the cherubim have eyes both before and behind (IV, 6).

The seven-sealed book, from its position in the right hand of the enthroned Glory, may be seen to be a fresh interpretation of the seven stars in Taurus, the seven-faceted seal of the Living God. When the Lamb appears, he will be directly before the throne, very slightly to the right of him who sits there. He is said to be within the throne, among the four cherubim and among the elders. Since the periphery of the square has been treated as (a) the surrounding ring of 24 thrones, (b) the limits of the central throne, marked by the cherubim, and since the Lamb is a sign in the periphery of the square, it cannot be denied that he is among the elders, among the cherubim, and within the limits of the throne. But St John chooses actually to force the paradox of location arising out of his several successive interpretations of the symbols, to express the mystery of divine omnipresence.

More astonishing and more illuminating still is the triple interpretation of the Seven Stars. They are (a) the fires of the Holy Ghost, burning before God's throne. They are (b) the seven-sealed Book, the plenitude of Divine Spirit as communicable truth. They are (c) the Sevenfold Spirit resting upon the head of the Lamb, to be his vision and his strength, whereby he 'prevails to open the book and to read it'. It is one Holy Ghost who is a lamp of life before the Father, the sense of revelation (we must know

240

not the letter, but the Spirit in it, and that Spirit is the very mind of God), and the indwelling power by which the Mediator interprets the revelation. And the threefoldness of the Spirit is expressed by St John's mystical geometry. The same seven stars are before the throne, when the throne is seen to stand back in the midst of the twenty-four; and in the right hand of him who sits, when the throne extends to embrace the cherubim; whereas, no sooner does the Lamb appear, than the seven stars are seen to rest upon his head.

None of the picture in IV–V is cancelled, it merely fades, as the first four seals are opened one by one, and one by one the cherubim cry. But with the fifth seal we leave the cherubim behind, and we begin to see the place of the Lamb as the altar of slaughter, a representation irreconcilable with the interpretation of the Seven Stars as the candlestick: the altar of slaughter is not beside the candlestick: the candlestick is within the temple.

The new form of representation begins to work itself out when the seventh seal is broken: over against the altar of slaughter in Aries is set the altar of incense in Virgo. It is not yet said that the second altar is within the shrine, though it must be so. The throne of God is to be located at the apex of the square, the height of a 'heaven' which is set over against an 'earth' below: the two altars are equally 'before' him: the one stands for Christ and the Saints, the other for the angels—it will presently be seen as the region of the stars; and stars are angels (I, 20).[1]

The form created by the incense-vision lasts anyhow to the sixth trumpet, when the incense-altar cries aloud. In the extra visions following that trumpet a new form is substituted. St John measures a line between the 'temple-and-altar' and the outer court. The incense-altar has now become the temple which houses it. Temple and altar still stand beneath and before the Lord, but they no longer represent angels and saints, they represent the character of the apostolic witness as that of 'a kingdom, a priesthood' (I, 6), Judah and Levi.

The sounding of the seventh trumpet continues the evolution

[1] At the blasts of the first three angelic trumpets fiery things fall on earth, sea, and rivers, but at the blast of the fourth nothing falls—the stars, where the angels are, simply turn pale.

241

from altar towards temple which we have witnessed in VI, 9 (altar), VIII, 3-5 (altar and altar of incense), and XI, 1 (temple and altar). Already in the last of these texts the balance has tipped in favour of 'temple'; one cannot couple temple and altar without putting 'temple' first. Now (XI, 19) the altar is quietly let go. We no longer consider the relation of the temple to anything outside it, but only to the Ark of the Covenant which expresses God's presence within it. The development we have followed is in accordance with the calendar. We were at Passover, when the Sun (Christ) is in the Altar (Aries). We advanced to midsummer, where the sun in Gemini is equally balanced above Aries and Virgo. At the seventh trumpet we reach the equinox. The sun is in Virgo, the ark of the covenant is in the temple, and Emmanuel is in the Virgin's womb. The temple now means the Church of God, especially expressed in her divinely-chosen daughter, Mary.

The sun falls away towards midwinter, and on the eve of Dedication (XIV, 13–20) we have the temple and the altar in equipoise once more. We see from this point of vantage a recapitulation of the year's reaping: how the Son of Man reaped corn in Aries, exhorted by an angel from the *temple* opposite, and then how the relation was reversed—an angel from the temple gathered grapes in Virgo, exhorted by an angel from the *altar* opposite him. We have then the Dedication-visions proper, in which the pattern of VIII is carefully rebuilt. We have (*a*) the levitical choir standing against the altar, and interpreted as the triumphant *saints*: (*b*) the incense-ministers coming forth from the temple: these are still liturgical *angels*. The two visions are carefully balanced against one another, the saints by the altar, the angels from the temple. But this is Dedication, in which all parts of the temple should be remembered; Dedication, which in St John's scheme dominates especially the winter quarter; and the position of the saints at the altar is defined by reference to the winter symbol, the 'sea' of glass. They stand above it, as purified in it.[1]

In this way the pattern of VIII is enriched with an element borrowed from IV—nowhere else is the 'sea' of glass mentioned. But it also borrows from XII: the incense is no longer a Godward

[1] The Levitical choir actually stood before the altar, and had the 'sea' or laver to the north-west of them, and so 'below' them according to St John's figure.

242

movement, a presentation of prayers: it is a manward movement, the coming of God into the temple: in XII we saw him in a symbolical Ark, now we see him in the Glory-cloud of power. Thus the Dedication-liturgy is an epitome of all the previous liturgies, Passover (IV–V), Midsummer (VIII), Feast-Season (XII).

The scheme of images thus set up in XV remains in force as far as the seventh vial, when a voice from the throne comes 'out of the temple', for the throne is there, hidden by the cloud. But this is the last we hear of the temple. There is no explicit mention of it or its appurtenances in the setting of the Alleluia-Psalmody out of which Advent breaks (XIX, 1–10.).

After the New Creation, Virgo reappears as the New Jerusalem —St John shews us a Virgin who has expanded to embrace the whole zodiac, and to wear it as a crown about her brows; a temple which has extended over the whole area of the city; jasper-stone which has become the fabric of the whole wall, incorporating in it the twelve jewels as its foundation-blocks. Because the temple swallows up the city, St John sees no temple in it. If we ask, 'What is the city's temple?' the answer will be, 'The throne of God and of the Lamb,' which is also her source of light. And since this is now *the temple*, the enthroned glory is seen in his jasper-aspect, not his sardius-aspect. 'Her luminary is as a stone most precious, a jasper crystal-bright.' Not that the sard of the redeeming Lamb can ever be forgotten: on his last page St John works round once more into the paschal quarter, looking for the Rider on the Horse, and hears the voice of Jesus through his angel: 'I am the root and child of David, the bright and morning star,' i.e. the sardius of Judah, of the altar and of the sunrise.

If we ask the question, 'What is the temple of God and the Lamb?' the answer must be, 'The city.' And therefore the whole city has the dimensions of the Holy of Holies, she is a perfect cube: 'the length, the breadth and the height thereof are equal.' And, like the Holy of Holies, she is lined with gold. But it is gold as clear as glass, like the invisible architecture of the firmament.

Does St John see the throne as occupying the centre of the city, or the place where the temple would be, if there were a temple (Virgo), or the usual place of the throne (Gemini)? Perhaps there is no consistent picture: but since the throne is so emphatically

243

'the throne of God and the Lamb' in the latter half of the vision (XXI, 22–XXII, 5) one would be inclined to see St John's mind settling upon Gemini there. If so, we may see the River of Life as the Milky Way. It comes out by Gemini, a little to the right, i.e. on the side of the quarter of rivers and springs, and flows right across the golden floor of the city-square ($\pi\lambda\alpha\tau\epsilon\iota\alpha$), i.e. the open space in the midst of the zodiacal circle. It cuts the circle again a little to the right of Sagittarius, thus having six of the months (zodiacal signs) to its right, and six to its left: these are, presumably, by a new interpretation, the trees of life. 'He shewed me a river of water of life bright as crystal, issuing from the throne of God and of the Lamb, in the midst of the city square: and, on the one side of the river and on the other, Tree of Life (a collective, as we might say "alder" or "poplar") bearing twelve fruitings, yielding her fruit month by month.'

The vision of the city contains the list of stones. Just as, in a paschal vision (VII) St John counted the tribes from Judah and Aries, so here in a Tabernacles-Dedication vision, he counts the jewels from Virgo and Levi, preserving balance. Following the precedent of VII he goes round anticlockwise. But he seems to use this order of counting generally when he is not following the calendar, but giving a static description: the four cherubim are counted anticlockwise in IV, 7.

244

which the Lamb receives is the antitype to the tables of the Law given to Moses at Sinai and to the scroll of prophecy given to Ezekiel by the River Chebar: it is also the pattern of the temple. We remember that Moses, too, when he had received the tables of the law, was shewn a pattern of the tabernacle in the mountain. Law is a design for the life of God's people under his covenant, and the word of prophecy declares how it will and must be executed; the temple of the New Covenant is no other than the living Israel; law, prophecy and pattern are all one. It is a New Testament commonplace that the word of Christ in the mouth of apostles, prophets and teachers builds up the spiritual house, or 'edifies' the Body of Christ.

St John shews us the great assembly: there is the throne of the royal Father, there are (a) the twenty-four elders also enthroned, in antitype to the twenty-four elders of priesthood in Chronicles. We hear next (b) of the four cherubic guardians antitypic to the Levitical guardians of the four-sided precinct. At this point the giving of the book takes place, and is greeted by the hymn which was provoked by the enthusiasm of the scene in Chronicles: 'Blessed art thou,' said David, 'O Lord God of Israel, our Father, from everlasting to everlasting: to thee, Lord, the greatness and the power and the exultation and the victory and the might. . . . From thee the wealth and the glory.' 'Worthy is the Lamb that was slain,' sings the angelic host, 'to receive the power and wealth and wisdom and might and honour and glory and blessing.' The same form of praise is repeated to the Enthroned Glory and the Lamb together: just before the appearance of the Lamb the En-throned Glory receives it alone. The benediction of David is the ultimate model for their hymns: there is nothing else of the same style in the Old Testament.

After this St John proceeds with the opening of the book, and the accompanying visions. With VII he resumes the theme of the Israelite muster. We now witness (c) the census and sealing of the twelve thousand from each tribe. The impressive repetitions of the catalogue echo the style of Chronicles. 'Over the first course for the first month Jeshboam the son of Zabdiel, and in his course twenty and four thousands. And over the course of the second month Dodiah the son of Ehohi, and in his course twenty and

247

four thousands' and so on. There can be no doubt that the sealing of the twelve twelve thousands follows the model of the twelve twenty-four thousands in Chronicles. (e) But, as in Chronicles, the numbered thousands are not Israel: Israel is numberless as the stars of the sky, and so St John proceeds direct from the vision of the 144,000 to the vision of the host that no man can number.

There is no need to labour the evidence for the parallel. If St John was not using Chronicles here, then no argument of the type we are constructing can have any validity. Let us pass to the more interesting work of interpretation.

The $12 \times 12,000$ is obviously the perfect number of a 'four-square Israel'. It is the number which Chronicles approaches, as it were, from both ends in the 24 courses of 12 Levites, and the 12 courses of 24,000 Israelites. Why does not Chronicles get rid of the last shred of asymmetry and use the simple 12×12? Because, as a matter of hard fact, there were 24 courses of the priesthood, supposed to belong to 24 priestly families. So Chronicles sets out with the task of establishing a balance between the 24 elders and the 12 patriarchs, and does it in the figure:

XXIV ELDERS
XXIV courses of XII Levites
XII courses of XXIV thousands
XII PHYLARCHS

St John states the perfect square twelve of thousands, denying the number twenty-four its claim to belong to the essence of Israel: and yet he keeps the twenty-four elders. How can that fit? Surely the figure

XXIV ELDERS
XII tribes of XII thousands
XII PATRIARCHS
is intolerable.

The awkwardness is removed by the symbolism of the city on St John's last page, which exhibits the twenty-four as no sum of twenty-four equal and identical units, but as the manifestation of a fundamental twelve in two aspects. Within the city, as in the heavenly assembly in IV–V, is the throne of God and the Lamb, and around it is the circle of twenty-four, in antitype to the twenty-four presbyteral thrones. The number is made up of twelve blocks of continuous foundations, with the twelve gaps between forming the city's gates. Every block of continuous foundation is built of one sort of precious stone, every gate is closed by a single pearl. So we have a necklace of alternate pearls and precious stones, laid in a square figure:

This necklace, or to use St John's language, this coronet, is not of twenty-four things in any one class of thing, but of twelve stones interset with pearls. The twelve stones are inscribed with the names of the apostles, the pearly gates with those of the tribes, whose angels guard them. But the stones are essentially tribal emblems too. The twelve apostles are the tribal chiefs of the new Israel: he who ordained them declared that they should sit on thrones, judging the twelve tribes. The city's coronet, therefore, consists of the twelve tribes, each with its ruler, and each with its angel: just as each of the seven churches has its angel and, we must suppose, its presiding elder or bishop too.

To St John's mind, we must conclude, the twenty-four of Chronicles is one of the opaque figures of the old covenant which has become perspicuous in the new. The old covenant had no twelve names which were the doubles of the twelve tribes: the only names comparable with the tribes were those of the patriarchs, but the names of the patriarchs *are* the names of the tribes, and, on the level of symbolism, the patriarchs are the tribes themselves. There were tribal captains who changed from generation to generation, and Chronicles gives a list of those for Solomon's time; but their names were really nothing. Now every tribe has its apostle, and the 24 elders turn out to be a sign of this fulfilment. In IV St John repeats the sign without comment in describing the heavenly 'Church' of the present age: in the city of the age to come he shows the fulfilment.

We may consider next what the relation is between the 144,000 of the sealing vision and the countless multitude of the vision succeeding it. The modern literalist will naturally incline to say that the 12,000 from each Israelite tribe represent the Israelites converted to Christianity, and the countless multitude from every nation, tribe, people and tongue the whole Catholic Church. But this interpretation leads to impossible difficulties. Not to mention the fact that most of the literal twelve tribes had apostatized and disappeared, leaving at the most Simeon, Levi, Judah, Benjamin, and an Ephraim whose credentials would not bear inspection, we have the more formidable difficulty that in XIV, 1–5 the 144,000 represent the Kingdom of Christ set over against the Kingdom of Antichrist. The Kingdom of Christ cannot by this time consist wholly or even 'in principle' of Israelites by blood. Moreover, in the city of the World to Come the 12 × 12 thousand remains the basis of all measurement.

The text of Chronicles supplies us with the answer. The 144,000 are the heads of families, the patriarchal *cadre* of the numberless host. It is the heads of families who above all others must appear at Zion for the set feasts: we have seen that the 144,000 who stand with the Lamb on the holy mountain keeping the feast of Passover in Apocalypse XIV are all adult males, 'he-lambs without blemish.' Now the ancient Israel was propagated according to the flesh, the new Israel is propagated according to the spirit: Christians are begotten not by natural fathers, but by apostles (as St Paul tells the Corinthians), or anyhow by elder Christians already possessed of the Faith and Spirit. So then the first fruits of the Church are also

250

its heads of families, begetting the rest. Stephanas's household, being the 'firstfruits of Achaea', are appointed by St Paul to preside over the family of God in Corinth (I Cor. XVI, 15). So the Church has 12 apostles and 12 × 12 thousand firstfruits, who both beget and preside over the countless harvest. In Apocalypse VII, 1–8 we have the sealing of the firstfruits, in 9–17 the vision of the harvest. The final vision of the Bride shows under the imagery of a city the countless host brigaded under the twelve princes and the twelve-times-twelve thousand fathers. From beginning to end we are dealing with a new spiritual Israel, for in Christ there is neither Jew nor Greek, circumcision nor uncircumcision.

The application of the numbers to the measures of the city is quite straightforward. 'The city lies four-square, and the length of it equals the breadth. And the angel measured the city with his reed to the measure of twelve thousand furlongs' involving a square measure of 144 thousand *thousand*: we have already multiplied by a thousand, already we are advancing from the numbered *cadre* to the numberless host. But we have further to go, for St John adds: 'The length and the breadth *and the height* of it are all equal,' which gives us the cubic number, 12 × 144 thousand thousand thousand. For fear that we should fail to see the point, he proceeds: 'And he measured the wall thereof' (a comparison with Ezekiel's measuring vision shows that the thickness is meant) 'as 144 cubits, in man's measure, that is to say, the angel's'. This sentence, to begin with, puts us in mind that the previous twelves in the square measures are to be multiplied by one another (12 × 12 = 144). It also conveys a mystery in the phrase 'measure of man'.

The phrase has a plain literal meaning, as Deuteronomy III, 11 shows. It means that the 144 cubits are just cubits measured on a man's forearm—a piece of information of which the practical value may seem to be nullified by the added note, that the 'man' is in this case the angel: for who has measured an angel's forearm? Obviously, then, the sentence, being geometrical nonsense, must be spiritual sense. The phrase 'measure of (a) man' has a mysterious ring. Deuteronomy in the text from which the idea is borrowed uses the straightforward 'cubit of man', which suggests no mysteries. St John's mysterious equivalent echoes the darkest riddle of his whole book, the number of the Beast: 'He that hath

251

understanding, let him reckon the number of the Beast, for it is number of (a) man. His number is 666. And I beheld, and lo, the Lamb standing in Mt Zion, and with him 144 thousands.' The 666 is opposed, it would appear, to the 144: the 666 is 'number of man' in XIII, 1 and the 144 is 'measure of man' in XXI. The mystical suggestion of the phrase in XXI is, presumably, that the measures, the squared 12,000 and its cube, are to be taken out in men, rather than in literal stones or gold: and that since measure of man is now measure of angel, the men are to be considered as of angelic stature and glory.

'The length, the breadth, and the height are all equal.' When St John a few verses back put the names of the apostles on the foundations of a living city, he appeared to be quoting St Paul to the Ephesians. 'Ye are fellow-*citizens*' (we speak of a city, then) 'of the saints, and denizens of God's house, built up upon the *foundation of the apostles* and prophets, Christ himself being the chief corner-stone, on whom the whole building is fitted, and grows into a holy temple in the Lord; in whom ye are built up together for a habitation of God in Spirit.' (In spirit in this age: in substance and person in the age to come.) St Paul resumes this theme in the next chapter: 'That Christ may dwell in your hearts; with your root and *your foundation* in love, that ye may be able to comprehend with all the saints what is the *breadth and length and height* and depth, to know the love of Christ which surpasses knowledge, that ye may be filled with all the fulness of God' (Eph. II, 19–22, III, 17–19).

These texts from Ephesians were doubtless well meditated by St John, and they express exactly what his imagery means. The city which is also a temple is the Body of Christ, which now grows, but will be seen to have reached its fulness in the World to Come. This fulness is 'the fulness of God', that is to say, all of the divine life that can be poured into the creature. The recipient is made perfect, in quality as well as in number, for 'she has the glory of God'. But in number as well as in quality: for it takes all the saints, each in his special way reflecting God and reflecting the others, to set forth the fulness, the length and the breadth and the height of 'Christ-in-us', now 'the hope', but then the substance, 'of glory.'

252

'The length and the breadth and the height are equal.' A cubic city is not so much impossible as meaningless: one can have a cubic structure, even a structure measuring fifteen hundred miles each way where the miles are paced out in angel's paces, but it will not be a city. No: it will be a sanctuary, and that is exactly what St John means, for the Holy of Holies had the dimensions of a cube. The city is all a sacred precinct: the sacred precinct is all a Holy of Holies, and therefore the length, the breadth, and the height are equal. Like the Holy of Holies, it is lined, even paved, with gold: but the gold is transparent as glass, like the sky. It is walled about with precious stones: of Solomon's temple we read that it was built wholly of 'squared precious stones', and though 'precious' here has not the technical sense, and simply means 'costly', it is still the same word.

Across the golden paving of the city square runs the river of life, poured from the throne of God and of the Lamb, watering on either side the tree of life. The tree has twelve fruitings, one every month, for the twelve mystical tribes of the New Israel. The comparison of the tribes with the months is old. In Chronicles the twelve courses of twice twelve thousand men are on duty month by month. In the Apocalypse the many times twelve thousand receive the fruit of immortality month by month. The river and the trees shew that the city, or precinct, or sanctuary is also the garden of Paradise.

St John does not measure the flow of the river here. Elsewhere he does. Since the great river is the Milky Way, it runs from Gemini to Sagittarius, and coincides with the upright diagonal of St John's cornerwise square. The square has a side of twelve thousand furlongs, and therefore it has a diagonal of seventeen thousand furlongs. The ratio between the diagonal and the side is well known to be an awkward one. If we have the side and want the diagonal, we must square the side, double the square, and take the square root of the product. $12^2 \times 2 = 288$, $17^2 = 289$. So seventeen is very nearly the exact diagonal of the square twelve. It is, indeed, one of the mathematical beauties of the square upon twelve, that its diagonal is so nearly a whole number. None of the smallish numbers can compare with twelve in this respect.

St John's Gospel, like his Apocalypse, ends with an appendix-

253

scene. The Apocalypse appears to be ending at XXI, 8, when the Enthroned Glory himself says Amen to the fulfilment of all his words; yet it opens out afresh into the vision of the Bridal City. And the Gospel appears to be ending at XX, 31, when the apostolic witness has testified to the purpose of all that he has written; yet it opens out afresh into the scene of the miraculous fishing. Sir Edwyn Hoskyns points out in his commentary that the symbolism of the miraculous fishing depends upon the text about the River of Life in Ezekiel XLVII; whithersoever the waters came, the Dead Sea was healed, and swarmed with every kind of fish. So Jesus is seen directing his fisher-disciples to cast their net where the living currents are, that is, to missionize where the Holy Ghost prepares their hearers. Very well, then; Apocalypse and Gospel not only both end in appendix-scenes, the two appendices both allegorize the appendix-visions of Ezekiel (XL–XLVIII). The Apocalypse concentrates more on Ezekiel's city, the Gospel wholly upon his river. The Apocalypse measures the city, the Gospel measures the river: Ezekiel measures both.

Sir Edwyn shews that the number of the miraculous catch, 153, is what the ancients called the triangular power of 17. (Of the nature of triangulars we shall speak directly.) Here Sir Edwyn stops, because 17 considered in itself is a meaningless number. But we do not need to consider it in itself; we may consider it as the diagonal of the square twelve, as the measure of that river which, issuing out of the throne of God and of the Lamb, cuts Paradise from top to bottom. It is then obviously good sense to see the fishes as the 'fullness' or 'complement' of the River of Life, just as the citizens are the fullness or complement of the square city.

But why, we may still ask, does St John take the *triangular* power of 17 as its 'fulness', rather than the square? The answer is that the square (289) is a meaningless number, whereas the triangular (153) receives an appropriate sense from that very treatise of numbers which St John found in Solomon's temple-building. The labour of the building was done by the non-Israelites of Solomon's dominions; 153 thousand and some odd hundreds were set to work (II Chron. II, 17-18: VIII, 7-8). What could be more appropriate to St John's purpose? The miraculous catch, as has long been recognized, signifies Gentile converts: it is these, rather than the Jews, who build up the temple of God, the Church. There are other interesting features in the 153, but it is beside our purpose to consider them here.

Since we have touched upon the measure of the River of Life, which is not to be found in the Apocalypse, it would be unreasonable to leave uncommented the measure of the river of death, which is. 'The winepress was trodden outside the city, and blood came out of the winepress to the height of the horses' bridles and to a distance of 1,600 furlongs' (XIV, 20). The number must be a mystery, but what is the mystery? The city outside whose walls the vintage of wrath is trodden is a mystical Jerusalem, yet not the Jerusalem of the World to Come. The final Jerusalem measures 12,000 stades along the side. Perhaps the mystical Jerusalem of this age measures 1,200. Then her square measure will be 1,440,000. Alas, that is a nought too many: her square is 144,000. Yes, but we must choose, it would seem, between $120 \times 120 = 14,400$ and $1,200 \times 1,200 = 1,440,000$, for the square root of 144,000 is an agony to extract and has no appearance of being a power of 12 when we have got it. We shall naturally prefer the fuller number, 1,200 not 120. So let 1,200 be the side of the city. Then each of the three tribal units of which the side is made up will be 400. So 1,600 takes us all along the side, and one unit round the corner. The place of the horsemen (IX, 16, XVI, 12, XIX, 11, 14) is in the spring quarter from Aries upward: the place of the winepress is Gehenna at the bottom corner of the square. So up the side and round the

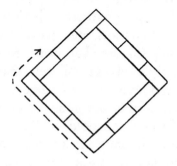

corner the blood will have to flow, to reach 'the bridles of the horses'. That is the best we can do with the 1,600. Let us hope someone will soon do better.

255

We must turn back to the 666, the most notorious of the riddles, and to the history of Solomon, which is its source. Solomon is a type of Christ, but he is a type of Antichrist also. Almost every type has this doubleness. Adam is the type of the Son of God, and also of the sin that lost the garment of glory. Eve is the bride of the heavenly Adam and the mother of the Seed who crushes the Serpent's head: she is also the woman who makes common cause with the Serpent and offers the fruit of sin to all mankind. We see the holy Eve in Apocalypse XII and XXI, the wicked Eve in XVII. Solomon is the son of David, of whom God said through Nathan, 'I will be to him a Father, and he shall be to me a Son.' He is the man of peace; his hands, free from David's bloodstains, are fit to build the temple of God which is the type of the Church. Each new generation seems to bear the hope of purity because it has not yet been tried, it puts behind it the errors of its fathers and aspires to be the seed that shall crush the serpent's head. It fails when it is put to the test, for it is not Christ. Solomon built the temple, and then proceeded to apostatize at leisure.[1] The throne of David shook, the kingdom was divided, and messianic glory did not return for a thousand years.

The story of the good Solomon continues as far as the visit of the Queen of Sheba, whose converse with Solomon is a model of princely courtesy between man and woman in the service of wisdom. From the queen's departure onwards the King breaks the law of kingship[2] clause by clause. 'He shall not multiply horses to himself, nor cause the people to return to Egypt that he may multiply horses'—'Solomon gathered chariots and horsemen, a thousand four hundred chariots, and twelve thousand horsemen. The horses which King Solomon had were brought out of Egypt.' 'Neither shall he multiply wives to himself, that his heart turn not aside'—'King Solomon loved many strange women . . . and they turned aside his heart after other gods.' 'Neither shall he greatly multiply to himself silver and gold'—'The weight of gold that came to King Solomon in one year was six hundred and sixty-six talents of gold.' The damnable number appears in the very next

---

[1] This part of the story is not in Chronicles: we must turn to the equivalent part of I Kings.

[2] Deuteronomy XVII.

256

verse after the withdrawal of the Queen of Sheba (I Kings x, 14). The root of all evil begins the King's downfall.

St John's use of Solomon's history as a source-book of numbers makes it virtually certain that he found the number of the Beast here: but its mere occurrence where it stands is not enough to explain the use he makes of it. There is plenty in the Apocalypse about the money basis of worldly power: where the mark of the 666 is given, it is used to regulate commerce. But why should it express the person or the name of Antichrist? Why is it so deep and so blasphemous a mystery?

The answer is to be found in its opposition to the name of Christ. St John immediately opposes to the men marked with the 666 on forehead or hand the 144,000 marked with the name of the Lamb and of his Father. 888 is the number of the Name of Jesus, reckoned by the rabbinic device of *Gematria*. In Greek (and Hebrew) the letters of the alphabet are used for numbers. $IH\Sigma OY\Sigma$ (Jesus) in Greek is $10+8+200+70+400+200=888$. To one who worked with number symbolism as St John does, this piece of wisdom cannot have been lacking. So, as he reads the tenth chapter of I Kings, it occurs to him that the arresting number 666 is a parody of the Name of Jesus.

Well, you may say, if 888 is the numerical value of the Holy Name, of what name is 666 the numerical value? It is not necessary to find an answer to this question, and none ever has been found, except by cheating.[1] Irenaeus very wisely remarked (after explaining the method of translating into letters) that as Antichrist has not yet appeared, we do not know what his name will

[1] The noblest example is that which obtains 'Caesar Nero' by transliterating those names into Hebrew and taking the numerical values of the Hebrew letters. This is not, on examination, quite so impressive as it sounds. For (*a*) 'Caesar' is otiose: we select this name to fit our convenience from many possible names and titles of Nero; (*b*) in transliterating a foreign name into Hebrew you have great latitude in the way of putting in or leaving out or varying vowel-letters: there are two, or at a pinch, three alternative letters for the S: we can either take 'Nero' (Latin) or 'Neron' (Greek). If, under these conditions, we can get a result, it is not so remarkable as it looked at first. Jesus is 888 in Greek, not Hebrew. St John, the teacher of Asian Christians, calls on his intelligent (Greek) reader to 'work the sum' of the 666. St John puts a *Gematria* puzzle into his Gospel, and that too is Greek, not Hebrew (John v, 2).

be. There are many possible names that conform to the number. Irenaeus's judgement is absurd if it means that St John has been given an unfounded intuition of the number to which this name, when known, will be found to conform. But it is a very sensible judgement if it means that by an inspired calculation from existing data St John arrives at the number, and leaves history to supply the name. This appears to be the truth. He read the 666 in Kings with the 888 in his head. That is all.

St John asks himself next why the diabolic parody of 888 should be 666 rather than 555 or 777. Before he can answer this, he will naturally consider why 888 is divinely appropriate to the person of our Redeemer. This, surely, is plain. It is a most emphatic exposition of 8, and 8 is the number of the Sunday after Holy Week, the day of Resurrection, the day of the First-and-Last who died and lives. If we compare 666 with this, it is even more emphatically an exposition of 6, than 888 is of 8. For if we take 6 and square it, we have 36, and if we triangulate 36, we have 666.

Triangulation is an idea in which ancient mathematicians were more interested than our contemporaries are. A diagram will explain it at a glance:

The first figure shows how 25 is the *square* of 5, the second how the *triangular* of 5 is 15. When we say that 666 is the triangular of 36 we mean that it bears to 36 the same relation as 15 bears to 5 in the figure. As the figure shows, the triangular of a given number is the sum of all the whole numbers up to, and including, that number. $5tr. = 1+2+3+4+5$. The formula for finding the triangular of any number is $\dfrac{n(n+1)}{2}$. Then $\dfrac{36 \times 37}{2} = 666$. So 666 is an exposition of 6, both because of its apparent form, and because it is a 'power' of 6, viz. the triangular of its square.

Why should Antichrist be so emphatically *six*? The whole arrangement of the Apocalypse explains this. The divine work with which it deals is a work of judgement: it is judgement which has the sixfold pattern of the working-days, and always on the sixth day there is the culmination of judgement. On the sixth day of the week, and the sixth hour, says St John,[1] the kingdoms of Christ and Antichrist looked one another in the face in Pilate's court, and the adherents of the False Prophet (Caiaphas) firmly wrote on their foreheads the mark of the Beast, when they said, 'We have no King but Caesar.' Presently they saw the Lamb uplifted with his true Name over his head, 'King of the Jews': and for all they could do, they could not get it erased: 'What I have written,' said Pilate, 'I have written.' Christ's Friday victory is the supreme manifestation also of Antichrist.

The number of the Beast reveals him as both the instrument of judgement on the wicked and the object of judgement himself. But that is not all. St John takes up two mathematical properties of the 666. First, 666 is what we should call the recurrent decimal for $\frac{2}{3}$. St John's age did not talk about recurrent decimals, but of course St John could recognize 666 as two-thirds of that standard quantity, the thousand. Why is Antichrist *two-thirds*? Because the angels of the trumpets have destroyed one-third of everything before he begins to reign, and the angels of the vials return with total destruction as he comes to his end. In the interval he reigns over a kingdom of two-thirds.

Now for the second mathematical property of 666. A glance back at the triangular 15 in the figure above will show us that every triangular, as well as having a base (in this case 5) has a periphery or surround (in this case 12). As the base of 666 is 36, so the periphery is 105. The whole 666 is the 'filling in' or 'fulfilment' of the periphery 105. In the figure above we may remove the periphery, and then we are left with a single triangle of 3. In a bigger triangle one could obviously strip away triangle after triangle before one came to the last or nuclear triangle. 666 consists of *twelve* triangles one inside another, 105 being the number of units in the outermost triangle. And the factors of 105 are $30 \times 3\frac{1}{2}$.

666, therefore, is a 12-fold triangle with a periphery of $30 \times 3\frac{1}{2}$.

[1] John XIX, 13–22; cf. Apocalypse XIII, 16–XIV, 1.

259

St John's calculation of the period of the Beast's reign, in days, is 12 (months) $\times$ 30 (days) $\times$ $3\frac{1}{2}$ (years). The coincidence between this reckoning and the factors of the 666 triangle is no mere accident. St John's reckoning of the period of the reign is artificial, devised for the sake of conformity with the factors of the 666 triangle. There neither is nor was any calendar in which $3\frac{1}{2}$ years are $3\frac{1}{2}$ times twelve months of thirty days each.[1] The purpose of the artificial reckoning is to exhibit the Beast's fatally limited reign as a function of his number.

[1] A solar calendar requires that about every other month shall be of 31 days, not 30. A lunar calendar must have every other month of 29 days and an intercalary month a little more frequently than every third year. So by lunar reckoning, $3\frac{1}{2}$ years is either about 1,270, or about 1,300 days: or, if we neglect intercalation entirely, it is about 1,240 days. In no case is it 1,260 days.

CHAPTER X

There has sometimes been a fruitless debate as to whether St John's writings are 'rabbinical' or 'gnostical'. Neither aspect can, in fact, be denied to them. If we had been studying half a century ago, we might have been exerting ourselves to distinguish two strains of influence behind, or even two perceptible and undigested sources within, his written work, the one gnostic and Greek, the other Jewish and rabbinic. Nowadays it seems more fruitful to look into the thought-process, and to find out, if we can, what St John *does*. If we have at all succeeded in this attempt, we may hope to have shewn how gnostical rabbinism worked, when it had been baptized into Christ.

The rabbinic tradition, with its holy book, its methods of inspired analogizing from text to text, its formal elaboration and its lack of philosophical discipline, was, on the face of it, a perfect raw material for theosophy. It hardly needed to be infected from without to become a full-blown *gnosis*. What may surprise us is the success of orthodox Pharisaism in confining and suffocating such vagaries. Yet there is evidence that the success was not so complete as the Talmudic literature would suggest. Under the shadow of Pharisaic rabbinism there was always a mystical activity, taking different forms at different times. It touches apocalyptic in II Enoch, Platonism in Philo; it finds its own form in later Jewish Cabbalism. Much of it spilt over into downright gnostic heresy by the way. Like other strands of Jewish spirituality which Pharisaic orthodoxy could not fully accommodate, it found its happiest and safest escape into Christianity. The teaching of St Paul must have seemed to the other old pupils of Gamaliel a combination of everything they had been taught to think unsound, and, not least, of gnosticism.

We certainly distinguish between heretical gnosticism and orthodox Christian spirituality. St Paul drew the line himself, in his epistle to Colossae. Mystical interpretation, mystical activity, must centre on, and be absorbed by, Christ. By this principle the rank growths of gnostic elaboration are cut. Christian *gnosis* is of Christ's person, and of the extension of his person, the Church; heretical *gnosis* erects a cosmic frame in which Christ must find his place. If one is trying to make up one's mind whether, say, Origen was heretical or orthodox, one finds oneself considering whether his system is a gnostical Christology expanding to cover everything in the universe, or a gnostical cosmology which determines the place of Christ within itself. It is this issue, rather than his method or temper of mind, which is decisive for his orthodoxy.

St John is extremely rabbinical, extremely gnostical, and extremely orthodox. His material is rabbinic, his method gnostical, his substance massively Christian. He marshals his scriptural figures with the mind of a rabbi, he divines from them like a gnostic, by means of a magic diagram. But every method of divination is no more than a means by which inspiration is liberated: it in no way determines what the inspired mind will conceive. A man might sit down before St John's diagram and run the point of his pen round the figures, and see any number of different visionary worlds. St John sees what he sees, because his mind is controlled by the Spirit of Christ. The Spirit passes through the divinatory technique like sunlight through clear glass, and falls straight upon the scriptural images behind, which are the natural types of Christian fact.

Those who explore the Jewish mystical tradition which lies behind the ultimate emergence of the Cabbala, find a special place to be occupied in it by the Tetragrammaton, the first words of Genesis, and the Chariot-vision of Ezekiel. The first words of Genesis are a staple of St Paul's more gnostical flights; Colossians I, 12–20 contains a multiple exposition of them. The Johannine Gospel springs out of the same text, as out of a well. We know that the Chariot-vision of Ezekiel was meditated by Jews who wished to 'ascend into heaven' by the Spirit: it was a technique of ecstasy. St John makes the meditation in Apocalypse IV, and into heaven he ascends. St Paul had ascended there before him, whether in Ezekiel's Chariot or no, we cannot tell, for he refuses to write the vision (II Cor. XII, 1–5).

It seems necessary to suppose further that St John speculated on the letters of the ineffable Name: for otherwise it is difficult to

262

understand his use of the title, 'the A and the Ω.' St John employs it in contexts of the greatest possible solemnity. In I, 8 and XXI, 6 alone the Father is directly said to speak. In I, 8 he says: 'Yea, Amen: I am the A and the Ω, saith the Lord God, the IS and WAS and COMETH, the Almighty.' In XXI it is: 'He that sitteth upon the throne saith: I make all things new. And, saith he, Write that these words are faithful and true' (i.e. Amen). 'And he saith to me: They are done. I am the A and the Ω, the beginning and the end.' There is only one other occurrence of the phrase, XXII, 13, in a text which transfers to Christ the lordship and the majesty. He says: 'Lo, I come quickly, and my reward is with me, to pay every man as his work is. I am the A and the Ω, the first and the last, the beginning and the end.' In all three texts it is God, or Christ in the full glory of his godhead, who speaks.

It is difficult to believe that in these texts 'the A and the Ω' is a mere paraphrase of 'the first and the last'. 'The first and the last' is a self-description of God in the prophecies of Isaiah: are we to believe that St John felt himself to have added to it by 'the A and the Z', to use our own alphabet? It would be risky to settle such a point by appeal to one's own impression of St John's sense for style. We can, in fact, do better. It appears that Talmudic writers use the Hebrew equivalent 'the A and the T', but they do not use it as a title of God. 'He made everything,' they say, 'from the A to the T,' and find a symbol of this in an unimportant and almost redundant particle following 'made' in Genesis I, I, 'In the beginning God made heaven and earth'; for the particle consists of an A and a T. They said also that God's seal is truth, and his truth is the beginning, middle and end, because the letters of the word 'truth' are AMT, the first, middle and last letters of the alphabet. Here we are very close indeed to St John. A connected word for truth, AMN (Amen), is made a name of God by Isaiah, and St John has several allusions to it. But AMN is not AMT, it has the wrong letters for our purpose: the Rabbis can say that AMT is the *seal* of God, they have no authority for making it his Name, and in consequence they do not apply the 'A and T' formula to him direct.[1]

[1] For a useful summary of the facts, see Dr Oesterley's article 'A and Ω' in the *Encyclopedia of Religion and Ethics*.

If the Rabbis (we shall naturally conclude) had used a form of divine Name which began with A and ended with T, they would have felt that God's being the first and the last could be read off from his Name: and then they might have used 'the A and the T' as a solemn title. This would have been especially probable, if the ineffable Name itself were of such a form. In fact, of course, the Name JHVH does not even contain either letter. But St John is writing in Greek. We know from a good deal of scattered evidence that the Gentile world accepted $IA\Omega$ as the expression of the sound of the ineffable Name. That Jahoh or Jahuh had been one pronunciation of the Name in Israel seems highly probable: it may have been commoner than the form IAVE which Origen accepted from certain Rabbis, and we have accepted from him. It would be absurd to enter here into the merits of such a question: for it is of no interest to us here to prove that the current Greek form $IA\Omega$ was correct: all we need to know is that it was current. If it was current, St John is most likely to have used it, and if he used it, there is nothing surprising about his sacred formula, 'I am the A and the Ω.'

There is a further confirmation. Reitzenstein,[1] thinking to show that St John was subject to Gentile influences, cites evidence for 'the A and the Ω' as a title of the somewhat shadowy God $AI\Omega N$, or *Eternitas*. It was natural for Reitzenstein to see St John as a simple borrower here, because he had not had leisure to make the minute examination of St John which would have shewn him that St John never just borrows, he always thinks. The name $AI\Omega N$ is an example of a short name largely composed of the letters A and Ω; the Name $IA\Omega$ is an even more striking example. That St John was thinking of God and Christ under the name $AI\Omega N$ is a suggestion not worth considering. That he was thinking of them under the Name JHVH is quite certain; and that he used the Greek equivalent $IA\Omega$ is probable in itself, and strongly confirmed by what we can see him to have done.

St John does not write the Greek Trigrammaton $IA\Omega$. He was probably still enough of a Jew to feel that it would be profanation to do so. He is, however, prepared to hint at it in riddles. The Trigrammaton, if we do dare to write it down and look at it,

[1] R. Reitzenstein, *Das Iranische Erlösungs-mysterium*, p. 244.

264

seems every bit as mysterious as its Hebrew original, the Tetragrammaton JHVH. Here is a word composed wholly of vowels, vowels not taken at random, either, but the middle one, the first, and the last, as we can see by simply writing out the vowel list, $A\epsilon\eta I o\upsilon\Omega$. Moreover, the first and last of the vowels are also the first and last letters of the whole alphabet. The Name seems providentially designed to express 'Him first, him last, him midst, and without end'.

But is it not a pity that the order is $I A\Omega$, not $A I\Omega$? Here Reitzenstein's $A I\Omega N$ seems to have an advantage which does something to balance the disadvantage of its superfluous N. Yet the $I A\Omega$ order has its own merit: for do we not naturally begin with the present, with what God is, before going on to speak of what he was or will be? The Name JHVH ($=I A\Omega$) was divinely interpreted to Moses as 'He that is' ($\dot{o}$ $\ddot{\omega}\nu$). Under the influence of the $I A\Omega$ St John develops it in the three tenses, 'the IS, WAS, and COMETH.' Exodus and the $I A\Omega$ are at one in demanding that the IS should stand first. When St John writes

> I AM the A and the Ω
> Saith THE LORD God
> the IS and WAS and COMETH
>   the Almighty

we ought to see that he is writing a triple parallel:

> I AM . A . Ω
> saith I A Ω
> IS . WAS . COMETH
>   Almighty.

There is a strong confirmation of this interpretation in the other two A and Ω texts, those in XXI and XXII. In a Greek predicative sentence the verb *to be* may be written or omitted at will. For the purposes of a parallel with the three-part IS, WAS, COMETH it is necessary for St John to express the verb in the sentence 'I am the A and the Ω', or he has nothing to parallel the IS. But in XXI and XXII he uses the short form of sentence without the verb expressed, and having done so, supplies it with a two-part parallel only, as it is appropriate that he should:

265

I (am) the A and the Ω,
> the beginning and the end,

and

I (am) the A and the Ω,
> the first and the last,
> the beginning and the end.

'But', it may be objected, 'if the connexion between the $IA\Omega$ and the A and Ω is so close as you allege, how can the A and Ω be allowed to degenerate into a simple two-part formula at the end of the book?' That is what we shall try to explain presently. We will attend now to the first chapter, in which anyhow the phrase is minted.

'I AM the A and the Ω, saith THE LORD God,
The IS and the WAS and the COMETH, the Almighty.'

The logicians tell us that the verb *to be* as used in predicative sentences does not assert existence, but simply joins the predicate to the subject. If, for example, we say that mermaids are fish-tailed girls, we are not held to assert that mermaids enjoy an existence that is fish-tailed and girlish, for they enjoy no existence at all. We mean merely that the notion of mermaid includes the notions expressed in the two descriptions. The logicians may say what they choose, and we may talk as we choose. However it may be with speaking of mermaids, it is natural enough for a man who has read the third chapter of Exodus to feel that every sentence in which the verb *to be* joins an attribute to the Name of God asserts, above all, his infinite existence, and secondarily a mode in which that existence is expressed. This, anyhow, is the mind of St John. When Jesus at Gethsemane says, 'I am (Jesus of Nazareth),' the assertion of absolute existence so overshadows the admission of human identity, that those who have come there to arrest Jesus of Nazareth fall on their faces before HIM WHO IS. The emphasis on the verb *to be* is strengthened by the option of omitting it in Greek: its presence may appear all the more significant when it is written. We can begin with the form: $\dot{\epsilon}\gamma\dot{\omega}\,IA\Omega$, 'I (am) THE LORD,' and then expand it as: $\dot{\epsilon}\gamma\dot{\omega}\,\epsilon\dot{I}\mu\iota\,\tau\dot{o}\,A\,\kappa\alpha\dot{\iota}\,\tau\dot{o}\,\Omega$, 'I AM the A and the Ω,' the IS, the WAS, and the COMETH. We begin with the attempt to

266

assert a mere equivalence between the subject and his Name, without asserting his existence, and then find that his existence is asserted in the Name itself. St Anselm mistook this for philosophy, and gave the world the Ontological Proof. It is bad philosophy, for one may disbelieve in God. It is good divinity, for one cannot believe in the God of Abraham, Isaac and Jacob, and at the same time disbelieve that whatever is truly asserted of him is a partial expression of his act of infinite existence.

The order of the three letters is significant for St John. They do not stand in the order of the alphabet as $AI\Omega$. God is not the WAS, IS, and SHALL BE, as though his being were merely the present phase of something previous and the preliminary phase of something still to be. He simply IS, and for that reason he WAS (our beginning) and COMES (to be our end). Of Antichrist it is said that he WAS and IS NOT and WILL BE HERE, for his present not-being is nothing but the cancellation of his WAS, and the delay of his WILL BE. Yet to state the opposition between the divine formula and the demonic formula as baldly as this is an over-simplification. It is true that the only formula for Antichrist is in this order, and that the characteristic and proper formula for the Divine Name is $IA\Omega$. But after the $IA\Omega$ order has been firmly established—it occurs under various disguises six times in the first chapter—St John rings the changes on the letters. In IV we have $AI\Omega$, to express the sempiternity of God's praise, 'as it was in the beginning, is now, and ever shall be, world without end,' and this is the last complete formula of the three tenses before the occurrence of the $AI\Omega$ antichrist formula in XVII, as the direct blasphemy of it. (Of incomplete formulas we will speak presently.) In the last chapter of all we have $A\Omega I$, 'the first and the last. . . . I AM.'

The WILL BE form of Ω is wholly reserved for Antichrist. There is nothing in the being of God which allows of future actualization. On the contrary, his infinite Act of being is so full, that it IS COMING upon the future of his creatures. The form used of Antichrist, WILL BE HERE ($\pi\acute{a}\rho\epsilon\sigma\tau a\iota$) would otherwise seem to recommend itself. It is a word actually associated with primitive Christian Advent-hope—it yields the common verbal noun Parousia which is almost technical for 'Advent'—and it is a proper partner to IS and WAS, because it also contains the verb to be. But St John will not use it of Christ and God. He prefers a form which directly answers the Maranatha-prayer: 'Come Lord'—'I come', 'I am the IS, WAS, and COMETH'. The answer to the prayer is the energy of the divine actuality, extending into man's future.

The ineffable Name is sometimes written short (JH) in the Old Testament, and then it appears in our Bibles as JAH. This will mean for St John a two-letter form IA alongside the three-letter form $IA\Omega$. The two letters, paraphrased according to St John's rules, will mean 'the IS and WAS'. The scripture, then, permits the worship of God for what he is in himself, and for what he has shewn himself in his works, without consideration of the future; a worship of gratitude and adoration, without explicit remembrance of hope or fear. Yet IA is in fact also $IA\Omega$, as is shewn by the two texts of Isaiah which conjoin the two forms of the Name in that order[1]: when we have worshipped in gratitude and reverence, we cannot long exclude the worship of hope and fear.

In accordance with the Biblical usage, St John twice praises 'the IS and the WAS' (in XI and XVI) for what he is, and what he has already done: our minds inevitably strain forward in expectation of the COMETH, and, as we shall see, they are not destined to disappointment. He never uses any other abbreviation; God is never 'He that is' simply, though the text of Exodus so plainly authorizes the title: nor is he any other pair but IS and WAS.

The Name of God is the Name of the infinite Act, and it was the thought of Israel that if one truly comprehended the Name of the God of Israel, one would comprehend the activity in which he overflowed upon the existence of Israel. God gave two expositions of his Name to Moses. He appeared symbolically in the flame of a bush burning unconsumed, a symbol which expresses the sheer energy of the divine Act in conjunction with his creaturely habitation. A flame of fire would be simply God, a flame in a bush burning unconsumed is God-in-Israel, the Lord JHVH. The expositions given at that time were simply 'I AM' and 'The God of Abraham, Isaac and Jacob' (Exod. III). After the Law-Giving, Moses desired a closer intimacy with God, and a vision of his Glory: and God descended to him as though in human form, though he would not suffer his face to be seen. This was the self-

<hr>

[1] JH JHVH, Isaiah XII, 2, and XXVI, 4.

revelation of the God who deals humanly with human creatures—with Moses, indeed, 'as a man with his friend'—and he gave an exposition of his Name in accordance with it, expressing an abundance of personal act within the sphere of Israel's life. 'The Lord . . . proclaimed the name of the Lord: JHVH, JHVH, a God full of compassion and *gracious*, slow to anger, plenteous in mercy and *truth*, keeping mercy for thousands, forgiving iniquity and transgression and sin, but that will by no means clear the guilty. . . .' (Exod. XXXIV.) St John refers to this passage in the end of the prologue to his gospel: 'And the Word became flesh and tabernacled among us, and we beheld his Glory, Glory as of the Father's only-begotten, "full of *grace* and *truth*." John beareth witness of him and crieth: This is he of whom I said, "He that COMETH after me is become before me," for he WAS before me: for of his fulness have we all received, and grace for grace. For the Law was given through Moses, *grace* and *truth* came through Jesus Christ; no man hath seen God at any time; the only-begotten God, he that IS in the bosom of the Father, he hath made the exposition of him.'

This text means that the angel or similitude in which Moses saw the Glory was but a shadow of the Word made flesh. He, revealed as IS, WAS and COMETH, exhibited grace and truth in action, and made thereby the true and living exposition of the Name. For the Only-Begotten Son reveals the Father by being his express image, and possessing the fulness of his Name in the acts of grace and truth.

We perceive that the threefold form, 'Is, was and cometh,' mediates between the sheer 'He that is' of Exodus III and the enumeration in Exodus XXXIV of the acts of mercy and truth. For the threefold form shows the divine Act already displayed in the history of the creature: the enumeration tells us the several qualities of this activity. And so we see the providentially-governed history of the world emanating, as it were, by stages out of the very Name of God: and this takes place through the Name's being conferred upon the Son.

When the Cabbalistic tradition later developed, the masterpiece of subtlety was to take the first words of scripture, and show from the very letters how the creation of the world was prefigured or contained in the Tetragrammaton. St John is not concerned with

269

the beginning of creation in his apocalypse, but he takes pains to exhibit the accomplishment of history as a new Genesis, a new six days' work, having the formal pattern of the old. At the same time he takes pains to show that the work is the expression of the Name of God by extending the Name throughout the work in a significant pattern.

The pattern appears directly after the title of the book.

'John to the Seven Churches that are in Asia:

Grace to you and peace
from the IS, WAS, and COMETH, and from the Seven Spirits before his throne,

and

from Jesus Christ the witness, the faithful, the firstborn of the dead, and prince of the kings of the earth.

To him that LOVETH us and LOOSED us from our sins by his blood, making us a kingdom of priests to God his Father, to him be the glory and the might for ever and ever. Amen.
Lo, he COMETH with clouds, and every eye shall see him, theirs also that pierced him, and all the tribes of earth shall wail because of him. "Yea, Amen; I AM the A and the Ω," saith God the Lord, "the IS and the WAS and the COMETH, the Almighty."'

This pattern consists of the following parts: (1) Blessing in the Name of $IA\Omega$, and of his faithful witness. (2) Doxology to the Name of IA, displayed in the IS of the witness, his love, and in his WAS, his redemptive acts. (3) Completion of the three-letter Name by the COMETH of Christ. (4) Solemn Amen to the advent-promise, confirmed by the Lord's full declaration of his Name. (This declaration is an elaborate paraphrase of 'Amen; I am the Lord[1], saith the Lord God of Sabaoth'. We have seen that 'Am the First and Last' and 'IS, WAS, and COMETH' are both paraphrases of 'Lord'; and 'Almighty' is the standing Greek translation of 'Sabaoth'. The natural form 'Lord God Almighty' appears in IV, 8, XV, 3, XVI, 7 and XIX, 6.)

The pattern is written again in the same order over the face of

[1] Or alternatively, I am the First and Last.' St John's formula, as we have seen, means both equally.

270

the whole Apocalypse. (1) God, revealed with the Seven Spirits before his throne, is proclaimed the WAS, IS, and COMETH at the Firstfruits-Pentecost vision (IV–V). (2) God is praised as the IS and WAS for his achieved work in the New Year vision (XI). (3) IS and WAS recurs in the third Vial, but the sixth adds at last the COMETH (XVI). (4) The Amen of him who is the A and the Ω receives three-fold expression in the visions of the Last Things, at XIX, XXI and XXII. The texts in which the pattern is thus displayed exhaust the allusions to the ineffable Name which the Apocalypse contains.

The pattern is not merely fact, it is also good sense. In the First-fruits-Pentecost vision the Kingdom of God is simply displayed: the whole three-letter Name belongs here. But when the Lamb takes the book, a drama of movement is initiated in which we are acutely aware of the temporal gap between what God has done and what he will do, between his IS-and-WAS, and his COMETH. The tension is not resolved nor the gap closed until the end of the Vials, when we know that HE COMETH indeed; nothing but the interlude (XVII–XIX, 10) then stands between us and his having come. When he has come, mounted upon the white horse, it is no longer COMETH, but AMEN, for all is fulfilled: from that moment until the end of the vision the Amen is unfolding itself.

In the simple analysis above, we have used four numbers to cover the application of the pattern to Apocalypse IV–XXII. We require a previous number to stand for the treatment of the Name in I–III, before the great eschatological movement begins. We will use the number 0 for this purpose. Let us now take the sections 0, 1, 2, 3 and 4 in order.

(0)

In the first section of the Apocalypse, that is to say, the first three chapters, the Name is declared, and related to the Person of Christ. This is in accordance with the significance of the section. In the scheme of the creation-week, it expresses the begetting of the pre-cosmic light, before the fabric of the world began. On this day the Name simply shines out by its own radiance, and reveals its connexion with the Word: for it is written, 'God *said*, let there be light, and there was light.' The festal scheme is in perfect accordance with this, for the dedication-festivity (Num. VII) is immediately preceded by the Aaronic Blessing, and immediately succeeded by the lamp-lighting (VI, 22–27, VIII, 1–4). 'Speak unto Aaron and his sons, saying, On this wise ye shall bless the Children of Israel. Ye shall say unto them, JHVH bless thee and keep thee, JHVH make his face to shine upon thee and be *gracious* unto thee, JHVH lift up his countenance upon thee and give thee *peace*. So shall they put my Name upon the children of Israel, and I will bless them. And it came to pass on the day that Moses had made an end of setting up the tabernacle . . . that the princes of Israel, the heads of their fathers' houses, made offerings. . . . This was the dedication of the altar, after that it had been anointed. And when Moses went into the tent of meeting to speak with God, then heard he the voice speaking unto him from above the mercy-seat . . . saying: Speak unto Aaron and say unto him, When thou settest on the lamps, the seven lamps shall give light in front of the candlestick. And Aaron did so.'

The putting of the Name upon the children of Israel is equivalent to the shining of the countenance upon them. The High Priest imposes the Name, and the High Priest sets up the sevenfold light. St John returns to this idea when he returns to Dedication in his last vision: 'They shall see his Countenance and his Name shall be upon their foreheads; and night shall be no more, and need have they none of lamplight or sunlight, for God the Lord shall shine upon them.' In Apocalypse 1 the High-Priestly Jesus of Zechariah's vision is revealed as the living expression of the Name, as the Countenance which shines as the sun shines in his strength, and as the setter-up of the sevenfold light.

St John begins from the Aaronic blessing. By the threefold use of the Name of JHVH it bestowed, among other things, Grace and Peace. So St John, adapting his formula to epistolary style, sends grace and peace to the Seven Churches from him whom he names threefold; and threefold in two several ways. He is the IS, WAS, and COMETH, but he is also he that sitteth on the Throne, the Seven Spirits that are before it, and Jesus Christ the faithful witness.

What is the relation between the threefold Name and the three Persons? Indiscreet theologians have sometimes assigned the IS to the Father, the WAS to the Redeemer, and the COMETH to the Paraclete. St John has too firm a grasp on the divine realities to fall into such error. Each of the clauses of the Aaronic Blessing is in the Name of JHVH, that is, in St John's translation, of $IA\Omega$, the IS, WAS, and COMETH. The Name belongs primarily to the Father, who is alone called by it in St John's three-line blessing; it descends in fullness upon the Son, as he is about to shew; if it did not, he would not be the Son. As to the Spirit, St John would not so much say that the Spirit also has the Name, as that the Spirit *is* the Name. In so far as Christians are sealed with the Spirit, the Name is on them: Christ has the plenitude both of the Spirit and the Name.

St John did not conceive of the Trinity as a society of three Persons. The society was of the eternal Father and the eternal Son, a society and a filiation perfected by the eternal indwelling of the very Spirit of the Father in the Son. The Spirit was no abstraction, but a real manifestation of the Godhead: and doubtless if we philosophize on his reality, we shall be led to the intellectual conclusion that he subsists *personally*, for how else can the Godhead really subsist? But to the mind of St John it was not as a third Person that he entered into the society of the Father and the Son, so as to make it in any way analogous to a human society of three individuals. The proper analogy is a society of two. The Spirit enters into the relationship not person-wise but spirit-wise, not by being begotten alongside of the Son, but by being inbreathed into the Son by the Father. His especial way of manifesting the always personal being of God is the most impersonal that is possible—that of self-identification with the person of another; for the action of the Spirit in us is moulded upon the form of our acts, he works in us as *we*, even in the process of divinizing us. This we believe in ourselves: the eternal archetype we see in the eternal Son of God.

St John's Trinitarian blessing has a most subtle balance, holding the duality of the Father and the Son alongside of the Trinity of Persons. This can be put in literary terms as a conflation of the triadic form of the Aaronic Blessing with the dyadic form of St Paul's epistolary greeting. For example, St Paul writes thus to the Galatians:

'Paul . . . to the Churches of Galatia: Grace to you and peace from God the Father and our Lord Jesus Christ, who gave himself for our sins that he might take us out of the present evil world,

273

according to the will of God our Father: to whom be the glory for ever and ever. Amen.'

St Paul, like St John, runs on from an elaboration of the description of Christ into a doxology, but he turns the doxology to the person of the Father, as Jewish form required. St John can follow St Paul by passing straight from the titles of Christ into thanksgiving for his redemption of us, in spite of the pattern of the Trinity, for he places Christ last of the Three. This would scarcely be possible to a Christian, unless he were also to annex the Spirit very closely to the Father; one way of expressing the Trinity is to write: 'The Father, and his Holy Spirit; and the Son (on whom the Spirit is fully bestowed).' St John gives the Name and the Spirit to the Father, for, like everything else, they are his first: and then proceeds to speak of Christ, beginning to show in the Doxology how he partakes in the Name, and in the following vision how he partakes in Name and Spirit. The annexing of the Spirit to the Father is emphasized by verbal form:

John, to the Seven Churches that are in Asia:

Grace to you and peace
from the IS, WAS, and COMETH, and from the Seven Spirits that are before his throne,

and from Jesus Christ, the witness, the faithful, the firstborn from the dead, and prince of the kings of the earth.

The verbal parallel between 'the Seven Churches that are in Asia' and 'the Seven Spirits which are before the Throne' holds the clauses about the Father and the Spirit together in a single line, matching the line about John and the Churches. The line about Father and Spirit is then more than balanced by the line containing the name and titles of Christ alone. Moreover the Spirit is explicitly annexed to the Father's throne, whereas so far as verbal form is concerned, Christ stands beside the Father as a co-ordinate source of grace and peace, just as in St Paul's greeting. And so we see how St John balances duality and Trinity, in a fashion which perfectly expresses the Biblical faith.

The IS, WAS, and COMETH begins to be applied to Christ in the LOVETH, LOOSED, and COMETH of the doxology and of its appendix,

274

the advent promise. 'Loveth' expresses the act of the divine Being, especially as manifested in Christ, and so St John writes elsewhere: 'God is love: herein was manifested the love of God for us, that God sent his only begotten Son into the world, that we might live through him' (I John IV, 8–9). We perceive that the 'loveth' like the 'is' has its tenses; the past tense describing what Christ did in human flesh. But the application of the Name and its tenses to Christ does not stand out from the doxology. It becomes plain in the sequel. For when the Son of Man, revealed among the Seven Candles, opens his lips, it is that he may say: 'Fear not; I AM the FIRST and the LAST' words which challenge exact comparison with the only other divine voice we have so far heard, 'Amen; I AM the A and the Ω.' If St John did not mean by this to give the IAΩ to Christ, then he wrote for the purpose of being misunderstood. 'I AM the FIRST and the LAST,' says the Son of Man, 'and the LIVING, and BECAME DEAD and lo, AM ALIVE INTO AGES UNENDING and have the keys of death and hell.' Here the IS of God is conjugated in terms not of love, but of life. 'He that lives', ὁ ζῶν, is as near a sound to 'he that is', ὁ ὤν, as the Greek tongue can pronounce: and 'the Living (God)' is a scriptural synonym for JHVH.[1] The past tense is a divine paradox, 'became dead': this is the true act of infinite life in mortal flesh, to conquer it and death by dying. 'Am alive into ages unending' is no more nor less a future tense than 'cometh' is: the act of infinite life invades the whole future of the creatures. The 'Lo' is interesting, for it places the triad we are examining in parallel with the triad of the doxology: 'That loveth us, and loosed us from our sins. . . . Lo, he cometh with clouds'— 'That live, and became dead, and lo, am alive into ages unending.'

When we were examining the Seven Messages, we saw how St John found the titles of Christ which head them by proceeding backward through the features of the Candlestick-vision, and how, when he had traversed them in four steps, he went over them again, combining with them elements from still further back in the Trinitarian Blessing and the Doxology. What he in fact does with the materials in the Doxology and Blessing amounts to

[1] Cf. Apocalypse X, 6. 'He that liveth into ages unending' = God as the Name invoked in the greatest oath, i.e. JHVH. Cf. also VII, 2, 'Seal of the Living God.'

275

this: he seizes the attributes of the Father in the name of the Son. 'He that hath the Seven Spirits of God'—they are not, then, simply the adjunct of the Father's throne. There the Son was named 'the Witness, the Faithful', but now we have the paraphrase 'the Holy, the True', both names of God himself. There we read, 'Amen: I am the A and the Ω, saith God the Lord'; but here 'Thus saith the Amen, the witness faithful and true, the beginning of the creation-work of God' is the voice of the Son of Man.

(1)

The Firstfruits-Pentecost vision returns to the first line of the Trinitarian Greeting. We see at last that Throne before which the Seven Spirits shine, and him that sits upon it, hailed in the never-ceasing cry of the Cherubim as the thrice-holy, the Lord God Almighty, the WAS, the IS, and the COMETH. St John is paraphrasing, according to his rules, the cry of the six-winged Seraphim in Isaiah VI. 'JHVH of Sabaoth' becomes 'Lord God Almighty', and the threefold 'Holy', like the threefold form of the Aaronic Blessing, calls for exposition in the three tenses, 'was, is, and cometh'. Here alone St John puts the WAS before the IS. The context explains it. The many eyes of the Ezekielian cherubim are interpreted as the organs of unceasing wakefulness, like the hundred eyes of Argus. 'Outwards and inwards[1] they are full of eyes, and have no rest day or night, saying, Holy, holy, holy. . . .' The divine eternity is here seen reflected in the endless worship of the creatures: to them God's worshipfulness was and is, and stretches into a future without end. This is to see God in the angels, rather than to hear what his Name is in itself. The vision is a vision of heaven, the principal vision of heaven as heaven which the Apocalypse contains, and the changeless sempiternity of its life is exactly what has to be expressed. It is against this background that the appearance of the slaughtered Lamb, and his taking of the book, is so dramatically set. The paradox of the Ascension is that something has *happened* in heaven, that the process of our salvation becomes event on high as well as beneath: and from this point onwards to the marriage of heaven and earth through the descent of Jerusalem, there

[1] St John is thinking of the Cherubim and their wings as a fence about the throne. The outward- and inward-looking sides are equally full of eyes.

276

is a double series of actions, heavenly liturgy being accompanied by earthly effect, as a flying bird by its shadow on the ground.

Firstfruits contains the antitype to the whole Trinitarian Blessing, not to its first line only. We begin with the first line—the Lord God and the Seven Spirits before his Throne: but in the second part of the vision the second line finds expression—Jesus Christ the faithful martyr for the truth of God, the first-begotten from the dead, enthroned as prince of kings.

(2)

All the series of seven visions which the Apocalypse contains begin with great festival liturgies except the trumpets, for the very simple reason that the quarter of the year which it represents has no considerable feast in its first month, whereas the others have. The mystery of the divine Name appears in all the festal liturgies, but not at the beginning of the trumpet-series, for there, instead of the praises of the Name, there is half an hour's silence. So, having dealt with the liturgy of IV–V, we pass next to that of XI, 15 ff., the liturgy of New Year.

In this liturgy the whole context of the Thrice-Holy is recalled —once more the four and twenty elders leave their thrones to fall upon their faces before God, blessing the Name in the form which the Thrice-Holy gave to it, 'Lord God Almighty' followed by the several tenses. All this identity of form only throws into the more significant relief the single difference: instead of 'was, is and cometh' we have 'is and was'. For, as St John works through his book, he is working through the pattern of the Name in I, 4–8 and he has now reached the Doxology, with its *IA* form, 'LOVETH, and LOOSED.' There the form turned our thoughts in the direction of those saving acts in which the eternal love of Christ *has* expressed itself towards us. The effect here is the same. The new year *has* dawned, the great trumpet at last *has* sounded, God *has* taken up his great power and established his kingdom, and the hour for the great consummation *has* struck. This many-sided fact is then seen to be grounded in the saving acts of the Incarnation: the travailing woman has given birth, Christ has been born and reached the all-ruling throne, the saints have been justified and Satan cast down. It is only from this point that we begin to move again into a prophesied future, as we see the setting up of the kingdom of Antichrist for a time, times and a half.

(3)

The kingdom of Antichrist appears to occupy a gap between two divine interventions. Because God is what he is, Christ came to save us, and again because he is what he is, Christ is coming to execute the judgement of quick and dead: but meanwhile the Beast comes up from the sea, and Satan gives him that throne of general dominion which he offered to Christ, if Christ would have worshipped him (Matt. IV, 8–10). To the eye of faith the setting up of this wicked kingdom is the indirect result of the first Advent; if Satan had not been cast out of heaven he would not have adopted the desperate and last expedient of open rebellion on earth. So we see the first Advent, as it were, working itself out in the time, times and a half; and the ungodly nature of the visible effect does but emphasize the newness and abruptness of the second Advent which will suddenly terminate it.

The Antichrist, therefore, stands after the IS and WAS and before its inevitable supplement, the COMETH. 'Cometh' belongs to the last moment of action preceding the Advent, for when it is come, it is come. The last moment of action before Advent is the end of the Vials. St John trails the theme of the Name all through the vial-series. For this is Dedication, and Dedication is the Feast of the Name. He takes up the form of IV and XI, 'Lord God Almighty, the IS and WAS (and COMETH).' In the introductory Sabbath to the Vials the mention of the sea of glass carries us back to the vision of glory in IV, the only other place where the sea is referred to. Again we hear the praises of the Name: 'Great and marvellous are thy works, Lord God Almighty, righteous and true are thy ways, King of the ages. Who will not fear, O Lord, and glorify thy Name, for thou only art holy. . . .' Our ears are attentive for 'the IS and WAS', but they do not hear it. They have only to wait until St John's cycle brings him back into the same quarter of the square. A voice at the third vial picks up the theme: 'Righteous art thou, the IS and the WAS, the holy, in judging so,' and another voice replies: 'Yea, Lord God Almighty, true and righteous are thy judgements.' We go on round the square again, and return into the same quarter with the sixth vial.

278

Under the sixth vial the course of the description throws up quite naturally the title *God Almighty*, and this acts as a sort of trigger to release the long-restrained COMETH, and it bursts out with explosive force in a direct word of Christ. 'They go forth to the kings of all the world, to gather them to the battle of the Day, the great day of *God Almighty*. LO, I COME AS A THIEF. BLESSED IS HE THAT WATCHETH AND KEEPETH HIS GARMENTS THAT HE WALK NOT NAKED AND THEY SEE NOT HIS SHAME. And he gathered them to the place called in Hebrew, Armageddon.'

Does the text fall away again after the tremendous word into flat narrative? Only for one line. Then, the seventh vial being flung upon the air, there comes forth a great voice out of the temple from the throne, saying, 'It is done'; the conclusion of the whole work, short of the Advent itself.

We may observe that 'Lo, I come' matches the 'Lo, he cometh with clouds' which is its archetype in I. Indeed the two texts are not unlike in form and spirit.[1]

Lo, he cometh with clouds: Lo, I come as a thief:
and every eye shall see him, Blessed is he that watcheth,
they also that pierced him; and keepeth his garments;
and all the tribes of the earth that he walk not naked
   shall wail because of him.   and they see not his shame.[2]

[1] The connexion between these two texts is cemented by the name of Armageddon which directly follows the second. 'Ar-mageddon' means 'Mount Megiddo'. The prophecy which says that 'They shall look on whom they have pierced' and that 'all the tribes of the earth shall wail over him' says also that the wailing shall be 'as the wailing of Hadadrimmon in the valley of Megiddo'. (Zech. XII, 10–14). Thus if St John had I, 7 in mind when he wrote XVI, 18, it is natural enough that he should have gone straight on from 'Lo I come' to mention Megiddo. The author of II Chronicles XXXV, 20–25 appears to have interpreted Zechariah's reference of the wailing for Josiah, who went up to Megiddo and met his doom there through an infatuation. God had commanded Necoh to march that way, and warned Josiah not to meddle. But Josiah went to his Armageddon there (unmindful of how, by the waters of Megiddo, 'the stars in their courses' had fought against Sisera). The kings in Apocalypse XVI commit folly of the same kind. It seems possible to treat the Hebrew name Megiddo as a double pun on 'mustering for battle' and 'wailing', but perhaps St John had not thought of that. As to why *Mount* Megiddo' rather than 'Vale of Megiddo', see below, p. 287.

[2] The parallel with III, 3–5 is, of course, more striking: see above p. 187.

This 'Lo, I come' answers, at length, the cry of the cherubim from which the whole drama of judgement began. 'Come,' they had prayed, 'Come, Come, Come.' St John draws the two liturgical words 'Maranatha' ('Come, Lord') and 'Amen' ('The words are faithful and true') into the power of the Sacred Name: Maranatha asks that he who IS and WAS should manifest his COMING; and when he is come, he becomes AMEN.

(4)

In the great Alleluia-liturgy of XIX the theme of the Name is re-introduced by means of the phrase which we have come to recognize as standing form: The *Lord* our *God Almighty* reigneth.' We may begin to listen for the IS, WAS, COMETH, but we shall not hear it, for it is now the turn of the Amen—the Amen which God himself pronounces. Because St John thinks he hears this Amen from the lips of his angel, he falls to worship him. The angel refuses worship, and the living Amen of God, Jesus Christ, breaks through the opened skies. We have had a hint of the mystery of word becoming flesh in the 'Lo, I come as a thief' of XVI. There the COMETH of the threefold Name came alive in the voice of Christ: here the Amen of God becomes flesh and blood in the person of Christ. Let us see how the mystery unfolds.

The Alleluia-liturgy of XIX, 1–10 falls into two parts. The former part receives its *Amen* from the elders and the cherubim, as they fall and worship. At the close of the second part the vial-angel makes himself felt and gives the Amen in paraphrase: '*These words are true words of God.*' St John falls before him who can thus pronounce the divine Amen, as the elders and cherubim had fallen before the throne. The angel hinders him; let him keep his worship for God.

Then, without pause, we read: And I saw the heaven opened, and behold, a white horse, and he that sat on him called *Faithful-and-True*. . . . And his name is called: *The Word of God.*

Since 'faithful-and-true' is elsewhere used with 'words' as a standing paraphrase for Amen (XXI, 5, XXII, 6); since in the messages Christ calls himself 'the Amen, the Witness Faithful and True' (III, 14); we can hardly escape the conclusion that Christ's appearance here is made in the person of the living Amen, in whom (unlike the angel) God can and must be worshipped: he is

280

the incarnate Amen, as he is the incarnate Word, for none but the divine Word can be the adequate witness or testimony to the truth of God. The angel has just said: 'I am thy fellow-servant, and of thy brethren that hold the testimony of Jesus: worship God—for the testimony of Jesus is the Spirit of prophecy.' This angel is the minister of the prophetic Spirit, the Spirit, that is, of St John's inspiration: St John, receiving this Spirit from the angel, is, with the angel, a fellow-minister: but that which, in or as the Spirit, is handled by the angel and St John and indeed by all faithful Christians, is the living testimony of Jesus, the Spirit-bearer: in him the testimony of God faithful and true, the testimony to God's truth and fidelity, exists personally, and is to be worshipped. The heaven rends, and behold him come.

So the Amen to the worship of the heavenly sabbath is, as it were, taken out of the lips of the congregation by Christ, the fulfilment of all the promises for which they blessed God. We have been hearing the benediction on those bidden in robes of white to the marriage-supper of the Lamb. We would say 'Amen' to that; but it is needless, for here is the Amen to it, Christ in the attributes of the warrior-bridegroom of the psalm *Eructavit* (XLV); and the white-robed host sweeps after him.

The Christ of Advent appears as the Amen, not only because he is the fulfilment of all God's promises, but also because Amen is the new Name of God in the World to Come, according to Isaiah LXV. 'Behold, my servants shall eat, but ye shall be hungry; behold, my servants shall drink, but ye shall be thirsty: behold, my servants shall rejoice, but ye shall be ashamed: behold my servants shall sing for joy of heart, but ye shall cry for sorrow of heart, and howl for vexation of spirit. And ye shall leave your name for a curse unto my chosen . . . and he shall call his servants by another name; so that he who blesses in the earth shall bless by the God Amen and he that sweareth in the earth shall swear by the God Amen, because the former troubles are forgotten and because they are hid from my eyes. For behold I create new heavens and a new earth, and the former things shall not be remembered nor come into mind. But be ye glad and rejoice for ever in that which I create, for behold, I create Jerusalem a rejoicing, and her people a joy.' (Isa. LXV, 13–18.)

281

To compare this with Apocalypse XIX: we have the contrast between damnation and felicity, with mention of the messianic supper, and the heavenly singing: we have the benediction pronounced in the Name of God who is the living Amen to it, and who shows himself to be such by performing the last act of the apocalyptic drama, the creation of new heaven and earth, and of the New Jerusalem. This, surely, is how St John reads his Isaiah, at a text as frequently alluded to in the Apocalypse as is any other. So here behold the incarnate God Amen: the New Creation is presently to follow.

To compare once more the texts we are studying with the archetypal pattern of the Name in I: 'Lo, he cometh with clouds' (I, 7) has found its antitype in 'Lo, I come as a thief' (XVI, 15), and 'Yea, Amen' in the incarnate Amen of XIX, 11. But the archetypal phrase is not simply 'Yea, Amen', it is (a) 'Yea, Amen; (b) I am the A and the Ω, saith God the Lord, (c) the IS, WAS and COMETH, the Almighty,' We have had (a) alone in XIX, we have (a) and (b) in XXI, and (a), (b) and (c) in XXII. That is Amen indeed, and the book ends.

XXI, 2 ff. picks up the theme of XIX, 5–16 through the figure of the Bride, and through the repetition of a formula: once more the command to write is followed up by a paraphrastic Amen. In XIX the Bride was promised in her wedding attire, and the angel said, 'Write: And he said, these words are the true words of God.' In XXI the Bride in wedding-attire has visibly descended, and the blessedness of the saints having been declared by a voice from the throne, God himself says, 'Write, for these words are faithful and true. And, said he to me, They are done. I am the A and the Ω, the beginning and the end.'

The A and Ω formula has occurred nowhere since we read it in the archetype at I, 8. But even now it is not completely rendered. There the verb *to be* was expressed, giving the full $IA\Omega$ form, but here it is not. That St John is perfectly aware of what he is doing is evident from the accompanying paraphrases in the two texts. In I, 8 it was, 'I AM the A and the Ω, . . . the IS, the WAS and the COMETH.' But here it is, 'I (am) the A and the Ω, the *beginning* and the *end*.' The formula is still incomplete, but this is not the final utterance of it; we have still to hear it once more. Its present form

282

is perfectly appropriate to its occasion, emphasizing simply that he who began all things has brought them to their end.

In the conclusion (XXII, 6 ff.) the two Amen-contexts of XIX and XXI are conflated. When the conclusion comes, we have just seen a second vision of the Bride, like that in XXI, 2, and the blessedness of those in whom God's throne is set has just been described in similar words: it is time for the divine Amen. But when it comes, it comes not from the enthroned Glory, as in XXI, but through the Angel, as in XIX, and St John once more attempts to worship him. He is told to direct his adoration rather to the divinity which speaks through the Angel; he listens, and the voice which he hears is that, not now of the Father, but of Jesus. 'Lo, I come quickly,' he says, 'and my reward with me, to give each man according as his work is: I the A and the Ω, the first and the last, the beginning and the end. Blessed are they that wash their garments, that they may have right to the tree of life. . . . I Jesus have sent my angel to testify these things to you in the Churches. I AM the root and child of David, the bright and morning star.' After this the book ends with a closely-woven pattern of 'Come, Lord', 'I come,' and 'Amen'.

The holding back of the AM to the very last is in agreement with the form of the Gospel-prologue: 'He that COMETH after me is become before me, for he WAS that first I follow. . . . God no man hath seen at any time: the only begotten God that IS in the bosom of the Father, he hath declared him.'

The incomplete formula in XXI ought plainly to be compared with the incomplete formula in XI. There we had 'the IS and WAS', to be followed in XVI by 'the IS and the WAS . . . Lo, I COME': here we have 'the A and the Ω' to be followed in XXI by 'the A and the Ω . . . I AM'. The dramatic effect is the same. Just as 'the IS and the WAS' has its scriptural authorization in the short form of the Name, IA, so 'the A and the Ω' has its authorization in the word of the Lord through Isaiah, 'I (am) the first and the last' (XLIV, 6).

283

CHAPTER XI

The Kingdom of Darkness is set by St John in elaborate antithesis to the Kingdom of Light. Just as Christ not only expounds the Name of God but is, in his action and his existence, an exposition of the Name, so Antichrist not only blasphemes the Name, he is a living blasphemy of the Name. We have observed several elements of the demonic parody in the course of running commentary on the text. We will now attempt a more systematic account of it.

We may begin by considering the triad, Dragon, Beast and False Prophet. Of what heavenly triad are they the travesty? We saw St John setting forth the kingdom of God in two triads, the threefold Name and the three divine Persons. It seems fitting that there should be three holy triads, not two; and in fact there is a third. When we were analysing the Trinitarian Blessing in I, we found in it a subtle balance between the triad (Father, Son, Spirit) and the dyad (God and Christ). What we have now to add is that this dyad is itself two-thirds of a triad, the three grades of derivation, God, Christ, his Servants. The Spirit and the Name descend in fullness from God to Christ, so that they are his Name and his Spirit. They descend to his servants, also, but not in fullness. The Seal of the Living God is his seal, not theirs, though it marks their foreheads. The brand they bear is Christ's and his Father's Name, not their own. God puts all revelation into the hands of the Son, but it does not descend to the servant save through the ministration of an angel. The complete indwelling of the Father's Spirit in the Son removes all inequality, while it confirms derivation; and so the first two grades are constituted, with the Spirit, a divine Trinity.

We must not ask, 'And of what grade is the Spirit?' for that would be to pass outside the form St John is using. The Spirit is precisely the divine Power in so far as he is undetermined to any grade, but passes through them all. If we say, 'But we are meta-

284

physicians, and we must have an answer: if the Spirit is an hypostasis of the Godhead, he must have his grade of derivation,' we shall, perhaps, be driven to something like the Western Scholastic conclusion—Since he presupposes the generation of the Son into whom he is inbreathed, we must derive him third, the Father sending him and the Son drawing him. But this is to advance into a speculation quite outside St John's forms. He simply sees the Father, with the Spirit beside him as communicable Godhead: and then he sees the two derived grades to which he is communicated, the derived equal, and the derived unequal.

The triad of the grades is, in fact, the triad with which St John begins, inlaying into it the triads of the threefold Name and the three Persons as he proceeds.

'Apocalypse of (2) Jesus Christ, which (1) God gave him, to show (3) his servants what must quickly be,

and he signified it by the message of his angel to (3) his servant John, who witnessed the word of God (1) and the witness of (2) Jesus Christ in all he saw. . . .

(3) John to the seven Churches that are in Asia: Grace to you and peace from (1) the IS, WAS and COMETH, and from the Seven Spirits that are before his throne, and from (2) Jesus Christ, the faithful witness. . . .

As revelation descends from God to Christ, and from Christ to his servants, for example, to John, but to him by the interposition of an angel; so grace and peace proceed *through* the three grades, but *from* the two alone, in whose Name the third blesses. All the saints who hold the word of God and the testimony of Jesus are servants, and partakers of the Spirit, but the inspired man in the act of his inspiration is pre-eminently or typically so. Then the 'servant' becomes 'the prophet'. St John himself is a prophet, and his book is 'this prophecy'.

The triad which the demonic figures blaspheme is the triad of derivation. Satan aspires to be a false God, the Beast a false Christ, and the second Beast a false prophet. Satan bestows on Antichrist 'his power and his throne, and great authority': the False Prophet 'executes all the authority of the first Beast in his sight, and makes the earth . . . to worship the first Beast'. In doing so they worship also the Dragon for having bestowed the power upon him. The

False Prophet himself is no more worshipped than the Christian prophet is.

Such is the demonic hierarchy, but it is, of course, a sham. There are no real grades in it. The Antichrist and the False Prophet are equally men: the False Prophet is to Antichrist simply what Goebbels was to Hitler (to take the modern example which is least likely to cause ill-feeling), or, as St John implies, what Balaam was to Balak and the magicians to Pharaoh. In being a demon, Satan has no superiority over the other two. Where men worship Satan, the image of God grovels before the serpent. The Satan of the Apocalypse is not the Miltonic archangel with tarnished wings. The Jews of St John's time commonly held a different account of the origin of demons. They were the damned souls of the dead giants, begotten once by the monstrous intercourse of the fallen angels with the daughters of men: the angels themselves had long ago been pinioned to the floor of the abyss. The demons were not what the heathen supposed themselves to be worshipping under the guise of Gods. They aspired to worship the angels of the stars and other parts of nature. But since the worship of the creature is a sin, the demons intercept it, turn it to their own advantage, and work the magic of the heathen cult. Demons are not stronger than men, their power is parasitical on the sin of men. Human error makes the godhead of idols, and human wickedness the sway of demons. Michael could cast down Satan at a blow, if men's sins did not give substance to his accusations in the court of heaven: and the Name of God would everywhere exorcise demonic mischief, if it were everywhere faithfully invoked. Satan is the vast image of a working lie, sprawled across half the heaven, and sweeping off with his tail a third part of the stars.

As there are no real grades of hierarchy in the Kingdom of Darkness, so there is no spirit which passes through them all and knits them into one. There are many demons, no doubt, in the fellowship of Beelzebub, and they will work their tricks in and for the Antichrist and the False Prophet. When the unholy three desire to bring the kings of earth to Armageddon each vomits a demon. These three demons may be felt as a faint parody of 'the Seven Spirits of God sent into all the earth', and one of the suggestions contained in the mysterious name of Armageddon supports

286

this line of thought. Ar-mageddon, i.e. Mount Megiddo, is not a name ever used in fact, but if it were, it would presumably describe the Carmel-range[1]; and it was to Carmel that Elijah persuaded Ahab to gather all the prophets of Baal (I Kings XVIII, 19); and there they contested with God, and met their doom. The spirit of deception which leads the false prophets to assemble against the prophet of God is presumably the vain confidence of their false inspiration, and therefore the spirit which is a parody of the Holy Spirit of true prophecy. Ahab bade the false prophets go to Carmel and perish; they were presently to do the like service for him, when with one voice they exhorted him to go up to Ramoth Gilead,[2] to perish there (I Kings XXII, 6). On that occasion Micaiah saw in a vision the lying spirit going forth by divine permission to be a spirit of false prophecy in their mouths: and the mission of this lying spirit is obviously antithetical to that of the Holy Spirit of true inspiration which Micaiah possesses. The false prophets sent the false Anointed to Ramoth Gilead, the false Anointed sent the false prophets to 'Mount Megiddo': the false Anointed and the False Prophet each vomit one of the spirits which leads the kings to Armageddon; thither they go themselves too, and there they perish. The third spirit is vomited by the Father of Lies. Ahab is a type of Antichrist in any case, being the husband of Jezebel, who is a type of the Wicked Woman (II, 20): and the Baal whom they and their prophets worship is, in St John's eyes, no mere type of Satan, he is Satan in person.

We may now consider the figures of the Beasts. Satan is 'the Dragon', i.e. Leviathan; he is also 'the serpent in the Beginning', the snake which misled Eve, and was doomed to warfare with her seed. The 'seed' was to strike his head, and he was to strike the 'seed's' heel. Antichrist is 'the Beast', i.e. Behemoth; he is also 'the seed of the serpent', joined with the serpent in the doom of fruitless war against the woman's seed. This means simply that he is the typical wicked man, the seed of Satan *par excellence* (see John VIII, 31 ff.).

---

[1] For the reason why Carmel is called Mt *Megiddo,* see above, p. 279.

[2] The LXX gives various forms of the name, among others Ramagalaad (II Chron. XXII), Aremoth-Galaad (Josh. XX). St John may have seen an assonance to such forms in the 'Armageddon' which he wrote.

There is an interchange of features between the Dragon and the Beast. The 'stricken head' becomes characteristic of the Beast, though it belongs primarily to the Oracle on the Serpent. The seven heads and ten horns are anticipated in the figure of the Dragon, though they belong properly to Daniel's oracle on the Beast (Dan. VII). Daniel, indeed, distributes the seven heads among four beasts; the great Beast of St John is to be understood as a summing-up ($\dot{\alpha}\nu\alpha\kappa\epsilon\phi\alpha\lambda\alpha\acute{\iota}\omega\sigma\iota\varsigma$) of them all, a quintessence of all the heathen tyrannies of history. The interchange of features between the Dragon and the Antichrist expresses the parody on the relation of the Son to the Father. The Father is mirrored in the Son: the Father's Seven Spirits descend to become the seven horns and eyes of the Lamb.

The heads and horns have in the Dragon no further meaning: they make him simply the archetype of the Beast.[1] In the Beast they receive their detailed exposition. Let us begin with the heads. They are seven kings, of whom it appears that the Beast himself is one. This is to our minds extremely confusing, but according to St John's symbolical conventions it is perfectly correct. The astral woman of XII wears the twelve zodiacal signs as a crown on her head, and this means that she is one of those signs (Virgo), and, from the point of view there taken, the chief of them (the sign of priestly Levi, the jasper). So, of the seven kings, the Beast is one, and the chief.

The seven are given a form which makes them a perfect parody of the week of divine action, as it occurs over and over again in the Apocalypse. Five have had their day, the sixth reigns: there will be a seventh whose reign, like the sabbath, will be but an interlude ('He must remain a little while'). The great manifestation of power awaits the eighth; but the eighth day is not a new day, it is an eighth-and-first, and this expresses the fact that it is a day of resurrection, for one of the seven is reborn in it. So too the Beast is an eighth, but only in being one of the seven returned from the Abyss, a demonic resurrection in parody of the resurrection of Christ.

[1] In St John's use of the diagram, however, it is the Dragon who arises out of the place of the Lamb, and so begins naturally enough the parody of his features which afterwards descends to the Beast. In the second Beast the parody continues, but in a slighter form: he has 'two horns like a lamb'.

288

At this point the Genesis-oracle on the Serpent and his seed comes to bear. 'The woman's seed shall strike thy head, and thou shalt strike his heel.' The serpent's seed *par excellence,* the Beast who is the eighth king, appears as the stricken head. The wound he bears is the stroke of the sword, the stroke of death; for it is written, 'God shall bring down his sword, the holy, great and strong, upon the Dragon, the fleeing Serpent, the Dragon the crooked serpent, and the Dragon shall he slay.' (Isa. xxvii, 1). And yet, according to Genesis, it is *after* the serpent has been so smitten by God through the hand of the woman's seed, that he strikes the woman's seed in the heel. How can he, bearing already the stroke of the sword which is the stroke of death? Here is a mystery: the deadly stroke has been healed, but only for a time.

The scriptures directly apply this mystery to the serpent, rather than to his seed. St John applies it to both. As to the serpent, he has been smitten through the merits of the Woman's Seed, and cast down from heaven to earth (as it is written, Upon thy belly shalt thou go, and earth shalt thou eat), before he ever turns to bite the heels of 'the rest of the woman's seed'. It is for the purpose of this heel-biting that he sets up the kingdom of the Beast; and the Beast is seen to be, like his master, one whom the sword of God has already smitten to death. The theme recurs in xx. When the Dragon raises the rebellion of Gog and Magog against the saints, he appears as one escaped by divine permission from the Abyss, into which he had been cast after the Sword of the Word of God had struck him down in the great battle. The stroke of his death has been healed; but only for a moment, and he falls into a worse death, the lake of fire which burns with brimstone.

The theme, then, is applied to the Dragon, but with even greater emphasis to the Beast, and that for two reasons: because the Beast is the parody of Christ, so that the return of his stricken head from the Abyss becomes the parody of Christ's passion and resurrection; and because the Beast is a mortal man, so that the stroke of death means in his case something to which a precise sense can be attached. If a man has died, he has died, and if he reappears and acts on earth, it is certainly a wonder. But if we are told that a demon has been mortally stricken by the sword of God, and yet has reappeared to plague us, we do not see at once what is meant.

Since he is not a bodily cretaure, his death-stroke cannot mean that he was sundered from the body that owned him before: and if it does not mean that, what can it mean but the annihilation of the spirit? But that it cannot mean, for the annihilated cannot return. In fact, the 'deaths' of Satan are (a) his casting down from heaven, (b) his imprisonment in the Abyss: and these things befalling an incorporeal spirit do not have to our imaginations the force of death.

Christ, a Lamb standing as slaughtered, is the symbol of all saving power: Antichrist, a Beast slaughtered to the death and healed, is the quintessence of demonic unreality. How does St John conceive the nature of the difference between the two deaths? The key to it lies in the several qualities of death recognized by Jewish belief. The Old Testament for the most part regards death, and especially violent or premature death, as simply penal; the typical reward of virtue is length of days. This simple phase of belief belongs properly to the age before resurrection has been revealed. The Judaism of the First Century believed passionately in resurrection. But the text of the Old Testament still stood: the doctrine of penal death could not be wholly evaded, but it could, and must, be qualified. There are several qualities of death. First, there are the exemplary sinners like Korah (Num. XVI, 29–35) struck down red-handed by divine justice, and dying 'both to this world and to that which is to come'. Second, there are sinners like Achan, who die a death of discipline, giving glory to the God of Israel (Joshua VII, 19–26). They are happy in receiving their punishment here: they die to this world, but live to that which is to come. (The class, somewhat surprisingly, includes many of the impenitent dying under discipline. St Paul thinks it likely that the excommunicate sinner may suffer 'the destruction of the flesh, that the Spirit may be saved in the day of Jesus Christ' (I Cor. v, 5); for we 'being judged by the Lord, are chastened that we may not be damned with the world'—*ibid.*, XI, 32). Third, there are premature deaths which are not visibly penal, but may be regarded as an atonement for sins—for who has not sinned?—and as a prevention of evils. Fourth, there are heroic and meritorious deaths, 'hallowings of the Name,' which atone for the sins of others, and obtain for the martyr peculiar rewards in the world to come. Such deaths are in no sense penal.

290

St John moved in this circle of ideas, as we can see from his adoption of the Rabbinic distinction between the first death (to this world) and the second (to the world to come). He even adds his own elaboration, a parallel doctrine of two resurrections. The first resurrection (to this world, in the millennium) is the privilege of martyrs, and also assures a part in the second resurrection (to the world to come, at the last day). The violent death of Antichrist, which terminated his first earthly reign, was like the death of Korah. He is a heathen man, and an enemy of God, and by his violent death he dies to this world, and to that which is to come. Thus, if he is allowed to return to earth, it is as a man already dead and damned, his name utterly expunged from the Book of Life. In relation to God's world, he is nothingness incarnate, he is already annihilated: and those who take part with him and take his name upon them take upon themselves an already achieved annihilation. Christ's death is of the opposite quality. It is wholly heroic, wholly meritorious, in dying it he has put death already behind his back, both the death to this world, and the death to that which is to come. Those who partake with him and take his Name upon them, take on themselves victorious and eternal life. Christ 'lives, and became dead, and lives into ages unending': Antichrist 'was, and is not, and will be here, and goes his way to perdition'. As the epitome of not-being, as the type of a working lie, he is the perfect object of idolatrous worship, for the idols, we know, are nothing in the world, and those that worship them are like unto them.

It remains to consider the historical application of St John's figure. We have hoped to show that all the features of it are significant, apart from any particular historical facts. St John has applied it to history: he did not shape it from history. The application may seem to us a trifle arbitrary, but that will not, in the circumstances, be surprising. The scheme of the seven heads is being fitted upon the Roman Emperors ready made, almost as it has been since by perverse expositors on an Antichrist at Rome or Paris or Berlin.

Irenaeus says that the Apocalypse was seen under Domitian, and almost any other date presents difficulties of an internal kind. So let Domitian be 'the sixth who now is'. If we consider the scheme of the week in general, we shall presume that the sixth represents a climax only second to the final climax in the eighth. Thus what St John will be saying to the Christians is this: 'Things are as bad as they ever have been, but this is not the end. This monster will die, and be succeeded by a short-lived emperor. After him will come the Antichrist, and the appalling three-and-a-half years of unrestricted persecution. Then your deliverance will be.'

If Domitian is the sixth, who are the previous five? It is impossible to be sure, because we do not know what to do with the three pretenders who succeeded Nero. If we count none of them, the five are Caius, Claudius, Nero, Vespasian and Titus, the 'bestial' phase of the empire being dated from the beginning of open self-deification by an Emperor. If we count two of the three pretenders (a reasonable thing, perhaps, since Vitellius was never recognised by the ultimately victorious party), we shall have Nero, Galba, Otho, Vespasian and Titus, and we shall date 'bestiality' from the beginning of organised persecution against the Church. No third solution appears to have much to be said for it. In any case the scheme of the week requires that the one of the seven who returns as an eighth should be in fact the first. Thus according to the one hypothesis the Antichrist will be Caligula *redivivus,* on the other he will be Nero *redivivus.*

Between these two suppositions there is little to choose. Both emperors received the death-wound. On the side of Caligula it may be said that he more exactly fits the type of Antichrist—that is to say, the type of Antiochus Epiphanes, both as himself and as projected back upon the person of Nebuchadnezzar by the author of Daniel. On the side of Nero it may be said, and has been said a great many times, that there was, anyhow, an expectation of his mysterious return; whereas no such expectation was ever held about Caius Caligula. It is also said that the 666 is to be extracted from 'Nero Caesar' in a Hebrew form. We have objected to the last point as unnecessary: the 666 already has an embarrassing number of senses apart from it, and anyhow St John does his cryptograms in Greek, not Hebrew, even including his divinations from the ineffable Name. The argument from the expectation of Nero's return is somewhat impaired by the date at which we must suppose the Apocalypse to have been composed. The original form of Nero-legend was simply that he had never died, but was in

292

hiding with the Parthians: there actually appeared false Neros in the East. This form of the legend will do at a pinch, but it is not perfectly appropriate; for according to it Nero is not 'dead and damned' when he returns. At a later date, when one had to admit that Nero must have died, a fantastic belief arose in Jewish (and Christian) circles, that he would return from the dead. This is the form of the legend which we really want; but it is difficult to suppose that it had got going before the beginning of the second century. In 95 (supposing that St John wrote about that year) Nero would not even have been an old man if he were alive, so why should the myth yet have abandoned its original and natural form, the restoration with Parthian aid of a Nero in hiding?

In view of these considerations, it may be wise to allow superior weight to the claims of Caligula. If it can be said that Nero made an impression on subsequent tradition in the role of Antichrist and *revenant*, it can be said with equal assurance that Caligula had left his mark on previous tradition; and it can be added with no hesitation at all that St John is more likely to have been influenced by his predecessors than by his successors. Caius Caligula, among his other foolish ideas, revived the exact project of Epiphanes, to bring the Jews to heel by erecting a heathen image bearing his own features in the City of Jerusalem. The scheme was never carried out, because the imperial official whose business it was prudently temporized, and meanwhile Caligula received the stroke of death, he was smitten by the Providence which had saved the Temple out of the hands of Sennacherib. But the event naturally revived the Epiphanes-idea in the minds of Jews and Christians. St Paul, writing to the Thessalonians, tells them that the Lawless One has yet to be manifested, one who sets himself up against everything called divine or worshipful, so that he even seats himself as God in the Temple of God. At present, says the Apostle, he cannot appear because of a restraining force or person, presumably the more sober spirit which suppressed Caligula and still held sway in the person of the reigning monarch. But a time will come when the hindrance will be removed. And then, presumably, one will appear who will execute all that Caligula dreamed.

It is reasonable to recognize the influence of the Caligula episode in the verbal form of the Lord's Prophecy as it is reported for us in Mark XIII. Since the Son of Man figure has the Antichrist expectation for its background in Daniel, it is natural that the Antichrist-emblem should play some part in Christ's prediction of the Son of Man's advent; but the particularity of reference in Mark XIII, 14 suggests something more. 'When ye shall see the abomination of desolation standing where he ought not—let the reader divine the sense!—then let those in Judea flee to the mountains. . . .' The Emperor, St Mark wishes surely to say, is going to try it again one day, and he will succeed—for a while.

The simplest view, therefore, to take of the historical prediction in the Apocalypse is that it is the continuation of the Christian tradition which we read in St Paul and St Mark. The advent of the Son of Man will be the termination of a reign of Antichrist of which Epiphanes was the type, and Caligula the threat. Caligula was struck down by the sword, but he will, as it were, return from the dead. His blasphemy was against God's 'Name and Temple' in Jerusalem: now the visible Temple has disappeared, he will return to blaspheme the invisible, 'God's Name and Tabernacle, even them that tabernacle in heaven,' the spiritual temple which is the Church (Apoc. XIII, 6).

Since the details of the figure of Antichrist are so evidently worked out on the plane of symbolism, it is almost useless to ask precisely what St John meant by the statement that Domitian's next successor but one would be Caligula back from the dead. According to St Mark, Herod said that Christ was the Baptist risen from death, even though the two preachers were close contemporaries. If we rationalize this, all it can mean is that the power and spirit of John had transferred themselves to Jesus, with force redoubled by John's martyrdom; but the rationalization does not do justice to the spirit of the text. The Synoptic Gospels themselves teach that John Baptist was the returning Elijah. Elijah's having been exempted from physical death had something to do with the expectation of his return. And yet the Baptist did not fall ready-grown from the sky, he was begotten by natural generation. It is, in fact, impossible to say what visible token, if any, St John would expect the Antichrist to show of his being Caius Caligula *redivivus*: or even in what he conceived the identity between the one person and the other to consist.

294

The question how far St John is tied down to particular historical prediction, has often been debated. It seems proper to give an antithetical answer. On the one hand he writes out of scripture, theology, and spiritual principle: he is writing about the Antichrist, not about the tendencies of Roman Imperial history. On the other hand the few verses in XVII concerned with the Seven Heads either mean nothing, or they mean quite precisely that the second successor of the reigning monarch will be the Antichrist. St John is not to know that Domitian (if he is writing under Domitian) is going to be cut off by violent death, perhaps in a matter of months, or that he will be succeeded by so very short-lived a ruler as Nerva. In the event, the historical prediction of Antichrist was disappointed with surprising swiftness by Trajan's accession.

We, presumably, are unlikely to feel that the particular prediction as such was part of divine revelation; Providence has not permitted it to become a clear part of the inspired text, and we might even wonder how firmly St John himself was attached to it. The Antichrist-scheme is a mode of representation, an inspired way of reviewing the existence of the Church under imperial rule. St John himself could give his figures several applications. In John IV the images of Apocalypse XVII return. The sinful woman seated on many waters becomes the Samaritaness by the well. It is the *sixth* hour. The Samaritan 'harlot' has suffered under five 'men' since she first, as Ezekiel says, wantoned with the Assyrian: Assyria, Babylon, Media,[1] Persia and Greece have all possessed her. She disowns Caesar, the sixth who now is, and looks for the Messiah; already she accepts him in the Spirit, though his visible kingdom has not yet displaced that of Rome. (By contrast, her unhappy sister, Jerusalem, rejects Messiah at the same *sixth* hour, crying, 'We have no king but Caesar'). Here the woman is still a city (not Babylon, but Samaria-Shechem). Her royal lover is still imperial tyranny, but the succession which brings us to 'the sixth who now is' is a succession of empires, not of individual monarchs. The principle is still the same: we are in the end of the working week of political slavery. The final struggle and the victory of the Son of Man is upon us, whatever temporary disasters may preface it.

[1] The Median Empire did not include Palestine, but the Jews thought it had done so. This is plain in Daniel.

So much for the seven heads. There is less to be said about the ten horns. Various scriptures suggest a league of kings against the Lord and his Israel at the last battle, Psalms II and cx, to search no further. The Daniel prophecies, on the other hand, give the Beast a monopoly of world power. St John reconciles the two pictures. The imperial power appears, in fact, to be absolute (there is, of course, Parthia, but that is only one king more). But in the last days ten kings who have as yet received no power will receive it, and make no use of it save to make common cause with the Beast in all things. If St John is thinking politically at all, he may be thinking of Antichrist as the orientalizing type of Emperor who substitutes subject kingdoms for provinces, so that he may rejoice in the title 'King of Kings'. And this agrees with the suggestions of the context: 'They will war with the Lamb and he shall conquer them, for he is Lord of Lords and *King of Kings*.'

If it is true for the most part that the Beast is written out of scripture and principle rather than out of contemporary history, the same is even more generally true of the False Prophet. It has often been suggested that he stands for the official priesthood of the Emperor-Cult, but the picture of such decorous and mundane dignitaries invoking fire from heaven or conjuring a voice out of a statue hardly fits. St John is thinking rather of the text of Deuteronomy, where we are warned that those who preach idolatry are not to be followed, whatever prophetical signs they may give. The False Prophet is to be set in contrasting parallel with the Two Witnesses, as the Beast is with the Lamb. St John himself is, indeed, a Christian Prophet, but the image-type of the function obtains free expression in the symbolical pair of martyrs. They also call down fire, not as a strengthless sign, but, like the fire of Elias, to devour their enemies. The False Prophet causes breath to enter the image of the Beast, that it may command those who refuse idolatry to be slain. When the true prophets have been slain for this very cause, and have lain three days and a half unburied, the Breath of God enters into them and raises them up.

Why, we may finally ask, does the divine Goodness permit the great rebellion of Antichrist? It is, we must answer, part of the economy of judgement. When Elijah on Mt Carmel said to the people, 'How long halt ye between two opinions? If the Lord is

God, serve him, if Baal, serve him,' they answered never a word, for it seemed to them very natural that the God of Israel should be worshipped on his days at Bethel or Dan, and the Baal of Tyre on his days in Jezebel's embassy-chapel. Elijah forced a trial of strength with Baal, and the men of Israel were compelled to choose: divine mercy sealed the seven thousand who bowed not the knee to Baal, and divine vengeance cut off all whose lips had kissed him. The world commonly presents the outward appearance of so many million lives evading from the cradle to the grave every fundamental decision, and even the self-knowledge whether they are servants of God or of Mammon. The great drama of Christ and Antichrist forces the issue: there is no motive for refusing the mark of the Beast except that one bears the mark of Christ, nor any, heaven knows, for receiving the mark of Christ except that one loves him. The demons and their human instruments make saints of the believers, and heroes of the saints: and by their industrious scavenging they collect all the refuse of the world, and pile it conveniently for the fires of gehenna.

The saints are secure in their predestination. The demonic attack is directed against them, but it turns always upon the wicked. The Dragon attacks the woman crowned with stars: he cannot touch her, and the swinging of his tail brings down the apostate third, already ruled out of the heavenly temple by the word of God in the measuring vision. Defeated in the court of heaven, he falls to earth full of wrath. A heavenly voice declares that his descent is a matter of rejoicing for those who tabernacle in heaven, and of woe to men whose only home is earth. He pursues the heavenly woman into the wilderness, and shoots a river after her, which the earth-angel swallows, and the woman is saved. But when with his confederates Satan gathers the wicked Kings to Armageddon, the angel has been beforehand with him: he has dried the river to ease their passage, before the deceiving spirits have even started on their mission of persuading the kings to come. The Mother of Messiah is pursued by the 'floods of Belial', but they do not come nigh her: the Great Harlot is peaceably enthroned on the many waters, yet they rise against her. Evil turns always against evil.

The two constituent parts of pagan power are military kingship and urban wealth. Ever since the days of Alexander the two have been unhappily adjusted. The military emperor is a god and protector to the city, he woos and flatters her, she affects to worship him. But she hopes devoutly that he will keep his armies at a comfortable distance. From time to time, whether through lack of money or through the mutiny of his troops, or through his own cruelty or spite, he moves against the city and pillages her. Such are the loves and the quarrels of the Beast and Babylon, the parody of that marriage that there is betwixt Christ and his Church, the heavenly Jerusalem. Jerusalem is a city, yet she is also the garden of Paradise, fresh and clean. Cast forth from her gates, consigned to outer darkness and consuming fire, are all the filth and perversion of the life of cities.

CHAPTER XII

(1)

The Apocalypse wears the superficial likeness of a prophetic narrative, the description of an order of events about to be unrolled. We look more closely, and find it almost impossible to make sense of the continuous story as it stands. We prudently decide to suspend the enquiry, until we have thoroughly examined the trains of symbolism and the formal patterns out of which the book is woven. They prove to be worth examining for their own sakes: but we cannot be satisfied wholly to lose sight of the original question. It may be that St John is not so seriously concerned with straight prediction as we once supposed, but it remains that he has used the predictive convention, to say the least of it, and we must try to state what it is that he apparently predicts.

He predicts in the end, 'What eye hath not seen, nor ear heard, nor hath it entered into the heart of man to conceive,' and if we are to attempt to give further precision to that, we shall need to see a better apocalypse than his. But there is a more modest enquiry we can undertake. How many distinct stages of event, we may ask, does St John's prediction describe, and how are they related to one another? When we have eliminated all the anticipations, recapitulations, and asides, how many things succeed one another in the prophecy?

We have one fixed rule and guide, the sequence in climax of the seals, trumpets, vials, and last things. The woes of the seals destroy a quarter, the woes of the trumpets a third, the woes of the vials destroy all. These judgements are all of them ministered by angels and belong to this world. The last things are effected by direct intervention of Christ and introduce the world to come. No interpretation which confuses these four stages can be allowed to stand. With this rule in mind, let us turn to the text.

The first three chapters hardly concern us. Here the Christ of the First Advent speaks to his Churches in the present time. The movement of the things to come springs out of the heavenly vision of the fourth and fifth chapters; not even that vision is itself in future time. The glorious Throne is timeless, and so is the hymn of the cherubim. The manifestation of the Lamb, and his taking of the Book, if we can talk at all of dating them, must be timed either at Christ's Ascension and the first Christian Pentecost, or at St John's experiencing of these mysteries. Not until the seals break under the hand of the Lamb, does the prophetic story begin to unroll.

(a) The visions of the seals have their centre in the present, and their conclusion in the end of all things: a conclusion which is therefore cancelled or suspended, and does not belong to the straight march of events. As to the centre—can anyone read the vision of the martyr-souls, and suppose that St John is predicting a time when they *will be* crying, 'How long?' The contrast is simply between present expectation and future fulfilment. The present in which the martyr-souls cry is not to be dated to a month or a year, it is the whole room of time between the death of St Stephen and the opening of the next phase of Advent. Any month and year within this time martyrs may be made, and their souls may cry from beneath the altar of their sacrifice; they may be delivered from the general state of the dead, rewarded with white robes, and told to wait for the great access of martyrdoms under 'the great tribulation'. By contrast we may call the persecution against which these martyrs cry 'the lesser tribulation'.

It follows that the woes of the horsemen are also of the present age. The martyr-souls see imperial conquest followed by civil war, with its inevitable sequels of famine and pestilence; they see in these things the coming of the end, but they are disappointed. Imperial conquest degenerating into civil war had been the pattern of things in the first century B.C., and in the troubles after Nero's fall it had seemed that the new glories of the Principate were going the same way. The Flavian House re-established the Empire, and the souls of the martyrs cried, How long?

(b) The sealing of the saints has no historical date. In view of the Great Tribulation about to come, the general fact that Christians are baptised with water and sealed with the Spirit takes on a special character: it is the guarantee of their inviolable predestina-

300

tion. And so the woes of the trumpets can begin, for they cannot harm the saints. These woes are natural disasters, the immediate preludes of the Great Trumpet: they are the mere fevers of Nature at the approaching doom, and a last warning to the wicked that they should repent. The seventh trumpet sounds, and we expect to see the future unfold. But we are disappointed; the earlier of the succeeding visions fall back into the past, shewing the birth, ascension and enthronement of the Man-Child as the background for the revelation of Antichrist. God's Christ has been crowned: now let Antichrist set up his kingdom if he will. The enthronement of Christ being the justification of the saints, Satan is forthwith cast out of heaven. This is still in the past; it is only with Satan's evocation of Antichrist from the abyss, or sea, that the history advances, and we take up the story where the sixth trumpet left it. The kingdom of Antichrist is flanked by the woes of the trumpets before, and the vials after, a fact expressed by $666 = \frac{2}{3}$. The trumpet-angels have smitten the third; Antichrist reigns over the two-thirds, until the vial angels return with total destruction. The vials, like the trumpets, have disasters of nature for their effect.

Before the vials fall, the mysterious 'harvesting of the elect' (XIV, 14–16) is perhaps to be understood to have snatched away the righteous, alive or dead, from the scene of coming judgement. But the accompanying 'vintage of wrath' (XIV, 17–20) is certainly an anticipation of the Battle which will follow the Great Advent. As soon as the righteous have been snatched out of Antichrist's kingdom the vials of wrath pour down on 'the throne of the Beast'. They provoke first blasphemy, then rebellion: the kings of the earth go to Armageddon.

(c) The Babylon-visions of XVII–XVIII are seen by St John in present time, they do not enter the predicted history as a real pause. The Alleluia-liturgy of XIX, 1–9 is, like the other heavenly liturgies, an event in a celestial series parallel to the earthly, and upon which the earthly depends. On earth nothing intervenes between the gathering of the hosts to Armageddon under the sixth vial, and the descent of the Rider on the Horse to give them battle.

From this point, and within the sevenfold series which the Advent initiates, a vast development of prediction unrolls, and the

301

Millennium is comprehended in a span. But the order of events here presents no problems: it is simply narrated, and is nothing but the accepted stock of Rabbinic eschatology: the Great Battle, the Kingdom of Messiah, the Rebellion of Gog, the Last Judgement, and the World to Come. The Rebellion of Gog is placed after the gathering of the Dispersion into the kingdom of David and the resurrection of the privileged dead, because Ezekiel (XXXVIII–IX) places it after the gathering of the flock on to the mountains of Israel and the resurrection of the dry bones. The gehenna of corpses after the destruction of Gog's army may naturally be identified with the gehenna of the Great Assize, which had become an accepted article of belief since Ezekiel's day. So the Great Assize comes in here, and we proceed with the visions which follow Gog in Ezekiel's book—the visions of the Holy City, where God himself will fix his throne for ever.

We may draw the general conclusion that St John describes only two future stages of history, in addition to the present stage: the Advent of Antichrist and the Advent of Christ. The story is punctuated by outbreaks of natural disasters, but these are points rather than periods of time. The Advent of Christ releases the eschatological series proper, from the Great Battle to the World to Come. St John treats this as a unit, because to the Christian everything is secured once Christ has come. To attempt to raise a drama of hope and fear over the rebellion of Gog would produce nothing but anticlimax.

The general conclusion which we have outlined amounts to the same thing as saying that St John remains within the limits of the Christian tradition. Christ had prophesied in this form, according to Mark XIII. I should like to record the opinion, against all pleas advanced to the contrary, that this chapter of St Mark is in substance as authentic a record of Christ's teaching as we possess anywhere: but this is not the place to discuss that. It is sufficient if it is conceded that St John accepted it as such. In that oracle the Lord had given St John's namesake, the Son of Zebedee, and his three companions a threefold prophecy.

(a) Wars and rumours of war, the conflict of nations or of dynasties, earthquake and famine, must not mislead the disciples of Christ into the expectation of immediate Advent. These are but

302

the beginning-pains of the travail. Meanwhile persecution will arise, and martyrs will be multiplied.

(b) The appearance of Antichrist or his image in the Holy Place will initiate the 'shortened days' of the Great Tribulation. False Christ and False Prophet will appear, performing signs and wonders, to mislead, were it possible, the elect.

(c) Great natural disasters will be the sign for the appearance of 'the Son of Man with Clouds'. He will send forth his angels to harvest ($\epsilon\pi\iota\sigma\nu\nu\acute{\alpha}\gamma\epsilon\iota\nu$) the elect from the four winds.

This is the pattern of Christ's prophecy, and it is also the pattern of St John's prediction. He applies (a) to his own day. He prefaces (b) with 'the trump of the Archangel', accompanied by sevenfold portents. He rounds off (c) with the traditional picture of the Last Things, which would be taken for granted in the minds of Christ's hearers, though Christ in fact omitted the mention of them. St John remains faithful to the spirit of Christ's omission, by making the Coming of Christ to carry with it all that follows. St John did not set out to predict anything fresh, but to see and enter into those things which Christ had predicted. His elaborations are not new predictions, but interpretations and presentations of what had been predicted already. His privilege was to have ascended into heaven, and *seen* the things which the Lamb had already unsealed to the Church by the opening of the Book. The Apocalypse is related to Mark XIII much as St John's Gospel is related to the rest of the Marcan story. St John's namesake, the Apostle, in whom St John sees himself moving through the events of the Gospel, had also stood on the Mount of Olives, and heard the revelation of Jesus Christ, which God gave him, to show his servants what must quickly be. St John of Ephesus, one in spirit with the Son of Zebedee, relives his experience in both his books.

(2)

By what process was the Apocalypse composed? We have been studying little else: but we have still to stand back from the mass of detail and collect, if we can, a more orderly picture. Let us, first of all, set aside the theological question. We are not discussing whether, or how, St John's mind was moved by God. That is a different dimension of act, and is in any case invisible. The account

303

we are trying to give is not an account of the operation of the First Cause, nor is it alternative to such an account. To ask whether St John saw his visions by means of a mystical diagram or through the Holy Ghost, is like asking whether the flight of an eagle is sustained by his wings or by the air. On whatever wind of spirit St John ascended, he moved the sinews of his mind, and we can observe the motions.

Have we been in the habit of even considering the question which we are now trying to answer? The Apocalypse exists, it occupies twenty pages of our Bibles, and St John's having written it seems perfectly natural. An elaborate and unfamiliar hypothesis about his manner of working is put before us, and we say, 'How far-fetched, how unnecessary.' Well, the proposed hypothesis may, in fact, be a bad one, but if so, we have to find a better. It is no use saying that the erection of this extraordinary edifice was just common form. Conceive St John—conceive yourself—taking pen in hand and sitting down to write. How does one start? It is no good saying that such a work is the product of simple lyrical inspiration, as it might be Shelley writing about the skylark. You put down what has suggested itself in direct response to your experience and then you go on from there, developing and elaborating the images and reflections, as they themselves seem to demand, until the work (let us hope) rounds itself off, and you stop: then perhaps (but more if you are Keats than if you are Shelley) you go back over it, pruning, rewriting, rearranging, until you are content. This is an extremely superficial description of lyrical composition, but it will do for our purpose, since all we have to say is that nothing like the Apocalypse could be the result of the process so inadequately described.

What sort of task was St John undertaking, what was he trying to do? One might have supposed that he would write seven homilies for the Seven Churches, saying just what was appropriate to the needs of each, and follow them up with a plain and orderly statement of what ought to be believed about the relation of the present world-order to the coming of the end. But it is obvious that the Apocalypse is nothing like this. It is no use saying, either, that St John simply described visions which came to him: for the visions when examined appear to have little to do with the visual

304

imagination, they are 'seen with the mind'. But 'seeing with the mind' is just a bad metaphor. Things 'seen with the mind' are *thought,* not of course thought out by voluntary construction, but thought under some apparent compulsion: and if they are not thought in visual images, they are probably thought in words. Yet this thought-process cannot, we have said, be in this case the simple spontaneity of lyric inspiration. It is an elaborate formal process. It is, indeed, deeply experienced, and so obtains the quality of 'vision', but that does not explain the origin or nature of the formal process. No doubt St John felt the form itself to be prescribed by what was revealing itself through the form, but that does not excuse us from asking how he approached the reality, how he put himself in the way of experiencing it through such a form as this.

At this point in the enquiry we have probably been used to let ourselves off by an appeal to 'the apocalyptic tradition'. Where we find an elaborate and as it were artificial literary structure, we naturally suppose that its author was making his own use of a form already traditional. Virgil deeply felt many things about the destiny of nations and the qualities of personal existence, but he allowed all this to express itself in the process of rehandling the epic convention. Take an accepted fable and the traditional manner of developing it, and get to work, knowing that the content you have to express will become articulate in the process of imagination. The trouble is that the apocalyptic tradition contains nothing like the form of the Christian Apocalypse. It supplies plenty of material, but it does not supply the form. The Apocalypses we know are mostly formless as wholes: they obtain what form they have from the continuous paraphrasing of scripture or the use of simple lists, as when the Twelve Patriarchs make their testaments one by one. There is no analogy either to the many-sidedness of the continuous symbolical theme, or to the internal building up of pattern out of the elements of previous pattern, or to the systematic use of echo and refrain, or to the astonishing fertility of devices for maintaining suspense and piling up climax.

No one had tried to do what St John does, so far as we know. Naturally, if anyone wishes to sketch in a shadowy and unknown genius looking over St John's shoulder, he cannot be refuted. If

305

we suppose a whole succession of such men to stand behind St John, we may satisfy our craving for evolutionary gradualness, but we shall increase our burden of unevidenced hypothesis. There are those who like to see visible history as the result of invisible conspiracy, and those who like to see surviving literature as the creature of lost tradition. There are others who prefer working in the light to guessing in the dark. We have done some guessing ourselves, but we have guessed about the character of events which did anyhow take place: the Apocalypse was composed and written, for here it is.

St John was making a new form of literature: it happens that he had no successor. St Mark performed the same unimaginable feat, and he was followed by others. The comparison is an interesting one, and students of St Mark ought to ask the same question as we are asking here about St John. What did St Mark sit down to do? To us the idea of writing a memoir or a biography is perfectly familiar, and the literary men of the Hellenistic world had some notion of it too. But it is unlikely that St Mark had ever read such a work, and in any case his gospel had no resemblance to their efforts. There was oral material no doubt, but it had not the form or order of a narrative, until one came to the part of the tradition which recorded the Passion. So how did St Mark envisage his task? The question, taken seriously, may lead to results no less surprising, though certainly quite other, than those to which we are driven in the case of the Apocalypse.

In the context of this question, the hypothesis of the diagram is a Godsend. In the process of our exposition, the diagram may appear as one further complication. After tracing so many symbolical lines through the book, we add this beside the rest. The diagram complicates the exposition, but it does nothing but simplify the supposed process of composition. If St John is keeping so many concerns in mind, following the symbolical week and the sacred year, the scheme of traditional eschatology, of Christ's prophecy, and of multiple Old Testament typology, how can he move at all, and how can he keep his pattern firm? The diagram supplies the answer. He makes each movement of the poem by working round the diagram: each such movement, or group of such movements, is a day in the week, a quarter of the year, and so on—he

306

will never get lost. The diagram, as St John comes back over it, retains the enrichments of meaning with which the previous movements have overlaid it. These afford materials for the fresh movement and give rise to that continually varied embellishment of a standing cyclic pattern which is the literary miracle of the Apocalypse.

The diagram represents the final object of St John's vision, the Kingdom of Heaven. We have foretastes of it in the Firstfruits-Pentecost vision (IV–V) and in the 'cancelled conclusion' to the first spring quarter (VII), and the completion of its unveiling in the vision of the Bride after the second spring quarter. St John started with the diagram ready drawn, that is to say he started with the form of what he aspired to see, final blessedness. By many stages, no doubt, by many efforts of spirit, he was to be taken up into the meaning of the diagram, to possess in prophetic rapture the goal of his vision. For this purpose it was not enough to contemplate the diagram; the diagram must, as it were, be persuaded to speak, and, in its own order, to reveal its mysteries. As the mind passed over and over it, the several stages of ascent were built up, the depth and breadth of the divine Kingdom were made full, until the World to Come burst on the seer's vision, charged with the weight of all he had seen by the way.

What it is so hard for us to recover is the thought-world in which the diagram, and the diagram simply, could be viewed as a sacred and illuminating thing. Unless St John had had such an attitude to the diagram, it is incredible that he should have worked from it. It may seem to us that essentially the diagram was an instrument of projection—that it fulfilled the same function as the gazer's crystal, or any of those mazes in which divining minds have been able to pick out what lay unrecognized in the abyss of the unthought. But we cannot suppose that St John saw it as an arbitrary psychological device, no better than any other, or that it had no meaning for him in itself, before he began to manipulate with it for the evocation of prophecy.

What, then, does the diagram represent? Is there a name for it? It seems best to answer, the Pleroma. There is a common form of thought, in spite of all differences, giving shape to the systems of the gnostics, and to the anti-gnostical doctrine of Colossians and

307

Ephesians. The divine life, it is taught, either freely or by some sort of necessity, articulates itself into a system or communicates itself to a plurality which is perfect and complete. The salvation of the elect means their finding their place in the 'Fulness'. Somehow there is a duality between the Pleroma and a world which lies beyond it. One might have supposed that when Life had fulfilled the form of the Pleroma, it had found its own limits, and would acquiesce in them. But in fact it is not so. There is a world outside the Pleroma, and we have to make our way from this world into the Pleroma.

There is the greatest variety of doctrine about the way in which the plurality of the Pleroma is related to the unity of the Godhead —the system may be pantheistic, emanationist, creationist. There is equal variety of doctrine about the relations of the Pleroma to the world in which we live 'according to the flesh'. For St Paul the Pleroma is the Body of Christ, in which spiritual creatures of all grades are to find their place. It pre-existed dynamically from all eternity, but it is being actualized through the Incarnation, the Redemption, and the coming Advent. The 'fleshly' world is its raw material, a material, however, of which some has to be discarded and the rest recreated, because of the Fall of Man.

St John's doctrine does not differ from St Paul's, but he goes further than we know St Paul to have gone in adopting gnostic form—or is it that the form we are concerned with belongs to his generation of gnosticism rather than to St Paul's? However that may be, the diagrammatic presentation of the Pleroma became a stock part of the gnostic systems, reaching its highest elaboration in the Valentinian school. As we saw, the Pleroma is the notion of some intrinsically natural or perfect articulation of being, in which existence reaches the limits of a complete system, and acquiesces in them. This notion is either based on mathematical analogy, or at least finds its inevitable expression in it. We take a formula, and fill out on paper the system which it prescribes, and there we stop: the number or figure has attained its *pleroma*. But how, to start with, do we get our formula? Here the element of the arbitrary enters. Numbers and lists will be culled from fields which have an accepted sacred significance: the best numbers are those in which a harmony between nature and scripture finds expression, 'nature' meaning chiefly 'astrology'. Valentinus's ogdoad matches the eight skins of the glass onion which was his cosmos: when we have passed the seven planets we reach the fixed stars, when we have passed the seven planetary days we reach the day of eternal life (the eighth-and-first). The cosmos is, indeed, no more than a parable of the Pleroma, which wholly transcends it. Still, the parable teaches, and the scripture teaches more: so let *eight* be the basic number of the Pleroma. Yet this is not the fulness of the Pleroma, for the Apostle had written to the Ephesians 'for the building up of the Body of Christ, until we all attain to the unity of the faith and comprehension of the Son of God, unto a fullgrown man, to the measure of the age of the *pleroma* of Christ'. What the fullness of the mystical Body of Christ is, we shall surely judge from the measure of the age which was *pleroma* or fulness for the physical body of Christ; and St Luke tells us that it was at thirty years that Christ judged himself to have sufficiently 'advanced in wisdom and age' and so began his ministry. So as the body of Christ built itself up in thirty years, the Pleroma must eternally articulate itself in thirty aeons. By what mathematical pattern can we proceed from the basic eight to the thirty? Valentine distributes the principle of the 'mystical marriage betwixt Christ and his Church' throughout the Pleroma; everywhere there are pairs in which the duality of male and female is seen. If, then, we count in pairs, we reach the thirty by a simple arithmetical progression. The ogdoad is four pairs; if we add five, and then six, we have thirty. The eight are nobler than the ten, the ten

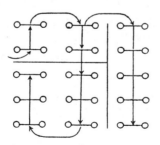

than the twelve: the ten are begotten from the last pair but one in the eight, the twelve from the last pair.

The Pleroma is now in principle 'full'; it must no doubt be

309

squared and cubed and have plenty of noughts added to the right-hand end of the resultant sum, to express the predestined number of those souls who find their mansions in the houses of the thirty aeons.

St John's book contains the same type of figure. The diagram represents the mathematical base of the Pleroma, and it is arrived at by a harmony of scripture and astrology, the twelve zodiacal signs and the twelve tribes. The twelve tribes are obviously the symbol of the Pleroma, the People of God, the Body of Christ; and scripture itself compares them with the twelve signs; the signs, or the segments which they mark, making up the Pleroma of the round heaven. They are to be viewed as a square, however, not a circle, because of the square Jerusalem on whose twelve gates the tribal names are inscribed, according to Ezekiel. If we want the fulness of the Pleroma, not simply the tribes but the men in the tribes, we take square twelves of thousands for the twelve fathers, and for the total of the 'families', we proceed into the dimension of the cube. St John is neither a pantheist nor an emanationist, but there is a sense in which for him too the Pleroma expresses the life of God; and so the diagram is in one aspect the Throne and in another the City.

Neither Valentine nor St John was content to leave the scheme of the Pleroma in mere mathematical emptiness. Valentine supplied a very handsome list of abstract nouns and philosophical adjectives to stand for his numerous aeons, and even concatenated them in an ingenious order which reminds one of the procession of categories in Hegel's logic. St John, being no gnostic heretic but an orthodox and apostolic man, accepts nature as the direct creature of the divine Goodness and the Old Testament as the expression of divine Revelation, and fills the places of his scheme with the tribal names and astral signs, symbols which God himself has appointed and ranged in order. This gives a solidity to his vision, and a docility to his attitude, which one would vainly seek for in heretical gnosticism, where inspiration makes up what it contemplates and dictates what it is going to believe.

The figure of the gnostic Pleroma did not simply stand there to be looked at, a motionless perfection of form; it generated a myth of fall and redemption, a drama which occupied a double stage partly in the Pleroma and partly in the outer dark. Thus, if we are viewing St John on a gnostic background, we shall find nothing to surprise us in the development of apocalypse out of the heart of the Pleroma, or the setting of the drama in the Pleromatic frame.

There is no need to elaborate further the parallel between St John's imagery and that of Valentinian gnosis. Perhaps we have already forced the comparison. We leave it to those who are competent to handle it. It will have served its purpose here if it has persuaded us that St John may very well have taken a serious interest in the diagram for its own sake, taking pains to construct it in such a way that the several mysteries it appeared to signify received their most appropriate and concordant expression. It was already there when, doomed to lonely reflection by his Patmian prison, St John was moved to enter upon the arduous path of meditated vision which produced the Apocalypse.

How did St John work in the formation of the book itself? Slowly, it would seem, and with deep recollectedness, casting every sentence into a mould of such finality that, once written, it became an oracle from which, in the sequel, fresh divinations could be made. For the already written part of his own work becomes formative of the rest, almost as though it were holy scripture. In writing the Candlestick-vision he underwent the control of Zechariah and Daniel, in writing the Seven Messages he underwent the control of the Candlestick-vision. His submission to its control was not voluntary, it was laid upon him. The vision thrust upon him the symbol of the lamps and stars, and of their mysterious equivalence. He learnt by the Word of Christ that they were the churches and their angels, and that Christ's presence among them in the forms of the vision affected their existence in a way which demanded to be expressed. Passing back over the text of the vision, he heard in it the messages of Christ to the Seven Churches.

Never for a moment, from the writing of the first line of the book, does St John escape from the control of the process he has initiated. When he greets the Seven Churches in the Name of the Three Persons, the Three Persons as they are in the diagram, elaborated further by the threefold exposition of the Name, everything that is to come is implicit in the few words he writes. The meaning of the Name works itself out in the short pattern of the Greeting, Doxology, Advent Promise and Amen. But this is

311

obviously no more than a sketch. The short pattern has set forth the Name, but a longer pattern must set forth the short pattern: and this takes place, as we have seen, in the whole book, in which the pattern of the Name is elaborated and fulfilled on the basis of the diagram.

The fulfilment must begin in further oracle or vision. To what vision shall we inevitably pass from the self-utterance of the Name in a blessing? Undoubtedly to the Candlestick-vision, which is the complement of the blessing with the Name, since both belong to the Dedication-feast and to Numbers VI-VIII. So St John's mind submits to another inescapable control, which will not release him until the book is done, the control of the festal series. Meanwhile, the Dedication-vision befell St John on a Sunday, and it was a revelation of light: so here is the beginning also of creation-week, and that series demands completion too.

The Dedication-vision has used the diagram, for the Churches which Christ addressed in Asia are an expression of the Pleroma. They are, however, a secondary and incomplete expression of it. It demands to be revealed in its heavenly being, and for this purpose the seer must ascend into heaven: which is very proper to the second day of the week when heaven was created, and to the Passover-Firstfruits feast, at which Christ himself ascended. The image of the door has already appeared and reappeared in the end of the Messages, a portent of what is to come. Inevitably St John falls into the meditation of Ezekiel's Chariot-vision, the traditional instrument of ecstasy, and passes through the heavenly door. The Chariot-vision belongs to Pentecost, not Passover, and so St John finds himself seeing the Passover-to-Pentecost period as one process, in which pentecostal revelation is gradually made full by the breaking of the seals of the Book.

The great movement of the Apocalypse is now launched; for the Pentecost we reach with the breaking of the seals is not yet fulfilment: the pattern of calendar in VI is a mere sketch, as the pattern of the Name in I was a mere sketch: and St John knows that it must be fulfilled in a vaster cycle. In making out his little calendar (VI) on the diagram, he has gone from Passover (Aries) on past Midsummer (Gemini) and right round the astral circle of the year past Aries and Gemini into Leo, there to end. This gives him the

312

model for his future progress: the New Year he stands before at the sixth seal is only the intermediate New Year of a cycle which has to run on through the whole year, past a second Passover to confront New Year again.

The unrealized potentialities of the diagram beckon him on. True, he ascended into heaven in IV, to behold a more adequate vision of the Pleroma than that provided by Christ indwelling on earth the Seven Asian Churches. Yet even this was not a fully adequate vision of what the diagram means: it was a vision of the bare diagram, not of the diagram 'made in all things full' by the twelve's being squared, multiplied in thousands, and then cubed, that is to say, by the completion of the world to come, the incorporation into heavenly Jerusalem of all those saved out of the earth. Many things must happen before the diagram can be seen as the fullness in all things made full. In IV we see the double twelve in heaven, in VII the twelve twelve thousands are sealed on earth; the two numbers have yet to be brought together. The countless multitude before the Throne, glimpsed in VII, are those that come out of the great tribulation into their glory. The great tribulation, therefore, that is, the days of Antichrist, must be revealed before the twelve twelve thousands from earth are incorporated into the heavenly twelve, and fulfilled in the cubic number which passes counting.

So we may see the Apocalypse articulating itself stage by stage: at no point is St John free to write what he chooses, but always what he must. He has only to greet his flock in the Name of the Trinity, and the Spirit grasps his pen and does the rest. The poem is the revelation, and the revelation is the poem. He sees what he writes, and writes what he sees. When the Son of Man stands before him his pen is in his hand, and the 'vision' is a compulsion to write thus and thus to the Seven Churches. When the Angel of the Oath appears in X, it is assumed that St John is writing: he has written that the seven thunders utter their voices, and hears a direction *not* to write what the utterance was.[1] All the past tenses,

---

[1] 'Not to write' really includes 'Not to listen for'. If St John concentrated his meditation upon the utterance of the seven thunders, a sevenfold series of visions or oracles would result, like those on the seals or trumpets. But that form is now to be discarded (until it returns in the seven vials).

'I was in the Spirit on the Lord's day . . . I heard . . . I saw . . . I saw,' are 'epistolary aorists', they take up the time-position of the reader, not of the writer, and might as well be rendered by presents or perfects: 'I have been possessed by the Spirit on the Lord's day . . . I hear . . . I see.'

How much of the compulsive thinking which gave rise to the Apocalypse took place on the level of conscious deliberation, how much in the subconscious levels of imagination, one cannot say. We must see St John moving over the face of his diagram with profound concentration, watching his ideas and listening to his heart, and writing only the words that had to be written so as to satisfy both. If we wish to appreciate the quality of the compulsion he experienced, we must take examples in which we appear able ourselves to experience it after him: for instance, how the mention of 'the Great Day of God Almighty' acts like a trigger to release the long held back 'I come', in the sixth vial: or how the Amen to the heavenly Alleluias first spreads in paraphrase on the angel's lips, and then takes flesh in the figure of the conquering Christ.

(3)

The question of St John's origin and affinities is one which it is impossible not to ask, but which I confess myself totally unequipped for answering. Only a scholar with expert knowledge of Hellenistic and especially Asian Jewry would be qualified. All I can do is to jot down certain limiting and elementary data.

First of all a negative. It is useless to try to decide the question by instituting a tug-of-war between St John's principal 'tendencies', in the hope of deciding that he is above all rabbinic or gnostic or an apocalyptist in the tradition of the great pseudepigrapha, or anything else. Such is the characteristically false approach of those who come to a work of literature from the outside. With our heads full of rabbinic lore, or whatever it may be, we read our author not in order to see what he does, but to pick out his borrowings and affinities. We see only what we come to find, and as there is plenty of it, we are quickly satisfied that he is fundamentally (say) a converted Pharisaic rabbi, and that all other affinities are quite secondary and superficial.

The truth is that St John's mental acts have an originativeness and an intensity which permits of borrowing to the limit from every side at once, without any loss of individuality or vitality. He may be as rabbinic as the orthodox synagogue, as gnostical as any gnostic: he synthetizes the previous Christian writings, he makes allusion to the whole of the Old Testament. And all this he does, because it is the perfect way for him to think his own thoughts.

St John's, then, is one of those strong minds in which many things meet to be fused and refashioned, and it is vain to claim him for this tradition or for that. As to the background of his earlier life, we must be content with formal and exterior indications. He is a Jew. The liturgy of the Synagogue through the cycle of the year is part of the standing furniture of his mind. He had not acquired his familiarity with it as an uncircumcised sympathiser, a numerous and very important type of worshipper in the synagogues of the Dispersion; for he has a Jewish name, and he is acquainted with the Old Testament in the Hebrew as well as in the Greek, as, to name but one instance, his use of Zechariah XII shows. His knowledge of the Hebrew of the chapter is not limited to the text, 'They shall look upon whom they have pierced': he might have had that already translated in a collection of proof-texts. He knows also about the presence of the name 'Magedon' in the context, a name which disappears in the Septuagint rendering. We cannot easily tell how well he understood the Hebrew in itself, and how far he was dependent on an Aramaic *targum*, customarily recited after it. The artificial language in which he writes is modelled upon the Greek of the Septuagint, but it is difficult to believe that it could have been handled with such good effect by a man who had not been used to think in a Semitic tongue, whether Hebrew or Aramaic.

It is easy and tempting to conclude that he must have grown up in Palestine: but we are probably not in a position to dogmatize as to what was or was not to be found hidden away in the ghettos of Asia. Were there no families, especially perhaps families of rabbis, in which Aramaic was talked in the home-circle? Were there no synagogues in which the Hebrew was still read out in front of the Greek paraphrase? Were all rabbinic schools in the Diaspora as Hellenistic as others?

If we are permitted to use the Johannine Gospel as evidence, we may be able to decide that St John had been in Palestine, but if so, was it as a citizen or as a pilgrim? Or was he, like St Paul, a rabbi from the Dispersion who studied in Jerusalem, or perhaps at Jamnia, if the city had already fallen? We should in any case be overstating the Palestinian hypothesis if we suggested that St John's acquaintance with the interior life of the synagogue was wholly Palestinian. For the speculations on the Name of God appear to belong to a habit of rabbinizing in the Greek tongue, which one would suppose to have been acquired in a Hellenistic, or at least bilingual, Jewish community. It is less likely that St John first began such ways of thought after he became a Christian.

If we insist on taking him to Palestine, perhaps we ought to take him to Egypt, too, to pick up a tincture of the sort of gnosticism which we find flowering there presently. And by the same reasoning someone coming across this book in the forgotten corner of a library one day may decide that the author undoubtedly studied in Cambridge, at the feet of this or that theologian whose writings on the Gentile-Jewish borderland happen in that distant day to have survived. It may be most sensible to see St John as an Asian Jew, brought up in a rabbinic school, where Hebrew was studied and Aramaic was not dead, but having for his everyday environment a more Hellenized Jewry which did its theology in Greek and was liable to develop gnostical tendencies; and, neither very early nor very late in life, converted to Christ. What he then became was not the effect of his background, but the act of his inspiration: we can see it coming to the birth under our very eyes.

THE TEXT

The Revelation of Jesus Christ, which God gave unto him, to shew unto his servants things which must shortly come to pass; and he sent and signified it by his angel unto his servant John: who bare record of the word of God, and of the testimony of Jesus Christ, and of all things that he saw. Blessed is he that readeth, and they that hear the words of this prophecy, and keep those things which are written therein: for the time is at hand.

John to the seven churches which are in Asia: Grace be unto you, and peace, from him which is, and which was, and which is to come; and from the seven Spirits which are before his throne; and from Jesus Christ, who is the faithful witness, and the first begotten of the dead, and the prince of the kings of the earth. Unto him that loved us, and freed us from our sins by his own blood, and hath made us kings and priests unto God and his Father; to him be glory and dominion for ever and ever. Amen.

Behold, he cometh with clouds; and every eye shall see him, and they also which pierced him: and all kindreds of the earth shall wail because of him. Even so, Amen. I am Alpha and Omega, saith the Lord God, which is, and which was, and which is to come, the Almighty.

I John, who also am your brother, and companion in tribulation, and in the kingdom and patience of Jesus Christ, was in the isle that is called Patmos, for the word of God, and for the testimony of Jesus Christ. I was in the Spirit on the Lord's day, and heard behind me a great voice, as of a trumpet, saying, What thou seest, write in a book, and send it unto the seven churches which are in Asia; unto Ephesus, and unto Smyrna, and unto Pergamos, and unto Thyatira, and unto Sardis, and unto Philadelphia, and unto Laodicea.

And I turned to see the voice that spake with me. And being

317

turned, I saw seven golden candlesticks; and in the midst of the seven candlesticks one like unto the Son of man, clothed with a garment down to the foot, and girt about the paps with a golden girdle. His head and his hairs were white like wool, as white as snow; and his eyes were as a flame of fire; and his feet like unto fine brass, as if they had been fired in a furnace; and his voice as the sound of many waters. And he had in his right hand seven stars: and out of his mouth went a sharp two-edged sword: and his countenance was as the sun shineth in his strength.

And when I saw him, I fell at his feet as dead. And he laid his right hand upon me, saying unto me, Fear not; I am the first and the last: I am he that liveth, and was dead; and, behold, I am alive for evermore, and have the keys of hell and of death. Write the things which thou hast seen, and the things which are, and the things which shall be hereafter; the mystery of the seven stars which thou sawest in my right hand, and the seven golden candlesticks. The seven stars are the angels of the seven churches: and the seven candlesticks are the seven churches.[1]

Unto the angel of the church of Ephesus write; these things saith he that holdeth the seven stars in his right hand, who walketh in the midst of the seven golden candlesticks; I know thy works, and thy labour, and thy patience, and how thou canst not bear them which are evil: and thou hast tried them which say they are apostles, and are not, and hast found them liars: and hast patience, and for my name's sake hast borne and hast not fainted. Nevertheless I have somewhat against thee, because thou hast left thy first love. Remember therefore from whence thou art fallen, and repent, and do the first works; or else I will come unto thee quickly, and will remove thy candlestick out of his place, except thou repent. But this thou hast, that thou hatest the deeds of the Nicolaitans, which I also hate. He that hath an ear, let him hear what the Spirit saith unto the churches; to him that overcometh will I give to eat of the tree of life, which is in the paradise of God.

[1] Italics here and elsewhere simply mark the passage upon which a fresh series follows.

And unto the angel of the church in Smyrna write; these things saith the first and the last, which was dead, and is alive; I know thy works, and tribulation, and poverty, (but thou art rich) and I know the blasphemy of them which say they are Jews, and are not, but are the synagogue of Satan. Fear none of those things which thou shalt suffer: behold, the devil shall cast some of you into prison, that ye may be tried; and ye shall have tribulation ten days: be thou faithful unto death, and I will give thee a crown of life. He that hath an ear, let him hear what the Spirit saith unto the churches; he that overcometh shall not be hurt of the second death.

And to the angel of the church in Pergamos write; these things saith he which hath the sharp sword with two edges; I know where thou dwellest, even where Satan's seat is: and thou holdest fast my name, and hast not denied my faith, even in those days wherein Antipas was my faithful martyr, who was slain among you, where Satan dwelleth. But I have a few things against thee, because thou hast there them that hold the doctrine of Balaam, who taught Balac to cast a stumbling block before the children of Israel, to eat things sacrificed unto idols, and to commit fornication. So hast thou also them that hold the doctrine of the Nicolaitans after the same sort. Repent; or else I will come unto thee quickly, and will fight against them with the sword of my mouth. He that hath an ear, let him hear what the Spirit saith unto the churches; to him that overcometh will I give to eat of the hidden manna, and will give him a white stone, and in the stone a new name written, which no man knoweth saving he that receiveth it.

And unto the angel of the church in Thyatira write; these things saith the Son of God, who hath his eyes like unto a flame of fire, and his feet are like fine brass; I know thy works, and charity, and service, and faith, and thy patience, and thy last works to be more than the first. Notwithstanding I have something against thee, because thou sufferest that woman Jezebel, which calleth herself a prophetess, to teach and to seduce my servants to commit fornication, and to eat things sacrificed unto idols. And I gave her space to repent of her fornication; and she will not repent. Behold, I will

319

cast her into a bed, and them that commit adultery with her into great tribulation, except they repent of their deeds. And I will kill her children with death; and all the churches shall know that I am he which searcheth the reins and hearts: and I will give unto every one of you according to your works. But unto you I say, the rest in Thyatira, as many as have not this doctrine, and which have not known the depths of Satan, as they speak; I will put upon you none other burden. But that which ye have already hold fast till I come. And he that overcometh, and keepeth my works unto the end, to him will I give power over the nations: and he shall rule them with a rod of iron; as the vessels of a potter shall they be broken to shivers: even as I received of my Father. And I will give him the morning star. He that hath an ear, let him hear what the Spirit saith unto the churches.

And unto the angel of the church in Sardis write; these things saith he that hath the seven Spirits of God, and the seven stars; I know thy works, that thou hast a name that thou livest, and art dead. Be watchful, and strengthen the things which remain, that are ready to die: for I have not found thy works perfect before God. Remember therefore how thou hast received and heard, and hold fast, and repent. If therefore thou shalt not watch, I will come on thee as a thief, and thou shalt not know what hour I will come upon thee. Thou hast a few names even in Sardis which have not defiled their garments; and they shall walk with me in white: for they are worthy. He that overcometh, the same shall be clothed in white raiment; and I will not blot out his name out of the book of life, but I will confess his name before my Father, and before his angels. He that hath an ear, let him hear what the Spirit saith unto the churches.

And to the angel of the church in Philadelphia write; these things saith he that is holy, he that is true, he that hath the key of David, he that openeth, and no man shutteth; and shutteth, and no man openeth; I know thy works: behold, I have set before thee an open door, and no man can shut it: for thou hast a little strength, and hast kept my word, and hast not denied my name. Behold, I will make them of the synagogue of Satan, which say they are Jews,

320

and are not, but do lie; behold, I will make them to come and worship before thy feet, and to know that I have loved thee. Because thou hast kept the word of my patience, I also will keep thee from the hour of temptation, which shall come upon all the world, to try them that dwell upon the earth. I come quickly: hold that fast which thou hast, that no man take thy crown. Him that overcometh will I make a pillar in the temple of my God, and he shall go no more out: and I will write upon him the name of my God, and the name of the city of my God, which is new Jerusalem, which cometh down out of heaven from my God: and I will write upon him my new name. He that hath an ear, let him hear what the Spirit saith unto the churches.

And unto the angel of the church of the Laodiceans write; these things saith the Amen, the faithful and true witness, the beginning of the creation of God; I know thy works, that thou art neither cold nor hot: I would thou wert cold or hot. So then because thou art lukewarm, and neither cold nor hot, I will spue thee out of my mouth. Because thou sayest, I am rich, and increased with goods, and have need of nothing; and knowest not that thou art wretched, and miserable, and poor, and blind, and naked: I counsel thee to buy of me gold tried in the fire, that thou mayest be rich; and white raiment, that thou mayest be clothed, and that the shame of thy nakedness do not appear; and eyesalve to anoint thine eyes, that thou mayest see. As many as I love, I rebuke, and chasten: be zealous therefore, and repent. Behold, I stand at the door, and knock: if any man hear my voice, and open the door, I will come in to him, and will sup with him, and he with me. To him that overcometh will I grant to sit with me in my throne, even as I also overcame, and am set down with my Father in his throne. He that hath an ear, let him hear what the Spirit saith unto the churches.

After this I looked, and, behold, a door was opened in heaven: and the first voice which I heard was as it were of a trumpet talking with me; which said, Come up hither, and I will shew thee things which must be hereafter. And immediately I was in the spirit: and, behold, a throne was set in heaven, and one sat on the throne. And he that sat was to look upon like a jasper and a sardine stone: and there was a rainbow round about the throne, in sight like unto an emerald. And round about the throne were four and twenty seats: and upon the seats I saw four and twenty elders sitting, clothed in white raiment; and they had on their heads crowns of gold. And out of the throne proceeded lightnings and thunderings and voices: and there were seven lamps of fire burning before the throne, which are the seven Spirits of God. And before the throne there was a sea of glass like unto crystal: and in the midst of the throne, and round about the throne, were four beasts full of eyes before and behind. And the first beast was like a lion, and the second beast like a calf, and the third beast had a face as a man, and the fourth beast was like a flying eagle. And the four beasts had each of them six wings; and they were full of eyes about and within: and they rest not day and night, saying, Holy, holy, holy, Lord God Almighty, which was, and is, and is to come. And when those beasts give glory and honour and thanks to him that sat on the throne, who liveth for ever and ever, the four and twenty elders fall down before him that sat on the throne, and worship him that liveth for ever and ever, and cast their crowns before the throne, saying, Thou art worthy, O Lord, to receive glory and honour and power: for thou hast created all things, and for thy pleasure they are and were created.

And I saw in the right hand of him that sat on the throne a book written within and on the backside, sealed with seven seals. And I saw a strong angel proclaiming with a loud voice, Who is worthy to open the book, and to loose the seals thereof? And no man in heaven, nor in earth, neither under the earth, was able to open the book, neither to look thereon. And I wept much, because no man was found worthy to open the book, neither to look thereon. And one of the elders saith unto me, Weep not: behold, the Lion of the tribe of Juda, the Root of David, hath prevailed to open the book, and to loose the seven seals thereof. And I beheld in the midst of the throne and of the four beasts, and in the midst of the elders, stood a Lamb as it had been slain, having seven horns and seven eyes, which are the seven Spirits of God sent forth into all the earth. And he came and took the book out of the right hand of him that sat upon the throne. And when he had taken the book,

322

the four beasts and four and twenty elders fell down before the Lamb, having every one of them harps, and golden vials full of odours, which are the prayers of saints. And they sung a new song saying, Thou art worthy to take the book, and to open the seals thereof: for thou wast slain, and hast redeemed men to God by thy blood out of every kindred, and tongue, and people, and nation; and hast made them unto our God kings and priests: and they shall reign on the earth.

And I beheld, and I heard the voice of many angels round about the throne and the beasts and the elders: and the number of them was ten thousand times ten thousand, and thousands of thousands; saying with a loud voice, Worthy is the Lamb that was slain to receive power, and riches, and wisdom, and strength, and honour, and glory, and blessing. And every creature which is in heaven, and on the earth, and under the earth, and such as are in the sea, and all that are in them, heard I saying, Blessing, and honour, and glory, and power, be unto him that sitteth upon the throne, and unto the Lamb for ever and ever. And the four beasts said, Amen. And the four and twenty elders fell down and worshipped.

And I saw when the Lamb opened one of the seven seals, and I heard, as it were the noise of thunder, one of the four beasts saying, Come. And I saw, and behold a white horse: and he that sat on him had a bow; and a crown was given unto him: and he went forth conquering, and to conquer.

And when he had opened the second seal, I heard the second beast say, Come. And there went out another horse that was red: and power was given to him that sat thereon to take peace from the earth, and that they should kill one another: and there was given unto him a great sword.

And when he had opened the third seal, I heard the third beast say, Come. And I beheld, and lo a black horse; and he that sat on him had a pair of balances in his hand. And I heard a voice in the midst of the four beasts say, A measure of wheat for a penny, and three measures of barley for a penny; and see thou hurt not the oil and the wine.

And when he had opened the fourth seal, I heard the voice of the fourth beast say, Come. And I looked, and behold a pale horse: and his name that sat on him was Death, and Hell followed with him. And power was given unto them over the fourth part of the earth, to kill with sword, and with hunger, and with death, and with the beasts of the earth.

And when he had opened the fifth seal, I saw under the altar the souls of them that were slain for the word of God, and for the testimony which they held: and they cried with a loud voice, saying, How long, O Lord, holy and true, dost thou not judge and avenge our blood on them that dwell on the earth? And white robes were given unto every one of them; and it was said unto them, that they should rest yet for a little season, until their fellow-servants also and their brethren, that should be killed as they were, should be fulfilled.

And I beheld when he had opened the sixth seal, and, lo, there was a great earthquake; and the sun became black as sackcloth of hair, and the moon became all as blood; and the stars of heaven fell unto the earth, even as a fig tree casteth her untimely figs, when she is shaken of a mighty wind. And the heaven departed as a scroll when it is rolled together; and every mountain and island were moved out of their places. And the kings of the earth, and the great men, and the rich men, and the chief captains, and the mighty men, and every bondman, and every free man, hid themselves in the dens and in the rocks of the mountains; and said to the mountains and rocks, Fall on us, and hide us from the face of him that sitteth on the throne, and from the wrath of the Lamb: for the great day of his wrath is come; and who shall be able to stand?

And after this I saw four angels standing on the four corners of the earth, holding the four winds of the earth, that the wind should not blow on the earth, nor on the sea, nor on any tree.

And I saw another angel ascending from the east, having the seal of the living God: and he cried with a loud voice to the four angels, to whom it was given to hurt the earth and the sea, saying, Hurt not the earth, neither the sea, nor the trees, till we have sealed the servants of our God in their foreheads. And I heard the number of them which were sealed: and there were sealed an hundred and forty and four thousand of all the tribes of the children of Israel. Of the tribe of Juda were sealed twelve thousand. Of the tribe of Reuben were sealed twelve thousand. Of the tribe of Gad were sealed twelve thousand. Of the tribe of Aser were sealed twelve thousand. Of the tribe of Nepthalim were sealed twelve thousand. Of the tribe of Manasses were sealed twelve thousand. Of the tribe of Simeon were sealed twelve thousand. Of the tribe of Levi were sealed twelve thousand. Of the tribe of Issachar were sealed twelve thousand. Of the tribe of Zabulon were sealed twelve thousand. Of the tribe of Joseph were sealed twelve thousand. Of the tribe of Benjamin were sealed twelve thousand.

After these things I beheld, and, lo, a great multitude, which no man could number, of all nations, and kindreds, and people, and tongues, stood before the throne, and before the Lamb, clothed with white robes, and palms in their hands; and cried with a loud voice, saying, Salvation to our God which sitteth upon the throne, and unto the Lamb. And all the angels stood round about the throne, and about the elders and the four beasts, and fell before the throne on their faces, and worshipped God, saying, Amen: Blessing, and glory, and wisdom, and thanksgiving, and honour, and power, and might, be unto our God for ever and ever. Amen. And one of the elders answered, saying unto me, What are these which are arrayed in white robes? and whence came they? And I said unto him, Sir, thou knowest. And he said to me, These are they which came out of great tribulation, and have washed their robes, and made them white in the blood of the Lamb. Therefore are they before the throne of God, and serve him day and night in his temple: and he that sitteth on the throne shall dwell among them. They shall hunger no more, neither thirst any more; neither shall the sun light on them, nor any heat. For the Lamb which is in the midst of the throne shall feed them, and shall lead them unto living fountains of waters: and God shall wipe away all tears from their eyes.

And when he had opened the seventh seal, there was silence in heaven about the space of half an hour.

And I saw the seven angels which stood before God; and to them were given seven trumpets.

And another angel came and stood at the altar, having a golden censer; and there was given unto him much incense, that he should offer it at the prayers of all saints upon the golden altar which was before the throne. And the smoke of the incense, at the prayers of the saints, ascended up before God out of the angel's hand. And the angel took the censer, and filled it with fire of the altar, and cast it into the earth: and there were voices, and thunderings, and lightnings, and an earthquake. And the seven angels which had the seven trumpets prepared themselves to sound.

The first angel sounded, and there followed hail and fire mingled with blood, and they were cast upon the earth: and the third part of earth was burnt up, and the third part of trees was burnt up, and all green grass was burnt up.

And the second angel sounded, and as it were a great mountain burning with fire was cast into the sea: and the third part of the sea became blood; and the third part of the creatures which were in the sea, and had life, died; and the third part of the ships were destroyed.

And the third angel sounded, and there fell a great star from heaven, burning as it were a lamp, and it fell upon the third part of the rivers, and upon the fountains of waters; and the name of the star is called Wormwood: and the third part of the waters became wormwood; and many men died of the waters, because they were made bitter.

And the fourth angel sounded, and the third part of the sun was smitten and the third part of the moon, and the third part of the stars; so as the third part of them was darkened, and the day shone not for a third part of it, and the night likewise.

And I beheld, and heard an angel flying through the midst of heaven, saying with a loud voice, Woe, woe, woe, to the inhabiters of the earth by reason of the other voices of the trumpet of the three angels, which are yet to sound!

And the fifth angel sounded, and I saw a star fall from heaven unto the earth: and to him was given the key of the bottomless pit. And he opened the bottomless pit; and there arose a smoke out of the pit, as the smoke of a great furnace; and the sun and the air were darkened by reason of the smoke of the pit. And there came out of the smoke locusts upon the earth: and unto them was given power, as the scorpions of the earth have power. And it was commanded them that they should not hurt the grass of the earth, neither any green thing, neither any tree; but only those men which have not the seal of God in their foreheads. And to them it was given that they should not kill them, but that they should be tormented five months: and their torment was as the torment of a scorpion, when he striketh a man. And in those days shall men seek death, and shall not find it; and shall desire to die, and death shall flee from them. And the shapes of the locusts were like unto horses prepared unto battle; and on their heads were as it were crowns like gold, and their faces were as the faces of men. And they had hair as the hair of women, and their teeth were as the teeth of lions. And they had breastplates, as it were breastplates of iron; and the sound of their wings was as the sound of chariots of many horses running to battle. And they had tails like unto scorpions, and there were stings in their tails: and therein was their power to hurt men five months. And they had a king over them, which is the angel of the bottomless pit, whose name in the Hebrew tongue is Abaddon, but in the Greek tongue hath his name Apollyon. One woe is past; and, behold, there come two woes more hereafter.

And the sixth angel sounded, and I heard a voice from the four horns of the golden altar which is before God, saying to the sixth angel which had the trumpet, Loose the four angels which are bound at the great river Euphrates. And the four angels were loosed, which were prepared for an hour, and a day, and a month, and a year, for to slay the third part of men. And the number of the army of the horsemen were two hundred thousand thousand:

and I heard the number of them. And thus I saw the horses in the vision, and them that sat on them, having breastplates of fire, and of jacinth, and brimstone: and the heads of the horses were as the heads of lions; and out of their mouths issued fire and smoke and brimstone. By these three was the third part of men killed, by the fire, and by the smoke, and by the brimstone, which issued out of their mouths. For their power is in their mouth and in their tails: for their tails were like unto serpents, and had heads, and with them they do hurt. And the rest of the men which were not killed by these plagues yet repented not of the works of their hands, that they should not worship devils, and idols of gold, and silver, and brass, and stone, and of wood: which neither can see, nor hear, nor walk: neither repented they of their murders, nor of their sorceries, nor of their fornication, nor of their thefts.

And I saw another mighty angel come down from heaven, clothed with a cloud: and a rainbow was upon his head, and his face was as it were the sun, and his feet as pillars of fire: and he had in his hand a little book open: and he set his right foot upon the sea, and his left foot on the earth, and cried with a loud voice, as when a lion roareth: and when he had cried, seven thunders uttered their voices. And when the seven thunders had uttered their voices, I was about to write: and I heard a voice from heaven saying unto me, Seal up those things which the seven thunders uttered, and write them not. And the angel which I saw stand upon the sea and upon the earth lifted up his hand to heaven, and sware by him that liveth for ever and ever, who created heaven, and the things that therein are, and the earth, and the things that therein are, and the sea, and the things which are therein, that there should be delay no longer: but in the days of the voice of the seventh angel, when he shall sound, the mystery of God should be finished, as he hath declared to his servants the prophets.

And the voice which I heard from heaven spake unto me again, and said, Go and take the little book which is open in the hand of the angel which standeth upon the sea and upon the earth. And I went unto the angel, and said unto him, Give me the little book. And he said unto me, Take it, and eat it up; and it shall make thy belly bitter, but it shall be in thy mouth sweet as honey. And I took the little book out of the angel's hand, and ate it up; and it was in my mouth sweet as honey: and as soon as I had eaten it, my belly was bitter. And he said unto me, Thou must prophesy again over many peoples, and nations, and tongues, and kings.

And there was given me a reed like unto a rod, with the saying, Rise, and measure the temple of God, and the altar, and them that worship therein. But the court which is without the temple leave out, and measure it not; for it is given unto the Gentiles: and the holy city shall they tread under foot forty and two months. And I will give power unto my two witnesses, and they shall prophesy a thousand two hundred and threescore days, clothed in sackcloth. These are the two olive trees, and the two candlesticks standing before the Lord of the earth. And if any man will hurt them, fire proceedeth out of their mouth, and devoureth their enemies: and if any man will hurt them, he must in this manner be killed. These have power to shut heaven, that it rain not in the days of their prophecy: and have power over waters to turn them to blood, and to smite the earth with all plagues, as often as they will. And when they shall have finished their testimony, the beast that ascendeth out of the bottomless pit shall make war against them, and shall overcome them, and kill them. And their dead bodies shall lie in the street of the great city, which spiritually is called Sodom and Egypt, where also their Lord was crucified. And they of the people and kindreds and tongues and nations shall see their dead bodies three days and an half, and shall not suffer their dead bodies to be put in graves. And they that dwell upon the earth shall rejoice over them, and make merry, and shall send gifts one to another; because these two prophets tormented them that dwelt on the earth. And after three days and an half the spirit of life from God entered into them, and they stood upon their feet; and great fear fell upon them which saw them. And they heard a great voice from heaven saying unto them, Come up hither. And they ascended up to heaven in a cloud; and their enemies beheld them. And the same hour was there a great earthquake, and the tenth part of the city fell, and in the earthquake were slain of men seven thousand: and the remnant were affrighted, and gave glory to the God of heaven. The second woe is past; and, behold, the third woe cometh quickly.

And the seventh angel sounded; and there were great voices in heaven, saying, The kingdoms of this world are become the kingdoms of our Lord, and of his Christ; and he shall reign for ever and ever. And the four and twenty elders, which sat before God on their seats, fell upon their faces, and worshipped God, saying, We give thee thanks, O Lord God Almighty, which art, and wast, because thou hast taken to thee thy great power, and hast reigned. And the nations were angry, and thy wrath is come, and the time of the dead, that they should be judged, and that thou shouldest give reward unto thy servants the prophets, and to the saints, and them that fear thy name, small and great; and shouldest destroy them which destroy the earth.

And the temple of God was opened in heaven, and there was seen in his temple the ark of his testament: and there were lightnings, and voices, and thunderings, and an earthquake, and great hail.

And there appeared a great wonder in heaven; a woman clothed with the sun, and the moon under her feet, and upon her head a crown of twelve stars: and she being with child cried, travailing in birth, and pained to be delivered.

And there appeared another wonder in heaven; and behold a great red dragon, having seven heads and ten horns, and seven crowns upon his heads. And his tail drew the third part of the stars of heaven, and did cast them to the earth: and the dragon stood before the woman which was ready to be delivered, for to devour her child as soon as it was born. And she brought forth a man child, who was to rule all nations with a rod of iron: and her child was caught up unto God, and to his throne. And the woman fled into the wilderness, where she hath a place prepared of God, that they should feed her there a thousand two hundred and threescore days.

And there was war in heaven: Michael and his angels fought against the dragon; and the dragon fought and his angels, and prevailed not; neither was their place found any more in heaven. And the great dragon was cast out, that old serpent, called the Devil, and Satan, which deceiveth the whole world: he was cast out into the earth, and his angels were cast out with him. And I heard a loud voice saying in heaven, Now is come salvation, and strength, and the kingdom of our God, and the power of his Christ: for the accuser of our brethren is cast down, which accused them before our God day and night. And they overcame him by the blood of the Lamb, and by the word of their testimony; and they loved not their lives unto the death. Therefore rejoice, ye heavens, and ye that dwell in them. Woe to the earth and the sea! for the devil is come down unto you, having great wrath, because he knoweth that he hath but a short time.

And when the dragon saw that he was cast unto the earth, he persecuted the woman which brought forth the man child. And to the woman were given two wings of a great eagle, that she might fly into the wilderness, into her place, where she is nourished for a time, and times, and half a time, from the face of the serpent. And the serpent cast out of his mouth water as a flood after the woman, that he might cause her to be carried away of the flood. And the earth helped the woman, and the earth opened her mouth, and swallowed up the flood which the dragon cast out of his mouth. And the dragon was wroth with the woman, and went to make war with the remnant of her seed, which keep the commandments of God, and have the testimony of Jesus Christ. And he stood on the sand of the sea.

And I saw a beast rise up out of the sea, having seven heads and ten horns, and upon his horns ten crowns, and upon his heads names of blasphemy. And the beast which I saw was like unto a leopard, and his feet were as the feet of a bear, and his mouth as the mouth of a lion: and the dragon gave him his power, and his seat, and great authority. And I saw one of his heads as it were wounded to death; and his deadly wound was healed: and all the world wondered after the beast. And they worshipped the dragon which gave power unto the beast: and they worshipped the beast, saying, Who is like unto the beast? who is able to make war with him? And there was given unto him a mouth speaking great things and blasphemies; and power was given unto him to continue forty and two months. And he opened his mouth in blasphemy against God, to blaspheme his name, and his tabernacle, even them that tabernacle in heaven. And it was given unto him to make war with the saints, and to overcome them: and power was given him over all kindreds, and people, and tongues, and nations. And all that dwell upon the earth shall worship him, whose name is not written in the book of life of the Lamb slain from the foundation of the world. If any man have an ear, let him hear. He that is for captivity shall go into captivity: he that is to be killed with the sword must be killed with the sword. Here is the patience and the faith of the saints.

And I beheld another beast coming up out of the earth; and he had two horns like a lamb, and he spake as a dragon. And he exerciseth all the power of the first beast before him, and causeth the earth and them which dwell therein to worship the first beast, whose deadly wound was healed. And he doeth great wonders, so that he maketh fire come down from heaven on the earth in the sight of men, and deceiveth them that dwell on the earth by the means of those miracles which he had power to do in the sight of the beast; saying to them that dwell on the earth, that they should make an image to the beast, which had the wound by a sword, and did live. And he had power to give life unto the image of the beast, that the image of the beast should both speak, and cause that as many as would not worship the image of the beast should be killed. And he causeth all, both small and great, rich and poor, free and bond, to receive a mark in their right hand, or in their foreheads: and that no man might buy or sell, save he that had the mark, either the name of the beast, or the number of his name. Here is wisdom. Let him that hath understanding count the number of the beast: for it is the number of a man; and his number is Six hundred threescore and six.

And I looked, and, lo, the Lamb stood on the mount Sion, and with him an hundred forty and four thousand, having his name and his Father's name written in their foreheads. And I heard a voice from heaven, as the voice of many waters, and as the voice of a great thunder: and I heard the voice of harpers harping with their harps: and they sung as it were a new song before the throne, and before the four beasts, and the elders: and no man could learn that song but the hundred and forty and four thousand, which were redeemed from the earth. These are they which were not defiled with women; for they are virgins. These are they which follow the Lamb whithersoever he goeth. These were redeemed from among men, being the firstfruits unto God and to the Lamb. And in their mouth was found no guile: for they are without blemish.

And I saw another angel fly in the midst of heaven, having the everlasting gospel to preach unto them that dwell on the earth, and to every nation, and kindred, and tongue, and people, saying with a loud voice, Fear God, and give glory to him; for the hour of his judgement is come: and worship him that made heaven, and earth, and the sea, and the fountains of waters.

And there followed another angel, saying, Babylon is fallen, is fallen, that great city, because she made all nations drink of the wine of the wrath of her fornication.

And the third angel followed them, saying with a loud voice, If any man worship the beast and his image, and receive his mark in his forehead, or in his hand, the same shall drink of the wine of the wrath of God, which is poured out without mixture into the cup of his indignation; and he shall be tormented with fire and brimstone in the presence of the holy angels, and in the presence of the Lamb: and the smoke of their torment ascendeth up for ever and ever: and they have no rest day nor night, who worship the beast and his image, and whosoever receiveth the mark of his name. Here is the patience of the saints, that keep the commandments of God, and the faith of Jesus.

And I heard a voice from heaven saying, Write, Blessed are the dead which die in the Lord from henceforth: Yea, saith the Spirit, that they may rest from their labours; and their works do follow them.

And I looked, and behold a white cloud, and upon the cloud one sat like unto the Son of man, having on his head a golden crown, and in his hand a sharp sickle. And another angel came out of the temple, crying with a loud voice to him that sat on the cloud, Thrust in thy sickle, and reap: for the time is come for thee to reap; for the harvest of the earth is ripe. And he that sat on the cloud thrust in his sickle on the earth; and the earth was reaped.

And another angel came out of the temple which is in heaven, he also having a sharp sickle. And another angel came out from the altar, which had power over fire; and cried with a loud cry to him that had the sharp sickle, saying, Thrust in thy sharp sickle, and gather the clusters of the vine of the earth; for her grapes are fully ripe. And the angel thrust in his sickle into the earth, and gathered the vine of the earth, and cast it into the great winepress of the wrath of God. And the winepress was trodden without the city, and blood came out of the winepress, even unto the horse bridles, by the space of a thousand and six hundred furlongs.

And I saw another sign in heaven, great and marvellous, seven angels having the seven last plagues; for in them is filled up the wrath of God. And I saw as it were a sea of glass mingled with fire: and them that had gotten the victory over the beast, and over his image, and over the number of his name, stand on the sea of glass, having the harps of God. And they sing the song of Moses the servant of God, and the song of the Lamb, saying, Great and marvellous are thy works, Lord God Almighty; just and true are thy ways, thou King of saints. Who shall not fear thee, O Lord, and glorify thy name? for thou only art holy: for all nations shall come and worship before thee; for thy judgements are made manifest.

And after that I looked, and, behold, the temple of the tabernacle of the testimony in heaven was opened: and the seven angels came out of the temple, having the seven plagues, clothed in pure and bright stones, and having their breasts girded with golden girdles. And one of the four beasts gave unto the seven angels seven golden vials full of the wrath of God, who liveth for ever and ever. And the temple was filled with smoke from the glory of God, and from his power; and no man was able to enter into the temple, till the seven plagues of the seven angels were fulfilled. And I heard a great voice out of the temple saying to the seven angels, Go your ways, and pour out the vials of the wrath of God upon the earth.

And the first went, and poured out his vial upon the earth; and there fell a noisome and grievous sore upon the men which had the mark of the beast, and upon them which worshipped his image.

And the second angel poured out his vial upon the sea; and it became as the blood of a dead man: and every living soul died in the sea.

And the third angel poured out his vial upon the rivers and fountains of waters; and they became blood. And I heard the angel of the waters say, Thou art righteous, O Lord, which art, and wast, because thou hast judged thus. For they have shed the blood of saints and prophets, and thou hast given them blood to drink; for they are worthy. And I heard another out of the altar say, Even so, Lord God Almighty, true and righteous are thy judgements.

And the fourth angel poured out his vial upon the sun; and power was given unto him to scorch men with fire. And men were scorched with great heat, and blasphemed the name of God, which hath power over these plagues: and they repented not to give him glory.

And the fifth angel poured out his vial upon the seat of the beast; and his kingdom was full of darkness; and they gnawed their tongues for pain, and blasphemed the God of heaven because of their pains and their sores, and repented not of their deeds.

And the sixth angel poured out his vial upon the great river Euphrates; and the water thereof was dried up, that the way of the kings of the east might be prepared. And I saw three unclean spirits like frogs come out of the mouth of the dragon, and out of the mouth of the beast, and out of the mouth of the false prophet. For they are the spirits of devils, working miracles, which go forth unto the kings of the whole world, to gather them to the battle of that great day of God Almighty. Behold, I come as a thief. Blessed is he that watcheth, and keepeth his garments, lest he walk naked, and they see his shame. And he gathered them together into a place called in the Hebrew tongue Armageddon.

And the seventh angel poured out his vial into the air; and there came a great voice out of the temple, from the throne, saying, It is done. And there were voices, and thunders, and lightnings; and there was a great earthquake, such as was not since men were upon the earth, so mighty an earthquake, and so great. And the great city was divided into three parts, and the cities of the nations fell: and great Babylon came in remembrance before God, to give unto her the cup of the wine of the fierceness of his wrath. And every island fled away, and the mountains were not found. And there fell upon men a great hail out of heaven, every stone about the weight of a talent: and men blasphemed God because of the plague of the hail; for the plague thereof was exceeding great.

And there came one of the seven angels which had the seven vials, and talked with me, saying unto me, Come hither; I will shew unto thee the judgement of the great whore that sitteth upon many waters: with whom the kings of the earth have committed fornication, and the inhabitants of the earth have been made drunk with the wine of her fornication. So he carried me away in the spirit into the wilderness: and I saw a woman sit upon a scarlet coloured beast, full of names of blasphemy, having seven heads and ten horns. And the woman was arrayed in purple and scarlet colour, and decked with gold and precious stones and pearls, having a golden cup in her hand full of abominations and filthiness of her fornication: and upon her forehead was a name written, Mystery, Babylon the Great, the Mother of Harlots and Abominations of the Earth. And I saw the woman drunken with the blood of the saints, and with the blood of the martyrs of Jesus: and when I saw her, I wondered with great admiration.

And the angel said unto me, Wherefore didst thou marvel? I will tell thee the mystery of the woman, and of the beast that carrieth her, which hath the seven heads and ten horns. The beast that thou sawest was, and is not; and shall ascend out of the bottomless pit, and go into perdition: and they that dwell on the earth shall wonder, whose names were not written in the book of life from the foundation of the world, when they behold the beast that was, and is not, and shall appear. And here is the mind, which hath wisdom. The seven heads are seven mountains, on which the woman sitteth. And they are seven kings: five are fallen, and one is, and the other is not yet come; and when he cometh, he must continue a short space. And the beast that was, and is not, even he is the eighth, and is of the seven, and goeth into perdition. And the ten horns which thou sawest are ten kings, which have received no kingdom as yet; but receive power as kings one hour with the beast. These have one mind, and shall give their power and strength unto the beast. These shall make war with the Lamb, and the Lamb shall overcome them: for he is Lord of lords, and King of kings: and they that are with him are called, and chosen, and faithful.

And he saith unto me, The waters which thou sawest, where the whore sitteth, are peoples, and multitudes, and nations, and tongues. And the ten horns which thou sawest, and the beast, these shall hate the whore, and shall make her desolate and naked, and shall eat her flesh, and burn her with fire. For God hath put in their hearts to fulfil his will, and to agree, and give their kingdom unto the beast, until the words of God shall be fulfilled. And the woman which thou sawest is that great city, which reigneth over the kings of the earth.

And after these things I saw another angel come down from heaven, having great power; and the earth was lightened with his glory. And he cried mightily with a strong voice, saying, Babylon the great is fallen, is fallen, and is become the habitation of devils, and the hold of every foul spirit, and a cage of every unclean and hateful bird. For all nations have fallen by the wine of the wrath of her fornication, and the kings of the earth have committed fornication with her, and the merchants of the earth are waxed rich through the abundance of her delicacies.

And I heard another voice from heaven, saying, Come out of her, my people, that ye be not partakers of her sins, and that ye receive

337

not of her plagues. For her sins have reached unto heaven, and God hath remembered her iniquities. Reward her even as she rewarded you, and double unto her double according to her works: in the cup which she hath filled fill to her double. How much she hath glorified herself, and lived deliciously, so much torment and sorrow give her: for she saith in her heart, I sit a queen, and am no widow, and shall see no sorrow. Therefore shall her plagues come in one day, death, and mourning, and famine; and she shall be utterly burned with fire: for strong is the Lord God who judgeth her. And the kings of the earth, who have committed fornication and lived deliciously with her, shall bewail her, and lament for her, when they shall see the smoke of her burning, standing afar off for the fear of her torment, saying, Alas, alas that great city Babylon, that mighty city! for in one hour is thy judgement come.

And the merchants of the earth shall weep and mourn over her; for no man buyeth their merchandise any more: the merchandise of gold, and silver, and precious stones, and of pearls, and fine linen, and purple, and silk, and scarlet, and all thyine wood, and all manner vessels of ivory, and all manner vessels of most precious wood, and of brass, and iron, and marble, and cinnamon, and odours, and ointments, and frankincense, and wine, and oil, and fine flour, and wheat, and beasts, and sheep, and horses, and chariots, and slaves, and souls of men. And the fruits that thy soul lusted after are departed from thee, and all things which were dainty and goodly are departed from thee, and thou shalt find them no more at all. The merchants of these things, which were made rich by her, shall stand afar off for the fear of her torment, weeping and wailing, and saying, Alas, alas that great city, that was clothed in fine linen, and purple, and scarlet, and decked with gold, and precious stones, and pearls! For in one hour so great riches is come to nought.

And every shipmaster, and all the company in ships, and sailors, and as many as trade by sea, stood afar off, and cried when they saw the smoke of her burning, saying, What city is like unto this great city! And they cast dust on their heads, and cried, weeping and wailing, saying, Alas, alas that great city, wherein were made rich all that had ships in the sea by reason of her costliness! for in one hour is she made desolate. Rejoice over her, thou heaven, and ye holy apostles and prophets; for God hath avenged you on her.

And a mighty angel took up a stone like a great millstone, and cast it into the sea, saying, Thus with violence shall that great city Babylon be thrown down, and shall be found no more at all. And the voice of harpers, and musicians, and of pipers, and trumpeters, shall be heard no more at all in thee; and no craftsman, of whatsoever craft he be, shall be found any more in thee; and the sound of a millstone shall be heard no more at all in thee; and the light of a candle shall shine no more at all in thee; and the voice of the bridegroom and of the bride shall be heard no more at all in thee: for thy merchants were the great men of the earth; for by thy sorceries were all nations deceived. And in her was found the blood of prophets, and of saints, and of all that were slain upon the earth.

And after these things I heard a great voice of much people in heaven, saying, Alleluia; Salvation, and glory, and honour, and power, unto the Lord our God: for true and righteous are his judgements: for he hath judged the great whore, which did corrupt the earth with her fornication, and hath avenged the blood of his servants at her hand. And again they said, Alleluia. And her smoke riseth up for ever and ever. And the four and twenty elders and the four beasts fell down and worshipped God that sat on the throne, saying, Amen; Alleluia.

And a voice came out of the throne, saying, Praise our God, all ye his servants, and ye that fear him, both small and great. And I heard as it were the voice of a great multitude, and as the voice of many waters, and as the voice of mighty thunderings, saying, Alleluia: for the Lord God omnipotent reigneth. Let us be glad and rejoice, and give honour to him: for the marriage of the Lamb is come, and his wife hath made herself ready. And to her was granted that she should be arrayed in fine linen, clean and white: for the fine linen is the righteousness of saints. And he saith unto me, Write, Blessed are they which are called unto the marriage supper of the Lamb. And he saith unto me, These are the true sayings of God. And I fell at his feet to worship him. And he said unto me, See thou do it not: I am thy fellowservant, and of thy brethren that have the testimony of Jesus: worship God: for the testimony of Jesus is the spirit of prophecy.

And I saw heaven opened, and behold a white horse; and he that sat upon him was called Faithful and True, and in righteousness he doth judge and make war. His eyes were as a flame of fire, and on his head were many crowns; and he had a name written, that no man knew, but he himself. And he was clothed with a vesture dipped in blood: and his name is called The Word of God. And the armies which were in heaven followed him upon white horses, clothed in fine linen, white and clean. And out of his mouth goeth a sharp sword, that with it he should smite the nations: and he shall rule them with a rod of iron: and he treadeth the winepress of the fierceness and wrath of Almighty God. And he hath on his vesture and on his thigh a name written, King of Kings, and Lord of Lords.

And I saw an angel standing in the sun; and he cried with a loud voice, saying to all the fowls that fly in the midst of heaven, Come and gather yourselves together unto the great supper of God; that ye may eat the flesh of kings, and the flesh of captains, and the flesh of mighty men, and the flesh of horses, and of them that sit on them, and the flesh of all men, both free and bond, both small and great.

And I saw the beast, and the kings of the earth, and their armies, gathered together to make war against him that sat on the horse, and against his army. And the beast was taken, and with him the false prophet that wrought miracles before him, with which he deceived them that had received the mark of the beast, and them that worshipped his image. These both were cast alive into a lake of fire burning with brimstone. And the remnant were slain with the sword of him that sat upon the horse, which sword proceeded out of his mouth: and all the fowls were filled with their flesh.

And I saw an angel come down from heaven, having the key of the bottomless pit and a great chain in his hand. And he laid hold on the dragon, that old serpent, which is the Devil, and Satan, and bound him a thousand years, and cast him into the bottomless pit, and shut him up, and set a seal upon him, that he should deceive the nations no more, till the thousand years should be fulfilled: and after that he must be loosed a little season.

And I saw thrones, and they sat upon them, and judgement was given unto them: and I saw the souls of them that were beheaded for the witness of Jesus, and for the word of God, and which had not worshipped the beast, neither his image, neither had received his mark upon their foreheads, or in their hands; and they lived and reigned with Christ a thousand years. But the rest of the dead lived not again until the thousand years were finished. This is the first resurrection. Blessed and holy is he that hath part in the first resurrection: on such the second death hath no power, but they shall be priests of God and of Christ, and shall reign with him a thousand years. And when the thousand years are expired, Satan shall be loosed out of his prison, and shall go out to deceive the nations which are in the four quarters of the earth, Gog and Magog, to gather them together to battle: the number of whom is as the sand of the sea. And they went up on the breadth of the earth, and compassed the camp of the saints about, and the beloved city: and fire came down from God out of heaven, and devoured them. And the devil that deceived them was cast into the lake of fire and brimstone, where the beast and the false prophet are, and shall be tormented day and night for ever and ever.

And I saw a great white throne, and him that sat on it, from whose face the earth and the heaven fled away; and there was found no place for them. And I saw the dead, small and great, stand before God; and the books were opened: and another book was opened, which is the book of life: and the dead were judged out of those things which were written in the books, according to their works. And the sea gave up the dead which were in it; and death and hell delivered up the dead which were in them: and they were judged every man according to their works. And death and hell were cast into the lake of fire. This is the second death. And whosoever was not found written in the book of life was cast into the lake of fire.

341

And I saw a new heaven and a new earth: for the first heaven and the first earth were passed away; and there was no more sea. And I saw the holy city, new Jerusalem, coming down from God out of heaven, prepared as a bride adorned for her husband. And I heard a great voice out of heaven saying, Behold, the tabernacle of God is with men, and he will dwell with them, and they shall be his people, and God with Them himself shall be their God. And God shall wipe away all tears from their eyes; and there shall be no more death, neither sorrow, nor crying, neither shall there be any more pain: for the former things are passed away. And he that sat upon the throne said, Behold, I make all things new. And he said unto me, Write: for these words are true and faithful. And he said unto me, they are done. I am Alpha and Omega, the beginning and the end. I will give unto him that is athirst of the fountain of the water of life freely. He that overcometh shall inherit all things; and I will be his God, and he shall be my son. But the fearful, and unbelieving, and the abominable, and murderers, and whoremongers, and sorcerers, and idolaters, and all liars, shall have their part in the lake which burneth with fire and brimstone: which is the second death.

And there came unto me one of the seven angels which had the seven vials full of the seven last plagues, and talked with me, saying, Come hither, I will shew thee the bride, the Lamb's wife. And he carried me away in the spirit to a great and high mountain, and shewed me that great city, the holy Jerusalem, descending out of heaven from God, having the glory of God: and her light was like unto a stone most precious, even like a jasper stone, clear as crystal; and had a wall great and high, and had twelve gates, and at the gates twelve angels, and names written thereon, which are the names of the twelve tribes of the children of Israel: on the east three gates; on the north three gates; on the south three gates; and on the west three gates. And the wall of the city had twelve foundations, and in them the names of the twelve apostles of the Lamb.

And he that talked with me had a golden reed to measure the city, and the gates thereof, and the wall thereof. And the city lieth foursquare, and the length is as large as the breadth: and he measured the city with the reed, twelve thousand furlongs. The length and the breadth and the height of it are equal. And he measured the wall thereof, an hundred and forty and four cubits, according to the measure of a man, that is, of the angel. And the building of the wall of it was of jasper: and the city was pure gold, like unto clear glass. And the foundations of the wall of the city were garnished with all manner of precious stones. The first foundation was jasper; the second, sapphire; the third, a chalcedony; the fourth, an emerald; the fifth, sardonyx; the sixth, sardius; the seventh, chrysolyte; the eighth, beryl; the ninth, a topaz; the tenth, a chrysoprasus; the eleventh, a jacinth; the twelfth, an amethyst. And the twelve gates were twelve pearls; every several gate was of one pearl: and the street of the city was pure gold, as it were transparent glass.

And I saw no temple therein: for the Lord God Almighty and the Lamb are the temple of it. And the city had no need of the sun, neither of the moon, to shine in it: for the glory of God did lighten it, and the Lamb is the light thereof. And the nations shall walk in the light of it: and the kings of the earth do bring their glory and honour into it. And the gates of it shall not be shut at all by day: for there shall be no night there. And they shall bring the glory and honour of the nations into it. And there shall in no wise enter into it any thing that defileth, neither whatsoever worketh abomination, or maketh a lie: but they which are written in the Lamb's book of life.

And he shewed me a pure river of water of life, clear as crystal, proceeding out of the throne of God and of the Lamb, in the midst of the street of it. And on either side of the river was there the tree of life, which bare twelve manner of fruits, and yielded her fruit every month: and the leaves of the tree were for the healing of the nations. And there shall be no more curse: but the throne of God and of the Lamb shall be in it; and his servants shall serve him: and they shall see his face; and his name shall be in their foreheads. And there shall be no night there; and they need no candle, neither light of the sun; for the Lord God giveth them light: and they shall reign for ever and ever.

And he said unto me, These sayings are faithful and true: and the Lord God of the Spirits of the prophets sent his angel to shew unto

343

his servants the things which must shortly be done. Behold, I come quickly: blessed is he that keepeth the sayings of the prophecy of this book. And I John saw these things, and heard them. And when I had heard and seen, I fell down to worship before the feet of the angel which shewed me these things. Then saith he unto me, See thou do it not: for I am thy fellowservant, and of thy brethren the prophets, and of them which keep the sayings of this book: worship God.

And he saith unto me, Seal not the sayings of the prophecy of this book: for the time is at hand. He that is unjust, let him be unjust still: and he which is filthy, let him be filthy still: and he that is righteous, let him be righteous still: and he that is holy, let him be holy still. And, behold, I come quickly; and my reward is with me, to give every man according as his work shall be. I am Alpha and Omega, the beginning and the end, the first and the last. Blessed are they that wash their robes, that they may have right to the tree of life, and may enter in through the gates into the city. For without are dogs, and sorcerers, and whoremongers, and murderers, and idolaters, and whosoever loveth and maketh a lie. I Jesus have sent mine angel to testify unto you these things in the churches. I am the root and the offspring of David, and the bright and morning star. And the Spirit and the bride say, Come. And let him that heareth say, Come. And let him that is athirst come. And whosoever will, let him take the water of life freely.

For I testify unto every man that heareth the words of the prophecy of this book, If any man shall add unto these things, God shall add unto him the plagues that are written in this book: and if any man shall take away from the words of the book of this prophecy, God shall take away his part out of the book of life, and out of the holy city, and from the things which are written in this book. He which testifieth these things saith, Surely I come quickly. Amen. Even so, come, Lord Jesus.

The grace of our Lord Jesus Christ be with the saints. Amen.

344

INDEX

347